evolution
or
creation?

Volumes in THE DOORWAY PAPERS series—

VOLUME IV: The Doorway Papers

evolution
or
creation?

ARTHUR C. CUSTANCE

Drawings by the Author

ZONDERVAN
PUBLISHING HOUSE OF THE ZONDERVAN CORPORATION
GRAND RAPIDS, MICHIGAN 49506

Part I — Issued 1959, Revised 1973
Part II — Issued 1968
Part III — Issued 1970
Part IV — Issued 1971
Part V — Issued 1972

EVOLUTION OR CREATION?
The Doorway Papers, Volume Four

Copyright © 1976 by The Zondervan Corporation
Grand Rapids, Michigan

Second printing 1979

In a number of places the author, who holds an M.A. in biblical Greek and Hebrew, while relying essentially on the King James Version of the Bible, has changed words where he feels some clarification of the Elizabethan English might be helpful on the basis of his study of the original languages.

Library of Congress Cataloging in Publication Data
Custance, Arthur C.
   Evolution or Creation?
   (His The doorway papers ; v. 4)
   1. Creation.   2. Evolution.   3. Monotheism.
4. Polytheism.   5. Man.   I. Title.
BS543.A1C87 vol. 4 [BL226]   230s [213]
ISBN 0-310-22980-4   75-23370
PRINTED IN THE UNITED STATES OF AMERICA

Contents

PART III

CONVERGENCE AND THE ORIGIN OF MAN

PART IV

THE SURVIVAL OF THE UNFIT

PART V

IS MAN AN ANIMAL?

Preface

THIS VOLUME contains two papers that are rather longer than usual, dealing with the earth's past geological history as it was being prepared for the introduction of man, and the unique constitution of man for whom the earth seems clearly to have been specifically designed. Three shorter papers deal with certain aspects of evolutionary theory to which not much attention is generally given in the literature of Christian writers.

In the first paper, "The Preparation of the Earth for Man," I have reexamined an older view of the earth's early history, which was actually in the process of being developed by some of the best minds in America and in Europe, and with great skill and clarity, when Darwin published his *Origin of Species*. Thereafter, unfortunately, this view was eclipsed by evolutionary thinking, because it advocated the twin concepts of divine intervention by direct creation and of providential planning and purpose, concepts which the scientific method was — and is — quite unable to accommodate. As our knowledge of the distant past increases however, this alternative view is seen to have more and more that should commend it for serious reconsideration; it can account for many geological phenomena otherwise quite unaccountable. This view and these phenomena are examined.

The second paper, "Primitive Monotheism and the Origin of Polytheism," gathers together some of the evidence now available which clearly indicates that man's religious history has not been marked by a gradual purification of his faith from animism to polydemonism to polytheism and finally to a pure monotheism; but by a trend in the opposite direction, representing rather degeneration than upward evolution.

The third paper, "Convergence and the Origin of Man," is a discussion of one aspect of the evidence from the fossil record and from the living world that similar needs and similar environmental

7

pressures act upon living organisms to mold them along similar lines so that they tend to converge in structural form, and that this takes place in such a way as to present the appearance of genetic relatedness where no such relatedness has ever actually existed. The bearing of this on the argument for descent based on similarity of form is obvious. The extent to which convergence can be shown to have occurred is proving something of an embarrassment to evolutionists.

The fourth paper, "The Survival of the Unfit," provides some information on the large number of cases in Nature where cooperation and even self-sacrifice are found to be by no means uncommon among animals in the wild, both between members of a single species and between members of different species. Animals are seen to feed the wounded, guide the blind, help the disabled, and upon occasion even to sacrifice themselves for those in need of care. In Nature, the unfit by Darwin's definition, do indeed very often survive. His view of Nature as a ruthless battleground was really quite unrealistic.

The final paper, "Is Man An Animal?" is important because it shows that man is not merely quantitatively different from all other creatures, but qualitatively different. The differences are examined in some detail from a large number of less familiar sources. The conclusion is that man was created a unique creature because he was to become a "house" for God Himself to be manifested in the flesh as man, without violence being done to His own Person as God. It is seen that the Incarnation really demands a uniqueness in the constitution of man, which puts him in a category by himself completely separated from all other animal forms.

The final chapter of this last paper is, in some ways, a summation of the whole series of sixty Doorway Papers. It shows that in the final analysis the universe must have been made for the world and the world for man, and man was made specifically for God — not merely that he might worship and enjoy Him (because of his spiritual nature) but that God might redeem him by becoming one with him in his world of time and space (because of his physical nature), thus to demonstrate His love before the whole host of heaven in a way not otherwise possible.

It is all of a piece: herein is the meaning of reality and experience. Truly we are far too wonderfully and fearfully made for any blind evolutionary process to prove a sufficient explanation.

The reader will note that each of these papers was previously published separately by the author, and thus there is some duplication of material.

Through faith, we understand that the worlds were planned by the word of God, so that what is seen was not made out of things that do appear.

— *Hebrews* 11:3

I will praise thee; for I am fearfully and wonderfully made: marvellous are thy works; and that my soul knoweth right well.

My substance was not hid from thee, when I was made in secret, and curiously wrought in the lowest parts of the earth.

Thine eyes did see my substance, yet being imperfect; and in thy book all my members were written, which in continuance were fashioned, when as yet there was none of them.

How precious also are thy thoughts unto me, O God! how great is the sum of them!

— *Psalm* 139:14-17

I beseech thee, my child, to lift thine eyes unto heaven and earth; and to see all things that are therein; and thus to recognize that God made them not of things that were, and that the race of men in this same way came into being.

— *II Maccabees* 7:28

Part 1
The Preparation
of the Earth for Man

Blind unbelief is sure to err,
And scan His work in vain;
God is His own interpreter,
And He will make it plain.

— *William Cowper*

Preface

IF ANYONE who has read this paper concludes that I am, after all, merely presenting a kind of theistic evolution, the fault will be entirely mine in not having made clear what the fundamental difference is between my own views and this rather popular alternative. As I understand it, theistic evolutionists are essentially orthodox evolutionists — except that they believe God was behind it all, from the appearance of the first amoeba to the appearance of the first man. The term "evolution" is still taken to mean the gradual transformation of one species into another by natural means without any genetic discontinuities. These means are understood to be explainable in the terms of natural processes, the only supernatural element being the initiation of the process and the evidence of purpose throughout; the only intervention on God's part was a kind of nudging of events. In due course it is hoped to demonstrate this in the laboratory. When this happens we shall know "how God did it." The Creator started it all off, and then withdrew from any further direct interference in it except on very rare and special occasions when miracles occurred, having assured Himself, as it were, that it would end up as He planned.

This is not my view at all, how ever much it may superficially seem to be. I believe that *God acted creatively, in the most distinct and positive manner conceivable, throughout the whole of geological history, introducing new species as they became appropriate, and removing others when they ceased to be.*

No laboratory experiment can ever hope to elucidate this creative process, as I understand it. But because God was graciously willing to permit us to see the unfolding of His designs, the geological record can be read as a more or less continuous one, with evidence of the fitness and appropriateness of things throughout the whole process, as the earth was prepared for the introduction of man.

Because science must, of necessity, reject any appeal to the supernatural, the scientific account must accordingly give only a partial view of the meaning of the earth's past history, and of the universe as a whole. Revelation is essential to make the picture complete, and part of revelation is the method by which God redeemed man, a method which throws light upon his origin, and has a direct bearing on the structure and functioning of the bodies of all other animals. If man is evolved, I believe it can be shown that he is not redeemable at all, for his capacity for redemption is dependent upon the nature of both his spirit *and his body*.

Introduction

THE ISSUES in the conflict between science and Scripture with regard to the earth's earlier history during the ages which preceded the coming of man have become almost impossibly confused. On the one hand, we have the confirmed evolutionist who finds no place whatever for the supernatural in his scheme of things, and therefore no place for God. He holds that everything has happened purely by chance, and that the process has occupied an immense period of time to be measured in billions of years. He rigidly excludes anything that smacks of catastrophism, holding to Lyell's dictum that the present is the key to the past. The progressive change from simple to complex forms of life has neither involved unbridgeable discontinuities nor divine interferences. The apparent gaps in the record do not represent discontinuities in the great chain of life. At the other extreme are those who, as openly confessed creationists, believe that virtually all the past is in one way or another stamped with the hallmark of instantaneous creation. Everything that has existed — the universe, our solar system, the planets, trees, animals, and man — came into being by fiat creation not more than a few thousand years ago. They interpret the phenomena of stratified rocks containing fossils as evidence of a global catastrophe in Noah's time and are therefore commonly referred to as "flood geologists."

Then there are creationists who believe that evolution was God's way of "creating." This seems to me really an abuse of language, but those who hold this view look upon evolution as a kind of creative process in itself. But they would admit that fiat creation was probably involved in the origination of matter, of life, and possibly of man as well.

A fourth school, of which I count myself a member, holds that we simply do not know precisely how God ordered the world in geological times prior to man, whether by direct creative activity or

15

by something akin to evolution. Those in this group believe, as I do, that something went wrong and a catastrophic judgment brought that older world to a disastrous end, leaving it ruined and desolate, as Genesis 1:2 describes it. Then followed a re-creation at a tremendously accelerated rate, over a period of six literal days, at the end of which, as for a jewel, the setting was reconstituted. Man was then created to be the star of the piece and to dominate the stage thereafter. Much of the geological evidence of catastrophism that has been commandeered by the flood geologists is believed, by this school, to belong between Genesis 1:1 and Genesis 1:2. Such a concept is anathema to those creationists who believe in a very young universe, not because it is catastrophic, but because it makes concessions to the concept of a very ancient world — and this invites an evolutionary interpretation of that world. On the other hand, it is almost as unpopular with theistic evolutionists who see no need for it and no evidence of it, because it does involve the catastrophic and badly conflicts with current uniformitarian philosophy among geologists.

So we have certain atheistic and theistic alternatives, all of which are held by people who honestly believe that the evidence entirely supports their own particular view. And it is no longer possible, it seems, for the protagonists to really communicate with one another usefully. But being the creatures we are, we each hold fast to the view that best serves to integrate the knowledge we have of the evidence, and this paper is merely one man's attempt to do just this from a biblical as well as a scientific point of view. Frankly, I think it can be shown that the direction in which geological theory was heading just before Lyell and Darwin turned the tide was very much that which I am proposing in this paper. The evidence now has accumulated to such an extent that I believe this older view should be brought forward again and reexamined. Certainly the Lyellian view of geology is beginning to show signs of bankruptcy, even as I think the Darwinian view of paleontology has done.

The informed Christian assuredly has two great advantages over the non-Christian. In the first place, he almost certainly will have a rather good idea of the data upon which the evolutionist rests his case, whereas the non-Christian evolutionist has probably read almost nothing of a serious nature from the Christian point of view. In this respect, he is likely to be seriously unaware of the weaknesses of his own position. In the second place, the Christian has the tremendous advantage of being willing to accept the light of Revelation which, by its very nature, supplies data that cannot be obtained any other way.

So here is the situation as I see it: We have four basic alternatives — the purely nontheistic evolutionary view, the theistic evolutionary view, the young earth or flood geology view, and the view to be explored in some detail in this paper, which argues for that particular form of catastrophism that sees a discontinuity between our present world and "the world that then was" (II Peter 3:6), which was disastrously overwhelmed and left a desolation as described in Genesis 1:2 and reconstituted in Genesis 1:3-31.

Chapter 1
The Concept of
Supernatural Selection

THERE IS a broad measure of agreement among professional geologists that the evidence points to an orderly succession of stages through which the surface features of the earth have passed to reach their present form, and that this probably took a very long time to come about. It was matched by an orderly succession of living forms, which began to appear rather later in the presently accepted time frame but has nevertheless been going on for a very long time relative to the span of human history. These two broad conclusions, based on an enormous amount of research into the earth's past history, are accepted both by a very large number of informed Christians and by the vast majority of qualified geologists and biologists. This does not by any means guarantee that they are true: but it certainly represents the present consensus of opinion in both circles. The universe is probably very old, and life began a very long time ago and shows an orderly progression from simple to complex. We are talking *only* about the matter of a succession of forms; we are *not* talking about any linear evolution of these forms from one another.

When we come to consider the *how* of these immensely drawn out sequences of geological and paleontological events, we find somewhat less agreement among the scientists themselves, and even less among informed Christian people. The fact is that the evidence can be interpreted in more than one way, and the preferred interpretation always depends upon certain basic and usually unstated assumptions. These assumptions hinge upon the question of whether natural laws are sufficient to account for all past events or only for some of them.

The origin of matter out of nonmatter is clearly not one of these natural events, because it is an inconceivable phenomenon for which we have no experience whatever that would serve as a guide to

18

understanding it by analogy. It is inconceivable to us that matter *never* had a beginning; and it is equally inconceivable to us that matter came suddenly into being out of nothing. These are really the only two alternatives, and both are simply inconceivable. Yet one of them must be true.

So scientists accept what amounts to the eternity of matter, inconceivable though that is, simply because the only alternative, direct creation, is clearly incredible to them. In other words, they accept what is inconceivable rather than what is incredible, because they prefer a nonsupernatural explanation to what they view as a supernatural one. Having started along this route, they are bound to follow it consistently and thereafter to reject any concept of divine interference unequivocally — indeed, dogmatically. They really have no choice.

Many Christian people, however, do not find direct creation out of nothing objectionable at all, although it is still not something we can actually conceive of in our minds. Having admitted supernaturalism to this extent, we do not find it at all irrational to allow the idea of divine interference subsequently during the course of geological history. But there is from this point on much disagreement as to whether such intervention by God was either necessary or likely. Could He not have so designed the universe and our world so that it would be capable of unfolding according to His plan without any such intervention? The answer certainly is, Yes! Indeed, I am fully persuaded that God is an economist where miracle is concerned and that more than 99.9 percent of all events happen as the result of natural law. But, and this is the crucial point, God *has* intervened throughout past time (and still does!) to perform what can only be described as miracles — using this word in the present context as Augustine used it, i.e., to mean the bringing about of events which are not so much contrary to Nature but contrary to what we *know* of Nature. In God's view, there are no miracles, there are merely alternative routes to accomplishing the same end.

So the basic question really is this. Did God merely wind the clock of Nature up, adjust its tempo, and then let it run its course thereafter on its own? Or does He constantly intervene in a supernatural way to do things which cannot possibly be accounted for in terms of natural law as we understand it in the laboratory or in the field?

In this paper, my object is to show that God has intervened, not to disrupt the natural order but to introduce into it courses of events that make the whole process something more than simply a natural development. Such intervention made Revelation necessary in order to complete man's understanding of the mind of God, even as Revelation was *not* necessary for him to understand the workings of Nature wherever God has not intervened. As a consequence, so long as the scientific view maintains its integrity as truly *scientific*, it must conduct its search apart from Revelation and thereby impose limits upon its understanding, though what understanding it does achieve may well be very nearly correct as far as it goes. Revelation is needed to complete our understanding, particularly our understanding of God's creative acts and His acts in judgment.

I do not think these interventions were called for because God was unable to design a natural order that would suit His purposes without them. But I believe He chose to do otherwise so that we could see how He was quietly at work preparing the stage for the enactment of a drama which was to serve uniquely to display His love. This drama was to involve the special creation of a unique creature, man, with freedom of will and a moral sense. This was to be followed by the trial of that man and the working out of his redemption when he failed the test. This redemption involved, in turn, the coming of the Creator Himself as a man, into man's world to sacrifice Himself for man and as a man. Man therefore had to be quite an exceptional creature, a creature in which God could perfectly express Himself in terms of human personality. Man's body and man's spirit had to be such that God could do this as man and for man.[1] Moreover, the natural order had to be such that this tremendous event could be brought to pass without either violating that natural order *or* the person of the Creator Himself.

The Creator had to be born as man is born but without man's corruption, and He had to grow up and live as men might have lived, while still being subject to the physical world in which man labors, eats, grows tired, and sleeps. And in due time, He had to give His life voluntarily as the sin-offering which would be truly human (and therefore acceptably *substitutional*), yet far exceeding the value of any one human life (and therefore *sufficient* for all who would claim it for themselves).

And since this sacrifice was to be the sacrifice of a man on man's behalf, we must assume that there was a first true man who fathered all other men thereafter, whose family is unequivocally "the family of man," whom the Redeemer truly represented in His Person. There can be no half-men who are capable of some kind of half-redemption.

---

[1] "Is Man an Animal?" in this volume.

Nor can even the first man have been any less human that the last, for the Redeemer must be a redeemer in retrospect, back to the very first man, even as He must be in prospect forward to the very last.

Adam, then, was redeemable; and to be truly so he must have been potentially like the Lord Jesus Christ as Man. In this sense, Jesus Christ was the last *Adam*. But Jesus Christ was also the prototype of Adam since He was the Redeemer before the world began (Rev. 13:8). Adam was created in His image (Gen. 2:26). It could not be otherwise.

So I am proposing that God was at work from the very first, moving toward this objective, the preparation of the earth as a stage for the coming of such a creature as man is. And because He is God, He had the right to adopt any plan that seemed best to Him. The plan He did adopt has allowed secular man to uncover to a remarkable degree the workings of Nature and to be in a position to discern (if he would but do it) how much evidence there is of plan and purpose in the course of past events. Orderly preparation is everywhere apparent to the eye of faith; and throughout the whole process God has, I believe, combined creative activity with providential superintendence over the work of His hands.

But I think we need a new term to describe this providential creative superintendence, and I am proposing that we call it *Supernatural Selection*. This is what the present paper is really about. Let me just state as briefly as I can what I mean by this term. Among living creatures, offspring differ from their parents, and this fact provides a means whereby select lines may be encouraged and unwanted lines may be allowed to disappear. If this occurs by accident, it is termed "Natural Selection." When it is performed by man, it is termed "Artificial Selection." Natural Selection is a purely fortuitous process involving no conscious direction as its strongest proponents see it. Artificial Selection depends upon the presence of man and cannot therefore have been operative prior to his appearance. But I believe there is evidence that the progress of forms from simple to complex has not been by chance but by design. This process has resulted, I suggest, from the operation of Supernatural Selection, a form of selection which has the purposefulness of Artificial Selection but also introduces supernatural forces.

It is widely agreed that Natural Selection is not strictly creative. Artificial Selection in a way is creative, but only in the sense that it is directed consciously toward a foreseen objective. Supernatural Selection differs from the other two in that it is a creative process whereby are introduced entirely new forms and therefore, presumably, new genes and new gene combinations. The natural order is not the *cause* of this introduction of novelty, but it is rather the *condition* of it. By combining these three kinds of selective processes — natural, artificial, and supernatural — I believe we have a much better account of the way in which God prepared the earth for the coming of man.

I am proposing that the term "Supernatural Selection" be taken to mean that God intervened within Nature, sometimes by acting directly upon the environment to change the *conditions of life,* sometimes providentially to change the *directions of life* (as when overruling the chance division of genes in the dividing cell), and sometimes creatively to introduce *entirely new forms of life* when the total ecology had been suitably prepared to accommodate them. And I believe that this makes better sense of the evidence and is more in harmony with the Christian world view than either blind evolution or fiat creation.

Chapter 2
Two World Views:
The Christian and the Naturalist

THE fundamental difference between the Christian and the purely naturalistic view of the world in which we live is simply that the former sees the world as having been deliberately planned as a habitation *for man,* whereas the naturalistic view sees man only as an accidental by-product of an entirely purposeless process. These two diametrically opposed views are epitomized by juxtaposing two quotations, one from the Word of God and one from man. The Word of God reads:

> For thus saith the Lord God that created the heavens, God Himself that formed the earth and made it; He hath established it, He created it not in vain, *He formed it to be* inhabited (Isa. 45:18).

According to man, in this instance G. G. Simpson:[2]

> There was no anticipation of man's coming. He responds to no plan and fulfils no supernal purpose. He stands alone in the universe, a unique product of a long unconscious, impersonal material process, with unique understandings and potentialities. These he owes to no one but himself, and it is to himself that he is responsible. He is not the creature of uncontrollable and indeterminate forces but is his own master.

Now, why is there such violent opposition between these two views? I think it exists for several reasons. To begin with, the first world view clearly introduces plan and purpose (what is technically known as the concept of *teleology*), and plan and purpose involve a Planner and a Purposer who stands above and outside of the program. And the existence of such a creative agency inevitably introduces the probability of supernatural intervention. Supernatural intervention, no matter how infrequent it may be, if it occurs at all, effectively removes the possibility of any complete scientific under-

---

[2] Simpson, G. G.: quoted by John Pfeiffer, "Some Comments on Popular Science Books," *Science* 117 (1953):403.

standing by pure intellect alone. Such intervention will inevitably involve events which can only be explained by reference to forces beyond experimental control because they are outside the system. In addition to this, the introduction of a personal Planner at once brings up the question of human responsibility in cooperation or opposition to the plan, since man clearly has the ability to perceive the purpose and therefore to advance or retard it. Both G. G. Simpson and Sir Julian Huxley, the great prophets of the naturalistic world view, have openly acknowledged this fact. For example, Sir Julian speaks of the "glorious paradox" of a process which through eons of time, though quite without direction, finally produced a creature, man, who by reason of his possession of self-consciousness and the ability to make delayed decisions is freed from the previous all-pervasive determinism of the natural order and can therefore undertake that which no creature before him had been able to undertake, namely, the directing of his own future. Indeed, he sees man as the introducer of purpose into a hitherto purposeless universe.[3] Henceforth man will direct evolution.

So these two views are indeed diametrically opposed. The second has really rejected the first for two stated reasons: supernatural intervention is a scientifically unmanageable concept, and moral responsibility to some Agency other than man is psychologically unacceptable. Scripture is clear in saying that man is both spiritually and intellectually in need of redemption, and so long as he is unredeemed, his spiritual and intellectual perceptions and tendencies are distorted.

The very existence of a Purposer introduces a whole "other world," interacting with this world to place either complete understanding or complete control out of man's reach unless he cooperates with God. And it calls man to humble himself, to place his will and his intellect at the service of the Lord instead of attempting to act as an entirely autonomous and self-sufficient creature. Unless he will accept the lordship of Christ in his life, a bondage which is really a freedom, he is forced to accept bondage to himself with his fallen nature, a bondage which is fatal. The naturalistic world view parades as an objective exercise of the intellect but is really the display of a rebellious spirit pretending to be self-sufficient and omnicompetent, cloaking itself in the garb of an unselfish humanitarianism that is entirely deceiving and self-deceived. Naturalism or scientific materialism is, in fact, a false religion, based on a

---

[3] Huxley, Sir Julian, *Rationalist Annual*, 1946, p. 87.

faith which, like the Christian faith, is supported by a creed and a hierarchy (evolution and the contemporary evolutionary authorities), and is every bit as dogmatic and narrowminded as it rightly accuses the medieval church of having been. As H. J. Eysenck said, "The mantle of the Inquisition sits uneasily upon the shoulders of the scientific establishment."[4] Or as R. E. Gibson put it, "The present tendency is for the scientific community, now grown powerful, to behave much as the Church did in Galileo's time."[5]

It, too, has its "scriptures," the pronouncements of its recognized authorities. It believes in miracles and has its shrines (and its sacred bones): and it has its prophets and its martyrs. In short, it is simply another religious world view, for man is indeed incurably religious. Only, it is pretending not to be religious and has so far been highly successful in maintaining the pretense.

Now the question is, Which religious world view is the most reasonable one? An examination of the evidence shows increasingly that the truth lies clearly in the Christian world view, in the view reflected in Isaiah 45:18. The world was indeed formed as a habitation for man, though it is to be gratefully acknowledged that we owe to science much of our understanding today of how this fitness for habitability by man has come about. If we once allow that the whole process of preparation *was* teleological, did have an end in view from the beginning, did involve divine intervention often creatively and sometimes in judgment, and that the world was prepared as a stage for the acting out of a drama specifically involving the confrontation of man and God under unique circumstances, then many striking phenomena in the preparation of the earth are wonderfully illuminated.

These phenomena can be usefully reviewed even within the confines of such a short paper as this. The phenomena to be considered are three. First, very briefly, the evidence that our world was specifically prepared *to sustain life*. Secondly, that *creative activity was clearly demanded* at many stages along the way, because there are an enormous number of critical missing links between groups of animals which evolutionists hold must have been related to one another by intermediate forms but which are nowhere to be found. Thirdly, that there has been a direction fo the course of events, which supports the view that the earth was being furnished specifically *for the coming of man*. In short, the impression of plan and purpose pervades the whole program to such an extent that it becomes virtually unintellig-

---

[4] Eysenck, H. J., in a letter in *New Scient.*, May 29, 1969, p. 490.
[5] Gibson, R. E., "Our Heritage from Galileo Galilei," *Science* 145 (1964):1275.

ible unless they are admitted, and all explanations which exclude them become stilted and artificial. The evolutionist must really commit a kind of intellectual suicide in order to maintain his position that the whole drama has been the result of a freak accident. Scientific materialism constitutes a darkening of the intellect, so that its proponents, though professing to be wise, really become foolish, degrading their spiritual nature by worshiping the human intellect of the creature rather than the wisdom and greatness of the Creator.

So we have these three matters to consider in order to make a reasonable assessment of the relative merits of the two world views.

Chapter 3
The Fitness of the Earth

I T IS a curious thing that so long as man was viewed as the center of the universe because of his unique relationship to God, the earth which is his home automatically achieved its special status by association, and very little thought was given to its peculiar fitness in performing this function. It was only after man had been dethroned and the geocentric concept of the universe had been abandoned, that man suddenly began to realize what a unique body the earth really is.

The uniqueness of the earth as a setting for life is indeed quite extraordinary and the fact is very widely recognized among scientists who nevertheless view it as a purely accidental circumstance. The kind of uniqueness here in view involves a number of factors: (1) its size, (2) its rate of revolution, (3) its mean distance from the sun, (4) the variations in its distance as it circles the sun, (5) the constitution of its surface, and (6) its satellite, the moon.

(1) *The size of the earth* determines the constitution of its atmosphere, and the constitution of its atmosphere determines the nature of the living forms upon it.[6] If it were much larger, it would have retained a large percentage of gases inimical to life. If it were much smaller, its gravitational forces would have been insufficient to retain virtually any atmosphere at all. The smaller planets with smaller gravitational fields lose a large proportion of their lighter elements during the cooling process. The larger planets retain most of their original atmosphere . Actual measurements show that although the weight of Jupiter is only 317 times that of the earth, so great is the amount of atmospheric strata around it that its volume appears to be 1300 times greater than that of the earth. The planet Mercury, on the other hand, has a mass approximately one twenty-third that of the

---

[6] Farmer, F. T., "The Atmosphere: Its Design and Significance in Creation," *Trans. Vict. Instit.* 71 (1939):38f.

earth and is known to have no appreciable atmosphere surrounding it, its gravitational field being too weak to retain nitrogen, oxygen, and water vapor.

The earth has, as a result, just sufficient mass that it is able to hold around itself a blanket of gases which both supports life and shields it from lethal rays of the sun. Its size is such that poisonous gases which formed as the earth cooled were not held in the atmosphere but escaped into space. The carbon dioxide, which *was* held, ultimately supported luxuriant vegetation, which in turn purified it for animal life by setting oxygen free through photosynthesis. Gases, like all other things, have mass, some being heavier than others. It so happens that the gases unsuitable for life were light enough and the earth's gravitational pull small enough that they were lost into space and thereby eliminated.

(2) *The rate of revolution* of the earth is just right for the continuous renewal of the atmosphere for animal life. Nothing gets too cold or too hot over most of its area, and plants have just sufficient times of light and of darkness to perform their function of regenerating the air (since the unique stability of carbon dioxide depends upon alternating light and darkness[7]).

(3) *The distance from the sun* determines the mean temperature of the atmosphere and the earth. The pliable materials of which living tissue is composed are made up of chains of molecules which retain their physical characteristics within a comparatively narrow range of temperature variation. It appears that apart from the very exceptional properties of carbon in forming these long chainlike molecules, such structures as ourselves and all other pliant forms would not be possible at all. It is only in a very restricted range of temperature that these carbon compounds are stable. If the temperature becomes too cold, these chains become inflexible, and if the temperature becomes too high, they lose their bonds and disintegrate. The range of temperature within which living flesh can continue without artificial protection is quite small relative to the ranges of temperature which may exist on a body in space.

(4) *The seasonal variations* which take place throughout the year, due to the 23⁰ axial tilt of the earth, are very important for the continuance of human life. Were it not for these changes, microorganisms which cause diseases and which are favored by certain environmental conditions, would multiply so extensively that the

[7] Henderson, Lawrence, *The Fitness of the Environment, An Inquiry Into the Biological Significance of the Properties of Matter*, quoted by K. Walker in *Meaning and Purpose*, Penguin Books, Harmondsworth, England, 1950, p. 102.

human race might very well suffer extinction because of them.[8] Man is not the only animal to suffer on this account. Consider what would happen to the mosquito population if the conditions ideal for their multiplication were to persist throughout the year all over the globe. Surgeon-General C. A. Gordon pointed out that not only does the persistence of a particular temperature and humidity have to be taken into account here, but even the length of day. The length of day, of course, is governed by the rate of revolution of the earth about its axis. In his paper, Gordon gave a chart showing the distribution throughout one year of some of the major diseases caused by these microorganisms.[9] Were the conditions favoring any one of the disease microorganisms maintained throughout the year, the consequences would probably be disastrous for man.

(5) *The surface of the earth* is part water, part dry land, in a ratio of approximately 3 to 1. The uniqueness of water has been pointed out by countless authorities so that the existence of water in a fluid state is itself fundamental to the continuance of life. On this point Harold Blum makes the following observations:[10]

> Water makes up perhaps 80 to 90% of all living organisms, and may be regarded as their principal environmental component, since even forms living in air maintain an aqueous internal environment in one way or another. Most of the water on the earth is in the liquid state, but it is also of importance as an environmental factor when in the vapor state and even as a solid.
>
> Water seems admirably suited for the major role it plays in maintaining a relatively constant temperature for the earth's surface, a matter of paramount importance to living organisms, which can serve only within a very restricted range of temperature. It owes this aspect of its fitness to several properties.

Blum then elaborates upon these properties. His elaboration leaves one filled with wonder at the power and wisdom of God in creating such a medium. But this medium requires a quite specific environment for its continued usefulness. That is to say, it is useful in a unique way — in a unique environment. Blum sums this up by saying:[11]

> So fitness partakes of the nature of uniqueness, the uniqueness of the earth as an abode of life is a matter that strikes one more forcibly the more he tries to break out of the circle. Not only is the earth as it is, but it has reached that state through an evolutionary process, each step of which has been dependent upon the one preceding it.

---

[8] Gordon, C. A., "Climate in Relation to Organic Nature," *Trans. Vict. Instit.* 17 (1883):33f.

[9] Ibid., pp. 51,52.

[10] Blum, Harold, *Time's Arrow and Evolution*, Princeton U. Press, 1951, p. 62.

[11] Ibid., p. 76.

> The stage upon which living systems bowed their debut was set by all the preceding events in the history of the earth — or, for that matter, of the Universe. These events placed important restrictions upon the nature of life and its evolution.
> Life, it seems, did not arise and evolve as a system free to vary in any direction whatever; but as a system upon which great restrictions were placed, some of them even before the earth came into existence.

Harold Blum concludes his chapter "Fitness of the Environment" with these words, "This aspect of fitness is not, then, universal, but exists only in relation to the planet Earth, or to planets that are very nearly like the Earth."[12]

Water is the most universally effective chemical solvent known, dissolving more substances than any other liquid, though being itself exceedingly stable chemically. It thus provides the fluid medium in which extremely slow chemical reactions may proceed rapidly. It constitutes the fluid medium in the body which makes the body a functioning chemical plant of high efficiency. Water also has almost the highest heat capacity of any known substance and therefore is probably the ideal stabilizer of the temperature of the planet, absorbing enormous amounts of heat without itself becoming too warm for life and then surrendering that heat without itself becoming too cold. Its unusual properties in all three states — solid (ice), liquid, or gaseous (vapor) — within the temperature ranges common to the earth make it tremendously important as a mechanical agent in modifying the earth's surface, weathering the rocks and creating a bed for the first plants, and allowing for its own recirculation by evaporating into cloud formations and then being condensed and precipitated. Its ability to absorb large quantities of oxygen at comparatively low temperatures guarantees survival of living organisms in oceans and lakes. Its exceptional property of expanding slightly just above the freezing point allows it to form a protective layer of ice that floats on the surface and prevents large bodies of water from freezing solid and destroying marine life.

Meanwhile, the earth has a proper relative proportion of land and water surface in order that the land may be neither parched through insufficient precipitation nor turned into a swamp through excess. The topography of the land is such that it assists in the process of watering the earth by causing turbulence in air currents which pass over it, thus bringing about the breakup of cloud formations.

(6) *The existence of the moon* is also of fundamental importance to

---

12 Ibid., p. 85.

the earth. As far as is known, it is the largest satellite relative to the size of its parent body. From this point of view it is, in fact, huge. The moon has sufficient mass to cause tides, and tides are of great importance in keeping the oceans fresh. The possession of a moon of such a size by our earth is of importance in more than one way to life as we know it. What currents do in vitalizing rivers, tides do for the oceans.

All these coincidences add up to an impressive testimony to the uniqueness of the earth as a theater for the unfolding of God's plan. In his book *Man on His Nature,* Sir Charles Sherrington remarked:[13]

> A great American physiologist, Lawrence Henderson, has set forth the particularity of the physical and chemical conditions whose occurrence on the face of the earth render possible the existence of the systems we call living. Certain anomalous properties of water in conjunction with universal powers and space-relations of the carbon atom, along with exceptional conditions of radiation and temperature, are shown to form a sort of conspiracy of circumstance allowing life to be, both here and now.

Dean H. Kenyon and Gary Steinman, in their book *Biochemical Predestination,* would go one step further and argue that the raw materials for life were created in such a form that life must have been predestined by them.[14] They put it this way: "Biochemical Predestination means that the limits beyond which evolutionary processes could not stray, would be determined largely by the properties inherent in the evolving bodies as preset by the (raw) materials from which the (finished) materials were fabricated."

We are often told that the chances of life on other planets like the earth are very considerable, and there is no need to suppose that the existence of life here is really so exceptional. I think the total situation is more complex than the public has been led to believe. In a paper entitled, "Some Cosmic Aspects of Evolution," which G. G. Simpson contributed to a symposium held in Europe in 1968, he dealt with some aspects of the possibility of life elsewhere in the universe and concluded with the following remarks:[15]

> The chances that anything like man, or for that matter like any other terrestrial species except perhaps the most primitive, exists elsewhere in the universe are, I think, the same as the chances that any other planet has had exactly the same history as earth — and as its inhabitants — in every essential detail for two billion years and more.

---

[13] Sherrington, Sir Charles, *Man on His Nature,* Cambridge U. Press, 1963, p. 80.

[14] Kenyon, Dean, and Steinman, Gary, *Biochemical Predestination,* McGraw-Hill, New York, 1969, p. 268.

[15] Simpson, G. G., "Some Cosmic Aspects of Evolution," in *Evolution and Hominization,* ed. Gottfried Kurth, Fischer, Stuttgart, 1968, p. 15.

In my opinion those chances are effectively nil for the mere one hundred million planets of Shapley's minimum or even for Hoyle's less reasonable billions of billions.

I therefore earnestly doubt whether there are any manlike beings waiting to greet us anywhere in the universe. The opposite opinion, even though it has been advanced by some eminent and sensible men, seems to me to underestimate either the complexity or the rigidity of historical causation.

Our earth therefore may be somewhat more significant than we might suppose, even though astronomers have shown that it is such a tiny speck of material in an inconceivably vast universe. The question arises, Can such a tiny speck, looked at from this point of view, be really so important? The answer, I think, may be found this way: There are two alternatives. One would be to make the earth much larger relative to the universe. And the other would be to make the universe much smaller relative to the earth. As we have seen, the first alternative is out of the question; the size of the earth cannot be changed very much. Then what of the latter alternative? What would happen if the universe were made smaller? Is it not true that in due time we should pierce through space until we have found its boundaries? Then suddenly it would not seem so big after all. At first this might not matter very much. But in the end and in a subtle way, when we found we could comprehend the whole of it, our view of the Creator would begin to contract and He would seem to become smaller as our exploration became more complete. In a way, man's greatness is sensed by the magnitude of his achievement, and the immensity of the universe, for the Christian, adds not a little to our sense of awe and our worship of the Creator. If it is true that the universe is expanding, there is little need to fear that we can ever catch up to, or overtake the greatness of God.

And this touches one other point. We are making an assumption that the universe was created a very long time ago. It is quite conceivable that God could have created everything instantaneously and set the stage for man in a moment. Yet this would have two effects: First, it would have prevented us from seeing how wise, methodical, and orderly is God's work. The suddenness of instantaneous creation is frightening rather than reassuring, and as a rule, God has only adopted this method when He desired to make a special impression. It is not His normal way. Moreover, "taking time" implies a certain determination, forethought, and unchangeableness of purpose, as though the end result was something greatly to be desired how ever long it took to achieve. It seems to have taken a long time to prepare the earth for man, and so long as we believe it *was* a preparation for man, we can derive considerable assurance and comfort from the knowledge that God was prepared to work so patiently. Yet from His point of view, there may have been no delay involved. Le Comte du Nouy made this remark:[16]

> To an imaginary being, with a life span of ten thousand million years, evolution would seem very rapid. To God, whom we cannot even conceive in relation to time, it may well have been instantaneous.

—— There is no doubt, of course, that God could have created the world instantaneously, although this would have involved the making of many things in such a form that they would appear to have an age which they did not, in fact, actually have — trees with tree rings that did not signify age, humus which was not constituted of decayed vegetation, and so forth. Scripture shows that this kind of "creation with a history" has often occurred in a miraculous way *whenever it was absolutely necessary*. Thus Moses' rod became a serpent (Exod. 4: 2-4) which was probably of comparable length, and therefore of a specific age, since serpents grow with age continuously. When the Lord restored Malchus' ear (Luke 22:51), it was the ear of a man, appropriate to his age even though it had certainly been created instantaneously. There are many such illustrations in Scripture. Undoubtedly the Lord could have accelerated the preparation of the earth for man in the same way, but evidently a better purpose was served by working in a manner more in keeping with human experience in order that man could, if he would, see that it was all done specifically in preparation for his own coming.

Unfortunately, for a little over one hundred years, since Lyell and Darwin's time, man has *not* been willing to see the whole process as purposeful with respect to himself. The insights of previous generations of naturalists have been, and largely continue to be, laid aside as inappropriate to the naturalistic world view. But the categorical denial of teleological explanations, a denial which at first seemed so stimulating to our understanding of the natural order, is now beginning to prove to be a barrier to further advances in understanding, and there is a new wind blowing.

---

[16] Du Nouy, Le Comte, *Human Destiny*, Longmans Green, Toronto, 1947, p. 200.

Chapter 4
Foresight and the Concept
of Teleology

ALFRED KUHN pointed out that modern objections to the inclusion of the concept of *purpose* to account for any phenomenon in Nature are traceable to Emmanuel Kant's "Critique of Teleological Judgment."[17] Kant held that such a concept really explains nothing, because it makes the "end," or objective, the *cause*. The end becomes the beginning. The argument is circular and therefore without force.

However, not all agree. Indeed, in recent years the older teleological view is regaining favor, especially among those whose main concern is with the origin and the nature of life, where behavior at a molecular and cellular level, as well as at the whole animal level, is increasingly difficult to explain in purely mechanistic terms. Thus Peter T. Mora of the National Institutes of Health, Bethesda, Maryland — during the discussion which followed a paper entitled "The Folly of Probability,"[18] which he presented at a conference on the general subject of the origin of prebiological systems — argued that the present insistence among biochemists that the concept of purpose must be rigidly excluded from all research into the origin and nature of life is proving just as defeating and unhealthy as the medieval insistence was that no other concept was acceptable. It is interesting to note that Dr. Mora's paper, according to the chairman (J.D. Bernal of England), raised "the most fundamental questions of the theory of the origin of life that have been raised at this conference, or as far as I know elsewhere." Mora's conclusion is that "a certain type of teleological approach must be pertinent to the study of living systems," and therefore we ought to "dare to ask whether there is

---

[17] Kuhn, Alfred, *Lectures on Developmental Physiology*, Springer-Verlag, New York, 1971, p. 4.

[18] Mora, Peter T., in *The Origin of Prebiological Systems*, ed. Sidney W. Fox, Academic Press, New York, 1965, pp. 57, 52.

something special in the living which cannot be treated by physics as we know it. . . . "[19]

This is in marked contrast to the views of an older generation. Leo Berg in his *Nomogenesis* observed:[20] "The history of science has taught us that vitalism, as a hypothesis, is valueless, it has in nowise aided us in making any progress in the interpretation of facts." Later he said:[21]

> We are enabled to work fruitfully in the field of natural science only by the aid of forces recognized in physics, and every naturalist should endeavour to interpret nature by mechanistic means. . . .

This could be true if the *only* object of research is the collection of measurable data for the purposes of prediction, if the only *tools* of research are those that measure and weigh, and the only way of obtaining a hearing among one's peers is to adopt an entirely mechanistic approach or else find oneself without a voice and a hearing.

It is true that the teleological explanation may be a lazy man's way out of an intractable problem. But it may also be the worshipful man's insight. The difficulty is to find the balance. But one does not find the balance by simply denying the alternative route to understanding. Sir Alister Hardy said in his book *The Living Stream*, that while we may regard the fabric of an organism as a mechanical configuration, "I would not for the world be thought to believe that this is the only story which life and her children have to tell. One does not come by studying living things for a lifetime to suppose that physics and chemistry can account for them all."[22] And Susanne Langer, with her characteristic eloquence and insight, pointed out:[23]

> Since the assumption of a Divine Creator, who might exercise the required foresight and ingenuity, is proscribed in the scientific sphere, the analogy of the industrial plant can be carried out only with a replacement in the managerial and planning departments; and this is commonly made surreptitiously by a literary trick of using what purports to be a mere figure of speech — the introduction of "Nature" or "Evolution" as the agent who supplies the blueprints and materials and guides the attainment of her (instead of His) purposes. This ready evasion of a difficulty, which really shows up the weakness of the machine model, has become the stock in trade

[19] Ibid., p. 51.

[20] Berg, Leo, *Nomogenesis: or Evolution Determined by Law*, Mass. Instit. of Tech., reprint 1969, p. 6.

[21] Ibid.

[22] Hardy, Sir Alister, *The Living Stream*, Collins, London, 1965, p. 182.

[23] Langer, Susanne, *Mind: An Essay on Human Feeling*, Vol. I, Johns Hopkins Press, 1967, p. 360.

not only of science writers, but of excellent, authoritative scientists writing on problems of adaptation, organic integration and evolutionary tendencies.

Langer gives one example: A. von Szent-Gyorgyi in his book *Oxydation and Fermentation* wrote: "Nature discovered oxydation by molecular oxygen . . . ." And again, "We usually find that the way Nature reaches its purpose is the only possible way, and yet, in spite of its simplicity, the most admirably ingenious way."[24] Surely these things could *only* be said of a personal agent, and who else could this possibly be but God Himself? Langer says, "The factory manager is left nameless."

Andre Schlemmer pointed out long ago that life behaves so *unlike* a machine in so many ways, that the mechanistic approach simply has to be abandoned again and again. Thus the body has very unmachinelike powers to heal itself, to repair and renew its parts, to make compensatory adjustments in order to insure the same work output. And "the most materialistic biologist cannot refrain from falling into teleological language as soon as he turns to explain the process."[25] He is simply *forced* to personify the agent who oversees it all.

Max Kleiber, an internationally renowned physiologist, brought up in the school of claude Bernard, objected strongly to any such course of action by a scientist. Science must rid itself of any appeal to a "personal" agency in the works. Thus he said:[26]

In an attempt to clear science of theology, the postulate that man is a machine is a rather tricky analogy, because an essential characteristic of a machine is that it is planned for a purpose, which implies a designer. . . . The study of man as a machine leads to teleology, and that leads naturally to the question of the mind of the designer of man. This mind must work in a way similar to that of the human mind, if we are to understand its planning; we understand the planning of the machine because the designing engineer thinks as we think. So we are back to theology.

He then observed that as an evasion of this rationale, some atheistic teleologists deified Nature itself! But he asked, "Can a biologist learn to understand what the inventor of a fish or a man had in mind when he designed these creatures?"[27] How blind can one be, indeed! Subsequently, he noted that there *is* a frank return to teleology by such outstanding workers as H. Krebs,[28] and more recently A. V.

[24] Von Szent-Gyorgyi, A.: quoted by Susanne Langer in a footnote, ref. 23, p. 360.

[25] Schlemmer, Andre, *The Crisis in the World of Thought*, IVF, London, 1940, p. 30.

[26] Kleiber, Max, "An Old Professor of Animal Husbandry Ruminates," *Ann. Rev. Physiol.* 29 (1967):11.

[27] Ibid., p. 14.

[28] Krebs, H., "An expansion into the borderline of biochemistry and philosophy," *Bull. Johns Hopkins Hosp.* 95 (1954):19-51.

Hill,[29] both Nobel Laureates. The latter referred to "innumerable examples" in both animal and plant life of what can only be described as evidences of superb engineering — which, of course, invites acknowledgment of a superb "Engineer." Kleiber would have none of this. He said, "Instead of accepting an analogy between a creator of organisms and a designer of machines and hunting for divine blueprints, the Darwinistically oriented physiologist is stimulated to search for causes, and even if he does not completely succeed he usually finds a lot of what is interesting on his way."[30] This seems to me a rather unsatisfactory motivation for the dedication of one's life to research. And if Krebs and Hill, and a growing number of other workers in the life sciences, are any indication, it is a *futile* approach as well.

But Kleiber was, it seems to me, fighting a losing battle, especially when dealing with the extraordinary abilities of the animal body to prepare itself for a role that is yet future. The embryologist sees this particularly — though he may be reluctant to say much about it because of the pressure of scientific opinion to the contrary. Sir Charles Sherrington expresses his wonder at it all, but is clearly not willing to acknowledge the existence of a divine Designer behind it. But his style of writing contrasts notably with that of, for example, G. G. Simpson writing on the same subject. Simpson exemplifies a peculiar blindness in a remarkable way. Thus in a paper entitled "The *Problem* of Plan and Purpose in Nature" (emphasis mine), he wrote:[31]

> An eye, an ear, or a hand is also a complex mechanism serving a particular function. It, too, looks as if it had been made for a purpose. This appearance of purposefulness is pervading in nature, in the general structure of animals and plants, in the mechanisms of their various organs, and in the give and take of their relationships with each other.

It is indeed.

Darwin said he never contemplated the design of the eye without a tremor. And Sir Charles Bell in 1832 wrote his Bridgewater Treatise, *The Hand: Its Mechanism and Vital Endowments as Evincing Design,* almost as an act of worship. Such was the spirit of the time which moved some men to praise and others to tremble. Other later men of equal stature with Bell, like Sir Charles Sherrington, acknowledged their unstinting admiration of the eye as an

---

[29] Hill, A. V., "Why Biophysics?" *Science* 124 (1956):1233.

[30] Kleiber, Max, ref. 26, p. 14.

[31] Simpson, G. G., "The Problem of Plan and Purpose in Nature," *Sci. Monthly,* June 1947, p. 481.

optical instrument and yet could no longer see it as evidence of design by the Creator.

One may compare Simpson's treatment of the eye in his *Meaning of Evolution* (pp. 169-175) and be impressed with his knowledge of the data on eyes in general. But one also senses the coldness, and one might almost say the disinterest of the writer, in the basic questions that such an organ raises.[32] If one reads, by contrast, Sherrington's treatment of the same subject in his *Man on His Nature* (pp. 105-109), one begins to capture something of wonder in the author's mind.[33] How sad, then, to find that he too was blind to the possibility that the designer was a Person, personally approachable and personally rejoicing in His own creations.

One writer of comparatively recent times, whose work is always a delight to read — perhaps because of his willingness to admit the fact of purpose — was F. Wood Jones of England. In his *Trends of Life*, he stated the present position very clearly when he said:[34]

> Against the tyranny of modern orthodox views on teleology there is no reason whatever why we should not rebel, for orthodoxy in this case, is not supported by scientific facts, but rests for the most part on prejudices inherited from the "intransigent materialism of the nineteenth century."

It is true. Prejudice, not scientific objectivity, has been the real reason for the rigid exclusion of the concept of design and purpose in accounting for natural phenomena. It certainly did not prevent Joseph Priestley in his research in chemistry, nor Sir Charles Bell in his research in physiology. Nor did Newton's faith prevent him from formulating his *Principia*, acknowledged to be one of the most extraordinary creations by the human mind in mathematics. There is really no sound reason to exclude the possibility of a Personal Creator superintending His own created order, though it may humble man a little by making him dependent upon revelation wherever his own limited means of exploration of the natural world prove inadequate.

---

[32] Simpson, G. G., *Meaning of Evolution*, Yale U. Press, 1952, pp. 169-175.

[33] Sherrington, Sir Charles, ref. 13, pp. 105ff.

[34] Jones, F. Wood, *Trends of Life*, Arnold, London, 1953, p. 58.

Chapter 5
The Setting of the Stage

THERE IS little doubt that the first step in preparing the
earth as a habitation for man must have been to clothe it with
vegetation as a source of food for the animals which preceded him.
The earth's earliest atmosphere was almost certainly not suited for
the support of animal life of any kind on land, though the seas could
do so. All animals which live on land must have free oxygen as a
source of energy. This oxygen can be breathed (or taken in through
the skin, as it is in insects) mixed with other gases such as hydrogen
or nitrogen, for instance. It appears that in the earth's atmosphere,
at the beginning, even after noxious gases had been removed chiefly
by loss from the earth's gravitational field, the available oxygen was
combined with carbon in the form of carbon dioxide. In order to free
the oxygen, plants were created to perform this role by photosynthesis, taking in carbon dioxide and setting the oxygen free in the
atmosphere again, converting the carbon into usable form. Since all
— flesh is grass (I Pet. 1:24) in the sense that all animal life depends —
upon plant life for energy, plant life had to precede animal life not
only to make the atmosphere respirable for them but to supply them
with food energy.

But the first plants obviously had to be able to survive without
soil, since soil is composed of decayed vegetation. Once vegetation of
such a kind had multiplied sufficiently to create humus, then higher
forms of plant life more effective as sources of energy for animals —
and later for man — could be created and planted. That God should
create and plant is not strange, for this is what we are told He did
with respect to the Garden of Eden (Gen. 2:8).

The course of events was, then, somewhat as follows. The rock
at the surface of the earth was broken down into gravel and sand by
the action of waves, wind, gravitational shock (i.e., falling and
breaking), and by alternating heat and cold, which would fragment
the rock by expansion and contraction. In addition, volcanic action

39

contributed ash and certain chemicals. In due time such combined forces provided suitable beds for the creation and planting of vegetation capable of growing without soil. As W. Bell Dawson pointed out, to begin the process of clothing the earth, God designed plants that could grow in pure sand; and these gradually made soil for plants of higher classes to grow in. There is, for example, one species of pine which is used extensively in France in the dunes along the coast, for the purpose of preventing them from drifting back over the cultivated fields.[35]

These first plants were reeds, rushes, and ferns, and although they often grew as large as trees, they were not the kind of vegetation which higher forms of animals use as food. They served a dual purpose, however. While they lived, they began to remove from the atmosphere its excess carbon dioxide; and when they died, they created a humus which when it had accumulated sufficiently provided the bed into which higher forms of plant life were introduced by creation. Lichens also enter this picture as fundamental to all that followed. "Lichens have no need for soil, but, preparing it, they lay the cornerstone for flowers and trees. They are the plant world's pioneers, bringing life where none existed."[36] When the time was fully come that animals should move out of the sea on to the dry land, there was both air fit for them to breathe and food suitable for them to eat.

George Wald, Professor of Biology at Harvard, speaks of the preparation of the atmosphere by plant life in the following way:[37]

> The atmosphere of our planet seems to have contained no (free) oxygen until organisms placed it there by the process of plant photosynthesis. . . .
>
> Once this was available organisms could invent a new way to acquire energy, many times as efficient. . . . This is the process of cold combustion called respiration.

Wald spoke of "inventing" a new way to acquire energy far more efficient than the methods by which plants acquire it. The word "invent" is inappropriate since it attributes to inanimate things a consciousness of purpose which they surely do not have. But his remarks serve to point out that the liberation of free oxygen for cellular respiration allowed for the introduction of living forms with immensely increased energy potential. The lowest, and thus pre-

---

[35]Dawson, W. Bell, *Forethought in Creation*, the Bible Instit. Colportage Assoc., 1925, p. 18. See also Dale Swartzendruber, "Wonders of the Soil," in *The Evidence of God in an Expanding Universe*, ed. J. C. Monsma, Putnam, New York, 1958, pp. 188f.

[36] Platt, Rutherford, "A Visit to the Living Ice Age," *Nat. Geog. Mag.*, April 1957, p. 526.

[37] Wald, George, "The Origin of Life," *Sci. American,* August 1954, pp. 49,52.

sumably the oldest, deposits of minerals are found in nonoxidized form, which seems to demonstrate the initial absence of free oxygen. It is evident, therefore, that animal life could not have existed until the plants had transformed the atmosphere.

This step thus opened the way for the introduction of creatures which were far less tied to their environment, one further step in the unfolding of God's purposes in the ultimate creation of man. As Wald put it:[38]

> Photosynthesis made organisms self-sustaining; coupled with respiration, it provided a surplus (of energy). To use an economic analogy, photosynthesis brought life to the subsistence level, respiration provided it with capital.

But this is not all. The new atmosphere thus generated had an equally important function of another kind:[39]

> The entry of oxygen into the atmosphere also liberated organisms in another sense. The sun's radiation contains ultraviolet components which no living cell can tolerate. We are sometimes told that if this radiation were to reach the earth's surface, life would cease. That is not quite true. Water absorbs ultraviolet radiation very effectively, and one must conclude that as long as these rays penetrated in quantity to the surface of the earth, life had to remain under water.
>
> With the appearance of oxygen, however, a layer of ozone formed high in the atmosphere and absorbed this radiation. Now organisms could for the first time emerge from the water and begin to populate the earth and the air. Oxygen provided not only the means of obtaining adequate energy for evolution, but the protective blanket of ozone which alone made possible terrestrial life.

These stages of preparation reinforce the concept of purpose, because they indicate the timed introduction of the requisite elements in the economy of Nature at each step as required — and very frequently without predecessors. The appearance of lichens, for example, looks much more like deliberate creation than the outcome of pure chance. Similarly, later on, lungs seemed to be in the making at the same time that the atmosphere was being prepared for creatures that could make full use of such structures, a circumstance which again looks much more like planning than the operation of pure chance.

Everything is orderly and purposeful, there is nothing accidental about the order in which forms of life appear from amoeba to man.

---

[38] Ibid., p. 53.
[39] Ibid.

The Evidence for a Succession of Forms

In giving introductory courses in the life sciences, which are naturally presented from the evolutionary point of view, university professors often refer to the "Evolutionary Base Line." By this is meant a succession of forms of life which are chosen to represent what are believed to be the basic steps in the process of development from amoeba to man.

This base line begins with unicellular forms such as Paramecia, but it is worth noticing that an authority like Gaylord Simpson considers the step from no life to amoeba as being as great as the whole passage from amoeba to man. In order to make the picture more or less complete, the Evolutionary Base Line will be given very briefly with a note explaining the advance represented by each form in the series.

The line is traced from the invertebrates to the vertebrates through Amphioxus, a creature which stands lowest in the phylum Chordata. This creature lacks a brain in the accepted sense, all its controls being distributed along the dorsal cord. It differs from other invertebrates in the possession of a pharynx perforated by gill slits which, however, serve to strain food rather than to provide an oxygen supply. Next in this base line it is customary to place the Lamprey, which has its notochord apparently encased in part in bony segments. Lampreys have "nostrils," rudimentary eyes, ears under the skin, and a single nasal pouch. These animals have a brain, but no movable jaw and no fins. Next comes Climatius which, like the former, is quite small but now has a kind of primitive jaw. Then comes Cladoselache, with paired fins, fully developed jaws, jointed and muscled, and with both upper and lower segments free to move. We are then introduced to Crossopterygians. Here we find the presence of bony structures underlying the fins constituting them genuine limbs. These are viewed as the forerunners of legs in amphibians. Unlike the animals which preceded, they possessed a simple lung. Associated with these representative creatures in the base line are the Dipnoi, or lung fishes, which are at a similar level of development except that they have a modified mouth construction in which there is an opening from the nasal sac (now a kind of lung) to the inside of the mouth. This enabled the animal for a limited time to dispense with the use of the gills and use oxygen stored in the nasal sac. In conjunction with the development of fins with a bone substructure, it became possible for these creatures to make short trips out of the water. It is generally held that, in Devonian times, extended drought dried up many rivers leaving only stagnant pools.

When these became depleted of oxygen, the lung fishes were able to move to new pools. Thus began, supposedly, the conquest of the land.

The most primitive amphibians appear in the Carboniferous Era, namely, the labyrinthodonts, in which appear rudimentary legs with five webbed digits and a more highly developed olfactory sense. Later in the Carboniferous Era, the Cotylosaurs are first discovered. One particular species, the Seymouria, have genuine legs which, however, were very squat and suggest that the possessor was not really at home on land. Nevertheless, the Seymouria produced the first land-type eggs in which the water environment is contained within the egg and surrounded by a "shell."

Up to this point, all living creatures were cold-blooded. So long as they stayed in the water, this was no disadvantage, a water environment being probably the most stable environment conceivable. In very hot weather, the deeper waters remain cool and in sub-zero weather, the ice which forms on the top protects the water beneath from dropping too low. It is generally thought that this accounts for the persistence of many fishes, such as Coelacanths, through millions and millions of years with virtually no change in form. However, when the environment over land areas had been prepared by plant life and the atmosphere had been made fit for animals that breathe air, it was then possible for living creatures to leave their watery home and come up to stay on the dry land. At first these had been forays only, then some of the first pioneers began to lay their eggs on the land, though they and the young returned to the water as a natural habitat. Longer and longer stays were made by such creatures in this new environment, but so long as they were cold-blooded, they were at the mercy of the elements, for when the sun went down or cold weather came, their energy was reduced to a very low level.

There is an early creature occasionally mentioned in the Evolutionary Base Line, the Dmetrodon, that was apparently supplied with a strange sail-like structure along its back supported by a number of "masts." Sometimes it looks as though God took delight in experimenting. It is not certain what purpose these served, but it has been thought that they were heat exchangers, a kind of network of arteries set in a thin membrane stretched out to present the maximum surface area to the sun, thus providing the animal with heat more rapidly than otherwise. Presumably, when cold temperatures came, the reverse process was avoided by a form of vasoconstriction so that deep body heat was not lost to the cool air through the heat exchangers. But no cold-blooded animal can remain active and alert outside of a fairly narrow range of temperature variation. Such creatures could never, therefore, become complete masters of the environment.

At this point, it is customary to follow a sideroad in the Evolutionary Base Line. Warm-blooded animals as a class bear their young alive. The egg, as such, is never "laid." But there was a stage — and representatives still exist — in which the transition was not completely made, as represented by the Duckbilled Platypus and the Spiny Anteater, both of which are egg-laying mammals. These creatures are truly mammals and warm-blooded, yet the young they bear appear first as reptilian eggs. A further stage is represented by the Marsupials. These are pouched animals which, like the Duckbilled Platypus and Spiny Anteater, are not included in the base line; but they are also referred to as transitional forms, because although the egg is never laid in this case, the young are nevertheless hatched "too soon" and have therefore to be returned to a kind of "shell" to complete the full process of embryonic development. They are not included because they are too "late" in the series.

Transitional forms between cold-blooded animals and mammals are sometimes represented by the Therapsids, of which one particular species, the Cynognathus, is customarily singled out. It is not necessary here to detail the reasons why this species is considered transitional, except to mention that it has a number of mammalian features, especially in the mouth region. And although it is cold-blooded, it appears to have been highly active — which most cold-blooded land animals are not.

Among the earliest representatives of the Placentals, which bear their young in a fully developed state are Hedgehogs, Ground Shrews, and Tree Shrews. The Evolutionary Base Line is traced through the Tree Shrews for several reasons, one of which is its completely unspecialized form. These little animals enjoy the privilege of being able to sit upright and use prehensile front feet to feed. While they have an exceedingly simple brain, they are highly mobile, with limbs capable of complex movements and a fair range of stereoscopic vision.

On a rung nearer the top of the ladder are placed the Lemurs, in which there is a development of fingernails and well-formed "hands," with opposable thumbs widely separated and separable from the rest of the fingers. They appear to have a wide range of vocalization and their eyes are closer to the front than similar mammals which preceded them. They were quite common in Eocene times. Their facial appearance was somewhat foxlike, a fact which has led some authorities to question whether they should be classed as Primates.

Soon after the appearance of the Lemurs, we find the Tarsioids. These creatures are placed much higher in the scale of evolution and are classed as Primates. Their eyes are turned completely forward, the nose is very short, and the flattening of the face is taken to mean that the sense of smell has become less important and stereoscopic vision has now taken over.

We come, then, to monkeys and apes which appear next in the geological time scale and seem to stand quite close to man in many interesting ways. It is now customary to complete the Evolutionary Base Line tentatively by passing from monkeys and apes through the South African man-apes (Australopithecinae) and certain Far Eastern fossil men (Sinanthropus and Pithecanthropus) to modern man.

In looking over this thread of progress, which is presented in slightly variant forms depending upon the authority, one can discern a certain purpose throughout the story. Sir Julian Huxley formulated a very simple definition of what is meant by progress from this biological point of view. He said: [40]

> We have thus arrived at a definition of evolutionary progress as consisting in a raising of the upper level of biological efficiency, this being defined as increased control over and independence of the environment.

Possibly there are many faults in this provisional base line. The order may be incorrect, and it is admitted at once that some of the stages are represented by animals which are still with us, though "ideally" they should long since have left the scene, having once fulfilled their role in the chain of events. But one can discern an apparently orderly progression which is intellectually satisfying and not at all unreasonable. This allows us to see that God may have acted in setting the stage for man through a series of steps which, if we ourselves had had His creative power, we too might have adopted as being entirely appropriate. If one thinks about it, there is really no reason why we ourselves should not have been so designed that embryological and foetal development, instead of taking nine months to complete, might have been completed in a matter of minutes. It is a startling thought and one can think of all kinds of physiological difficulties, but with His infinite design capacity God could easily have overcome any such difficulties, and this accelerated gestation would seem the most natural thing in the world. There are

---

[40] Huxley, Sir Julian, *Evolution: The Modern Synthesis*, Harper, New York, 1942, p. 564.

social implications, of course, in such a program, and I am entirely ignoring these by this proposal. But the fact remains that God could have appointed this as the normal method. That He did not do so, that He made it a drawn-out process, suggests to me that He also had a good reason for making the preparation of the earth for man a drawn-out process. It is not altogether impossible that David, by inspiration, may have penned his words in Psalm 139:14-16 in such a way that they could have a kind of double meaning to reflect some such thought as this:

> I will praise thee; for I am fearfully *and* wonderfully made: marvellous *are* thy works; and *that* my soul knoweth right well.
>
> My substance was not hid from thee, when I was made in secret, *and* curiously wrought in the lowest parts of the earth.
>
> Thine eyes did see my substance, yet being unperfect; and in thy book all *my members* were written, *which* in continuance were fashioned, when *as yet there was* none of them.

The process of the preparation of the earth for the coming of man was not altogether unlike the process of the preparation of the organs and tissues in the womb which, when the time has come for birth, will all be perfectly suited for the role they are to play in the introduction of a human being into the world.

If there is any sense in which later forms of life were "higher" than earlier forms, it may not be so much in their complexity as it is in their increasing independence of the environment. With the appearance of man, we have a creature who, though by no means wholly independent of the environment, yet is so constituted structurally and functionally as to be superior to the environment in an entirely new way. He is, or may be, more independent geographically by being ubiquitous, dietetically by being omnivorous, environmentally by being master of land and sea and air — and now even of space also — and governmentally by his acquisition of superior means of achieving dominion over all other contestants. In a manner of speaking, each of these areas of superiority was apportioned a little at a time to animals which preceded him, though to none of them was given superiority in them all.

The nearer the time came for the playing out of the final act of the drama, the more nearly can the stage be seen to have achieved its final setting. It is not therefore surprising that just before the appointed time for the creation of man, there were already in existence manlike creatures whose presence demonstrated how nearly ready the setting of the stage was. Such creatures were in existence by then not because some blind evolutionary process was about to cast man up as a final gesture in fulfilling its own destiny, but rather because

God had now deliberately and purposefully brought the world to that condition of preparedness appropriate for the introduction of man, the crown of creation. The idea that this vast display of creative activity in thus setting the stage, occupying an inconceivably great span of time, could be likened to the gestation period in the birth of a human being, may seem farfetched indeed, and yet it is an idea that has appealed to many minds in the past — until Darwin turned men's thoughts into the barren channel of atheistic evolution. Somewhere during the Middle Ages an anonymous writer, without benefit of the knowledge of the past which we now have, set forth this concept very simply and with great beauty when he said, "The Cosmos was pregnant with man."[41]

[41] Ramm, Bernard, *The Christian View of Science and Scripture,* Eerdmans, Grand Rapids, Mich., 1954, p. 227.

Chapter 6
The Growing Evidence
of Creative Activity

FOR MANY years paleontologists have been remarking upon the absence of certain essential links with which to complete, in Arthur O. Lovejoy's phrase, "The Great Chain of Being." There is something disturbing about these breaks in the record, and great rejoicing has occasionally resulted from finding some transitional form, such as the Polyp Hydra (linking animal and vegetable),[42] and the Archaeopteryx which bridged the gap from reptiles to birds—or so it seemed. Moreover, where such links were still missing, there were often those who were willing to supply them. One very famous practical psychologist, P. T. Barnum, did just this, supplying many such missing links in an exhibit which was part of a larger collection of curiosities the public was invited to see in 1842, seven years before Darwin's *Origin of Species* was published.[43] The advertisements of the day heralded this exhibition in New York City, which began the American Museum, formed by combining Scudder's and Peele's Museums. It was enlivened with freak shows and stage entertainment. Perhaps some of the reconstructions in present day museums are still in the Barnum tradition!

Gaps in the Record

At first the authorities, faced with the existence of such gaps, attributed this to the "incompleteness of the geological record." When one or two of these missing links were later discovered, their plea seemed to be quite justified. Given time, the chain would be forged completely. But this has not proved to be the case. The missing links persist at many critical points, and there are not a few authorities today who believe that they never will be found. Either they have been destroyed, or evolution has been discontinuous. This

---

[42] Lovejoy, A. O., *The Great Chain of Being*, Harvard U. Press, 1942, p. 233.
[43] Ibid., p. 236.

does not mean that they now believe in direct creation by a personal Creator, but rather that the small jumps resulting from mutations as currently observed have at times and for unknown reasons been much larger — large enough, in fact, for a reptile at one fell swoop to suddenly become a warm-blooded feathered fowl. This kind of jump was not termed a mutation but a saltation by R. Goldschmidt.[44] A single quotation from this authority will serve to show what he had in mind when he spoke of saltations:

> At this point in our discussion, I may challenge the adherents of the strictly Darwinian view, which we are discussing here, to try to explain the evolution of the following features by the accumulation and selection of small mutants; hair in mammals, feathers in birds, segmentation in arthropods and of vertebrates, the transformation of gill-arches in phylogeny, including the aortic arches, muscles, nerves, etc.: further, teeth, shells of molluscs, ecto-skeletons, compound eyes, blood circulation, alternation of generations, statocysts, ambulacral system of ecinoderm, pedicellara of the same, enido-cysts, poison apparatus of snakes, and finally, primary chemical differences like hemoglobin versus hemocyanin, etc. No one has accepted this challenge! Corresponding examples from plants could be given.

In other words, Goldschmidt argues that there have occurred at many points sudden and radical changes of form involving at times the whole organism, so pronounced as to be quite unexplained by gene mutations. His major antagonist, Dobzhansky, completely disagrees. But on one thing both concur, namely, that blind evolution accounts for everything.

At first, Christians were quick to underscore the gaps as evidence of the intervention of God. Here, they felt sure, evolution must be abandoned and creative activity introduced. But then inevitably some of the gaps began to be filled in. Those who were a little more far-seeing warned that it was dangerous to emphasize these gaps as evidence of creative activity for two reasons: first, because if they were reduced in number, God would be made smaller and smaller; and secondly, because it tended to minimize the continuous sustaining activity of the Creator in the day to day workings of Nature, reducing God's activity not to sustaining the world but to special interferences in it. In recent years this warning has been issued more and more loudly in spite of the fact that evolutionists themselves have been more and more ready to admit the persistence of the gaps.[45]

---

[44] Goldschmidt, Ralph, *Material Basis of Evolution*, Yale U. Press., 1940, p. 6.

[45] Lack, David, *Evolutionary Theory and Christian Belief*, Methuen, London, 1957, pp. 62,63, in which several quotations give warning against constituting the Creator as "God of the Gaps."

The question is, then, do we need to surrender this evidence of creative activity? If we are careful to remain aware of the fact that God is not merely the God of the gaps but the God of the continuities also, we shall not need to relinquish what seems to me a very strong evidence of direct creation.

We do not believe in God simply because gaps exist, which seem to demand a God to fill them. We know these gaps exist at present, and there seems every likelihood that they will persist, and so we merely say as Christians, "Such gaps may well be points at which God was at work by directly creative means." But the fact is that the scientist with a Christian faith does not actually find himself any less eager to fill in the gaps if he can. It is true that his faith may make the search less important, but it may supply him with a compensating drive — the desire to explore God's handiwork in creation simply because it *is* His handiwork. Moreover, few if any paleontologists ever set out specifically to discover a missing link whose form they have already conceived as intermediate between two other divergent forms. They search for fossil animal remains and if they happen to come across an intermediate form, they rejoice as one who finds great spoil. But so would the Christian paleontologist! One's faith in the reality of a Creator who had a purpose really has no bearing on it. Finding an intermediate form like an Archaeopteryx is not really the reward of diligence (though diligence is required), but simply good fortune for the finder. It may seem otherwise with supposed intermediate forms between man and the apes, but here the situation is a little different, because any fossil ape is taken almost automatically as a missing link, even though the finder knows perfectly well that given a certain basic skeletal structure of similar proportions, a like habitat, and a similar source of food, convergence will almost guarantee parallel development. It is only what one might expect. It would be surprising if this were *not* so.

In some ways, the Christian research worker is in an advantageous position: he may be kept, by his knowledge of the Bible, from making some of the ludicrous mistakes made by eager exponents of man's animal ancestry, such as the construction of Mr. and Mrs. Hesperopithecus out of the tooth of a wild pig. And in so far as he reports upon findings of fossil remains of creatures below man, he may — like Hugh Miller[46] — achieve an eloquence unattained by

---

[46] Miller, Hugh, *The Testimony of the Rocks*, Nimmo, Edinburgh, 1874. A similar literary eloquence will be found in two other books written in a like spirit: Prince Petr Kropotkin, *Mutual Aid,* Extending Horizon Books, Boston, reprint 1955, and F. Wood Jones, *Trends of Life*, Arnold, London, 1953.

the indifferent evolutionist, who sees only data in what he finds. Modern works on geology or paleontology are, by and large, atrociously dull and have none of the eloquence of, for instance, Miller's *The Testimony of the Rocks.*

Gaps exist all down the line from the very beginning to the very end of the record, from the Cambrian Era to the Pleistocene Age, from nonliving to living, from vegetable to animal, from invertebrate to vertebrate, from cold- to warm-blooded, from animal to man. These are merely the major areas in which gaps exist. Gaps appear also between Orders, Classes, Families, Genera, and Species. In the total view it could quite reasonably be argued that there is not one missing link, i.e., between animals and man, but a least a million missing links since there are over a million species. Of course, gaps between species are not really admitted, they are supplied by imagination. But at the other levels they are acknowledged.

Between the nonliving and the living, there is a gap. There are some who hold that the viruses supply a bridge, but this is not generally conceded. We have already spoken of this gap earlier. Gaylord Simpson had an illuminating statement about this.[47]

> Above the level of the virus, if that be granted status as an organism, the simplest living unit is almost incredibly complex. It has become commonplace to speak of evolution from amoeba to man, as if the amoeba were a natural simple beginning of the process. On the contrary, if, as must almost necessarily be true short of miracle, life arose as a living molecule or protogene, the progression from this stage to that of the amoeba is at least as great as that from amoeba to man.

Many other writers have underscored Simpson's words, stating that in fact the amoeba had "solved" all the problems of living successfully and that the rest of evolutionary history is merely an elaboration, adding virtually nothing that is absolutely new. We hear much these days, especially since Oparin's work, of the possibility of synthesizing life in the laboratory. Supposing a protogene or living molecule were so constructed, would it really be alive? Is life merely chemistry and physics? Is not one of the characteristics of living things a kind of will to continue alive? Where does this "will" come from? Is it conceivable that it arises automatically if you can just get molecule bonds of the right kind in a test tube? Whether there is really a gap here, or not, depends to some extent on how comprehensive one's definition of life is to be. The power to adjust, to propagate, and to heal, and not merely the power but the will — the urge — to do these things is part of life.

---

[47] Simpson, G. G., ref. 32, pp. 15,16.

Equally inexplicable is the sudden profusion of life when we first meet it. The controversy as to the reality, or otherwise, of pre-Cambrian fossils continues unabated, not so much because there is an increasing amount of evidence but because the Cambrian rocks which appear next in time and are in some places found imposed directly upon them, contain fossil remains representative of all the principal phyla of animals.[48] It used to be thought that the vertebrates were not represented but there are today some who believe they were.[49] This leaves evolutionists with the embarrassing problem of accounting for practically all the major types of animals appearing suddenly without forebears, a situation which is hard to explain except by postulating creation on a grand scale in the beginning. This being unacceptable, it becomes essential somehow to find at least some evidence of prior stages of development in pre-Cambrian times. Hence the plea that certain inclusions found in these earliest of all rocks are actually the remains of very simple forms of life metamorphosed during the subsequent history of these rocks. Douglas Dewar gave an excellent treatment of these finds, giving the nature of them, the claims made for them, and the authorities who held them to be organic.[50] He then showed the extreme precariousness of such claims. In this Gaylord Simpson agreed:[51]

> It is true that most pre-Cambrian rocks have been so altered as to be unsuitable for the clear preservation of fossils. This, however, is not true of all of them, and the exceptions have been so carefully searched, that fossils other than algae should have been found if present. There must be some special reason why varied fossils are suddenly present in the Cambrian and not before.

We must begin of course with the major divisions, the phyla. Here there is no doubt about the problem of gaps. The case was stated succinctly by Buchsbaum, in a standard textbook:[52]

> Everyone enjoys the unravelling of a good mystery, but no one would like to read on from clue to clue, until the earliest and most important events seemed about to be disclosed, only to find that the rest of the pages in the book were missing. Just this kind of exasperating situation confronts us when we try to relate animals to one another in an orderly scheme.
> Anyone can see that honeybees are much like bumble bees, that bees resemble flies more than they do spiders, and that spiders are more like lobsters than like clams.

---

[48] Shull, A. F., *Evolution*, McGraw-Hill, New York, 1936, p. 46.
[49] Romer, Alfred, *Vertebrate Palaeontology*, 2nd ed., U. of Chicago Press, 1945, p. 36.
[50] Dewar, Douglas, "The Earliest Known Animals," *Trans. Vict. Instit.* 80 (1948):12-32.
[51] Simpson, G. G., ref. 32, p. 18.
[52] Buchsbaum, R., *Animals Without Backbones*, U. of Chicago Press, 1938, pp. 334,335.

But when we attempt to relate the phyla, which, by definition, are groups of animals with fundamentally different body plans, there is little we can say with certainty. Arthropods are clearly allied to annelids, but how they are related to such utterly different animals as starfishes or vertebrates is quite obscure. The fossil record, which in many cases provides us with a whole series of gradually changing specimens from which we can work out the evolution of one small group from another, is of practically no use in relating the phyla to each other. For, as we dig deeper and deeper into the rocks, expecting to find a level at which the most recently evolved phyla no longer appear, we find instead that the fossil record is obliterated.

Buchsbaum then explained this for his readers by stating that the record fails us here because the rocks have been so altered in various ways that any fossils they contained have been changed beyond recognition as such. But this is an entirely gratuitous assumption. There are pre-Cambrian rocks at great depth which have not been so metamorphosed, and yet they still contain no such missing links. Unfortunately the student is not told that at this point in his education. When his mind has been thoroughly set to accept with conviction the theory of evolution then he can be casually told that there are problems. This is almost deliberately misleading. Buchsbaum says "We must assume a relationship." *Must* we?

Vast masses of unmetamorphosed pre-Cambrian sediments, like the huge Cuddapah series of India, over 20,000 feet thick, which are perfectly suited to have preserved fossil traces of life — had it existed — are known.[53] It has also been claimed that the early seas were deficient in lime, and that on this account the hard parts which are normally fossilized were not developed during this period. But the suddenness with which they appear in Cambrian rocks is hard to explain on this basis, for it seems unlikely that the lime salts were so suddenly increased in the interval. And the existence of extensive coastal fauna — missing earlier — adds to the difficulty, since this could not be accounted for by such a means. Moreover, as has been pointed out on numerous occasions, jellyfish, which have no hard parts at all, are found in Cambrian rocks as fossils. So the total absence of fossils in pre-Cambrian times is not merely due to the absence of hard parts.

The problem is real enough. Recently Daniel I. Axelrod wrote:[54]

One of the major unsolved problems of Geology and Evolution is the occurrence of diversified multicellular-marine invertebrates in Lower Cam-

---

[53] Davies, Merson, "The Present Status of Teleology," *Trans. Vict. Instit.* 79 (1947):80.
[54] Axelrod, Daniel I., "Early Cambrian Fauna," *Science*, July 1958, p. 7.

brian fossils including porifera, coelenterates, brachiopods, mollusca, echinoids, and arthropods.

In the Arthropoda are included the well known trilobites which were complexly organized, with well differentiated head and tail, numerous thoracic parts, jointed legs, and — like the later crustaceans — a complex respiratory system. From a phylogenetic standpoint the Early Cambrian faunal assemblage is generally interpreted to represent rather simple ancestral types in their respective phyla, which rapidly diversified into numerous types (species, genera, families, orders) during and following the Early Cambrian.

Their high degree of organization clearly indicates that a long period of evolution preceded their appearance in the record. However, when we turn to examine pre-Cambrian rocks for the forerunners of these Early Cambrian fossils, they are nowhere to be found. Many thick (over 5000 feet) sections of sedimentary rock are now known to lie in unbroken succession below strata containing the earliest Cambrian fossils. These sediments apparently were suitable for the preservation of fossils, because they are often identical with overlying rocks which are fossiliferous, yet no fossils are found in them. Clearly, a significant but unrecorded chapter in the history of life is missing from the rocks of pre-Cambrian time.

Numerous theories have been advanced to explain this hiatus. . . .

Axelrod then listed these, which include such theories as that the fossils were destroyed by changes in the rock, that the fossils had no skeletons because there was no calcium in the sea, that the sea was acid preventing the formation of calcarious skeletons, that the marine life originated in fresh water only reaching the oceans in Cambrian times, that pre-Cambrian life lacked hard parts because life was confined to surface water where skeletons would have been of little use, or that skeletons suddenly appeared due to the adoption of a sluggish mode of existence at the bottom of the sea. These and other theories are examined and the general conclusion is that in due time evidence will be forthcoming to show how the evolution took place. It seems to me that it is proper to continue this search and unless those who undertake it adopt an essentially hostile attitude towards creation, the search will not be thorough. Until they find what they are looking for, we have as much right to believe in direct creation as they do in evolution — indeed more right, because the sudden appearance of living forms is a fact, but their supposed evolution is still only a theory.

Merson Davies pointed out that it is not merely a case of the absence of a few simple transitional forms. What is missing is virtually 99 percent of the earlier stages of development of all kinds of forms, insects, birds, mammals, reptiles — all sorts of highly organized and presently represented living creatures. Thus he wrote:[55]

---

[55] Davies, Merson, ref. 53, pp. 81,82.

Essentially new types always appear suddenly; the greatest problems being solved outright, without any clue as to how they were solved. Nobody knows how crinoids originated. The first amphibians have true feet, there being nothing to show how any fin became a foot. Swimming molluscs (Pteropods) appear at the base of the record; while their supposed ancestors, the Opisthobranchs, do not appear until the Carboniferous, some two hundred million years later. . . .

The first birds have large and perfectly formed feathers, there being nothing to put between a feather and a scale. The first bats are perfect bats, and even include a still existing family (the Vespertilionidae). The first whales are as true whales as any existing today, and include quite different types, one of which belongs to the existing order of Odontoceti, and seems to have no connection with the others. . . .

The first insects include the largest ones known to us — Meganeura — or monster dragonflies, with a wingspan of nearly a yard in extent; also numerous cockroaches of many kinds. The earliest known scorpion is hardly distinguishable from existing ones, and has such a well-developed poison apparatus that it is named Palaeophonus, or ancient murderer. It is the same with the whip scorpions, which are fully characterized from the first. Spiders also appear suddenly, and are practically unchanged from the start. Among the first water fleas we find the modern genus Estheria.

Wood Jones was of the opinion that the vertebrates did not evolve out of invertebrates. He said:[56]

Since the acceptance of Darwin's theory of evolution, many attempts have been made by distinguished biologists (such as Gaskill and Patten) to prove that the invertebrates did indeed evolve into vertebrates: but all the available evidence makes it quite certain that the two great phyla arose in complete independence of one another.

Nor can the vertebrates be derived from the arthropods, which are also found in Cambrian rocks, as A. L. Kroeber put it:[57]

No arthropod can give rise to a vertebrate, their patterns are separated by profound, unbridgeable clefts.

The same is true in the plant world. C. R. Metcalfe and L. Chalk had this to say:[58]

All views which have been expressed concerning the phylogenetic interrelationships of plant families are largely a matter of personal opinion. To the authors, as indeed to many other botanists, it appears highly improbable that the families of flowering plants have been evolved one from another.

In the same connection, A. F. Shull said:[59]

[56] Jones, F. Wood, ref. 34, p. 74.
[57] Kroeber, A. L., *Anthropology*, Harcourt, Brace, New York, 1948, p. 315.
[58] Metcalfe, C. R., and Chalk, L., *The Anatomy of Dicotyledons*, Clarendon Press, Oxford, 1950, quoted by Irving W. Knoblock, *Jour. Amer. Sci. Affil.* 5, no. 3 (September 1953):14.
[59] Shull, A. F., ref. 48, p. 57.

The true flowering plants appeared suddenly in such abundance and variety in late Cretaceous that it is generally assumed they originated much earlier, though little fossil evidence of them in earlier periods has been obtained.

Agnes Arber, in a remarkable book *The Natural Philosophy of Plant Form*, goes even further and argues that it has been to the detriment of botanical research that evolutionary ideas and the determination to trace continuous lines has governed the thinking of contemporary students in this field.[60] Similarly, Ronald Good pointed out that at least some of the best-known speculations about organic evolution are less generally applicable in botany than is usually claimed. He observed:[61]

Little or nothing in this picture of Evolution in the Flowering Plants supports the view that they are the products of any highly competitive and illiminative plan of nature. On the contrary it suggests that no matter what new characters or combinations of old characters change with time may effect, they are all able to find an existence somewhere in the scheme of things.

It seems, therefore, that not only are representatives of many of the stages of supposed plant development missing, but even those which are available are not to be accounted for by currently accepted evolutionary theory. J.W. Klotz emphasized the problem here when he stated:[62]

One of the big problems of plant evolution, and especially the evolution of flowering plants, is the fact that the latter appear so suddenly in the geological record. . . .

Darwin called their origin an "abominable mystery," and most evolutionists today still agree. It is generally assumed that they must have originated earlier, not because fossils have been found, but because it is inconceivable that it should have originated so suddenly. Sprague says that apart from the Caytomailes, which occupy a rather isolated position, the earliest angiosperms recorded in the fossil state belong largely to recent families and genera. He also points out that fossils afford no clue to the inter-relationships of the families.

Scott says much the same thing. He points out that the fossil history of the flowering plants shows no sign of a beginning, for with few exceptions all these specimens can be referred to families still existing.

D. H. Scott's actual words are striking.[63] He said that the flowering

---

[60] Arber, Agnes, *The Natural Philosophy of Plant Form*, Cambridge U. Press, 1950, 240 pp.

[61] Good, Ronald, *Features of Evolution in the Flowering Plants*, Longmans Green, London, 1956, p. 388.

[62] Klotz, John, "Nature's Complexity and God," in *The Evidence of God in an Expanding Universe*, ed. J. C. Monsma, Putnam, New York, 1958, p. 433.

[63] Scott, D. H., *Extinct Plants and Problems of Evolution*, Macmillan, London, 1924, p. 57.

plants "appear suddenly in their full strength, like Athene sprung from the brain of Zeus. We know nothing of their evolution."

Walter Beasley has remarked upon the importance of the mutual adaptation in the middle part of the Cretaceous period of pollinating insects and honey-bearing flowers.[64] John Klotz pointed out that such interdependence between insects and flowering plants are extensive.[65] One of the best known of these is the Yucca moth and the Yucca plant in which the dependence is absolute. A similar situation exists in the relationship between the commercial fig and a group of small wasps; and likewise between the common Jack-in-the-pulpit and a species of tiny fly. There is a dual problem here. Not only is the origin of angiosperms and flowering plants a mystery, but so also is the origin of insects, which in this case are essential to them. Comte du Nouy stated that about one thousand species of insects have been identified in the upper Carboniferous, but nothing is known of their past. He said, "If they descend from the common stock we have no idea when they branched off to evolve in their own manner."[66]

Heribert Nilsson has published a monumental work entitled *Synthetische Artbildung*. In this massive volume (1,300 pages) Nilsson declared that having spent a long life in seeking experimental proof of evolution he now found himself forced to abandon it. He summed up his thoughts at one point in the following words:[67]

> My attempts to demonstrate Evolution by an experiment carried on for more than 40 years have completely failed. At least, I should hardly be accused of having started from a preconceived antievolutionary standpoint...
>
> It may be firmly maintained that it is not even possible to make a caricature of an evolution out of paleo-biological facts. The fossil material is now so complete that it has been possible to construct new classes, and the lack of transitional series cannot be explained as being due to the scarcity of material. The deficiencies are real, they will never be filled.

Earlier in his book a whole section was devoted to the origin of flowering plants. He spoke of the "incomprehensible appearance" of separately existing stocks in the plant kingdom:[68]

---

[64] Beasley, Walter J., *Creation's Amazing Architect*, Marshall, Morgan and Scott, London, 1955, p. 115.

[65] Klotz, John, ref. 62, pp. 78f.

[66] Du Nouy, Le Comte, ref. 16, p. 77.

[67] Nilsson, Heribert, *Synthetische Artbildung*, Verlag CWK Gleerup, Lund, Sweden, 1953, pp. 1185 and 1212.

[68] Ibid., p. 499. From page 447 onward Nilsson illustrates the discontinuities in the development of plant life with dozens of examples. The gaps are not minor ones, easily accounted for by an appeal to the "imperfection of the record," but major ones which force him to the conclusion that "there is not even a caricature of an evolution."

If we look at the peculiar main groups of the fossil flora, it is quite striking that at definite intervals of geological time they all at once and suddenly are there, and moreover, in full bloom in all their manifold forms. . . .

We have referred to the mystery of the origin of vertebrates. Alfred Romer stated that two subclasses of bony fishes were already quite distinct at their first appearance in the fossil record.[69] When we pass from cold-blooded vertebrates to warm-blooded vertebrates, we run into similar problems of the absence of transitional forms, nor can we even conceive of them. From the very beginning it has been recognized that the first baby mammal to be born could not have survived unless its mother was already a mammal also. But when this mother was a baby, it could not have survived unless *its* mother were a mammal.[70] And so the problem goes. Simpson held that the regular absence of transitional forms is not confined to any one class or order but is an almost universal phenomenon. He said, "It is true of almost all orders, of all classes of animals both vertebrate and invertebrate . . . and it is apparently true also of analogous categories of plants."[71] He stated that this is true of all the thirty-two orders of mammals and continued:[72]

The earliest and most primitive members known of every order already have the basic ordinal characters, and in no case is an approximately continuous sequence from one order to another known. In most cases the break is so sharp and large that the origin of the order is speculative and much disputed.

In another place, the same authority quoted D'Arcy Thompson in 1942 as follows:[73]

Eighty years of study of Darwinian Evolution has not taught us how birds descended from reptiles, mammals from earlier quadrupeds, quadrupeds from fishes, nor vertebrates from invertebrate stock. The invertebrates themselves involve the selfsame difficulties, so that we do not know the origin of the echinoderms, the molluscs, of the coelenterates nor of one group of protozoa from another. . . .

The failure to solve this, the cardinal problem of evolutionary biology is a very curious thing, and we may well wonder why the long pedigree is subject to such breaches of continuity. We used to be told, and were content to believe, that the old record was of necessity imperfect — we could not expect

---

[69] Romer, Alfred, ref. 49, quoted by Russell Mixter, "Creation and Evolution," monograph, Amer. Sci. Affil. Goshen, Ind., 1951, p. 21.

[70] Reddie, James, "On the Various Theories of Man's Past and Present Condition," *Trans. Vict. Instit.* 1 (1866):178. Wallace and Darwin both recognized this problem, but had no answer to it.

[71] Simpson, G. G., *Tempo and Mode in Evolution,* Columbia U. Press, 1944, p. 107.

[72] Ibid., p. 115.

[73] Thompson, D'Arcy, *On Growth and Form,* Cambridge U. Press, 1942, pp. 1092,1093.

it to be otherwise: the story was hard to read because every here and there a page had been lost or torn away. . . . But there is a deeper reason. A "principle of discontinuity" then, is inherent in all our classification. . . .

In natural history Cuvier's types may not be perfectly chosen nor numerous enough, but types they are; and to seek for stepping stones across the gaps between is to seek in vain forever.

I. Manton, in a book dealing with problems of cytology and evolution in the Pteridophyta,[74] came to the conclusion that phyletic trees resemble less a trunk with branches than a "bundle of sticks," a point of view with which W. Pauli agreed when he said, "The evolutionary tree proves not to be a tree at all but a profusely branched shrub."[75]

It had been hoped that time would correct the imperfection of the fossil record but this has not proved to be the case, and today it is being very widely admitted that the gaps are likely to remain. Indeed, a few paleontologists are even doubting whether they ever existed. . . . In a volume dedicated to Ernst Mayr, John Imbrie presented a paper entitled, "The Species Problem with Fossil Animals." Here he wrote:[76]

> The most serious limitation of paleontological data is the sparcity of fossils. It is true, of course . . . that future (search) will bring forth an unknown but certainly very large amount of new material from localities and horizons now unrepresented in evolutionary collections. Nevertheless, from general theoretical considerations on the nature of sedimentation and diagenesis, and from practical experience in portions of the geological column which have been thoroughly examined for fossils, most paleontologists and stratigraphers would predict that no amount of future field work will ever fill a majority of existing phyletic gaps between transient species.

In short, the intermediate forms, the missing links, are missing now and are never likely to be found. Perhaps they never existed? Belief in their existence is, then, faith in things not seen. . . .

And the gaps are extraordinarily widespread. Witness this broad confession by perhaps the greatest paleontologist in the United States at the present time, Gaylord Simpson of Columbia University and the American Museum of Natural History. In his *Tempo and Mode in Evolution*, he wrote:[77]

> On higher levels . . . continuous transitional sequences are not merely rare, but are virtually absent. These large discontinuities are less numerous so

---

[74] Manton, I., *Problems of Cytology and Evolution in the Pteridophyta*, Cambridge Univ. Press, 1950: quoted by Irving W. Knoblock, *Jour. Amer. Sci. Affil.* 5, no. 3 (September 1953):14.
[75] Pauli, W., *The World of Life*, Houghton Mifflin, Boston, 1949: quoted by Irving Knoblock as in ref. 74.
[76] Imbrie, John, "The Species Problem with Fossil Animals," in *The Species Problem*, ed. Ernst Mayr, Amer. Assoc. Adv. Sci., Washington, D. C., 1957, p. 142.
[77] Simpson, G. G., ref. 71, pp. 105,115.

that paleontological examples of their origin should also be less numerous; but their absence is so nearly universal that it cannot, offhand, be imputed entirely to chance and does require some attempt at special explanation as have been felt by most paleontologists. . . .

As it became more and more evident that the great gaps remained, despite wonderful progress in finding the members of lesser transitional groups and progressive lines, it was no longer satisfactory to impute this absence of objective data entirely to chance. The failure of paleontology to produce such evidence was so keenly felt that a few disillusioned naturalists even decided that the theory of organic evolution, or of general organic continuity of descent, was wrong, after all. . . .

The face of the record thus does really suggest normal discontinuity at all levels, most particularly at high levels, and some paleontologists (for example Spath and Schindewolf) insist on taking the record at its face value.

This was written in 1944. Ten years later Simpson reaffirmed this distressing situation. In his book *The Major Features of Evolution*, he wrote:[78]

In spite of these examples, it remains true, as every paleontologist knows, that *most* (emphasis his) new species, genera, and families, and that nearly all new categories above the level of families, appear in the record suddenly and are not led up to by known, gradual, completely continuous transitional sequences.

It is difficult to see how one could possibly ask for any more concrete evidence for the fact of actual *creation* than this.

And once again, several years later, he affirms that the situation still remains the same. In his paper "The History of Life," presented during the Darwin Centennial Celebrations, he wrote:[79]

It is a feature of the known fossil record that most taxa appear abruptly. They are not as a rule led up to by a sequence of almost imperceptibly changing forerunners, such as Darwin believed should be usual in evolution. A great many sequences of two or of a few temporally intergrading species are known, but even at this level most species appear without known *immediate* (emphasis his) ancestors, and really long, perfectly complete sequences of numerous species are exceedingly rare. Sequences of genera, immediately successive or nearly so . . . are more common. . . . But the appearance of a new genus in the record is usually more abrupt than the appearance of a new species: the gaps involved are generally larger. . . . This phenomenon becomes more universal and more intense as the hierarchy of categories is ascended. Gaps among known species are sporadic and often small. Gaps among known orders, classes, and phyla are systematic and almost always large.

It is intriguing to see how varied are the attempts to account for

---

[78] Simpson, G. G., *The Major Features of Evolution*, Columbia U. Press, 1953, p. 360.
[79] Simpson, G. G., in *Evolution After Darwin*, Vol. I, ed. Sol Tax, U. of Chicago Press, 1960, p. 149.

these gaps. There is no denying them any longer, and yet it is fatal to admit that they are real: so there must be found some way of explaining how they are missing from the record. There are two kinds of solutions which salvage the theory of evolution. The older one is that adopted by R. B. Goldschmidt who cut the gordion knot by saying that probably no intermediate forms were ever required. Animals changed by sudden monstrous leaps or *saltations*, rather than by many small barely observable *mutations*. He proposed, for example, that on one occasion a reptile laid an egg and to mother's enormous surprise, a bird hatched from it![80] All the phyla, classes, orders, and families arose instantaneously by this kind of saltation. Once it had occurred, the new "hopeful monster," as it has been called, sires a whole family of offspring which then quickly explore their genetic heritage and try out "explosively" all the variant forms allowed by the new constitution. This whole concept was seriously proposed by this very reputable geneticist and given a serious hearing by what must have been a rather desperate group of evolutionists. It is little short of miracle — or perhaps fantasy would be better. Theodosius Dobzhansky, in commenting on Goldschmidt's idea, which he described as "catapulting into being new forms of life," rightly observes "this theory virtually rejects evolution as this term is understood."[81]

A more recent "explanation" was discussed by Jonathan Roughgarden in an issue of *Science*. He wrote:[82]

> In one of the most interesting and provoking essays, Eldredge and Gould examine the importance of gaps in the phylogenetic record. . . . New species form in small populations separated from the main species population by a physical barrier to dispersal. Then . . . it is unlikely that (the fossil record) will sample the new species until some late stage in its formation when its range has increased. Hence gaps appear in the phylogenetic record.

This might help to account for gaps in the record between *species*, but surely not between higher classifications of animals? It is as Roughgarden observes: the idea of geographic isolation as the cause of speciation is "currently trading on its intuitive appeal, the authority of its proponents, and its power as a synthesizing principle. But its acceptance is transient."

[80] Goldschmidt, Ralph, "Evolution As Viewed by One Geneticist," *Amer. Scientist* 40 (1952):84-98.

[81] Dobzhansky, Theodosius, *Genetics and the Origin of Species*, Columbia U. Press, 1949, p. 53.

[82] Roughgarden, Jonathan: reviewing "Models in Paleobiology," ed. Thomas J. M. Schoff, in *Science* 179 (1973):1225.

Although I have a great admiration for Gaylord Simpson's clarity of thought and facility of expression, I cannot refrain from mentioning how he has proposed that these gaps occurred. As explained by G. Ledyard Stebbins in a paper entitled "The Dynamics of Evolutionary Change," Simpson's idea is that while "many examples are known in which a new type of animal or plant appears suddenly and seems to be completely separate in respect to many large differences from any earlier form,"[83] one must simply assume that "the fossil record contains many highly significant gaps." This is interesting as a scientific explanation. The record lacks the intermediate forms, and so we must conclude that the intermediate forms are lacking in the record!

There is an observation made by W.R. Thompson in a paper entitled "The Status of Species," which is particularly to the point in uncovering important hidden implications involved in any proposal that such missing links really did exist and really have been *lost*. He pointed out that the argument that "although fossils of types and species we need to complete a phylogeny cannot be found, these types and species did once exist " is a double-edged weapon.[84] If the types leading up to and very similar to ichthyosaurs, for example, existed *before* they are actually known as fossils, "why may not the vertebrates also have existed before the periods in which we find them as fossils, and may not the temporal succession, fish-amphibians-reptiles-mammals, also be an illusion?" The point is well taken. For we have as much right to argue that there could conceivably have been modern fossils alongside the very earliest ones, which would, of course, play havoc with the whole theory of evolution. Who is to say that these postulated modern fossils have not simply been lost along with all the rest of the missing links?

This, then, is the present position. It is not that we who believe in creation have distorted or misread the evidence. The fact is that it requires as much faith in miracles and as much faith in the reality of what still has not "been seen" to believe in evolution as it does in creation. The connection between different species, including man and the apes, looks very convincing, but it may well be merely a matter of common design by a single Creator.

---

[83] Stebbins, G. Ledyard, "The Dynamics of Evolutionary Change," in *Human Evolution: Readings in Physical Anthropology,* ed. N. Korn and F. W. Thompson, Holt, Rinehart and Winston, New York, 1967, p. 48.

[84] Thompson, W. R., "The Status of Species," in *Philosophical Problems in Biology,* ed. Vincent E. Smith, St. John's Univ. Philosophical Series 5, Jamaica, New York, 1966, p. 91.

Frank Marsh made a comment that is relevant here:[85]

> Evolutionists commonly explode at this point and say, "Well, if God created us separately and without evolution through the beasts, why did He deliberately deceive us by making us appear morphologically and physiologically as if we are blood relatives. . . ? The answer is that God has not deceived us. One reason why God gave us the Bible is to clear this very point. Although we may appear to be blood related to the beasts, the facts are that we are not. If we insist upon being deceived on this point, it is not our Creator who deceives us, but we ourselves.

Revelation was given where man's knowledge was limited. We cannot blame God if we choose simply to ignore it.

---

[85] Marsh, Frank L., *Life, Man and Time*, Pacific Press Pub. Assoc., California, 1957, p. 171.

Chapter 7
Natural or
Supernatural Selection

THUS FAR we have seen how the earth was prepared for life and how free living organisms were introduced as soon as the setting was properly conditioned to support them. And we have also reviewed the evidence that throughout the earth's subsequent history there have evidently been innumerable occasions when creative activity was witnessed by the sudden appearance without antecedents of forms of plant and animal life precisely adapted to thrive in a world at that particular stage of preparedness.

We can already discern at certain periods a grand logic in the order of events. Animals could not live on land without an atmosphere containing free oxygen and plant food. Because all animal energy is derived from the oxidation of foodstuffs in the animal body, both plant life and a respirable atmosphere were essential. Most plants need soil, especially plants which are to serve as animal fodder. To create this soil, specialized plant forms were designed that do *not* need soil to live in, and the decay of these slowly formed the soil for those plants which would serve as food. At the same time, all plant life began the process of preparing the atmosphere by ridding it of most of the carbon dioxide (all but .04 percent of it) and returning unwanted oxygen to it in a free form while converting the carbon into forms having usable energy.

All this we have already considered briefly. And then began the parade of animal life which was to culminate in man. These successive forms themselves contributed to the preparation and conditioning of the final environment, which such a creature as man would require. As the process of conditioning neared its completion, more and more manlike forms were introduced as part of the web of life and as witnesses to the imminent appearance of man. Such creatures were not man's ancestors, but man's heralds. They indicated that the conditions of life — of food, of atmosphere, of climate, and so forth — were virtually established to constitute the earth a fit habitation for the crown of creation.

Centuries ago Gregory of Nyssa,[86] long before man had any idea, except from Genesis, of the nature of geological history, penned these words with remarkable foresight:

> It was not proper that the chief should make his appearance before his subjects. The king should logically be revealed only after his kingdom had been made ready for him, when the Creator of the universe had, so to speak, prepared a throne for him who was to rule. . . .
> Then God caused man to appear in the world both to contemplate the marvels of the universe and to be its master. Man was last to be created, not that he should therefore be contemptuously relegated to the last place, but because from his birth it was fitting that he should be king of his domain.

As I see it, the gradual change from an environment such as one sees in reconstructions of early geological times into the kind of environment one now observes in travel literature, was brought about by a combination of natural and supernatural events. The Evolutionary Base Line, which we have already considered very briefly, may represent not so much a great unbroken "chain of being" (to use Arthur O. Lovejoy's phrase), with discontinuities or sudden jumps, but rather it may give us an approximate sequence of how the ages were characterized with respect to plant and animal life while God was introducing, successively, entirely new forms of life by direct creative activity, in each case only when the total ecology was fully prepared to accommodate them.

There were times when there seemed to have been unusual bursts of creative activity, and times of what seem like phases of global destruction. Throughout the process, the total environment seems to have been altered progressively and providentially, making many forms obsolete but clearing the way for the introduction of other and higher forms, which sometimes resulted in almost a different world. Now and then, the temporal order of events seems to throw the purposefulness of the process into sharp focus. We know this with reasonable certainty, for instance, in the period which immediately preceded the coming of man. Hugh Miller wrote on this with characteristic eloquence:[87]

> Not until we enter on the Tertiary period do we find floras, amid which man might have profitably labored as a dresser of gardens, a tiller of fields, or a keeper of flocks and herds. Nay, there are whole orders and families of plants of the very first importance to man which do not appear till late even in the

---

[86] Gregory of Nyssa: quoted by Charles Hauret, *Beginnings: Genesis and Modern Science*, Priory Press, Dubuque, Iowa, 1964, p. 53.

[87] Miller, Hugh, ref. 46, p. 45.

Tertiary. Some degree of doubt must always attach to merely negative evidence, but Agassiz, a geologist whose statements must be received with respect, finds reason to conclude that the order of rosaceae — an order more important to the gardener than almost any other, and to which the apple, pear, quince, cherry, plum, peach, apricot, victorine, almond, raspberry, strawberry, and various brambleberries belong, together with all the roses and the potentillas — was introduced only a short time previous to the appearance of Adam. While the true grasses — a still more important order which, as the cereals of the agriculturalist, feed at the present time at least two-thirds of the human species, and in their humbler varieties form the staple food of the grazing animals — scarce appear in the fossil state at all; they are peculiarly plants of the human period.

My understanding is that late Tertiary also saw the first appearance of such flora as the willow, myrtle, anemone, plum tree, magnolia, holly, rhododendron, azalea, and many other plants bearing fragrant flowers.

There is no doubt in my mind, though I realize that this is a somewhat subjective point, that at the same time He was preparing the plant world for man, God was also taking delight in introducing animals of special significance to him, not only as sources of motive power or for food but in other ways — as objects of companionship and for the enjoyment of their beauty and grace in their natural habitat. In the earlier stages of the preparatory process, animals seem to have been very largely without beauty by human standards, even ugly in fact, as though such things were not of any consequence at that time. The fact that ugly or ungainly creatures (like the crocodile, for example) are still with us in small numbers suggests that we should not make the mistake of supposing that the beauty of an animal, in man's eyes, contributes in any way to its survival, and it is reasonable for the Christian therefore, to view it as an expression of God's concern for man's pleasure — even as the fragrance of flowers seems to be.

We must suppose that God simply acted creatively in the most absolute sense, to introduce throughout this immensely long period of preparation those new forms of life which the fossil record tells us unequivocally came suddenly upon the scene without antecedents. But I do not think we need to assume that their explosive development into a multitude of variant forms thereafter was the result of a similar creative activity. I suggest that this proliferation occurred for reasons we can understand in terms of natural processes still manifestly at work in a natural order which no longer calls for such divine interferences. There is a principle widely recognized and experimentally verifiable that when a small population of animals is isolated or introduced into a new environment, its capabilities of variation are realized to the maximum extent as a direct consequence of inbreeding. The genetic reasons for this need not concern us here, but it is an important fact because this, in effect, is what would be the situation for every new animal or plant form introduced into the world by direct creation. Such a situation would lead as a natural consequence to what Ralph Goldschmidt termed "explosive diversification."[88]

This phenomenon has been observed for both plants and animals. Years ago Sir William Dawson, referring specifically to post-Pliocene molluscs and other fossils, observed that "new species tend rapidly to vary to the utmost extent of their possible limits and then to remain stationary for an indefinite time."[89] The circumstance was noted in connection with insect populations by Charles Brues, who adds that "the variability of forms is slight once the population is large, but at first is rapid and extensive in the case of many insects for which we have the requisite date."[90] Adolph Schultz confirmed it for primate populations,[91] and Mayr for birds.[92] Ralph Linton noted it in connection with man also,[93] and Lebzelter elaborated this into an interesting key to early human history by saying, "Where man lives in large conglomerations, physical form tends to be stable while culture becomes specialized; where he lives in small isolated groups, culture is stable but specialized races evolved."[94] The point is an important one for early human history, because fewness of numbers did indeed lead to an extraordinary variability in type as seen in early fossil remains but a remarkable uniformity in pattern as seen in early *cultural* remains.

Thus, the introduction of a newly created type, of which only a few would presumably be brought into existence, would result in close inbreeding at first and a consequent explosive diversification. Thereafter, it is quite possible that something akin to Natural Selection may have sorted out these diversified forms into appropriate habitats. Natural Selection is *not* creative; it is strictly selective. But it could serve as a sorting out mechanism.

---

[88] Goldschmidt, Ralph, ref. 80, p. 97.

[89] Dawson, Sir William, *The Story of Earth and Man*, Hodder and Stoughton, London, 1903, p. 360.

[90] Brues, Charles, "Contribution of Entomology to Theoretical Biology," *Sci. Monthly*, February 1947, p. 130.

[91] Schultz, Adolph, "The Origin and Evolution of Man," Coldspring Harbor Symposia on Quantitative Biology 15 (1950):50.

[92] Mayr, Ernst, *Mathematical Challenges to the Neo-Darwinian Interpretation of Evolution*, Wistar Instit., no. 5, 1967, p. 47.

[93] Linton, Ralph, *The Study of Man*, Appleton-Century, New York, 1936, pp. 26f.

[94] Lebzelter, V.: quoted by W. Koppers, *Primitive Man and His World Picture*, Sheed & Ward, London, 1952, p. 219.

The potential for variation would allow newly introduced forms to spread rapidly, and successfully fill niches in the total ecology, thus modifying the environment and opening the way for the introduction of even further created forms. At the same time, God may have modified the environment by changing temperature, climate, altitude, or any of the other components, simply by acting upon the physical aspects of the world. These two counterbalancing forces, the physical and the biological, under the guiding hand of the Creator would be quite capable of bringing about a slow change, always in the same direction, toward living forms of greater independence, and toward man. Speaking as an evolutionist, Wood Jones says, "Indeed, it seems hardly too much to say that evolution is ultimately no more than the adaptation of organisms to environment."[95] If Jones had said *Change* instead of evolution, I think he would have been nearer to the truth. And to make his observation even more complete, it would only be necessary to add ". . . and the environment responds in turn to the animals within it."

It is no wonder, since God had planned everything ahead of time, that there are numerous occasions upon which animals seem to be actually making preparations or being prepared by the development of new organs or new capabilities *for changes which have yet to be introduced.* This phenomenon is referred to as "preadaptation." Preadaptation, a not infrequent phenomenon by any means, is one of the mysteries in the story of life, which the evolutionists who cannot accept the idea of plan and purpose find virtually impossible to account for. The best that Simpson could do was to suggest that there is really no preadaptation involved, but only an accidental development which evolution then takes advantage of. This he termed the "opportunism" of the evolutionary process.[96] Le Comte du Nouy was in some ways a little more honest in facing up to the problem when he said:[97]

> To a Biologist who knows how to look at Nature, she is a constant source of wonder. . . . Throughout the development of Evolution the Scientist finds himself facing this unaccountable mystery, the creation of organs destined to improve sketchy solutions so as to increase the freedom of the individual, his independence with respect to his environment. . . .
>
> The same holds true for the appearance of homoiothermism (constant temperature) in birds. This is an immense and unquestionable liberation from the servitude of the environment and has, it must be admitted, all the

[95] Jones, F. Wood, ref. 34, p. 154.
[96] Simpson, G. G., ref. 32, pp. 160-186.
[97] Du Nouy, Le Comte, ref. 16, pp. 70,72.

characteristics of absolute creation, whereas we feel that such cannot be the case. This stands today as one of the greatest puzzles of Evolution.

Anyone unfamiliar with the subject might wonder why birds rather than mammals are mentioned. The fact is that current theory derives birds from reptiles, i.e., warm-blooded feathered creatures from cold-blooded scaled ones. There is a big controversy as to how feathers could be evolved out of scales. Those of us who disagree with evolution are not supposed to use our imagination too freely. If we do, we are accused of being unrealistic and unscientific. But imagination has had a holiday among evolutionists in this little problem. F. B. Sumner,[98] after considering the currently available explanations, concludes that "nothing but the guiding hand of a designer, here, if not the direct intervention of the Creator Himself . . . could have transformed the scales of a reptile forthright into the plumage of a bird." And more recently still, W. E. Swanton, of the British Museum of Natural History, emphasized the problem by saying, "Nothing in the series (of fossil remains) helps us with the vexed evolutionary and chemical problem of the transition of scales to feathers."[99] The plausibility of the scales-to-feathers transformation theory rests in the fact that both apparently spring from the epidermis and that on certain parts of the bird, feathers gradually give way to scales where the upper leg portion becomes the lower leg portion. But merely pronouncing the magic word *Evolution* really explains nothing. It is much more reasonably taken as evidence that a wise Creator designed a basic structure out of which He could subsequently create either scales, or feathers, or both at will. Even if by some chemical process it should be possible in time for scientists to induce scales to become feathers, or feathers scales, this would in no way weaken the evidence of creative activity, it merely gives us an insight into the wisdom of God in designing a basic living substance out of which He could later derive two very different structures as He saw fit.

Another reason for choosing birds in this context is that they may have been the first warm-blooded creatures to be introduced, and this transformation is so profound that it requires far less faith to attribute it to the direct creative activity of God than it does to pure chance. A cold-blooded bird would be a very different creature both in form and habit from those with which God has beautified our world.

---

[98] Sumner, F. B., *Science* 93 (1941):522.
[99] Swanton, W. E., "Critical Steps in Evolution from Fish to Birds, Mammals to Man," in *Times Science Review*, Summer 1953, p. 11.

To my mind, the evidence for a process of Supernatural Selection is abundant, and I believe, if the concept were once allowed (which seems unlikely at the present time), a great deal more evidence would be found almost immediately. Supernatural Selection has operated in Nature to bring about changes in form before those changes were entirely necessary, thus preparing an animal species for its own future and not merely for its immediate present. Le Comte du Nouy, because his philosophy allowed him to give recognition to this kind of evidence, not unnaturally has made a greater appeal to the common man, who is apt to find a purposeless universe a distressing thought. Thus he wrote of one stage of animal life:[100]

> Amphibians are terrestrial when they reach their full development, but aquatic till then. Reptiles, on the contrary are completely terrestrial. The development in the aerial medium necessitates an apparatus to enable the embryo to breathe air directly. Needless to say, the history of the development of this mechanism is entirely obscure. This is an example of a transformation *which does not confer an immediate advantage on the animal endowed with it* (his emphasis) but which represents a necessary step to attain a still distant but superior stage: that of mammals. . . .
>
> Everything always takes place as if a goal had to be attained and as if this goal was the real reason, the inspiration of Evolution.

In an article on fossil man, Loren Eiseley referred to the same phenomenon, though his interpretation was slightly different:[101]

> The reason why a given form of life chooses to launch upon a new adventure is always apt to remain mysterious. One thing, however, seems rather plain: animals do not evolve new organs for the specific purpose of intruding into a new environment. Instead they start with what the Biologist calls a "pre-adaptation" — an existing organ, habit, or other character which offers the possibility of being used successfully under new environmental circumstances.
>
> The first vertebrates to leave the water successfully, for example, had already acquired a primitive lung, utilized for survival in swamp waters of low oxygen content. Other pre-adaptations, such as a muscular fin capable of being transformed into a primitive foot, contributed to the success of the venture.
>
> What we cannot so readily clarify in certain of these instances is whether events *forced* the movement across into the new corridor, or whether the restless impetus, the exploring curiosity, the vital drive of the animal promoted the crossing.

From their different points of view both writers discern the essential appropriateness of the pattern of change. In the long view, the end seems clearly to be the cause of the beginning, a concept which Gaylord Simpson felt was quite unacceptable. Yet for all his

---

[100] Du Nouy, Le Comte, ref. 16, pp. 73,74.
[101] Eiseley, Loren, "Fossil Man," *Sci. American,* December 1953, p. 70.

feelings of distaste, this great authority admitted that the evidence is there.

Starting with a very simple environment and introducing into it just such forms as could live — and, in time, leave their impress upon it, thereby modifying it slightly — God began to prepare the stage for man. The modification of the earliest environment allowed the introduction of new species more complex in form but now able to survive where they could not have survived earlier. These in turn left their mark and prepared the environment so that the Creator could introduce even more complex forms of life both plant and animal. And so the process continued through millions of years. Every now and then some whole fragment of this system that had been introduced deliberately but had now completely served its purpose was removed from the picture to be replaced by some other form, which consequently appeared upon the scene without any introduction, except that the stage was ready to receive it.

For the study of this interacting system in the past, we have only the fossils. And these can be interpreted in the light of the present. But the study of ecology today shows that in many instances several new forms must be introduced together and cannot be introduced separately. For example, honey-bearing flowers and pollinating insects are entirely dependent upon one another, and must both have been introduced together. These are only two such dependent forms. There are many others known, and undoubtedly many more unknown. And the possibilities for concomitant development purely by chance are slim indeed. To my mind, Natural Selection is a far less reasonable explanation than Supernatural Selection, because both insects and flowers were preceded by long lines of other insects and other flowers whose stages of development were so timed as to produce at the critical moment forms which must thereafter exist together.

Both Darwin and Romanes agreed that if it could ever be shown that any two forms of life were fundamentally dependent upon each other and could only survive together, the theory of evolution by Natural Selection would no longer be tenable. In the course of time, a number of examples of interdependence came to be known to both these men. But in spite of their previous assurances, the discovery did not induce them to surrender their faith. Today it is known that Nature is full of such examples.[102] Some of these are dealt with in the

---

[102] Darwin, Charles, *Origin of Species*, Ward Lock, London, 1901, p. 161; and George Romanes: quoted by Walter Kidd, "Plan and Purpose in Nature," *Trans. Vict. Instit.* 31 (1897):216.

Doorway Paper entitled "Nature as Part of the Kingdom of God" (in Volume III, *Man in Adam and in Christ*).

Natural selection is held to operate randomly. That is to say, variations which prove a selective advantage to a living organism are quite random, and as it were accidental. But according to the view we are presenting, variation is not random. It takes place within certain predetermined channels divinely appointed to make the end result possible. The fact that mutations are reversible is evidence of this. Mutations give rise to variant forms, and these variant forms may revert back to the exact original form.[103] To my mind, this indicates that the change was controlled so that its exact reversion was possible. Let me illustrate. If I throw a baseball, and then run to where it lands and throw it back again, and an observer notes that the ball lands exactly at the point where I was standing for the first throw, he might say, "This was pure coincidence." But if I did this three or four times, he would be apt to say, "You are controlling the ball deliberately, and putting a measured amount of effort into the throw each time." In the same way, if a mutation led to a form which in mutating back again, returned the organism only part way back to its original form, and upon different occasions the extent of reversion was different, one could assume that such jumps or mutations were quite random. But apparently this is not so. Therefore variations resulting from this cause are according to law, and God stands behind the law.

The nonrandomness of variation in Nature has been underscored by several authorities. A. J. Cain has this to say:[104]

> In view of the complexity of living things and their environment, a more cautious approach should be used. So far, every supposed example of random variation that has been properly studied has been shown to be non-random...
>
> Those characters or variation patterns that have been described as non-adaptive or random should properly be described as "uninvestigated." One must not assume randomness without proof.

In a nutshell, the present controversy among the authorities is

---

[103] This fact is now generally acknowledged in the literature. Cf. D. Lewis and Leslie Crowe, "Theory of Revertible Mutations," *Nature*, September 12, 1953, p. 501; and John Sinclair, "The Nature of the Gene and the Theory of Evolution," *Jour. Amer. Sci. Affil.* 6, no. 3 (1954):3. Sir Gavin de Beer remarks upon it in mammals (*Embryos and Ancestors*, Oxford U. Press, 1951, pp. 96,97); also S. L. Washburn (*Appraisal of Anthropology Today*, Univ. of Chicago Press, 1953, p. 151); Francis Ryan in connection with bacteria ("Evolution Observed," *Sci. American*, October 1953, p. 80); and Theodosius Dobzhansky ("The Genetic Basis of Evolution," *Sci. American*, January 1950, p. 35); John Klotz in insects (*Genes, Genesis and Evolution*, Concordia, St. Louis, 1955, p. 229); William Tinkle and Walter Lammerts in plants (*Modern Science and Christian Faith*, 2nd ed., Van Kampen, Wheaton, Ill., 1950, p. 90 fn.).

[104] Cain, A. J., "So-called Non-adaptive or Neutral Characters in Evolution," *Nature*, September 8, 1951, p. 424.

not whether evolution has taken place, but rather whether the observed progression of forms has resulted by accident or by design. If the latter is true, a factor is introduced which is no longer capable of complete explanation in terms of physics and chemistry, and it is for this reason that evolutionists have fought against it. They insist that progress results from natural and not supernatural selection. This feeling goes right back to the beginning of the controversy.

Thus, for example, Wallace, who shared with Darwin the credit for launching the theory in a more or less polished form, finally became disillusioned as to the ability of the principle of Natural Selection to provide an adequate explanation. He concluded that "superior intelligence" must also be involved. After Wallace's death, Osborn wrote of "transformations which become more and more mysterious the more we study them." Although he did not join with Wallace by an appeal to a directing supernatural principle,[105] he came in the course of his long life to explain evolution as the result of an organizing and directing principle (which he refused to call supernatural) for which he found no naturalistic basis or explanation.

The well-known South African paleontologist, Robert Broom, held that there was "some spiritual power which has planned and directed evolution, and that below this there are other spiritual agencies, some good and some evil, which in turn direct "partly intelligent" inferior spiritual agencies associated with various animals and plants."[106]

Broom, with Sir Charles Bell, suggested that a study of one's own fingers and hand with its intricacy of bone, muscle, tendon, blood vessels, and nerves, and the delicacy and complexity of its conscious control, will convince anyone of the improbability that such a structure arose by sheer accident or by a continued series of accidents short of infinity. He then pointed out that whatever improbability one assigns to the random origin of a hand, this must be multiplied by a billion billion to express the improbability that Nature as a whole is the result of a sequence of accidental and random events.

Yet Simpson was still convinced:[107]

Adaptation is real, and it is achieved by a progressive and directed process. This process is natural, and it is wholly mechanistic in its operation.

---

[105] Quoted by G. G. Simpson, "The Problem of Plan and Purpose in Nature," *Sci. Monthly*, June 1947, p. 488.

[106] Broom, Robert, "Evolution as the Paleontologist Sees It," South Africa Journal, *Science* 29 (1933):54f.

[107] Simpson, G. G., ref. 105, p. 489.

This natural process achieves the aspect of purpose without the intervention of a purposer, and it has produced a vast plan without the concurrent action of a planner.

This seems a fantastic faith, but it is adopted by some kind of compulsion — the refusal to believe in any supernatural interference.

The great geneticist, Weismann, argued in the same way. He wrote:[108]

We accept Natural Selection not because we are able to demonstrate the process in detail, not even because we can with more or less ease imagine it, but simply because we must — because it is the only possible explanation that we can conceive. . . .

It is inconceivable that there could yet be another capable of explaining the adaptation of organisms without assuming the help of a principle of design.

William Bateson likewise accepted Natural Selection only because he considered the concept of separate creation "absurd."[109] And more recently we find examples of the same frantic refusal to face the possibility of God's creative activity. Patterson and Stone, in a book dealing with experiments with fruit flies, put the matter this way:[110]

The only alternative to evolution by selection among random mutations with the majority of mutations detrimental at the time and place of their occurrence, is directed mutations to fit the need of the organism, possible only under supernatural guidance, although this is seldom the name applied to such a concept.

One gathers from the context that this only alternative is completely unacceptable.

In summary, then, although, to the seeing eye, there is really plenty of evidence of a Planner behind the process, this evidence must officially be ignored or denied, because the only currently acceptable explanation is the scientific one and science cannot allow anything which is not defined purely in terms of physics and chemistry. So long as this remains true, the concept of Supernatural Selection must be flatly rejected. But it is not rejected because the evidence is against it. The evidence of progress is undeniable. To believe that such progress could continue for millions of years by pure chance requires great faith. If natural forces are inadequate to account for the process, the only alternative is the existence of

---

[108] Weismann, A.: quoted by Philip Fothergill in *Historical Aspects of Organic Evolution*, Hollis and Carter, London, 1952, p. 118.

[109] Bateson, William; see P. Fothergill, ref. 108, p. 173.

[110] Patterson, J. T., and Stone, W. S., *Evolution in the Genus Drosophila*, Macmillan, New York, 1952, p. 235.

supernatural forces, and to reject these on a priori grounds is irrational. In short, the Christian is far more rational than the evolutionist, and because he is, his understanding of the process of biological progress may be nearer to the truth.

Natural Selection: An Unproven Hypothesis

Although most authorities would find the concept of Supernatural Selection quite unacceptable and although they agree that Natural Selection is the cause of evolution, it has never really been possible to demonstrate it. About the only example of Natural Selection in action is thought to be the case of the spread of melanism in a species of moth. This is a case where some years ago a black variety of an otherwise white moth appeared in England for the first time. It was a rarity at first, valued by collectors. In the course of time, these black moths began to multiply at a greater rate than the parent group, until in certain areas the tables were turned and the white variety became quite rare.[111]

This phenomenon is usually explained as follows: In an industrial atmosphere, the background tends to be dirty. And when the white moths settle, they stand out clearly and are picked off in greater numbers by the birds which eat them than the darker ones which are less clearly visible. So we have a clear-cut case of the operation of Natural Selection.

However, for several reasons the problem is a little more complex. In the first place, the black moths are exceeding white moths in numbers in the countryside also, where a dark color in itself may not be of any advantage at all.[112] In the second place, there is some evidence that darkness of color may be associated with superior viability.[113] The reasons for this are not understood at present, but there are other cases where the darker species is superceding a light one in which Natural Selection does not seem to be the affective cause. George Carter, after speaking of these things, said frankly:[114]

> It must be admitted that even today our belief in the efficiency of selection depends on logical deduction rather than on the results of observation or experiment.

Even Natural Selection, therefore, is an article of faith. But there is

---

[111] Carter, G. S., *A Hundred Years of Evolution*, Sidgewick and Jackson, London, 1958, pp. 133f.; and David Lack, *Evolutionary Theory and Christian Belief*, Methuen, London, 1957, pp. 44,45.

[112] Klotz, John, *Genes, Genesis and Evolution*, Concordia, St. Louis, 1955, p. 284.

[113] Carter, G. S., ref. 111, p. 139.

[114] Ibid., p. 140.

a double weakness in this doctrine. For, not only is it still un-demonstrated in fact, even the basis of the argument for it is very often irrational. Natural Selection is supposed to be acting upon mutant forms which, having once appeared, are subsequently en-couraged to multiply in a population, because the mutations have conferred some advantage on them. But the likelihood of mutant genes finding expression is very small, since mutations are almost always found to be harmful and disadvantageous. So the useful materials offered to Natural Selection to operate upon are exceed-ingly scarce.[115] Also mutations artificially generated in the labora-tory throw little light on how Nature has been able to create new forms. Nature has tended to resist change by mutation, not to encourage it. Thus, as has been pointed out many times, Natural Selection can only select (or reject) what is there already; it does not, apparently, have the power of creating new *genes*. Yet geological history is filled with examples of the sudden appearance of new forms.

Almost every supposed illustration of Natural Selection used in standard textbooks can be shown to be quite unreasonable, although the average student is seldom aware of it. On one occasion, a professor of mine was illustrating Natural Selection with the familiar example of the tiger and the horse. The theory is that tigers easily overtook the slower horses with shorter legs and thereby eliminated them while the longest legged got away. These in turn sired the next generation in which many shorter legged offspring were soon de-stroyed. Thus Nature selected automatically the horses with longer legs, eliminating the rest. This process, being extended over many generations is taken to account for the evolution of faster and faster horses.[116] While I was listening to all this, it occurred to me that only the faster tigers would ever get enough to eat; and they too, therefore, ought to have been developing longer and longer legs. I asked the professor about this point. For a moment there was silence, and then the whole class (about 300 students) burst out laughing — and the professor finally joined in. He then lectured us for about 20 minutes on the need of being critical of accepted views, although he had not been too critical himself.

Another classic example tells how the giraffe got his long neck.[117] Recurrent and extended drought apparently reduced the

[115] Ibid., pp. 141,142.

[116] For textbooks using this illustration, see E. O. Dodson, *A Textbook of Evolution*, Saunders, Philadelphia, 1952, p. 275; and W. Howells, *Mankind So Far*, Doubleday, New York, 1945, p. 7.

[117] Reproduced in all seriousness in *Life*, May 18, 1953, in a UNESCO article on "Race."

supply of green things until the animals, including the giraffes, took to eating leaves from the lower limbs of trees. When these were eaten off, the animals with longer necks had the advantage and those with shorter necks died off. This continued for years and years, and for many centuries only those giraffes which could reach above their fellows could sire the next generation. Thus, their fantastic form resulted by Natural Selection. Unfortunately, the female giraffe is about twenty-four inches shorter than the male, a fact probably fatal to the theory, unless the males were uncommonly gentlemanly.[118]

Sometimes Natural Selection has not operated where it seems obvious that it should have done so. The shrew is one of the tiniest of mammals. Its rate of metabolism is so rapid that it must eat twice its weight every day, and dies if denied food for only a few hours. Yet James L. Baldwin pointed out:[119]

> Although only a slight increase would relieve its hunger pinch (by reducing heat losses), it ceased to evolve long ago. . . . Despite its severe handicap, Selection has not been able to add a fraction of an inch to its size in 55,000,000 years. Nevertheless, the smallness of this species has enabled it to survive and outlive all the huge species of dinosaurs.

Not only is Natural Selection unable to do any more than select what is available, there are limits even to the powers of "Artificial" Selection. In Human Selection, it is possible to introduce purpose, but there is still no creativity in the strictest sense. A bewildering variety of dogs is possible, but nothing that is not still "dog." And probably in a remarkably short time, if they were all turned loose, the various lines would disappear or would revert to a wild type somewhat like a wolf or wolfhound.

Moreover, breeding experiments are limited in quite specific ways. W. R. Thompson pointed out in his introduction to a new edition of Darwin's *Origin of Species*, published in honor of the Darwin Centenary by J. M. Dent in Everyman's Library:[120]

> In a certain pure line of the housefly, those with the longest wings may conceivably have an advantage — though I cannot see how this can be demonstrated — but we cannot, by choosing and mating those longwinged flies, produce a progressive increase in the proportion of longwinged flies or a progressive increase in wing length.

This observation is important. For example, with respect to the giraffes, Natural Selection could only favor those with long necks

---

[118] Jones, F. Wood, ref. 34, p. 93.
[119] Baldwin, James L., *A New Answer to Darwinism*, publ. privately, Chicago, 1957, p. 69.
[120] Thompson, W. R., Introduction to Darwin's *Origin of Species*, Everyman's Library, Dent, London, 1956, p. xii.

already. It could not increase neck length in each generation. If it did, we ought still to find, occasionally, that giraffes are born with quite short necks, unless one can assume that all the genes of the original line have disappeared.

Selection, then, is not a creative but merely a sorting-out process. Nothing actually new can be added to the sum total of potential at any given moment. Advance in the evolutionary sense is quite out of the question by such a means. Francis B. Sumner put the matter this way:[121]

> Another advance over the Selection view as conceived by Darwin, is a clearer realization of the limitations of Selection, in producing continuous change in a given direction. The great majority of experiments in this field have shown that the effects of selection while at first they may be rapid, soon come to an end. A level is reached in the character dealt with at which it ceases to advance, at least with any regularity or certainty.
>
> This situation is now explained on the basis already indicated, that we have to do with a sorting-out process, by means of which particular genetic combinations are separated out from a mixed population and perpetuated. In the course of this process no new elements commonly appear upon the scene though new combinations of previously existing elements may give rise to strikingly new qualities.

Similarly, in the case of Artificial Selection, as L. B. Walton said many years ago, the supposed progress made in the improvement of domesticated animals and plants is nothing more than the sorting out of pure lines and thus represents no actual advancement.[122]

There is a further consideration. It is often found that a single environment has favored the introduction of a diversity of living forms each of which has found an entirely different — and sometimes fantastic — means of perpetuating its species. For example, the methods by which plants disperse their seeds are legion, and so diverse are they that one has the feeling God must have taken a sheer delight in exploring all the possible solutions. There are plants in which the seedpod lies at the junction of a leaf with the main stem. When the weather becomes dry, at this point the leaf begins to coil itself like a spring, and this process continues until there is a length of quite sharp and well-defined corkscrew. The formation of the corkscrew appears to result from the structure of the stem. Two layers of different material react to the drying process in building up tension until the arrangement breaks free and flies off with some

[121] Sumner, F. B., "Is Evolution a Continuous or a Discontinuous Process?" *Sci. Monthly*, July 1929, p. 75.

[122] Walton, L. B., "The Evolutionary Control of Organisms and Its Significance," *Science*, April 3, 1914, pp. 479-488.

force, carrying it a fair distance from the parent plant. Then two things take place: first, the ground is softened by rain at the same time to receive the seed pod, and secondly, moisture begins to act upon the coil in such a way that it starts to unwind itself. The whole structure is of such a form that the somewhat pointed seed pod is resting point down and at a slight angle to the soil. The gradual unwinding of the coil serves to drill the pod into the soil where it takes root in such a way that the old withered leafy end becomes the visible stem of the new plant.[123]

To conceive of this extraordinary mechanism by which a plant propagates itself as having arisen purely by chance, by the action of Natural Selection, seems most unreasonable. But it is by no means alone. The more carefully Nature is studied, the more wonderful and varied are its devices. A single environment cannot surely be accounted the sole inspirer of such a multitude of mechanisms. How does such variety arise? Is it not quite as reasonable to recognize a Creator, not only with infinite power but with infinite resourcefulness also?

Wood Jones has described a quite fascinating series of special structures, which appear usually in the later stages of embryonic development, and serve a special purpose, but only for an exceedingly short time. These structures are essential to the survival of the newly born animal, but then serve no further purpose. They consequently disappear without leaving a trace. To give one example from Wood Jones:[124]

> Much has been written concerning the birth of Marsupials, and for a century or more it has been known that, although the newly born young is in a singularly immature state, its forelimb and hand are relatively well developed. The question as to how it becomes translated from the cloacal orifice, at which it is born, to the marsupial pouch in which it continues its immature existence, has long been settled, since, from several observations, it is known that it climbs from the cloacal orifice and into the mouth of the pouch by its own efforts. Many have considered that it is incredible that the very immature and ill-formed creature could make so long a journey through the fur of the mother's ventral surface without some maternal aid. It is only very recently that it has been shown (Lyne) that upon the rudimentary fingers of the immature young at birth there are very highly perfected little claw-like nails developed especially to enable it to make this one journey. The journey being safely accomplished and the immature creature having found sanctuary in the pouch, these temporary claws are shed, before the definitive nails, formed in accordance with the adult animal's needs, are developed.

---

[123] A number of species are known, a characteristic example being a member of the geranium family (Erodium sp.), commonly called Cranesbill, found in Europe as a weed.
[124] Jones, F. Wood, ref. 34, p. 113.

It may be that my imagination is inadequate, but it is very difficult to conceive of such a momentary development resulting from Natural Selection. Unless the nails begin to grow in a form exactly suited to the incompletely born animal's needs, what could Nature select? It therefore throws no light upon how such structures were introduced for such a short journey and short period of time. The whole complex stands or falls as one. The pouch is useless unless the animal completes the journey, and the journey is made in vain unless the pouch is ready to receive its occupant. Moreover, it is suited for an occupant only halfborn and yet in one essential this halfborn creature must be, as it were, "adult."

In summary, then, Natural Selection cannot be demonstrated to be operative at the present time, the usual illustrations of its operation in the past being very doubtful. Even if it were operative, it has little or nothing to work on in Nature, it is in no sense creative of new forms. Where it seems most obvious that it should have acted, it evidently did not do so, and it is totally incapable of explaining many of the devices by which species perpetuate themselves. Altogether a most unsatisfactory theory, as Thompson has put it:[125]

> The position, therefore, is that while the Modern Darwinians have retained the essentials of Darwin's evolutionary machinery, to wit, Natural Selection, acting on random hereditary variations, their explanation, plausible in Darwin's day, is not plausible now.

In short, Natural Selection is not really a reasonable doctrine any longer: it is little more than an article of faith.

---

[125] Thompson, W. R., ref. 120, p. xiii.

Chapter 8
Creation and Divergence

NATURAL SELECTION acting upon random mutations is still the only viable option for most evolutionists at the present time. This is current orthodoxy. But it is widely admitted, nevertheless, that the concept is of doubtful validity. Sir Julian Huxley in 1943 said frankly, "the direct and complete proof of the utilization of mutations in evolution under natural conditions has not yet been provided."[126] And Theodosius Dobzhansky said in 1962, "No satisfactory theory of mutations has yet emerged."[127] One year later, Ernst Mayr, perhaps the greatest authority on speciation, admitted candidly: "Mutations merely increase the heterozygosity of a population but do not lead to the production of new species. . . . Mutations cannot produce new species in sexually reproducing species."[128]

Artificial selection is admittedly a different matter, for the operation of human planning and conscious purpose make things possible which pure chance has little if any likelihood of achieving, as Leo Berg put it:[129]

> Artificial and Natural Selection are two very different things. In the first, the intelligent will of man operates; in the second, blind chance. Man engaged in the improvement of his breed in a rational manner, crosses *only* what is useful, selecting from the offspring *only* the useful, removing *all* else (his emphasis throughout). Nature can do nothing of the kind.

Nature may eliminate what is not immediately useful but it cannot by itself foresee what might be useful in the future unless one attributes to it some kind of purposeful planning, and this is precisely what the evolutionist is most anxious to avoid. Yet by capitalizing the word Nature and personifying it by referring to it as *her* or *she*,

---

[126] Huxley, Sir Julian, ref. 40, p. 116.

[127] Dobzhansky, Theodosius, *Mankind Evolving*, Yale U. Press, 1962, p. 46.

[128] Mayr, Ernst, *Animal Species and Evolution*, Belknap Press of Harvard U. Press, 1963, p. 432.

[129] Berg, Leo, ref. 20, p. 65.

evolutionists do really deify Nature while dethroning Nature's Creator.

Man is in the position of being able to see ahead and can therefore take advantage of chance mutations that are recognized to be of possible use sometime in the future. As a rule, Nature would merely eliminate them, for Nature's way is to discourage the exceptional and favor only the normal. Populations of animals do not encourage the persistence of the extremes of their range because they are constantly crossed with the normals which therefore overwhelm them and thus place natural limits on variability, once the form is established for any particular habitat. This is a kind of negative selection process and is everywhere to be observed both in the field and in the laboratory. Attempts to extend the range of variability are usually unsuccessful, or if the extremes *are* favored by controlled breeding, they almost always turn out to be less fit in the field — though they may have some particular value to man if he maintains the breed under unnatural conditions. Certainly the rule in Nature is to favor the mean, not the extremes.

Furthermore, mutant varieties of a particular species that have been produced in the laboratory by artificial controls differ in a very significant way from those mutant varieties observed in Nature, to which the artificial varieties are assumed to be analogous. C. P. Martin of McGill University,[130] has pointed out that in Nature varieties of certain supposedly closely related species are observed to anticipate the differences of the adult form *quite late in embryological development.* Up to a point, the embryos of subphyla, for example, are indistinguishable. Later, the characteristics that set apart the different orders make their appearance in the embryo, followed later still by generic differences, and finally by specific differences. Only in the last stages of prenatal development do specific differences, which will be observable in the adult, become apparent. In marked contrast, laboratory mutant forms which will be clearly distinguishable as adults, display their well-defined differences *in the very early stages of embryological development.*

Clearly, then, artificially induced mutant varieties tell us little or nothing of how the different varieties of animals arose under natural conditions. In short, the embryos of very different adult forms, such as a chicken and a man, follow a parallel course of development that is remarkably similar for a remarkably long time, considering the differences in adult forms. By contrast, adult forms

---

[130] Martin, C. P., "A Non-Geneticist Looks at Evolution," *Amer. Scientist,* January 1953, pp. 100-106.

which have been "engineered" in the laboratory by deliberately induced mutations, while they too as adults may diverge quite radically, are actually observed to begin this process of differentiation far earlier in embryonic development.

To put it very simplistically, divergent forms in Nature do not suggest by their embryonic development that they are divergent because they are mutant forms. Thus, artificially induced mutant varieties shed little or no light on how the different varieties of animals arose under natural conditions. It is not even sufficient to say that the Creator used some method for their production which was not unlike that which man may use. Superficially, about the only common element that one can point to with certainty at the moment is that Artificial and Supernatural Selection both involve forethought and planning. In this, at least, they are clearly to be distinguished from Natural Selection which, in the present state of our knowledge, seems almost to be a fantasy. It is doubtful if Natural Selection has in reality played any part whatever in the formation of species, and in so far as Darwin depended upon it as the prime agency in speciation, the title of his famous work, *The Origin of Species*, was a complete misnomer.

It is apparent from the discussion up to this point that in the past, in the geological period before the appearance of man, the stage was being prepared by the deliberate intervention of God who created, as occasion demanded, entirely new types and forms of life and, to use J. J. D. de Wit's apt terminology, invested them with "enormous genetic recombinational potency."[131] All that was needed for these potentials to be realized was that the newly introduced forms be set in appropriate niches, in which their capacities for variation would be most useful. We know from observation in Nature that this is a perfectly reasonable interpretation of the evidence. Ernst Mayr freely acknowledges the principle involved here,[132] and Sir Julian Huxley illustrates it thus: "It is indicated clearly in many island forms, which have diverged in isolation while their counterparts on the mainland have remained constant over wide areas in spite of a great diversity of environments."[133] Darwin's Galapagos finches are an excellent case in point. On the various islands where the birds introduced themselves, each community formed a distinguishable variety, while the original stock from which

[131] De Wit, J. J. D., "A New Critique of the Transformist Principle in Evolutionary Biology," *Philosophia Reformata* 29 (1964):55.
[132] Mayr, Ernst, ref. 128, p. 538.
[133] Huxley, Sir Julian, *The New Systematics*, Oxford U. Press, 1940, p. 288.

these local populations were derived, continued the original form with none of these divergences. Jens Clausen and W. M. Hiesey, in a paper entitled "Balance Between Coherence and Variation in Evolution," noted that shifts in the environment — which is, of course, an alternative to shifting the particular species to a *new* environment — tend to alter the balance between forces favoring persistence of the type and departure from the typical form. And such an alteration leads to change in the genetic constitution of the particular race and of the species itself.[134]

It is obvious, therefore, that if we can only supply some means of accounting for the introduction of an entirely new type of animal into a given habitat, the subsequent expansion and differentiation of that type into variant forms is not merely easily accounted for, it is virtually inevitable. The problem for the non-Christian naturalist is that he cannot account for the appearance of the new type. The Christian can allow creation as a reasonable explanation and can point out that it is, in fact, the *only* explanation, since all these new types appear to have been introduced without genetic antecedents. Yet because they were introduced by the same Creator, they often share many features which suggest an economy of planning. This parallelism of design in details is what has confused the evolutionist, because he is persuaded that the only way to account for it is to assume descent. Walter Lammerts and John Sinclair have suggested that groups of genes may have been designed *as groups* to carry the responsibility of looking after certain specific needs of the organism and that these can be rearranged to produce, for example, an eye suited to a particular animal. They put it this way:[135]

> Thus on the basis of economy of effort, a wise Creator would certainly use the same genes in all organisms wherever possible, i.e., wherever the same function was to be achieved.

A little over 200 years ago, such a concept had already been proposed by the perceptive Comte Buffon (1707-1788).[136] In his work *Of the Nature of Animals* he expressed the view that the Creator seemed to have employed but one idea, varying it *ad infinitum*, from plants to worms to reptiles to man, "to give men an opportunity of admiring equally the magnificence of the execution and the simplicity of the design." He viewed the design as really a mode of operation or a

---

[134] Clausen, Jens, and Hiesey, W. M., "Balance Between Coherence and Variation in Evolution," *Science* 130 (1959):1413.

[135] Lammerts, Walter, and John Sinclair, "Creation in Terms of Modern Concepts of Genetics and Physics," *Jour. Amer. Sci. Affil.* 5, no. 3 (1953):8.

[136] Buffon: quoted by J. C. Greene, *The Death of Adam,* Iowa State U. Press, 1959, p. 141.

system of processes rather than simply a pattern of structures. And he believed that the true aim of Natural History was to discover and understand these processes, and not merely to classify their end results. It all makes perfectly good sense to see the whole panorama in this light, granted the single premise that behind it stands a Creator with a purpose. One candid evolutionist, G. A. Kerkut, has written:[137]

> If living material had developed on several different occasions, one would expect to have a large number of distinct groups of animals whose relationships and affinities are difficult to discern. . . . This is the present situation.

Fair enough, as far as it goes: only it is surely a gross understatement to speak of "several different occasions" when in reality these gaps are a universal phenomenon, and such "occasions" must therefore run into the thousands. Moreover, their interrelationships are not only difficult to determine, they are in fact *impossible* to determine, except by ultimate reference in the mind of God.

So then, we can see this whole process as a series of creative acts which account for the introduction of new forms of life as soon as the setting is appropriate for them, followed by diversification due to the spread of these created forms with their high potential for variation into new habitats. Their introduction into the total economy of Nature will in turn change the system, tending it toward the formation of a habitat finally to be ideally suited for the introduction of man along with animal forms and plant forms of particular importance to the welfare of the human race. And all the while, the changes in the total environment involve a series of physical events which were laying in store for man's future use, the enormous reservoirs of energy in the form of fossil fuels (coal, gas, and oil) which were going to make possible his final dominion over the earth.

---

[137] Kerkut, G. A., *The Implications of Evolution*, Pergamon Press, New York, 1960, pp. 14,17.

Chapter 9
Supernatural Selection:
A New Name for an Old Concept

THE IDEAS set forth thus far in this paper are by no means new. There are many good reasons now to resurrect an older view which was eclipsed by Darwinism, and to reexamine its implications in the light of new knowledge and of the manifest bankruptcy of current evolutionary philosophy. Indeed, evolutionary philosophy has been so detrimental to society in terms of its influence on international politics and on the spirit of Big Business over the last sixty years since 1914, that it ought to be judged by its fruits and replaced.

Darwin himself was very conscious of his departure from a view of Nature which had previously been held by Naturalists regarding the purposeful preparation of the earth for man, and there are not a few who believe that this awareness was the cause of the dis-ease in his own spirit. Indeed, he seemed almost anxious to preserve the older view, if not to embellish it, in the second of two essays which he published in 1842 and 1844, which were really the forerunners of *The Origin of Species*. In these he admitted the reasonableness of the view which he was nevertheless destined to demolish. He proposed the existence of [138]

> a Being with penetration sufficient to perceive differences in the outer and innermost organization (of living things) quite imperceptible to man, and with forethought extending over future centuries to watch with unerring ease and to select for any object the offspring of an organism produced under the foregoing circumstances; I can see no conceivable reason why he could not form a new race (or several, were he to separate the stock of the original organism and work on several islands) adapted to new ends.
>
> As we assume his discrimination and his forethought, and his steadiness of object, to be incomparably greater than these qualities in man, so we may suppose the beauty and complications of the adaptation of the new races and

---

[138] Darwin, Francis, ed., *The Foundations of the Origin of Species: Two Essays Written in 1842 and 1844 by Charles Darwin,* Cambridge U. Press, 1909, pp. 85ff. in second essay.

their differences from the original stock to be greater than in the domestic races produced by man's agency. . . . With time enough, such a Being might rationally aim at almost any result.

Almost a century before, Comte George Louis Buffon had said he believed that man could effect the variation that he did by horticulture and animal breeding, only because the potential was there to begin with. Man did not really create anything new, but only permitted what was already present to find expression in new ways. As he put it, the basis of man's power to alter nature lay in natural variability. Man simply reinforced the agency of natural causes. He wrote: [139]

> Every animal was adapted to a particular region with a particular climate and food supply. When animals were forced to abandon their natural habitat, i.e., by human intervention or by any "revolution on the globe," they underwent changes in physique and appearance which in the course of time became hereditary; changes in one part of the body produced modifications in other parts, so that the whole appearance was materially altered.

Some fifty years later, we find a distinguished London surgeon, James Parkinson, writing in 1804: "If the fossil record should show progress from simple to complex forms of life, this progress must have been intended by God and He must have arranged a series of appropriate settings for each act of the drama. . . ." [140]

Fifty years later still, the renowned anatomist, Sir Richard Owen, addressed himself to the same issue but went somewhat further, since a great deal more was by then known of the nature of the fossil record, in elaborating what was just before Darwin's time to be a well-rounded and highly satisfying synthesis of Christian faith and geological knowledge. Owen wrote: [141]

> The recognition of an ideal example for the vertebrate animals proves that the knowledge of such a being as man *must have existed before man appeared;* for the Divine Mind that planned the archtype also foreknew all its modifications. The archtypical idea was manifested in the flesh, under diverse modifications, upon this planet, long prior to the existence of those animal species that actually exemplify it (emphasis mine).

In a similar vein, Sir Humphry Davy had written a few years before, "There seems, as it were, a gradual approach to the present system of things, and a succession of destructions and creations preparatory to the existence of man." [142]

---

[139] Buffon: quoted by J. C. Greene, ref. 136, p. 148.

[140] Parkinson, James, *Organic Remains of a Former World,* Vol. I, London, 1804, p. 467.

[141] Owen, Sir Richard: quoted by G. C. Gillispie, *Genesis and Geology,* Harper Torchbooks, New York, 1951, pp. 204,205.

[142] Davy, Sir Humphry, *Consolation in Travel,* Dialogue III, 3rd ed., London, 1831.

To Buffon, as to most of his contemporaries, it seemed obvious that such modifications due to environmental influences would naturally become fixed in the line. He did not stop to ask whether such modifications would become unfixed if the organisms were returned to their former habitat. It is known today that this does in fact happen, and such modifications are termed *dauermodifications*. Alfred Kuhn on this wrote:[143]

> The form and size of cells can be modified strongly and in various ways by environmental factors. Certain modifications of form are retained for a long time after the conditions change, and it often takes a large number of generations before a new form, corresponding to the new conditions, is acquired.

There cannot, therefore, be the slightest objection from the point of view of current biological theory to the concepts here under review, provided that we allow the possibility of creation with a purpose. Such a view meets all the requirements of the present evidence. And the idea of fiat creation is not as *verboten* today as it was even a generation ago. Certainly in explaining the existence of matter, fiat creation has to be introduced. H. Bondi, in his book *Cosmology*, went so far as to say in this regard, "The creation here discussed is the formation of matter *not out of radiation but out of nothing*" (emphasis mine).[144] And in his *Physics and Philosophy*, W. Heisenberg warned that science should be prepared for "phenomena of a qualitatively new character" upon probing deeper into the structure of things.[145] Thomas Huxley admitted in a letter to Darwin that creation in the ordinary sense of the word was perfectly conceivable. He felt that "the a priori arguments against theism and, given a Deity, against creative acts, are devoid of reasonable foundation."[146]

The temper of the times was then far more favorable to recognition of concepts of this kind. Long before this, Charles Lyell, in his famous *Principles of Geology*, had said:[147]

> We must suppose that when the Author of Nature creates an animal or a plant, all the possible circumstances in which its descendants are destined to live are foreseen, and that an organization is conferred upon it which will enable the species to perpetuate itself and survive under all the varying circumstances to which it must inevitably be exposed.

At about the same time, William Whewell, one of the keenest

[143] Kuhn, Alfred, ref. 17, p. 83.

[144] Bondi, H., *Cosmology*, 2nd ed., Cambridge U. Press, 1960, p. 144.

[145] Heisenberg, W., *Physics and Philosophy*, Harper, New York, 1958, p. 165.

[146] Huxley, Thomas, in *The Life and Letters of Charles Darwin*, ed. Francis Darwin, Vol. II, Murray, London, 1887, p. 187.

[147] Lyell, Charles, *Principles of Geology*, Vol. II, London, 1830-33, pp. 24,25.

minds of his day, was speaking boldly of the need to leave the option of divine creative activity open. In an essay entitled, "Indications of the Creator," when speaking of the sudden and explosive expansion of new lines, particularly just before the appearance of man, he wrote:[148]

> We may form various hypotheses with regard to the sudden or gradual manner in which we may suppose the distribution (of living things) to have taken place. We may assume that at the beginning of the present order, a stock of each species was placed in the vegetable or animal province to which it belonged by some cause outside of the common order of nature. . . .
>
> Hence, even on natural grounds, the most intelligible view of the history of the animal and vegetable kingdoms seems to be that . . . at the beginning of each cycle, a creative power was exerted of a kind to which there was nothing at all analogous in the succeeding part of the same cycle. . . .
>
> Thus we are led by our reasonings to this view, that the *present* order of things was commenced by an act of creative power entirely different to any agency which has been exerted since. None of the influences which have modified the present races of animals and plants since they were placed in their habitations of the earth's surface can have had any efficacy in producing them to begin with.

This reflects my own view that the demand for *creative* activity exists chiefly at the beginning of each of these cycles of new forms of life by which geologists are now accustomed to distinguish the successive ages or lesser periods. Only providential superintendence with respect to the physical changes in the environment and the division of the genetic materials in each generation would be needed in addition, to give the whole process the appearance of purposeful direction which it certainly has.

Lyell himself seems to have gradually changed his position however, for I can find nothing comparable to the admissions of his earlier *Principles* appearing in his somewhat later *Manual of Elementary Geology*, which was published in 1855. But Alfred Russell Wallace in 1870, in spite of his thinking which was following a line very similar to that of Charles Darwin, was still willing to acknowledge that there might have been divine creative activity, when he wrote, evidently with some trepidation:[149]

> We must, therefore, admit the possibility that, if we are not the highest intelligences in the universe, some higher intelligence may have directed the process by which the human race was developed. . . . I must confess that this has the disadvantage of requiring the intervention of some distinct individual

---

[148] Whewell, William: quoted by W. H. Hoare, *The Veracity of the Book of Genesis*, Longmans Green, London, 1860, pp. 165,166.

[149] Wallace, Alfred Russell, *Contributions to the Theory of Natural Selection*, Macmillan, London, 1870, page unknown.

intelligence to aid in the production of what we can hardly avoid considering as the ultimate aim and outcome of all organized existence — intellectual, ever-advancing, spiritual man.

Well, it was a noble try — but a rather timid one that could only speak of some distinct individual intelligence rather than a personal, omniscient God. My impression is that Wallace would have spoken a little more boldly in his later years. Even Darwin seems to have been troubled by the apparent atheism in his views and suggested that his concept was, after all, a grand testimony to the wise forethought and creative powers of the Almighty. But he clearly hoped by this statement to lessen somewhat the shock of his essentially non-Christian approach. Once he had discovered that the shock he feared was not too harmful to his own acceptance, he entirely dropped any appeal to the supernatural.

Charles Lyell, whose writings had tremendously influenced Darwin, still hesitated to relinquish the idea of creative intervention, even after he had observed the immediate success of Darwin's *Origin of Species*. On May 5, 1869, he wrote to Darwin:[150]

> I was therefore not opposed to (Wallace's) idea, that the supreme intelligence might possibly direct variation in a way analogous to that in which even the limited powers of man might guide it in selection, as in the case of the breeder and horticulturalist. In other words, since I feel that progressive development or evolution cannot be entirely explained by natural selection, I rather hail Wallace's suggestion that there may be a Supreme Will and Power which may not abdicate its (sic) functions of interference but may guide the forces and laws of nature.

For myself, the nearest reflection of my own views, in this earlier period in the development of geological theory, is to be found in the two works of Louis Agassiz who, after a most notable career in Europe, was in 1841 appointed to the Chair of Natural History at Harvard. The first is his *Essay on Classification*, published in 1859, and the second his *Principles of Zoology* published in 1907. In his *Essay*, he wrote:[151]

> Who can look upon such a series . . . and not read in them the successive manifestations of a thought, expressed at different times in forms ever new and yet tending to the same end, onwards to the coming of Man whose advent is already prophesied in the first appearance of the earliest fishes.

Subsequently, in his *Principles*, he wrote:[152]

---

[150] Lyell, Charles: quoted by R. T. Clark and J. D. Bales, *Why Scientists Accept Evolution*, Presb. and Reformed Publ. Co., Philadelphia, 1966, p. 17.

[151] Agassiz, Louis, *Essay on Classification*, Harvard U. Press, 1859, pp. 166,167.

[152] Agassiz, Louis, *Principles of Zoology;* quoted by an unnamed author (F.W.H.) in *God's History of the World*, Nisbet, London, 1907, p. 149.

It is evident that there is a manifest progress in the succession of beings on the face of the earth. This progress consists in an increasing similarity to the presently living fauna and among the vertebrates especially in their increasing resemblance to man. But this connection is not the consequence of a direct *lineage* between the faunas of different ages. There is nothing like parental descent connecting them.

The fishes of the Paleozoic Age are in no respect the *ancestors* of the reptiles of the Secondary Age, nor does man descend from the mammals which preceded him in the Tertiary Age. The link by which they are connected is of a higher and immaterial nature, and their connection is to be sought in the view of the Creator Himself, whose aim in forming the earth, in allowing it to undergo the successive changes which geology has pointed out, and in creating successively all the different animals which have passed away, was to introduce man upon the face of our globe. *Man is the end towards which all the animal creation has tended from the first appearance of the first paleozoic fishes* (emphasis mine).

That is where the picture was when Darwin shattered it. At the time the success of his *Origin of Species* was undoubtedly evidence of a widespread and growing dissatisfaction with the view that saw all natural history as divinely guided toward the coming of man. This inevitably led to the view that man had a special destiny, and this, in turn, underscored the fact of his moral responsibility and a probable judgment to come. This was an uncomfortable idea, and it is obvious that men were anxious to escape from it. But I believe we shall yet see a change — and a return to a view of the earth's past history that will be less hostile to certain basic elements of the Christian world view.

Chapter 10
Catastrophe and Reconstitution

THROUGHOUT THE whole process of the preparation of the earth for man, there seem to have been not merely periods of great creative activity but also periods of great destruction. And these periods of destruction seem to have been related in some way to the times of creative activity, not causally but as a kind of prelude or clearing-of-the-decks. Perhaps Agassiz was a little extreme in his view that there were innumerable such clearings-of-the-decks, believing as he did that there were at least hundreds of these catastrophes, wiping out every plant and animal over vast areas of the earth's surface, but he was by no means alone in recognizing the profound effect such would have upon the earth's ecology.

Like the other major interruptions in geological history, they seem to mark real boundaries between the eras, the largest divisions of geological time. Normal D. Newell of the American Museum of Natural History in New York has put it this way:[153]

> Abrupt paleontological changes at these stratigraphic levels are real, approximately synchronous, and recognizable at many places in different parts of the earth where fossiliferous rocks of approximately similar age are represented and have been carefully examined.

These are seemingly global events, which "are characterized by the abrupt dropping out of all the species, most of the genera, and many of the higher categories (superfamilies, orders, and classes) characteristic of the times." When the earth settled down again, we seem almost to be in a new world. Otto H. Schindewolf of Tübingen, who has been particularly concerned with this problem, noted that in the recovery period the new categories of life that suddenly appear without antecedents often seem to be representative of types in the later, more completely occupied world. It looks as though God was

---

[153] Newell, Norman D., "Catastrophism and the Fossil Record," *Evolution* 10, no. 1 (1956):97.

indeed introducing the archtypes that were to mark the new order, giving them the wide potentials for later diversification that my thesis proposes.

Newell notes such abrupt changes of scene, especially at the end of Permian, at the close of the Mesozoic, and just before the present order of life was introduced. He pointed out that "geologists have long supposed that rates of evolution and extinction are in some manner influenced by the ecological changes induced by orogeny (i.e., mountain-building)." But he added:[154]

> In recent years it has become increasingly evident that orogenic disturbances and associated ecological changes are actually rather restricted in extent and therefore of minor evolutionary importance. . . . Evolutionary episodes as revealed in the record of fossils apparently do not coincide closely with times of mountain building.

When the age of the great cold-blooded reptiles passed away and warm-blooded animals appeared on the earth in their place, there actually was one such abrupt discontinuity between the old and the new worlds on a global scale. Henry F. Osborn observed:[155]

> The most dramatic and in many respects the most puzzling event in the history of life on the earth, is the change which exterminated this vast array of creatures. These reptiles were in the climax of specialization and grandeur. . . . We have no conception as to what world-wide cause occurred. . . . We can only observe that the world-wide effect was the same: the giant reptiles both of sea and land disappeared.

Some of the proposed explanations could apply readily enough to the land animals, as for example the diminishing food supply in the form of plant life. But this does not help very much with respect to those animals which lived in the sea. Whatever the cause, it was one which operated equally on land and sea, and it was surprisingly sudden. George Gamow has put it:[156]

> The kingdom of giant reptiles with its innumerable representatives on the land, in the sea, and in the air, was certainly the most powerful and extensive animal kingdom during the entire existence of life on the earth, but it had also a most tragic and unexpected end. During a comparatively short period towards the end of the Mesozoic Era the Tyrannosaurus, Stegosaurus, Ichthyosaurus, Plesiosaurus, and all the other "sauri" disappeared from the surface of the earth as if wiped away by some giant storm. . . . The causes that led to such a sudden extinction of the most powerful animals that ever existed on the surface of our planet have remained rather obscure.

[154] Ibid.
[155] Osborn, Henry F., *The Age of Mammals in Europe, Asia and North America*, Macmillan, New York, 1910, p. 98.
[156] Gamow, George, *Biography of the Earth*, Mentor Books, New York, 1948, p. 173.

Not only do we have the evidence, of a negative kind, that such creatures suddenly vanished from the scene, but we have a more positive evidence in the existence of so-called animal cemeteries which are considerably later. These take the form of very extensive beds in which millions of bones of a very wide variety of species of animals are found indiscriminately mixed together. In these cemeteries there are the remains of herbivorous as well as carnivorous animals and the bones of the former apparently show no signs of having been gnawed. This is a proof that both types of animals perished together. Furthermore, there is little evidence of weathering, a fact which is taken to mean that they were buried almost as quickly as they were destroyed — perhaps by the very agency which destroyed them. And finally the bones are forcibly intermixed; that is to say, the leg bone of one species may be found rammed tightly into the eye socket of the skull of another species, a circumstance which suggests that these creatures were overwhelmed, not merely suddenly, but violently. Such cemeteries have to be seen to be believed. No simple explanation such as that the bones of centuries of dead creatures merely accumulated by being washed into a depression, or that they represent the after-dinner remains of generations of some particular local predatory species (such as hyenas for example) will suffice. These bones have not been exposed to the sun or the air for any length of time prior to burial, nor are they gnawed.

Newell leaned heavily on the work of Schindewolf (the importance of whose work, incidentally, has been recognized by G. G. Simpson) and emphasized the reality of these discontinuities and the widespread nature of them. And he admitted frankly that they seem (at least in some cases) to be caused by quite exceptional circumstances, circumstances not commonly observed at other periods of geological history or often affecting aquatic life as dramatically as terrestrial life. So exceptional are the circumstances, in fact, that according to Newell:[157]

> Schindewolf believes the best way to explain many of the innumerable small as well as the few large discontinuities in the fossil record . . . is by means of catastrophic extinctions and simultaneous creation of new faunas.

Of course, this kind of explanation is unacceptable to the great majority of recognized authorities on matters geological. Ernst Mayr felt that the explanation is really quite simple.[158] He said, "Ultimately their extinction is due to an inability of their genotype to

---

[157] Newell, Norman D., ref. 153, p. 100.
[158] Mayr, Ernst, ref. 128, p. 620.

respond to new selective pressures," an explanation which sounds impressive but merely pushes the problem one step further back to the prior question, Why this inability? There might also be many equally simple answers to this question in terms of current genetic theory, but the problem still remains as to why such an inability to respond should suddenly arise in hundreds of thousands of animals of different categories and all in the same geological time frame. It is not at all a comparable situation to the somewhat limited but none the less sad extinction of species which seem to be associated with the propensities for overkill by early man in his hunting forays,[159] or by the buffalo hunters of recent memory. These humanly induced extinctions had only a small effect on the total ecology, comparatively speaking, for they concern only a small number of species.

Perhaps the most striking extinction of all that is still essentially unexplained is the one which seems to have immediately preceded the appearance of true man and which is in some way linked to the coming of the Ice Age. It is difficult to discuss this particularly disastrous event without appearing to be overdramatic, and those who constitutionally find any kind of catastrophism distasteful try hard to play down the quite extraordinary character of the fossil record from which we must reconstruct the event. This catastrophe was sudden in the extreme. It was violent. It seems to have been very widespread. It was accompanied by a fundamental change in climatic conditions in many parts of the world. It wiped out enormous numbers of animals of all kinds — large and small, land and aquatic. And it literally marked the end of a whole world order. Look at some of the facts of the case as set forth by various authorities since the early years of the last century.

In 1821, Benjamin Silliman of the Department of Geology at Yale University, wrote of the large number of species which were apparently overwhelmed in this single catastrophe. He pointed out that whales, sharks, crocodiles, mammoths, elephants, rhinoceroses, hippos, tigers, deer, horses, various species of the bovine family, and a multitude of others were found in strata "in most instances indicating that they were buried by the same catastrophe which destroyed them all."[160] A contemporary of Silliman's, Granville Penn, wrote:[161]

---

[159] On the concept of overkill, see: *Pleistocene Extinctions*, ed. P. S. Martin and H. E. Wright, Jr., Vol. VI., Proc. of 7th Congress of the International Association for Quaternary Research; especially Martin's own paper, "Prehistoric Over-Kill," Yale U. Press, 1967, pp. 75-120.

[160] Silliman, Benjamin, in *Amer. Jour. Sci.* 3 (1821):47f.; 8 (1827):130f.

[161] Penn, Granville, *A Comparative Estimate of the Mineral and Mosaical Geologies*, Vol. II, 2nd ed., London, 1825, p. 81.

> The great problem for geological theories to explain is that amazing phenomenon, the mingling of the remains of animals of different species and climates, discovered in exhaustless quantities in the interior parts of the earth, so that the exuviae of those genera which no longer exist at all, are found confusedly mixed together in the soils of the most northerly latitudes. . . . The bones of those animals which can live only in the torrid zone are buried in the frozen soil of the polar regions.

And to quote one more contemporary, George Fairholme, who described similar evidence in Italy from the Arno River Valley:[162]

> In this sandy matrix bones were found at every depth from that of a few feet to a hundred feet or more. From the large and more apparent bones of the elephant, the rhinoceros, the megatherium, the elk, the buffalo, the stag, and so forth, naturalists were led by the elaborate studies of Cuvier and other comparative anatomists to the remains of the now living bear, tiger, wolf, hyena, rabbit, and finally the more minute remains even of the water rat and the mouse. In some places so complete was the confusion . . . that the bones of many different elephants were brought into contact, and on some of them even oyster shells were matted.

Both Darwin and Wallace were impressed by the evidence of mass destruction just before man appeared. In his *Journal of Researches*, the former wrote of his wonder at the picture presented by the fossil record in South America, which he visited on the voyage of the *Beagle* in 1845:[163]

> The mind is at first irresistibly hurried into the belief that some great catastrophe has occurred. Thus, to destroy animals both large and small in South Patagonia, in Brazil, in the Cordillera, in North America up to the Behring Straits, we must shake the entire framework of the globe. Certainly no fact in the long history of the world is so startling as the wide extermination of its inhabitants.

His contemporary, Alfred R. Wallace, in 1876 wrote in a similar vein:[164]

> We live in a zoologically impoverished world, from which all the hugest, and fiercest, and strangest forms have recently disappeared. . . . Yet it is surely a marvellous fact, and one that has hardly been sufficiently dwelt upon, this sudden dying out of so many large mammalia not in one place only but over half the land surface of the globe. . . .
>
> There must have been some physical cause for this great change; and it must have been a cause capable of acting almost simultaneously over large portions of the earth's surface.

---

[162] Fairholme, George, *New and Conclusive Physical Demonstrations of the Fact and Period of the Mosaic Deluge,* n.p., 1837.

[163] Darwin, Charles, *Journal of Researches,* Ward Lock, New York, 1845, p. 178.

[164] Wallace, Alfred Russell, *Geographical Distribution of Animals,* Vol. I, Hafner, New York, 1876, pp. 150,151.

One of the most thorough students of this last great catastrophe was Sir Henry Howorth whose works are now virtually unobtainable. Although his interpretation of the evidence was, and still is, rejected by geologists committed to Lyell's principle of uniformity, he nevertheless put on record a tremendous amount of data, much of it gathered at firsthand, which is not nearly as well known as it should be. In one of his major works, *The Mammoth and the Flood*, he collected data regarding the innumerable known cases of mammoths frozen in northern latitudes, particularly in Siberia.[165] And yet in spite of this information, which is always very well documented, a comparatively recent paper by William R. Farrand entitled, "Frozen Mammoths and Modern Geology," spoke of only some 39 known frozen carcasses, of which only four are by any means complete; and it never once mentions the books and papers published by Sir Henry Howorth.[166] To Dr. Farrand, there is no real evidence of catastrophe in spite of the extraordinary circumstances under which these giant creatures evidently died. Howorth, however, gives many details which it is quite impossible, I believe, to account for in any other way than by assuming a very sudden catastrophe followed almost immediately by *intense* cold. It was encouraging to see that a correspondent countered Farrand's statements very effectively:[167] but Farrand replied with considerable sarcasm, clearly being on the defensive.

In 1887 Howorth wrote:[168]

> In the first place, it is almost certain in my opinion that a very great cataclysm or catastrophe occurred . . . by which the mammoth with his companions was overwhelmed over a very large part of the earth's surface. This catastrophe, secondly, involved a widespread flood of waters which not only killed the animals but also buried them under continuous beds of loam or gravel. Thirdly, that the same catastrophe was accompanied by a very sudden change of climate in Siberia, by which the animals that had previously lived in fairly temperate conditions were frozen in their flesh under the ground and have remained there ever since.
>
> When the facts are stated, they are of such a nature as to be almost incredible and they are drawn from the works of such men as Wrangell, Strahlenberg, Witzen, Muller, Klaproth, Avril, Erman, Hedenstrom, Betuschef, Bregne, Gemlin, Brandt, Antermony, Liachof, Kusholof, Chamisso, Maljuschkin, Ides, Baer, Schmidt, Bell, Tatishof, Middendorf,

---

[165] Howorth, Sir Henry, *The Mammoth and the Flood: Uniformity and Geology*, London, 1887.
[166] Farrand, William R., "Frozen Mammoths and Modern Geology," *Science* 133 (1961):729-735.
[167] Lippman, Harold E., Letter to the Editor, under the heading "Frozen Mammoths," *Science* 137 (1962):449ff.
[168] Howorth, Sir Henry, ref. 165, p. 47.

von Schrenck, Olders, Laptef, Sarytschef, Motschulsky, Schtscukin, Maydell, besides the official documents of the Russian Government.

One of the rivers of Siberia that empties into the Artic is the Yenessei. Concerning the buried animals revealed in the strata along the sides of this river, Howorth remarked:[169]

> Pallas reports that the mammoth bones which fall out of the cliffs are so numerous that on decomposing they form a substance called "osteocolli" or "bone glue." The next great river eastward towards Alaska, emptying into the Arctic, is the Lena. It is a vast stream which consists of twists and turns, making a course of over 2000 miles. The natives who live in the regions of the Lena river make a living travelling up and down the river in boats, gathering up the ivory tusks that they see sticking out of cliffs along the river banks and which they find fallen to the edge of the water.

The number of animals that are buried in Siberia must be stupendous. Some conception can be obtained from the fact that since A.D. 900 men have made it a business to collect the ivory of the region and sell it in China, Arabia, and Europe. In one case where a record was secured, Lyddeker stated that in a period of twenty years tusks from at least 20,000 animals were taken from the Siberian mines to markets in Europe during the nineteenth century.[170] Howorth reported what has since been confirmed many times, that the contents of the stomachs of many of these giants had been examined carefully and been shown to contain undigested food, composed of leaves of trees now found in southern Siberia.[171] Microscopic examination of the skins of some of these animals has since revealed red blood corpuscles. This is thought to be proof, not only of sudden death, but death due to suffocation either by gas or water.[172] One particular animal with an undigested meal still in its stomach had been eating buttercups, sedges, grasses, the beans of wild oxytropis, and young shoots of fir and pine. In 1901 an expedition to Kolomysk was made by some Russian scientists to convey to St. Petersburg a particularly fine specimen with hair, skin, and flesh perfectly preserved — which also had the remains of undigested food in its stomach.[173]

---

[169] Ibid., p. 54.

[170] Lydekker, Richard, Annual Report, Smithsonian Instit., 1899, pp. 361-366.

[171] Undigested food: cf. Charles Lyell, *Principles of Geology*, Vol. I, p. 183, quoting a letter to Humboldt from Prof. Brandt of St. Petersburg; also *Sci. American*, August 1901, for a similar observation; and *Sci. American*, September 1951, p. 164.

[172] Death by suffocation: first remarked upon by Prof. Brandt in 1846 in the Proc. of Berlin Academy, p. 223.

[173] Brandt: quoted by Howorth, ref. 165, p. 61.

Fig. 1. Imperial Mammoth (Elephas imperator) of Nebraska and Texas, after a painting by C. R. Knight in the American Museum of Natural History, New York City. This is typical of specimens such as the various Siberian finds mentioned in the text. Photo used courtesy of the American Museum of Natural History.

Perhaps no one single discovery can ever quite convey so strong an impression of the suddenness and immensity of the catastrophe as one reported first by Brandt,[174] and subsequently accredited by others, in which three mammoth mummies were found *standing erect* and facing north. A similar discovery was made by Fisher of a single specimen in the same extraordinary attitude of arrested flight.

We have mentioned the existence of rhinoceroses in a similar condition. In a letter to Baron Humboldt from the same Professor Brandt (of St. Petersburg), particulars are given of a rhinoceros obtained by Pallas in 1772 from Wiljiusky (latitude 64°), from the banks of the Wiljiu, a tributary of the Lena. Brandt wrote concerning it:[175]

---

[174] Brandt, in Lyell's *Principles of Geology*, Vol. I, p. 183.
[175] Ibid.

> I have been so fortunate as to extract from cavities in the molar teeth of the Wiljiu rhinoceros a small quantity of its half-chewed food, among which fragments of pine leaves, one half of the seed of a polygonacious plant, and very minute portions of wood with porous cells or small fragments of coniferous wood were still recognizable. It was also remarkable on a close examination of the head, that the blood vessels discovered in the interior of the mass appeared to be filled, even to the capillary vessels, with a brown mass (coagulated blood), which in many places still showed the red colour of blood.

Before considering similar animal cemeteries in other parts of the world, it might be well to point out that it is not a normal occurrence to find dead animals *anywhere* – except on our highways! For example, Baron Nordenskiold remarked:[176]

> In the first place I must call attention to the extreme rarity of the occurrence of the remains of animals which have recently died. . . .
>
> During my nine expeditions in the Arctic regions, where animal life during summer is exceedingly abundant, I can recall very few occasions upon which I have found remains of vertebrate animals which could be proved to have died a natural death. Near hunting grounds there are to be seen, often enough, the remains of reindeer, seals, foxes, or bears that have died from gunshot wounds, but no naturally dead polar bear, seals, walrus, white whale, fox, goose, auk, lemming or other vertebrates. The polar bear and the reindeer are found there in hundreds: the seal, walrus, and white whale in thousands: and birds in millions. These animals must die a natural death in untold numbers. What becomes of their bodies? Of this we have for the present no idea. . . .

The only conclusion that one can draw from this is that the death of these hundreds of thousands of large animals was unnatural, and virtually simultaneous. How do we know it was simultaneous? Because, as we shall see, similar vast cemeteries are found elsewhere, in which the predators and the preyed upon died together, and there is no evidence of the bones of any of the animals having been gnawed. The only difference between these animal cemeteries in other parts of the world and those in Siberia is that the former were not preserved by refrigeration, and therefore appear rather as vast assemblages of bones.[177] In the Harvard Museum a slab six feet by ten feet contains bones so thickly packed and in such confusion that there is every evidence of violence in their compaction. In the Colorado Museum of Natural History a similar geological exhibit is to be seen, taken from an animal cemetery at Agate Springs, in which it is estimated that the bones of about 9000 complete animals are buried in one hill. One section of such a bone cemetery is shown in Fig.2.

---

[176] Nordenskiold, Baron N.A.E., *Voyage of the Vega*, Vol. I, 1881, pp. 322,323.

[177] Animal cemeteries: see more recently the New York *World*, reporting from Alaska, June 1, 1930, and Associated Press, April 16, 1949.

Fig. 2. Part of an animal cemetery taken from a quarry at Agate Springs, Nebraska, and now exhibited in the Denver Museum of Natural History. It contains bones of thousands of animals, extending over a wide area. Photo used courtesy of the Denver Museum of Natural History.

Howorth had this to say about these animal cemeteries:[178]

The most obvious cause we can appeal to as occasionally producing mortality on a wide scale among animals is a murrain or pestilence, but what murrain or pestilence is so completely unbiased in its actions as to sweep away all forms of terrestrial life, even the very carriers of it — the rodents — including the fowls of the air, the beasts of the field, elephants, tigers, rhinoceroses, frogs, mice, bison and snakes, landsnails, and every conceivable form of life, and this not in one corner only but, as far as we know, over the whole of the two great continents irrespective of latitude or longitude.

The fact of the bones occurring in great caches or deposits in which various species are mixed *pell-mell* is very important, and it is a fact undenied by geologists that whenever we find such a locality in which animals have suffered together in a violent and instantaneous destruction, the bones are invariably mixed and, as it were, "deposited" in a manner which could hardly be explained otherwise than by postulating the action of great tidal waves

[178] Howorth, Sir Henry, ref. 165, p. 180.

carrying fishes and all before them, depositing them far inland with no respect to order.

Howorth continued later:

> If animals die occasionally (in large numbers) from natural causes, different species do not come together to die, nor does the lion come to take his last sleep with the lamb! The fact of finding masses of animal remains of mixed species all showing the same state of preservation, not only points to a more or less contemporary death, but is quite fatal to the theory that they ended their days peacefully and by purely natural means.
>
> If they had been exposed to the air, and to the severe transition between mid-winter and mid-summer, which characterizes Arctic latitudes, the mammoths would have decayed rapidly. But their state of preservation proves that they were covered over and protected ever since.

This renowned but neglected authority concluded:[179]

> It is almost certain in my opinion that a very great cataclysm or catastrophe occurred by which the mammoth and his companions were overwhelmed over a very large part of the earth's surface. And that the same catastrophe was accompanied by a very great and sudden change of climate in Siberia, by which the animals which had previously lived in fairly temperate conditions were frozen . . . and were never once thawed until the day of their discovery. No other theory will explain the perfect preservation of these great elephants.

From the Antarctic also there is evidence, according to geologists of the Bryd Expedition,[180] of similarly different climatic conditions. Great coal fields, evidence of luxuriant growth, were discovered at the head of Thorne Glacier in the Queen Maude Range within 200 miles of the South Pole. Such conditions so near to that frightful wilderness of ice and snow, which is so much more terrible than the North Pole in its coldness and barrenness, is remarkable witness of a previous world which must have been a very different one. So numerous are the fossils there that the explorers actually had difficulty making a selection. Today life in these regions is conspicuously absent.

Evan Hopkins remarked that the fossil plants of north Greenland proved that the land has been favored with a climate at least 30° F. warmer than at present.[181] He pointed out also that among the animals entombed in the deposits in Siberia besides the mammoths are bears, hippos, hyena, lions, tigers, and others which can only live and flourish in or near the tropics. Moreover, the fossil forest at

---

[179] Ibid.

[180] Reported from Little America in the Toronto *Telegram*, December 13, 1933.

[181] Hopkins, Evan, "On Terrestrial Changes and the Probable Ages of the Continents," *Trans. Vict. Instit.* 2 (1867):4,8.

Atanekerdluk at a latitude of 70⁰ is indicative of a temperature of at least 30⁰ F. higher than is now found at that parallel. Similar conditions are likely to be found now at the 48⁰ parallel, a fact which shows a shift of climate with respect to the equator. What has been said of land animals is equally true of fishes and even of plants. Some years ago Philip Le Riche presented a paper before the Victoria Institute in London in which he made this statement:[182]

> It can easily be shown that many of the strata contain the fossil remains of fish which have been suddenly interred before putrefaction had acted upon their fleshy bodies, for their bodies are preserved as they were during life. And this remarkable state of preservation of fish life is also found in the flora. For plants as fine as maidenhair ferns are found embedded in the strata with even their venules intact, showing that they must have been buried very shortly after their deposition in the sediment, otherwise they would have become converted into leaf mold and indistinguishable, whereas a botanist can place the fossil plant in its proper order of plant life.

The suddenness of this destruction is further strikingly borne out by the fossil cuttlefish of Lyme Regis that were killed and entombed with such inconceivable rapidity that they still retain the dark fluid with which their ink bags are filled when alive.[183] But these animals when disturbed release this protective device within a matter of seconds. Speaking of fish, Howorth even recorded a whale which was found entombed with the elephants, a discovery which Pallas confirmed — mentioning also buffalo *in situ* with the heads of large fishes.

In spite of the fact that many of these authorities would now be considered quite out of date, so that their interpretations would almost certainly be rejected, the evidence itself remains undeniable; and it is difficult to explain it satisfactorily in any other way. In concluding this brief survey, and referring this time to accumulations of bones which were washed pell-mell into fissures and clefts in the rocks, one can reflect upon the words of the venerable Joseph Prestwich, affectionately styled the Father of the Geological Society. After speaking of such animal cemeteries and pointing out how the bones of carnivores are mixed indiscriminately with those of their natural prey, the bodies seeming to have been torn apart with violence, he summed the situation up by saying:[184]

---

[182] Le Riche, Philip, "Scientific Proofs of the Universal Deluge," *Trans. Vict. Instit.* 61 (1929):86.

[183] Cuttlefish of Lyme Regis: see Byron C. Nelson, *The Deluge Story in Stone*, Augsburg, Minneapolis, 1931, p. 113.

[184] Prestwich, Joseph, in the *Quart. Jour. Geol. Soc.* 48 (1912):326.

These bones cannot be of animals which fell into these fissures (where they are found in such profusion), for no skeleton is complete. They cannot have been brought by beasts of prey, for none are gnawed. They were not brought by streams (i.e., spring floods), for none are rolled. The bones could not have laid exposed for long, for none are weathered. They were not covered up normally, for they were broken by the violence of their deposition together with the associated rocks. . . .

The formation of these fissure deposits in so many places . . . seems to confirm the belief that the rubble drift itself did not owe its origin to normal causes, but to something catastrophic in the nature of earth movements.

Such, then, is the kind of evidence which is to be found all over the world of the sudden death of an enormous number of animals of very recent and modern times. Some of these creatures died in latitudes that were almost at once plunged into an Ice Age which preserved them by freezing. Some of them died in more temperate zones and were accumulated by the action of torrents of water sweeping hither and yon as the earth reeled, before the waters had been sufficiently gathered together in one place to expose the dry land. And, finally, some were accumulated and rammed together forcibly and indiscriminately into clefts in the rocks which served to sieve them out of the draining waters.

The suddenness of the event is everywhere attested, in the Arctic by the extraordinary state of preservation of mammoths and other creatures, and in the more temperate zones by the very fact that predators and preyed upon came to a sudden end together. Even within the waters, the movements of silt and water-washed materials were sometimes so sudden and overwhelming that fishes were trapped before they had the few seconds necessary to react in a characteristic defensive way. Some bivalved forms, in fact, were overwhelmed so rapidly that they did not have time to close.

Furthermore, we may conclude, I think, that the catastrophe which was worldwide profoundly affected world climate. There are some who believe that the Ice Age is bound up with the sudden subsidence of the waters. They argue that the effect of this subsidence was greatly to increase the exposed land area. I am not competent to assess the mechanics of this hypothesis, but there is little doubt that what has been observed was related to the coming of the great cold which brought ice down over half of the northern hemisphere and introduced the world to an Ice Age from which we really have not yet altogether recovered. We may say that the ice caps have merely retreated far enough to allow most of us to ignore them. And the event was recent indeed. The present is, geologically speaking, the end of the Pleistocene. It is as Shull has observed:[185]

> At few points in geological history has there been extermination comparable to that of mammals in the time just preceding the recent. In part this may be due to repeated glaciation, but most of it is unexplained. Only the tropical regions, notably Africa, escaped this great diminution of mammals, and the Pleistocene mammals of that continent were essentially the same as today.

A study of the rocks indicates that the same may be said largely of Australia. The pattern of fossil marsupials has continued on in that continent and is still with us. It is probably true, as Baker pointed out, that not a few species of animals — indeed, large areas of living things — might very well have survived the catastrophe. But those which perished irretrievably as species had to be re-created.[186] Those species which had not perished altogether began once more to multiply. Possibly this is why in Genesis 1 God said in some cases, "Let the earth bring forth. . . ," while in other cases Scripture says, "So God created. . . ," etc. Not everything had to be recreated; and as for plant life, the earth perhaps did indeed bring forth seed which was in itself — in the earth (Gen. 1:11).

Perhaps the tilting of the earth's axis by as much as 40^0 or more at the time of the last great convulsion of nature may have been partially responsible for the fact that in the New World, for example, the great ice sheet reached down over New York State. Possibly we shall yet discover what upset the earth's equilibrium at the time to cause this tilt. When — and if — this axis of rotation becomes completely vertical again, the ice caps will presumably disappear entirely and the whole earth could enjoy a temperate climate. The recovery at present is only partial (23^0), so that although the ice retreats annually, we still have polar caps with us. If we assume that the axis of rotation of the world that then was, was normal to the earth's plane of rotation around the sun, then that world would have enjoyed a much more temperate climate over its whole surface. This could have important theoretical implications, for as H. Hamshaw Thomas of Cambridge, in a letter to *Nature*, pointed out:[187]

> The possibility that changes have occurred during the past in the position of the earth's axis of rotation . . . is of great interest to all students of fossil plants.
> It has long been clear that the geological evidence of former vegetation shows that the lands around the Arctic Sea bore an ample covering of plants

---

[185] Shull, A. F., ref. 48, p. 65.

[186] Baker, Howard B., *The Atlantic Rift and Its Meaning*, publ. privately, 1932, with numerous illustrations and extensive bibliography, pp. 181-183 (obtainable only from Library of Congress).

[187] Thomas, Hamshaw, Letter to the Editor, *Nature*, August 20, 1955, p. 349.

during a long period, probably from Devonian to Tertiary times. This vegetation included many large trees and was very different from the scanty flora of these regions living today.

And so the Old World was suddenly brought to an end just when it had seemed ready to receive man as its paramount chief. But God had formed it and given it its appointments and established its natural order; and He had not created all this in vain (Isa. 45:18). He had intended it in the first place as a habitation for man, and although His intention had been forestalled by some counteragency, that intention stood firm: and so the process of reconstitution was once again undertaken by the Lord to put everything ready for the introduction of man, for whom it had all been planned.

Thus man finds himself in a world in which there are strange contradictions. Everywhere to the eye of faith there is evidence of plan and purpose — such evidence, in fact, that even the unbelieving find it hard not to recognize it. At the same time, equally ubiquitous, is the evidence of catastrophe and judgment, as though some contrary planner had been at work seeking to thwart the Creator's design, and more particularly and more dramatically just when man's coming was drawing near.

Perhaps it is time to reassess the geological evidence in the light of these two opposing forces, one for good and one for evil.

Epilogue

WHATEVER THE cause of the last great cataclysm that saw the end of "the world that then was," the result was to leave the globe in a chaotic state which required very extensive reordering before man could be introduced into it.

There is some justification for the view that Genesis 1:2 is a description of this scene immediately before the reordering began. Moreover, it can be shown that most present translations, with the exception of a few like that of Dathe or Rotherham, do not really do justice to the original Hebrew which would have been more precisely rendered as "But the earth had become a ruin and a desolation" rather than "and the earth was, etc."[188]

It will be noted that there are three changes here: the use of the disjunctive *but* for the conjunctive *and*, the use of *become* for *was*, and the use of the pluperfect (or past perfect, as it is alternatively called) instead of the perfect tense, i.e., *had become* instead of *became*. I have written at length on this matter and shown that this view was held by the earliest Jewish commentators.[189] It was adopted by many of the early church fathers, and it has been held in an unbroken tradition to the present time. It is, therefore, in no way a concession to geology, for it was clearly maintained in the Jewish rabbinical literature long before there was any geological knowledge of consequence to challenge the Scriptures.

The clear implication, an implication recognized by the Rabbis, is that the original created worlds which preceded were of no great concern nor in need of any revelation except to state simply that God created them (v.1). After them occurred the last great cataclysmic discontinuity leaving a desolated world needing to be restored. The process of restoration was evidently enormously accelerated, the task

---

[188] Custance, Arthur C., "Analysis of Genesis 1:1,2" in Doorway Papers, Vol. VI.
[189] Custance, Arthur C., *Without Form and Void*, publ. privately, Brockville, Ontario, 1970.

of renewal being completed within a period of six days. Furthermore, I do not think one *can* treat these days as anything but 24-hour periods. In the first place, usage elsewhere in Scripture shows that the word *day (yōm)* is to be taken as literal when accompanied by a numeral: the qualifying statement "the evening and the morning" reinforces this view, being the Hebrew equivalent of the New Testament term "a night and a day" (II Cor. 11:25: one word, i.e., *nuchthēmeron)*, which is similarly definitive. The Hebrew language also has a perfectly suitable word for an "age," namely, 'olām, which is almost precisely what we mean when we speak of a geological age. And finally, the original text is written as simple prose and not as poetry, so that an appeal to poetic allegory is really without foundation.

Moreover, we have a few hints in what follows, as to the reality of the reconstitutional nature of the process. Not everything was *re-created*. The phrase, "Let the earth bring forth," etc., is significantly different from the references to direct fiat creation. Furthermore, the seed of plant and tree which sprang up was "already in itself in the earth" (v.11). Finally, the garden was merely *planted*, suggesting that the soil itself was already available and prepared, a soil constituted from decayed vegetation of the previous creation.

That such a process of recovery could be so soon completed is by no means exceptional in Scripture, for the turning of water into wine, the multiplying of the loaves and the fishes, the restoring of Malchus' ear, and the raising of Lazarus requiring the complete re-creation of his decayed body, all demonstrate clearly that the same Creator, the Lord Jesus Christ, could indeed perform at an enormously accelerated rate the work which in previous geological periods had no *need* to be accelerated and, indeed, was better not so done.

This was the last great shaking of the earth alone. Next time the heavens, too, will be shaken (Heb. 12:26), and in their place will come a wonderful new heavens and a new earth in which there will never be sorrow or hurt, war or death, or any of those things which make this scene the "vale of tears" that it still is, for all its beauty.

But at that time the earth was finally ready to serve as the stage upon which was to be acted out the drama of man's redemption, as an everlasting display of the love of God for His creatures, a love which was great enough that He was willing to come in the Person of His Son Jesus Christ and lay down His life that all who would accept this sacrifice for themselves personally might be everlastingly saved.

Part II
Primitive Monotheism
and the Origin of Polytheism

Introduction

ONE HUNDRED years ago, when Darwin published his book, *The Origin of Species,* the climate of opinion was already tending towards the view that everything was in a state of improvement, that men were getting better and better, their ideals higher and higher, their religious faith purer and purer, their productivity greater and greater. The corollary of this, though it was not always worked out at first, was that in reverse everything must have been worse and worse as one passed back into history and prehistory. Even those who believed that occasionally in the past and in some parts of the world — notably where primitive people existed — degeneration had also occurred, were still emotionally persuaded that by and large progress was automatic. The persuasive philosophy of evolution seemed to have been contagious and one by one each branch of historical research succumbed to the temptation to reconstitute its data in ascending scales, starting with the simple, crude, or naive and leading to the complex, refined, or sophisticated at the present. The history of art, technology, social organization, everything in fact — including religious beliefs — was assumed to fall into this pattern. There was a logical compulsion about it all. Indeed, it appeared self-evident that it must be so.

Several theories about the origin of religious faith with an evolutionary slant preceded Darwin's classical work. Spencer wrote at some length on the subject, as did others, each setting forth what they supposed was "how it all began." It began with the worship of the dead, sometimes ancestors but not always, or it began with the feeling which early man was supposed to have that Nature was animated, that "things" had "wills" which one did well to reconcile oneself with, or it began simply because our earliest forebears lived lives which were so dangerous in circumstances so frightening and so constantly beset by unknowns that they cowered and trembled and were almost immobilized with fear throughout the better part of their lives. In these circumstances what was assumed to be a certain superstitious bent in human nature "naturally" gave rise to feelings of awe and dread, which slowly evolved into structured religious beliefs. This sounds like a frightful exaggeration of what otherwise intelligent men claim to have happened, but it is not really so. For example, Lewis Browne wrote in all seriousness:[1]

> In the beginning there was fear; and fear was in the heart of man; and fear controlled man. At every turn it overwhelmed him, and left him no moment of ease. With the wild soughing of the wind it swept through him; with the crashing of thunder and the growling of the lurking beasts. All the days of man were gray with fear, because all his universe seemed charged with danger. . . . And he, poor gibbering half-ape, nursing his wound in some draughty cave, could only tremble in fear.

Christian writers who believed that Scripture was a true record of man's early history viewed this tendency as a serious challenge, and with increasing frequency learned papers and scholarly books began to appear, in which precisely the opposite view was declared to be a far better interpretation of the available evidence. It was a time of great missionary expansion; and, it should not be forgotten, of expansion also in studies made by anthropologists of primitive people. Unexpectedly the best informed of the latter began to find themselves in nearer agreement with the former, and the result was the publication of the writings of such man as Andrew Lang. Lang greatly influenced a Roman Catholic writer, Wilhelm Schmidt, an anthropologist himself and founder of a justly famous journal *Anthropos*. The Transactions of the Victoria Institute in those earlier years were full of papers on the issue. A list of them will be found subsequently in this paper. Between the years 1900 and 1935 the whole subject was dealt with in a scholarly fashion by men committed to the view that the evolutionary reconstructions of man's religious beliefs were fundamentally erroneous, and they produced such an impact that evolutionary philosophers virtually abandoned the whole line of argument. From the mid-thirties on, the issue has been almost a dead one, although many theological colleges of liberal persuasion conduct their courses in the history of religion as though nothing had ever been written of this nature.

Because evolutionists have dropped the subject, there has come to be comparative unconcern about the issue on the part of many well-informed Christian readers and one hears very little about it

---

[1] Browne, Lewis, *This Believing World:* quoted by Samuel Zwemer in *The Origin of Religion*, Cokesbury, Nashville, Tenn., 1935, p. 53.

these days. This might lead one to the view that evolutionary philosophy has not altogether been a curse, for wherever it has been rigorously pursued and dogmatically asserted, evangelicals have been forced to think seriously and write seriously on the matter. Challenge has been a good thing, because the circumstances surrounding this particular study show that as soon as the threat is withdrawn the Christian is apt to go to sleep.

However, it is worthwhile perhaps to reconsider the matter once more from a slightly different point of view. And therefore in Chapter 1 of this paper I propose to set forth, briefly, the view that as far back as we can go by studying tradition, whether oral or written, and by analyzing the present beliefs or the recent beliefs of those who are still living comparatively primitive lives, a pure monotheistic faith seems to have preceded a superstitious, degraded, ineffective, and unreasonable system of beliefs later subscribed to. This is true of classical antiquity, not merely around the Mediterranean, but in India and in the Far East, and even — if the term *antiquity* applies — to the great civilizations of the New World. Then I propose in the second chapter to consider very briefly what I feel to be some of the implications of man's tendency towards spiritual degeneration to which history bears such a strong testimony. The first chapter is therefore intended as a kind of annotated bibliography, a resume of the evidence, a review paper with the appropriate documentation. Chapter 2 is more philosophical, an exploration of ideas rather than facts, of implications of events rather than the events themselves.

Chapter 1
From Monotheism to Polytheism

In Sophisticated Society

SOME YEARS ago Prebendary Rowe observed that it is more sensible to start with the known and reason upon it towards the unknown than to start with the unknown in the hopes of being able to explain the known. We now have a body of "knowns" which is substantial, and in some ways the most assured data are to be found in that quite vast literature which has been preserved from the Cradle of Civilization, Mesopotamia.

When the cuneiform literature first began to reveal its message, scholars of cuneiform and Egyptian hieroglyphics soon found themselves dealing with a tremendous number of gods and goddesses, and demons and other spiritual powers of a lesser sort, which seemed to be always at war with one another and much of the time highly destructive. As earlier and earlier tablets, however, began to be excavated and brought to light, and skill in deciphering them increased, the first picture of gross polytheism began to be replaced by something more nearly approaching a hierarchy of spiritual beings organized into a kind of court with one Supreme Being over all. One of the first cuneiform scholars to acknowledge the significance of this trend was Stephen Langdon of Oxford, and when he reported his conclusions he did so with a consciousness of the fact that he would scarcely be believed. Thus he wrote in 1931:[2]

> I may fail to carry conviction in concluding that both in Sumerian and Semitic religions, monotheism preceded polytheism. . . . The evidence and reasons for this conclusion, so contrary to accepted and current views, have been set down with care and with the perception of adverse criticism. It is, I trust, the conclusion of knowledge and not of audacious preconception.

Since Langdon took the view that the Sumerians represent the oldest historic civilization, he added:

---

[2] Langdon, Stephen H., *Semitic Mythology*, Mythology of All Races, Vol. V, Archaeol. Instit. Amer., 1931, p. xviii.

> In my opinion the history of the oldest civilization of man is a rapid decline from monotheism to extreme polytheism and widespread belief in evil spirits. It is in a very true sense the history of the fall of man.

Five years later in an article which appeared in *The Scotsman,* he wrote:[3]

> The history of Sumerian religion, which was the most powerful cultural influence in the ancient world, could be traced by means of pictographic inscriptions almost to the earliest religious concepts of man. The evidence points unmistakeably to an original monotheism, the inscriptions and literary remains of the oldest Semitic peoples also indicate a primitive monotheism, and the totemistic origin of Hebrew and other Semitic religions is now entirely discredited.

To my knowledge only one person has seriously challenged Langdon's conclusion since. And this was an old professor of mine, T. J. Meek.[4] The argument that Langdon used was based on the following circumstances: The Sumerian religion in its latest development before the people disappeared as an entity swallowed up by the later Babylonians, seemed to have involved about 5000 gods. The inscriptions of circa 3000 B.C. or perhaps a millennium earlier show only 750. The 300 tablets or so known from Jamdet Nasr in 1928 when Langdon published these texts, contained only three gods; the sky god Enlil, the earth god Enki, and the sun god Babbar. The 575 tablets from Uruk translated in 1936, which Langdon dated about 4000 B.C. but are now believed to be more accurately dated 3500 B.C., contain the names of only two deities: the sky god An and the mother goddess Innina. Meek's criticism of Langdon's essay was that the number of gods he mentions for the earlier tablets is in error. In the Jamdet Nasr text there may have been as many as six, not three. On this account Meek felt that he could accuse Langdon of gross inaccuracy and thus undermine the force of his argument. At the same time he admitted that at least one of these six is doubtful. Moreover, it is not always possible to be sure that a name which appears as someone to whom prayers are made is necessarily thought of as a deity. Praying to saints has been known even in modern days! In any case, when the forward view of history takes us from two deities to a small number — whether three or six 500 years later, to 750 a thousand years later, and to 5,000 before the picture becomes indistinct — the argument against Langdon's interpretation of the data based upon an error in counting of such small

---

[3] Langdon, Stephen H., *The Scotsman,* November 18, 1936.

[4] Meek, T. J., *Primitive Monotheism and the Religion of Moses,* U. of Toronto Quarterly 8 (January 1939):189-197.

proportions surely carries no weight at all. It does not seriously challenge his basic argument.

In any case, subsequent excavations at Tell Asmar from the period of the third millennium B.C. have fully corroborated his findings. Thus Henry Frankfort wrote in his official report:[5]

> In addition to their more tangible results, our excavations have established a novel fact, which the student of Babylonian religions will have henceforth to take into account. We have obtained, to the best of our knowledge for the first time, religious material complete in its social setting.
>
> We possess a coherent mass of evidence, derived in almost equal quantity from a temple and from the houses inhabited by those who worshipped in that temple. We are thus able to draw conclusions, which the finds studied by themselves would not have made possible.
>
> For instance, we discover that the representations on cylinder seals, which are usually connected with various gods, can all be fitted into a consistent picture in which a single god worshipped in this temple forms the central figure. It seems, therefore, that at this early period his various aspects were not considered separate deities in the Sumero-Accadian pantheon.

This raises an important point; namely, the possibility that polytheism never did arise by the evolution of polydemonism, but because the attributes of a single God were differently emphasized by different people until those people in later years came to forget that they were speaking of the same Person. Thus attributes of a single deity became a plurality of deities. It is not merely that single individuals laid emphasis upon different aspects of God's nature but whole families and tribes seemed to have developed certain shared views about what was important in life and what was not, and therefore, not unnaturally, came to attribute to their god and to put special emphasis upon those characteristics which seemed to them of greatest significance. For example, a warlike people are not too likely to emphasize the gentleness of God nor a legalistic people the forgivingness of God. They will rather emphasize His power in the one case and His justice in the other. In three other Doorway Papers[6] we have explored the possibility that the sons of Noah (Shem, Ham, and Japheth) each developed a bent towards life which led them to different emphases: Shem on the spiritual quality of life, Ham on the practical concerns of life, and Japheth on the philosophical aspects of life. It is not surprising, therefore, that the God of the Semites is a

---

[5] Frankfort, H., *Third Preliminary Report on Excavations at Tell Asmar (Eshnunna)*: quoted by P. J. Wiseman in *New Discoveries in Babylonia about Genesis*, Marshall, Morgan and Scott, London, 1936, p. 24.

[6] Part I, "The Part Played by Shem, Ham, and Japheth in Subsequent World History"; Part IV, "The Technology of Hamitic People"; and Part V, "A Christian World View: The Framework of History," all in Doorway Papers, Vol. I.

God of pure spirit. The gods of the Hamites, on the other hand, were gods of power. And the gods of the Japhethites or Indo-Europeans were gods of light, in the sense of being gods of "understanding." I think Matthew's Gospel was written for the descendants of Shem and is slanted towards their way of thinking about God. Mark's Gospel was written for the descendants of Ham and is full of action, of doings, of service, of authority — where the characteristic phrase is "immediately," "straightway," and similar terms. Luke's Gospel was undoubtedly written for the descendants of Japheth; and it may be merely coincidence, though I doubt it very much, that the writer's name means "light."

Long before Langdon had made his translations, Friedrich Delitzsch had made a rather similar proposal regarding the continuing tendency towards the multiplication of deities.[7] He refers to a tablet reported upon by T. G. Pinches which, though only fragmentarily preserved, tells us that all, or at any rate, the highest of the deities in the Babylonian pantheon are designated as one with and one in the god Marduk.

The god Marduk is set forth under the name "Ninib," as "the Possessor of Power"; under the name of "Nergal" or "Zamama," as "Lord of Battle"; under the name "Bel," as "Possessor of Lordship"; under the name "Nebo," as "The Lord the Prophet"; under the name "Sin," as "Illuminator of the Night"; under the name "Shamash," as "Lord of all that is Just"; under the name "Addu," as "God of Rain." Marduk therefore was Ninib as well as Nergal, Moon-god as well as Sun-god, the names being simply different ways of describing his attributes, powers, or duties.

The same historical process can be traced in Egypt. Renouf in his Hibbert Lectures for 1879 quotes M. de Rouge as having said that from, or rather before, the beginning of the historical period, the pure monotheistic religion of Egypt passed through the phase of Sabeism; the sun instead of being considered as the symbol of life, was taken as the manifestation of God Himself. Rouge observed:[8]

> It is incontestably true that the sublimer portions of the Egyptian religion are not the comparatively late result of a process of development or elimination from the grosser. The sublimer portions are demonstrably ancient; and the last stage of the Egyptian religion, that known to the Greek and Latin writers, heathen or Christian, was by far the grossest and the most corrupt.

---

[7] Delitzsch, Friedrich, *Babel and Bible*, Williams and Norgate, London, 1903, pp. 144f.

[8] Renouf, P. Le Page, *Lectures on the Origin and Growth of Religion as Illustrated by the Religion of Ancient Egypt*, Williams and Norgate, London, 1897, p. 90.

Renouf observed:

> M. de Rouge is no doubt correct in his assertion that in the several local (centres of) worship, one and the same deity re-appears under different names and symbols. . . .
>
> He infers from the course of history that since polytheism was constantly on the increase, the monotheistic doctrines must have preceded it.

A very sound argument indeed.

Again, as in Sumeria and Babylonia, so also in the course of time the Egyptians multiplied and broke up into factions with tribal loyalties and somewhat provincial religious preferences the purer concept of one God which they had all shared at the beginning and which involved some considerable knowledge of His attributes. This led to a confusion of attributes with different individuals, and descriptive terms became names of deities. Rawlinson wrote many years ago concerning this:[9]

> The deity, once divided, there was no limit to the number of His attributes of various kinds and of different grades; and in Egypt everything that partook of the divine essence became a god. Emblems were added to the catalogue; and though not really deities, they called forth feelings of respect which the ignorant could not distinguish from actual worship.

It was not perhaps unnatural that in order to symbolize God's various powers it would have been taught that His vision was as sharp as a hawk's, or He was strong as a bull, or that He watched unseen like the crocodiles whose eyes alone are to be seen. In time these symbols were mistaken by the common people as being gods in themselves; so was fulfilled that which Paul had written in Romans 1:18-23, that men turned from the worship of God Himself to the worship of His creatures and in due course became vain in their imaginings, and their understanding was darkened. In the second part of this paper we shall return to this subject again, because it is important to see why these grosser aspects of religious belief should have so completely swamped those loftier aspects which ancient Egyptian texts show clearly to have once been remarkably pure.

It might be thought that the picture has changed radically since the days of Renouf and his Hibbert Lectures. This is not the case. Sir Flinders Petrie, in an excellent little book on the subject of Egyptian religion, wrote as follows:[10]

> There are in ancient religions and theologies very different classes of gods. Some races, as the modern Hindu, revel in a profusion of gods and

---

[9] Rawlinson, George, ed., *Herodotus,* appendix to Book II, p. 250.
[10] Petrie, Sir Flinders, *The Religion of Ancient Egypt,* Constable, London, 1908, pp. 3,4.

godlings which continually increase. Others . . . do not attempt to worship great gods, but deal with a host of animistic spirits, devils, or whatever we may call them. . . . But all our knowledge of the early positions and nature of the great gods shows them to stand on an entirely different footing to these varied spirits.

Were the conception of a god only an evolution from such spirit worship, we should find the worship of many gods preceding the worship of one god. . . . What we actually find is the contrary of this, monotheism is the first stage traceable in theology. . . .

Wherever we can trace back polytheism to its earliest stages, we find that it results from combinations of monotheism. In Egypt even Osiris, Isis, and Horus, so familiar as a triad, are found at first as separate units in different places: Isis as a virgin goddess, and Horus as a self-existent God.

Each city appears to have had but one god belonging to it, to whom others were in time added. Similarly Babylonian cities each had their supreme god, and the combinations of these and their transformations in order to form them into groups when their homes were politically united show how essentially they were solitary deities at first.

Everywhere the pattern seems to have been much the same, wherever we have sufficient records to establish the historical sequence. It is not strange that a conquering people should set their own deity at the head of the pantheon, but it is also not strange either that for the sake of peace and harmony they should pay lip service to the deities of the conquered, though allotting to them inferior positions. This kind of broad-mindedness we would tend to commend today under the general heading of religious freedom. But the penalty of this broad-mindedness is that the truth is very quickly blurred. The solution is not simple: the Jesuits, as an example, have traditionally taken the stand that only the truth should be given complete freedom of expression and therefore religious tolerance is equated with lack of conviction. Any man who agrees that people may worship whatever they will is really confessing, so they argue, that he himself is not absolutely certain that he has the truth and therefore is willing to be broad-minded. They have a point. The monarchs of antiquity, like Cyrus for example, allowed complete freedom to conquered peoples to build their temples and establish their priesthoods as suited them individually. The consequence was that such men by their "enlightened" policy contributed to the tremendous proliferation of deities. As I have said, the problem is a difficult one: but ecumenism may be a worse menace in the opposite direction by insisting that everybody must agree to worship the same "God" who may be no God at all.

As we pass from these ancient civilizations toward the East we come to India. And although the literature from this land is very ancient, tracing the history of the origin of its religious beliefs is not as straightforward. Nevertheless, there is a measure of agreement that here, too, there has been a steady multiplication of deities through the centuries, until they are now like the stars in the sky for number. One of the best-known authorities in this area was Max Muller, who although he did not have the Christian convictions that many contemporary scholars had, nevertheless, reached certain conclusions that should be mentioned. Max Muller, born in Germany in 1823, studied in Paris and subsequently taught in London. He wrote many volumes among which *Chips from a German Workshop* is perhaps his best known. He also wrote *Lectures on the Origin and Growth of Religion, as Illustrated by the Religions of India*. Finally, he edited his great monument and life work, a series entitled *The Sacred Books of the East*. He did not believe that early India was monotheistic in its faith, but neither did he believe it was polytheistic — polytheism being a later stage which involved a process of degeneration. In his *The Science of Language* he wrote:[11]

> Mythology, which was the bane of the ancient world, is in truth a disease of language. A myth means a word, but a word which, from being a name or an attribute, has been allowed to assume a more substantial existence. Most of the Greek, the Roman, the Indian, and other heathen gods are nothing but poetical names, which were gradually allowed to assume divine personality never contemplated by their original inventors. Eos was the name of dawn before she became a goddess, the wife of Tithonos, or the dying day. Fatum, or Fate, meant originally what had been spoken; and before Fate became a power, even greater than Jupiter, it meant that which had once been spoken by Jupiter, and could never be changed — not even by Jupiter himself. Zeus originally meant the bright heaven, in Sanskrit Dyaus; and many of the stories told of him as the supreme god, had a meaning only as told originally of the bright heaven, whose rays, like golden rain, descend on the lap of earth, the Danae of old, kept by her father in the dark prison of winter. No one doubts that Luna was simply the name of the moon; but so likewise Lucina, both derived from lucere, to shine. Hecate, too, was an old name of the moon, the feminine of Hekatos and Hekatebolos, the far-darting sun; and Pyrrha, the Eve of the Greeks was nothing but a name of the red earth, and in particular of Thessaly. This mythological disease, though less virulent in modern languages, is by no means extinct.

Hence once more we see how polytheism develops subsequently. Reverting once more to Rowe's observation about arguing from the known to the unknown, it may safely be said without the slightest hesitation that monotheism *never* evolved out of polytheism in any part of the world's earliest history for which we have documentary evidence. As we shall see, this was true also in China.

---

[11] Muller, Max, *Lectures on the Science of Language,* 1st series, Scribner's, Armstrong, N.Y., 1875, pp. 21,22.

Many of his contemporaries disagreed with Muller's interpretation of the evidence, Andrew Lang being one of them. And since his time there has been wide acceptance of the idea that the history of religious beliefs in India has been characterized by the personification, often in gross physical forms and in increasing multiplicity, of a few concepts of the nature of God which at first saw Him as invisible and made Him so remote that He became virtually impersonal. Such lofty concepts do not appeal to ordinary men and what happened in the Middle East appears to have been repeated in India, except that the process proceeded much further because of the cultural continuity that circumstances allowed in that country. In the course of this, they reached the point where their gods were numbered not by the thousands as in Sumeria but by the tens of thousands. No doubt if Egypt had retained its original culture likewise, it too might have ended up worshiping 50,000 deities where once they worshiped perhaps only one. Edward McCrady, writing about Indian religious beliefs observed that even the Rig Veda (Book 1, p.164) shows us that in the early days the gods were regarded simply as diverse manifestations of a single Divine Being. He quoted:[12]

> They call him Indra, Mythra, Varunna, Agni — that which is One, the Wise name by different terms.

Scholars in the West incline to the opinion that the earliest of the hymns in the Rig Veda date from between 1500 to 1200 B.C.[13] Indian tradition, on the other hand, claims for them a much earlier antiquity. Whatever its date and however little Muller shared the Christian view of man's spiritual history, he nevertheless admitted freely:[14]

> There is a monotheism that precedes the polytheism of the Veda; and even in the invocation of the innumerable gods the remembrance of a God, one and infinite, breaks through the mist of idolatrous phraseology like the blue sky that is hidden by passing clouds.

When we come to China, the situation is even more confused, for the Chinese seem to have had a peculiar aversion to the worship of *personal* deities. Some of the older writers, nevertheless, were confident that they could discern evidence of a once pure monotheistic faith, which however was early lost sight of because of the extreme

---

[12] McCrady, Edward, "Genesis and Pagan Cosmogonies," *Trans. Vict. Instit.* 72 (1940):55.

[13] MacNicol, Nicol, ed., *The Hindu Scriptures,* Everyman's Library, Dent, London, 1938, p. xiv.

[14] Muller, Max, *History of Sanskrit Literature:* quoted by Samuel Zwemer as in ref. 1., p. 87.

practicality of the Chinese mind. Such a pure faith, as we have already seen, is not "useful," because one cannot hope to bribe, cajole, or in any way persuade to one's own advantage a Supreme Being who is absolutely pure and above bribery or cajoling. And therefore from a practical point of view one seeks the ear of lesser powers and forgets the Higher One. A notable work in this respect was written by John Ross of the United Free Church of Scotland entitled *The Original Religion of China*[15] (published in New York, no date), in which the author examined the underlying concepts of early Chinese religion as judged by their names or words for God by special reference to the hyphenated title, Shang-Ti. He interpreted these two words to mean "above" or "superior to" and "ruler," i.e., "Supreme Ruler." He said that the name "bursts suddenly upon us without a note of warning . . . with the completeness of a Minerva."

More recently a flood of fresh light on early Chinese faith has resulted from the discovery of the so-called "Oracle Bones." Chinese scholars have divided their ancient times into three separate periods: first, the primal-ancient; second, the mid-ancient; and third, the near-ancient. The first period stretches roughly from the 21st to the 12th century B.C. According to Ron Williams, who could read Chinese fluently, each of these periods possessed its own distinctive religious characteristics. The first was purely monotheistic. The second was dualistic with a tendency towards materialism but still retaining a flavor of the ancient monotheism. The third was completely materialistic. Professor Williams observed:[16]

> It would perhaps be desirable at this point to examine the terms used for God. Chinese writing, like the hieroglyphics of Egyptian or Cuneiform syllabaries of Mesopotamia, was originally pictographic. That is to say, each character was a picture or diagram describing the object or idea to be conveyed.
>
> There are two terms to be found at this early period. One is 天 Ti'en, or "heaven," occurring with great frequency in the Classics. It consists of two radicals, 人 jen, "man," and 二 shang, "above." That is to say, the sign for heaven, which is now an abstract idea, originated out of two signs meaning "The man above." In later times the Emperor was referred to as the 天 子 Ti'en Tzu, or "The Son of Heaven." This reflects views generally held in the ancient world regarding the divine origin of kings. The other name, which is the current one in use today in China, is (as mentioned by Dr. Ross) 上 帝 , Shang Ti. In the oldest inscriptions which we possess (this was written in 1938), these two characters are combined into a single pictograph 帝 , which is composed of three elements. The first is 亼 , which is the original

[15] Ross, John, *The Original Religion of China:* p. 25: quoted by Samuel Zwemer, ref. 1, p. 86.
[16] Williams, R., "Early Chinese Monotheism," a paper presented before the Kelvin Instit., Toronto, 1938.

form of 木 , *mu*, meaning "wood" and is a picture of three sticks or a faggot. The second, ⼓ , is the earlier representation of 束 , *shu*, meaning "to bind." Above this bound faggot is placed ⼆ , which is the ancient 上 , *shang*, meaning "above." The character 米 is the archaic form of 火 束 , meaning "to burn a faggot of wood." We therefore find the sign 桼 to mean "the burning faggot of a wood offering to the One Above," but also the "One Above to whom the burning faggot of wood is offered."

And there is in China today an ancient custom at the new year of first binding a bundle of sesame stalks or cedar branches with a red cord and then standing them up on end in the centre of the open courtyard and burning them as an act of worship. This was the sacrifice of the burning faggot to God Above, although now they often call it a sacrifice merely to heaven.

The terms Ti'en and Shang Ti might be compared respectively to the words *God* and *Jehovah* in the Old Testament. In the words of Professor Gile, "Shang Ti would be the God who walked in the garden in the cool of the day; the God who smelled the sweet savour of Noah's sacrifice, and the God who allowed Moses to see His back. Ti'en would be the God of Gods of the Psalms, whose mercy endureth forever."

Williams pointed out in his paper that the *Book of History* in its opening sentence states that the ruler, Shun, on his accession in 2255 B.C. "offered the customary sacrifice to God." This statement, made without introduction or explanation, implies an unknown series of antecedent events running back into the remoteness of antiquity. Habitual practice had made them so familiar that they needed no details of the ceremonies involved. Their authority was so unquestioned that there was no place for a preface. Williams continued:

In this period of Chinese history, God the Supreme Ruler was one and indivisible, incapable of change, having no equal, ruling absolutely and alone over all in heaven above and in earth beneath. He did what He willed and no power was able to hinder Him, and His will was always right. Yet He not infrequently permitted the wicked to flourish and in the *Odes* we frequently hear the voice of that complaining spirit which gave occasion to the book of Job.

Subsequently Williams noted that neither in the *Book of History* nor in the *Odes* can any reference to idols be traced. No representation to anything in the heavens above or in the earth beneath has ever been made in China to typify God. And He may be worshiped anywhere at any time, being everywhere present.

So far, our information has been gleaned solely from the pages of the Chinese Classics. There remains yet another source of information to which reference has already been made, the so-called Oracle Bones. As Williams observed, bones inscribed in ancient Chinese characters were found by J. M. Menzies of Cheeloo University in Tsinan, considered by sinologists to be the greatest living authority on the Archaic Chinese script. Over 20,000 fragments of these bones were found near An-yant in North Honan, the site of the early capital of the Shang dynasty. The bones are inscribed with questions asked by the king of his priest on the one hand and the answer which the priest received by divination on the other. They contain the name of God, Shang Ti, and in spite of their number no reference is made to any other deities whatsoever.

Let us examine a few of these inscriptions, the oldest Chinese writings which we possess. For clarification, the symbol for deity has been boxed in with a fine line.

1.
"Inquire about God ordering rain; there will not be full harvest."

2.
"God orders rain: a full harvest."

3.
"Inquire in this, the third moon, about God ordering much rain."

4.
"Inquire about the king building the city; God consents."

The form thus appears in these earliest of records as the only symbol for God, and it is completely free of all anthropomorphism.

In due time, this pure faith begins to be eclipsed as later documents of a similar nature reveal that prayers are now being made first of all *through* ancestors to God who is not addressed directly, and then in time to the ancestors themselves. Later still petitions to a personal God are replaced by petitions to heaven, and in due course to earth also. In the mid-ancient period the great philosopher Chu, the famous annotator of the Classics, defined heaven as "the blue vault above," or alternatively by some process of mental evolution as "the abstract right."

Very recently, a volume in the series "The Great Ages of Man" was published dealing with ancient China. The author was Edward H. Schafer. He traced this devolution as follows:[17]

---

[17] Schafer, Edward H., *Ancient China*, in The Great Ages of Man, Time-Life Inc., New York, 1967, p. 58.

One of the oldest and certainly the greatest of the deities was the Sky God Ti'en. In the very early days Ti'en was thought of as a great king in the sky, more magnificent than any earth bound king, more brilliant and more terrible. Later, many viewed him as an impersonal dynamo, the source of energy that animated the world.

So once again, therefore, where we can work from written records, we have evidence of the degeneration of religious faith, not its evolution upwards.

If we move from the Middle East into Europe, the story repeats itself once again. Thus Axel W. Persson, in his work *The Religious Beliefs of Prehistoric Greece*, remarked:[18]

Out of two deities, the great Goddess and the Boy God, there later developed a larger number of more or less significant figures which we meet with in Greek religious myths.

In my opinion, their multiplying variety depends to a very considerable degree on the different invocating names of originally one and the same deity.

The same basic process is apparent in early Italy. Rosenzweig,[19] writing about the Iguvine Tablets, the date of which is not certain but probably belonging within early Etruscan times, remarked upon "the curious flexibility" of the pantheon revealed in these tablets, in which "deities are distinguished by adjectives, which in their turn emerge as independent divine powers. . . ." The author considers this to be perhaps the most striking feature of these tablets.

It seems to me that from all that has come to light over the past hundred years from the study of ancient documents, that is to say, from the written records of ancient civilizations, the picture of man's spiritual history, in so far as his formalized beliefs are concerned, allows us only to conclude that he began with a pure faith in a God of justice and compassion, who was omnipresent, omnipotent, and omniscient, who could be worshiped in spirit without the necessity of images or other such paraphenalia. This concept, in fact, was too high to survive among ordinary men whose knowledge was not either being miraculously reinforced or continually added to by revelation. The gross polytheism of paganism in the classical world of Rome and Greece can be accounted for not as man striving to purify his faith but rapidly losing the truth he once had. The extent to which this classical world was indebted to the Middle East for its degenerate faith is amply borne out in Hislop's justly renowned study, *The Two Babylons*.[20]

---

[18] Persson, Axel, *The Religion of Greece in Prehistoric Times*, U. of California Press, 1942, p. 124.

[19] Book review, *Amer. Jour. Archaeol.* 43 (1939):170,171.

[20] Hislop, A., *The Two Babylons*, Partridge, London, 1903.

In Unsophisticated Society

We have no written records to cover the original beliefs of primitive people, but a tremendous number of detailed and sympathetic studies of their beliefs have been made during the past hundred years and collected notably by Wilhelm Schmidt. The evidence by inference allows us to say with confidence that the course of their religious history was precisely the same as that of the higher civilizations of antiquity — with this difference, that whereas in the civilized countries a pure faith was corrupted by faulty reasoning due to the sinfulness of human nature, among primitive people a pure faith was corrupted through ignorance and superstition, again reinforced by the sinfulness of human nature. If we are to follow Lyell's principle of interpreting the past in the light only of things happening within historic times, then we have no right whatever to make the assumption that man started by groping in the dark and has only now begun to approach the Light. The evidence shows that he began with the true Light and now has his understanding increasingly darkened. The evidence for this among primitive people is to be found in every corner of the world where such people now exist or have existed within recent times. And paradoxically, the more primitive they are, the simpler and the purer is their faith often found to be. We shall look very briefly at a few pieces of evidence, which are merely representative of a vast compendium of information now available in such volumes as are listed in the bibliography of this paper.

Without a doubt the most informative work on the monotheism of primitive people is that by Wilhelm Schmidt, which, though originally a many-volumed work in German, was published in 1930 in a condensed English translation as a single volume.[21] This is an excellent study, written with authority and fluency, having none of the stuffiness about it that one might expect with such an erudite author, and most informing.

Schmidt first traced the history of thinking on the subject of the origin of religion as it developed during the last century. He pointed out, briefly, that Spencer was largely responsible for the first evolutionary interpretation of "religion," noting that he anticipated Darwin by seven years as is shown by his article, "The Development Hypothesis," which appeared in *The Leader* for March 20, 1852. It

---

[21] Schmidt, Wilhelm, *The Origin and Growth of Religion: Facts and Theories*, tr. H. J. Rose, Methuen, London, 1931, xvi and 302 pp.

may be worth noting also, in passing, that Tennyson wrote "In Memoriam," with its erroneous description of Nature as "red in tooth and claw," ten years before Darwin's *Origin* appeared. Schmidt observed that Spencer made no effort whatever to employ genuinely historical methods to establish his thesis.[22] On the basis of present evidence it is now apparent that Spencer was completely wrong. Spencer held that primitive people began by worshiping ancestors, and that as civilization developed, ancestors "naturally" were formed into hierarchies, and hierarchies in turn led to rank, the highest ranks becoming deities.

What Schmidt was able to prove conclusively was that if primitive cultures are grouped on the basis of their cultural level and these groups are then placed in an ascending order, it is found that the lowest groups have the purest concept of God and that as one progresses from mere hunters, to food gatherers and storers, to food growers as pastoral nomads maintaining flocks, to food growers who have settled land use, and on up the scale to semiurban communities, one finds at first a simple faith in a Supreme Being who has neither wife nor family. Under Him and created by Him are the primal pair from whom the tribe is descended. According to Schmidt we find this form of belief among the Pygmies of Central Africa, the Southeastern Australians, the inhabitants of North-Central California, the primitive Algonkins, and to a certain extent the Koryaks and Ainu.

As soon as we come to the next order of primitive cultures, to use Schmidt's words, "conditions are entirely changed." It is no longer only the primal pair or the first father who received worship but a greater or smaller number of other dead ancestors. Moving on up the scale of cultural complexity, the worship of ancestors and other deceased persons supplants the worship of the Supreme Being entirely, and the anthropomorphization of the gods resulting from this equation gives rise to the making of "images" of various kinds. The pure spirit of the Supreme Being is reduced to a gross caricature of a dead man. The progress of man's spiritual understanding was really a degression, the first step sometimes being the transfer of worship from the Creator of the first man to the man himself first created as the head of the human race. This progenitor of the race then appears as an intermediary between God and men, but being more easily conceived in the mind's eye, he soon displaces God altogether. Thus, quoting Schmidt:[23]

---

[22] Ibid., p. 63.
[23] Ibid., p. 71.

The falsity of Spencer's theory is shown by the mere fact that ancestor-worship is very feebly developed in the oldest cultures while a monotheistic religion is already clearly and unmistakeably to be found there. . . .
It is also unfortunate for Spencer's theory that the highest development of ancestor-worship does not come till the most recent times. . . .

Schmidt then treated of a second alternative view of the origin of religion, the animistic concept proposed by E. B. Tylor. Tylor's view assumed that primitive man used his own existence as a measure of all other existences and came to think of everything, beasts and plants at first but even inanimate things in the end, as consisting of body and soul like himself. It was assumed that primitive man would soon discern by introspection that he had a soul, some kind of spiritual inner reality which could, for example, travel in dreams, or in ecstasy, or in hallucinations. He attributed to all forces of nature a soul life similar to his own, which could not be seen, but was assumed. From this animistic concept he moved "naturally" to the view that this spirit world was personal. Thus arose polydemonism. In due time as society became stratified socially, so did the "demon" world, until we arrive at a stage of polytheism in which many of the demons have been elevated into deities. The final stage was the acknowledgment of one spiritual being who became Chief, i.e., God, and to whom all other demons and lesser deities were subservient and in a lower category. Even after this rationalization had supposedly given rise to a monotheistic faith, Tylor maintained that such a Being would be too high, too exalted, too remote, to need human worship, "too indifferent to concern himself with the petty race of men."[24] So He was simply ignored. Thus a monotheistic faith which resulted from a process of rationalization became by a further process of rationalization a faith so removed from the exigencies of life that it came to be irrelevant.

Schmidt's massive work is concerned with showing that in spite of the reasonableness of Tylor's reconstruction which, incidentally, swept the learned world as persuasively as did Darwin's *Origin*, it is totally unsupported by the evidence, as he put it:[25]

Tylor's theory, like Spencer's, was produced during the heydey of Evolutionism, and has all the marks of its origin, especially its a priori assumption of an upward development of mankind along a single line, and the absence of any proof that the single stages of the process have any historical connection with one another. For indeed, no such proof is to be found for any step of Tylor's long evolutionary path. The order of the steps and their connection one with another is founded purely and simply on the psychologi-

---

[24] Ibid., p. 77.
[25] Ibid., p. 81.

cal plausibility of this connection; and the plausibility depends on the assumption that the simple always precedes the complex.

Schmidt considered one further view, that of Max Muller, who developed a complex theory which argues that the attempt to rationalize the natural forces at work in the world, the sun, moon, rain, thunder, earth, sky, fire, water, led to stories attempting to explain these forces which took the form of nature myths. The terms which were paramount in these myths, the word for fire for example, or the sky, came to be viewed by the less intelligent as the names of deities and these gave rise to the pantheons of classical antiquity. As Schmidt pointed out, however, in spite of his fame and his great learning Max Muller lived too long, long enough in fact to see his ideas gradually abandoned completely.

In Schmidt's closing chapter there are several eloquent passages in which he summed up what is known about the origin of the idea of the Supreme Being in primitive cultures. He said that man has social, moral, and emotional needs. The first or social needs were met by his early belief in a Supreme Being who is also the Father of mankind. The second, or moral needs, find their support in belief in a Supreme Being who is Judge of the good and the bad and is Himself free from all moral taint. The third group of needs, the emotional, were satisfied by his belief in a benevolent Supreme Being from whom comes nothing but good. Man has other needs, too. He seeks a rational cause and this is satisfied by the concept of a Supreme Being who created the world and who orders it in a way that makes sense, in a way that is dependable. Man also needs a protector and finds it in this Being who is omnipotent. And thus in all these attributes this exalted figure furnished primitive man with the ability and the power to live and to love, to trust and to work, and to sacrifice unworthy objectives for more worthy goals beyond. Schmidt said, "We thus find, among a whole series of primitive races, a notable religion, many-branched and thoroughly effective."[26]

In the intervening nearly 300 pages he showed that the more primitive the culture, the more clearly do these attributes of the Supreme Being show forth, being taken so much for granted that they are often scarcely expressed, a circumstance which led many investigators to assume that they didn't even exist. To sum up his findings very briefly, then, in his own words:[27]

---

[26] Ibid., p. 284.
[27] Ibid., p. 191.

Going back to the most primitive people, the Pygmies of Africa or the central Australians or the central Californian Indians — all have one Supreme Sky God to Whom they make offerings of their blood and their first fruits taken in the hunt or from the soil. All these peoples also have short prayers with, here and there, ceremonies, to the Supreme Creator God before Whom nothing existed.

Many writers on this subject have singled out these particular primitive tribes for a good reason. They are all people who have been in a sense isolated either by reason of island residence (such as the Andamanese or Madagascans), inhospitable forests (such as the Tierra del Fuegians), desert regions (such as the Australian aborigines or the Bushmen), inhospitable climate (such as the Eskimo or other Arctic people), or because of their frank hostility toward the white man (such as the Zulu in Africa or many American Indian tribes).

Andrew Lang, after pointing out that the Australian aborigines have probably the simplest culture of any people known to us, states that they have religious conceptions which are "so lofty that it would be natural to explain them as the result of European influence."[28] Yet at the time of writing he felt this explanation was quite unjustified. God is all-knowing, lives in the heavens, is the Maker and Lord of all things, rewards the good conduct of men and by His "lessons" softens the heart. Such was their belief.

The same author, speaking of the Andamanese whom he considered to be living at approximately the same cultural level though in somewhat more pleasant circumstances, states that their God is invisible, immortal, the Creator of all things except the powers of evil, knows the thoughts of the heart, is angered by falsehood and wrongdoing of all kinds, is pitiful to those in distress or pain and sometimes personally affords them relief. He is the Judge of souls and at some future time will preside over a great assize. The information supplied to Lang came from older members of the community who were not acquainted with other races at that time. As Lang says, foreign influence seems to have been more than usually excluded.[29]

Samuel Zwemer spoke of the truly monolithic character of the Supreme Being of the Pygmies of Africa, the Tierra del Fuegians, the Indians of North America, the Central Australian tribes, and the primitive Bushmen, as well as many peoples of the Arctic cultures,

---

[28] Lang, Andrew, *The Making of Religion*, Longmans Green, London, 1909, pp. 175-182,196.

[29] Ibid., p. 196.

which he maintained is "clear even to a cursory examination."[30] In his paper, he was not merely reiterating what others have observed, namely, that all these primitive peoples have knowledge of a Supreme Deity, but rather that the Supreme Deity they recognize is everywhere essentially the same figure with the same attributes.

Canon Titcombe,[31] speaking of the warlike Zulus who established such a reputation for themselves when British troops were battling with them, quoted a former Bishop of Natal who had a firsthand acquaintance with them while they were still culturally intact, as stating that they had no idols (a rather exceptional observation in Africa), but acknowledged a Supreme Being who was known either as the Great-Great One — equivalent to "The Almighty" — or as the First Outcomer — equivalent to "The First Essence." The bishop said that in spite of their reputation as being without even a concept of God, the Zulus repeatedly spoke of Him, and quite of their own accord, as the Maker of all things and all men.

The same author made an interesting statement about the Madagascan native beliefs, which he said are often found expressed in proverbial form.[32] They had such sayings as the following: "Do not consider the secret valley, for God is overhead" — in which the truth of divine omnipresence is clearly recognized. Another was, "The wilfulness of man can be borne by the Creator, for God alone bears rule" — which clearly recognizes the omnipotence of God. A third such proverb says, "Better be guilty with man than guilty before God," which clearly implies a belief both in divine holiness and justice.

Speaking of the American Indians, Paul Radin wrote:[33]

> Most of us have been brought up in the tenets of orthodox ethnology, and this is largely an enthusiastic and quite uncritical attempt to apply the Darwinian Theory of Evolution to the facts of social experience. Many ethnologists, sociologists, and psychologists still persist in the endeavour. No progress will be achieved, however, until scholars rid themselves once for all of the curious notion that everything possesses an evolutionary history.

The same writer some years later, speaking of Lang's view that polytheism did not precede and lead to monotheism, remarked, "his intuitive insight has been abundantly corroborated."[34]

In conclusion we may note that the *Journal of the Royal An-*

---

[30] Zwemer, Samuel, "The Origin of Religion: By Evolution or by Revelation," *Trans. Vict. Instit.* 67 (1935):189.

[31] Titcombe, J. H., "Prehistoric Monotheism," *Trans. Vict. Instit.* 8 (1873): 145.

[32] Ibid., p. 144.

[33] Radin, Paul, *Monotheism Among Primitive Peoples*, n.p., London, 1924, pp. 65ff.

[34] Radin, Paul, *Primitive Men as Philosophers*, Dover, New York, rev. ed. 1956, p. 346.

thropological Institute by 1950 was prepared to publish a paper by E. O. James in which the writer spoke as follows:[35]

> Thus, it is impossible to maintain a unilateral evolution in religious thought and practice in the manner suggested by the rationalistic classifications of Tylor and Frazer following along the line of the "Law of the Three Stages" enunciated by Comte. Nevertheless, neither the Euhemeran speculation that the idea of God arose in ancestor worship, revived by Herbert Spencer, nor the Frazerian evolution of monotheism from polytheism and animism as a result of a process of the unification of ideas, can be reconciled with the shadowy figure of a tribal Supreme Being now known to have been a recurrent feature of the primitive conception of Deity.

From high cultures and low cultures the same picture emerges. It is a picture of a remarkably pure concept of the nature of God and His relation to man being gradually corrupted on the one hand by rationalizations which resulted from the gradual substitution of man's own thinking in place of revelation and on the other hand by superstition which stemmed from ignorance and forgetfulness of the original revelation. As we shall see, briefly, in the following part of this paper, there is little to choose between rationalization and superstition. The end result in both cases is the same — man's foolish heart is darkened.

---

[35] James, E. O., "Religion and Reality," *Jour. Royal Archaeol. Instit.* 70 (1950):28.

Chapter 2
Some Implications

FROM THIS all too brief survey, several points of importance emerge. Most obvious, of course, is the evidence that at least with respect to man's religious history the theory of evolution is quite contrary to the facts. The most primitive people are still assumed to be a paradigm of early man, since the parallels between their art, their weapons, and their general cultural level and the art and weapons of prehistoric man are pretty well taken for granted. The Eskimo, in particular, is said to give us a very good picture of paleolithic man. Yet paleolithic man is supposed to have been almost a gibbering ape except for his possession of some tool-making skills and social organization which the apes never achieved, whereas his modern representatives in every part of the world have a highly developed religious sense which is totally at variance with any theory of animal origins.

It is true that today we find these people with religious beliefs encrusted over and almost totally submerged by superstitious fears and distortions that seem to us of the worst kind. It is easy to be horrified by some of their religious practices (ritual cannibalism, for example). But when such practices are compared with modern use of nuclear weapons, they could be more humane when viewed in the light of their object, since in this case it is not so much the destruction of their enemies as it is the acquisition of the strength they admire in them and wish to capture for themselves. And, of course, for reasons already noted, they have tended to neglect the benevolent and merciful heavenly Father of whom they seem once to have had knowledge and whom they believe they need not fear, and seek instead to appease the malevolent and more immediately present evil spirits which they believe they do need to fear.

It seems clear now that man must have begun with a pure concept of a Supreme Being, a great God, Lord of all, Creator of the world, merciful and just and all-seeing, omnipresent, and omniscient. This was the faith of primitive people whom evolutionists themselves hold to be our "contemporary ancestors."

Where did this pure faith come from? It was revealed from the very beginning, and such a revelation demonstrates that man's mind at the very beginning was clearly capable of spiritual comprehension. Adam and Eve were not exceptional animals barely escaped from some primate herd, but creatures of another order by an act of divine creation which prepared them to enjoy a unique relationship with God and to be the recipients of a much fuller revelation than appears from a superficial reading of Genesis. They walked with God in the Garden and communed with Him.

Moreover, as for existing primitive people themselves, I believe, culturally speaking, that they once knew better things.[36] What the evidence does show is that men may preserve certain recollections of man's original faith if they have not been corrupted by the sophistications of high civilization. Civilization tends rather to cloud than to clarify true faith. Lord John Avebury observed: "Materialism is one of the latest products of the human mind; spiritualism (he did not mean what we mean now by this word) is one of the earliest." Primitive people are far more disposed to attend to matters of the spirit, to accept God as real, than civilized man is. Civilization robs man of his spiritual perception, rather than enhancing it.

This is an important fact because it is contrary to what we generally assume. It always comes as a shock, for some reason, to find that the cultured genteel individual may be totally untaught in the things of God and even hostile to spiritual truth. It is the "nice" people who are so often spiritually unconcerned. Somehow, God still seems able to speak more easily and directly to people who are less culturally sophisticated. Not many noble are called (I Cor. 1:26).

As a consequence, one has to face the anomalous fact that in that very aspect of human behavior which most completely distinguishes man from the animals, namely, his religious sense, man appears to have had his clearest insights when he had, supposedly, barely repudiated his animal heritage. On the other hand, when he had struggled "upwards" after millennia of civilization he had in fact lost his initial vision and become spiritually decadent. At the same time the very people who propose this anachronism would also like us to believe that as man has culturally evolved, his spiritual insights have gradually been purified until he has now achieved a monotheis-

---

[36] Custance. Arthur C., "Primitive Cultures: A Second Look at the Problem of Their Historical Origin," Part II in Doorway Papers, Vol. II.

tic and elevated concept of the nature of God. Yet in the same breath we are assured this process of "improvement" will only reach its climax when man no longer has any such religious beliefs at all! The logical extension of a false premise inevitably leads to such contradictions.

Again, the history of man's religious insights underscores a further fact of profound significance. To hold part of the truth but not the whole of it may be as dangerous as holding no truth at all. It is said that heresy is part of the truth carried to its logical conclusion. The great "ecumenical" heresy is that God is benevolent. God is indeed benevolent, though merciful would be a much better word; but God is also just. The unthinking individual who knows only that God is good will be misled into feeling safe no matter what he does. He can with equanimity ignore the worship or recognition of God altogether. God won't mind how he behaves, for no matter what he does he can assure himself that he has had nothing to fear and that God will fully understand even if he forgets Him completely. He need only fear evil.

The Christian concept of God as loving and merciful has been welcomed by society because it is such a "comfortable doctrine." Part of the truth carried to its logical conclusion gives an entirely false view of man's relationship with God. And, there is every reason to suspect, it is an entirely unsatisfactory view in point of fact. The very idea of God being displeased with man's conduct, or judging his motives, or intending to reward his life appropriately at some great Assize is safely dismissed. At first, such a liberation from the fear of consequences can be a tremendous relief. But just as the man who falls freely in space is temporarily liberated from the conscious effects of gravity — until he hits the ground — so a man thus "liberated" from the burden of unforgiven sin will feel a tremendous sense of relief until, suddenly, the illusion of "weightlessness" is destroyed. Most men have this awe-ful sense of "reckoning" at times — some with an appalling sense of terror. Psychiatrists actually have been gradually coming to the conclusion that man is unhealthy without some fear of the consequences of sin. Freedom from gravity even in the physical world may yet prove to be unexpectedly upsetting to man's well-being.[37] It is not healthy to live in a dream world where all is forgiven and dismissed as though nothing had ultimate significance nor will ever be brought before some higher Court of Justice.

---

[37] *M.D. Canada* 11 (1968):70.

One of man's strange problems is the persistent feeling that in some way he really ought to be punished and not merely forgiven, otherwise he cannot forgive himself. To feel the urge to punish oneself, to make some kind of expiation, while at the same time believing that there really is no one in heaven or on earth who cares whether such an expiation is made can be very disturbing. It leaves man with a sense of guilt but no sense of sin — the modern dilemma. We are so constituted that there is a greater sense of release in falling down before a God of justice and appealing for mercy, than there is in trying to persuade oneself that no wrong has been done at all because there is no ultimate source of righteousness. The burdened conscience remains as a mockery, but it remains burdened. So the most primitive people, like the most civilized, have neber been quite able to rid themselves of the feeling that it is necessary to make sacrifices which cost something. But because God is thought of as benevolent only and therefore not requiring sacrifices, such sacrifices are made to devils — for to whom else can they be made?

So, originally, man's faith in the goodness of God was balanced by an equal knowledge of His holiness and justice. But one of the effects of civilization was to "play down" the more demanding side of God's nature, until His justice has become entirely lost sight of and conscience has become the plaything of cultural values which are relative. Nobody minds one saying today that God is love, but one is not considered very civilized if one says that God is also just. In short, a part of the truth is a dangerous thing, and we need to restore the equally important truth that God is not only benevolent and forgiving but just and demanding also. I suspect that rather extraordinary things would happen for good, if God's ministers were once more to proclaim the message of judgment as Jonathan Edwards did. The fear of the Lord is the beginning of wisdom. . . .

And this brings me to the final point. As we have seen, there is every reason to believe from the study of the "faith" of primitive people that man once shared a revelation of the nature of God and man's relationship to Him. Yet we know from Scripture that even by the time of Abraham there was scarcely an individual alive to whom that revelation was of any vital consequence. How did this come about? Is revealed truth itself powerless? The answer, I think, must be Yes, such truth *is* powerless. It is powerless, unless it is freshly revealed in every generation and to the individual personally. A knowledge of the truth, no matter how precise and accurate it is, if it has been acquired merely by oral transmission or by reflection, is powerless to engender genuine spiritual understanding. The truths we inherit do not provide real insight. Thus the same truths may survive for several generations and yet be spiritually sterile, and being sterile will become of little consequence, something preserved by habit but without power to affect conduct. One sees this in the lives of young people who have been brought up in a godly Christian atmosphere, where they have become familiar with truth, the real significance of which is lost to them entirely, because they have been taught only by man and not by the Holy Spirit.

This is what I mean by the necessity of inspiration. We may be told a saving truth, perhaps in Sunday school, until we are word perfect, and yet be totally unresponsive to it, until one day the Holy Spirit opens our understanding. It is clear that the Holy Spirit cannot open our understanding to truths that we have never heard, and to this extent the memorization of Scripture is a kind of guarantee that at least the vehicle for the communication of spiritual insight will be available to the Holy Spirit. The danger, however, is that truth with which one becomes familiar in this way may cease to convey any meaning whatever, so that the mind becomes hardened against that which ought to enlighten but doesn't. It is even more unfortunate that the Truth itself acquires the reputation of being inconsequential by reason of its powerlessness. The crucial point here is that spiritual truth *is* powerless, and it is even a hindrance unless and until the Holy Spirit has opened our real understanding to its true meaning. Though this may appear as bordering upon heresy, it seems to me that there is more hope for those who have never heard the truth of the gospel than there is for those who have heard it all their lives. Perhaps, in the wisdom of God, there is more hope for the present generation of biblical illiterates than for the generation which lived in the borrowed light of Victorian times.

Thus, in summary, the evidence shows unequivocally that man cannot have evolved in his religious insights in the kind of a way he has evolved in his technical skills, for example, because while these skills steadily improved, his insights did precisely the opposite. Man evidently started with a vital faith in God and a conception of his own relationship to Him that must have been revealed, since it has never been improved upon nor even maintained unless continually strengthened by or confirmed by revelation.

In the possession of a capacity for spiritual understanding man is a unique creature, but he is also a fallen one, constantly needing the renewing of his mind because constantly plagued by the noetic effects of sin. Neither the enlarging influence of civilization, which frees him from some of the burdens of daily living, nor the softening and restraining effects of culture, which set some limits to his evil propensities are adequate to dispel his spiritual blindness or set him free from superstition, fear, and idol worship.

The original revelation of which so many nations and tribes have a dim recollection must be renewed by the Holy Spirit in the heart of the individual to be effective in transforming his life, enlightening his mind, and bringing peace into his soul. Without this divine inspiration, neither traditional knowledge nor personal reflection will return man to fellowship with his Creator. Except a man be born again (John 3:3), he cannot see nor can he enter into the kingdom of God.

Appendix:
Additional Bibliography

Collins, Roy, "Some Characteristics of Primitive Religions," *Trans. Vict. Instit.* 19 (1884):216-252.

Frankfort, Henry, and Frankfort, H. A., *The Intellectual Adventures of Ancient Man,* U. of Chicago Press, 1946, 401 pp.

Jevons, F. B., *An Introduction to the History of Religion,* Methuen, London, 1896, 443 pp.

Keary, Charles F., *Outlines of Primitive Belief,* Scribner's, New York, 1882, xxii and 534 pp.

Kellog, S. H., *The Genesis and Growth of Religion,* Macmillan, London, 1892, xiv and 275 pp.

Koppers, Wilhelm, *Primitive Man and His World View,* Sheed & Ward, London, 1892, xiv and 275 pp.

Lang, Andrew, *The Origins of Religion,* Watts, London, 1908, 128 pp.

Langdon, Stephen H., "Monotheism as the Predecessor of Polytheism in Sumerian Religion," *Evangelical Quarterly,* London (April 1937).

Muller, Max, *Origin and Growth of Religion as Illustrated by the Religions of India,* Hibbert Lectures, Longmans Green, London, 1878.

Rawlinson, George, *The Prevalence of Early Monotheistic Beliefs,* Present Day Tracts, Vol. II, Rel. Tract Soc., London, 1883, p. 41.

Thomson, J. Radford, *The Prevalence of Early Monotheistic Beliefs,* Present Day Tracts, Vol. II, Rel. Tract Soc., London, 1883, tract 11.

Further papers of the Victoria Institute:

Avery, J., "The Religion of the Aboriginal Tribes of India," *Trans. Vict. Instit.* 19 (1885-86):94-121.

Brown, R., "The System of Zoroaster Considered in Connection with Arabic Monotheism," 13 (1879-80), paper no. 51.

Rule, W. H., "Monotheism, a Truth of Revelation and Not a Myth," 12 (1878-79):343-369.

Welldon, Rt. Rev. Bishop, "The Development of the Religious Faculty in Man, Apart from Revelation," 39 (1907):7-21.

Whitley, D. G., "Traces of a Religious Belief of Primeval Man," 47 (1915):125-148.

Samuel Zwemer has an excellent bibliography: see pp. 241-248 of *The Origin of Religion,* Cokesbury, Nashville, Tenn., 1935.

Part III
Convergence
and the Origin of Man

The phenomenon that has caused the most trouble in attempts to determine evolutionary affinities is convergence: the development of similar characteristics by organisms of different ancestry.

— *George Gaylord Simpson,*
Biology and Man

Chapter 1
The Meaning of Convergence

CONVERGENCE IS a phenomenon in Nature which, according to some of the best authorities, is to be found in all living things, whether plant or animal. It is exactly the opposite of *Divergence,* which is really only another name for evolution. By convergence is meant the observed tendency of living forms, which are quite unrelated phylogenetically, to respond to similar contingencies of life by developing similar structures. These "structures" include not merely features of the skeleton itself but internal organs, organs of sense, body fluids, and even (in birds at least) such things as calls, coloration, and habits of nest building. It is as though there were in Nature some built-in mechanism whereby any animal or plant, faced with a problem that must be solved if it is to survive, can develop a structure, using this word in the wide sense indicated above, which solves that problem in a most economical and efficient way. But we may go further than this and say that such solutions have a remarkable tendency to conform so closely to a pattern, depending upon the nature of the challenge, that widely different types of animals (placentals and marsupials, for instance), which have no linear relationship as far as current evolutionary thinking is concerned, develop independently along lines so similar that if we did not have other information to the contrary they would be erroneously assumed to be very closely related.

The two diagrams in Fig. 3 illustrate the fundamental difference between divergence and convergence.

Because of the tremendous emphasis placed by evolutionists upon the importance of structural similarity (morphology) to establish lines of derivation, the fact that similarities can arise by entirely nonevolutionary means offers a serious challenge to current theory. Since, in the very nature of the case, evolutionists have no other convincing way of building their "trees" than by studying morphol-

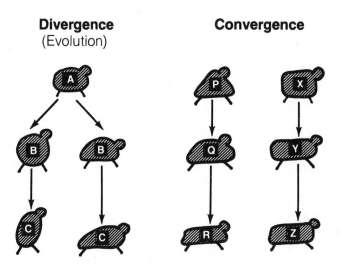

Fig. 3. These two diagrams are intended to illustrate the fundamental difference between divergence and convergence. The former is merely another word for evolution and makes the assumption that starting with a single animal form A one may observe that in succeeding generations descendants differ somewhat until at B and at C they are found to be quite different in form. In convergence, by contrast, after a period of time the descendants of quite different and quite unrelated forms P and X will be observed to have come to be quite alike so that R and Z would be assumed to be derived from some common ancestor . . . which in fact is not the case.

ogy (at least, as far as the fossil record is concerned), the challenge of convergence is a very embarrassing one. As a consequence, in spite of a tremendous amount of research into the fact itself, the phenomenon of convergence has in recent years been softpedaled. In many textbooks it is, in fact, entirely ignored. In the 1950 edition of Chambers' Encyclopedia, although evolution is treated with the usual thoroughness, biological convergence is not even listed in the general index. The thirteen-volume Oxford English Dictionary does not mention convergence with a biological meaning as occurring in the English language. In the 1964 edition of the Encyclopedia Britannica which has pages and pages of text on the theory of evolution,[1] convergence is covered (under morphology) by a single paragraph of eighteen lines, of which one third are actually given to

---

[1] Encyclopedia Britannica, 1964 edition, Vol. XV, under "Morphology," p. 819.

the subject of divergence which, as the author notes, is simply another word for evolution. We are told that convergence is not only rare, but involves only superficial resemblances, whereas divergence is, of course, said to be everywhere pervasive in Nature.

As we can easily show, however, the truth is precisely the opposite. On the one hand, convergence is, as a well-known authority on evolution has said, almost universal. This is an established fact. Animals which can be shown to be unrelated have developed precisely similar structures or mechanisms which are so complex that the possibility of their having emerged purely by accident is quite inconceivable. Nor are such convergences in any way superficial. They frequently are of such a nature as to involve the whole animal.

On the other hand, divergence (or evolution) is in no sense a demonstrable fact. If by "evolution" we mean merely the variations which may be observable between animals known to belong to the same species (varieties of dogs, for example) and still capable under proper conditions of interbreeding and produce fertile offspring, then we are dealing with a fact. But this kind of evolution throws no light upon the origin of species in the broader sense. To this extent, where convergence is an established fact, evolution is merely an "attractive theory."

Probably no theory based on such tenuous grounds has even been promoted with such fervor, argued so dogmatically, and accorded such universal recognition on such slender grounds as the theory of evolution. One suspects that the fundamental weaknesses in current theory, which are already being admitted in many quarters, account for the increasing hostility on the part of its chief proponents towards every serious attempt made to reexamine its basic assumptions. In one of his latest works, G. G. Simpson,[2] like a man whistling in the dark, found it necessary to assure his readers again and again that evolution is true, is a fact, is unchallengeable. In *This View of Life*, Simpson repeats his "variations on a theme" *ad nauseam*, on pages vii, 10, 12, 40, 51, 62, 63, 151, and on page 193 five times within the space of fourteen lines!

Ralph Gerard some years ago made this significant statement which is particularly appropriate in the present context:[3]

> When we find ourselves entertaining an opinion about the basis of which there is a quality of feeling which tells us that to enquire into it would be

[2] Simpson, G. G., *This View of Life*, Harcourt, Brace & World, New York, 1964.
[3] Gerard, Ralph, "The Biological Basis of Imagination," *Sci. Monthly*, June 1947, p. 499.

absurd, obviously unnecessary, unprofitable, bad form, or even perverse, we may know that that opinion is a nonrational one and probably therefore founded upon inadequate evidence.

It is a comment upon the extent to which the public has been hoodwinked by evolutionists that librarians are in the habit of filing books on evolution under the heading of Science, Biology, or some such thing, whereas books which are a serious attempt to show the fallacies or weaknesses of current evolutionary thinking are apt to be filed under the heading of Religion.

It is widely agreed among those engaged in research that the uniqueness of the scientific method lies in the fact that it is fundamentally a search for error rather than truth.[4] Twenty-five years ago we were commonly led in the university to believe that the proper method of research was first of all to accumulate all the data possible and then, having done this, the truth would become self-evident.[5] By this means one was supposed to introduce strict objectivity. No one could challenge the truth thus arrived at. What has since become increasingly apparent is that no scientist ever operates in this way. There is no mere "collecting of data." We look at Nature with blinders on, guided by preconceptions of what we expect to find. And our extraction of the data is, whether we like it or not, always a selective process. We end up with *capta* ("takens") not *data* ("givens"). There are no "givens" — or it would be more truthful to say, *everything* is "given," and consequently we are forced to select, because we are not capable of seeing the whole. So the method of science, as we understand it now, is not to act as a kind of empty box into which we invite Nature to pour its substance, but to act as a filter. This filter is structured by our preconceptions, our bias, by the set of our minds, which is, in fact, the motivating force which gives us the energy for research in the first place. Nature abhors a vacuum and will not usefully inform the mind that is itself a vacuum. So the evidence we find in Nature is always "for" or "against" some par-

---

[4] Rudolph Flesch wrote: "For the layman, the most important thing about science is this: that it isn't a search for truth but a search for error. The scientist lives in a world where (the whole) truth is unattainable, but where it is always possible to find errors in the long-settled or the obvious. . . . So-called scientific books that are supposed to contain final answers are never scientific. Science is forever self-correcting and changing; what is put forth as gospel truth cannot be science." Quoted by Hillier Kreighbaum in *Sci. Monthly*, April 1952, p. 240, from Flesch's *The Art of Clear Thinking,* Harper, New York, 1951.

[5] Evans-Pritchard, E. E., wrote: "The whole history of scholarship, whether in the natural sciences or in the humanities, tells us that the mere collection of what are called facts, unguided by theory in observation and selection, is of little value." *Social Anthropology,* Cohen and West, London, 1951, p. 64.

ticular idea which consciously or unconsciously prompts us to make the search.[6]

If research is therefore such a biased process, how is objectivity achieved at all? The built-in safety device which forms an essential part of the scientific method is the determination, if it is at all possible, to discover the error in an hypothesis. We make an assumption that we know what the "truth" is, and then we search with all the sincerity and honesty of purpose of which we are capable to find contrary evidence. The scientific method is in this sense a search for error, not a search for truth. And any hypothesis which does not encourage its proponents to conduct this honest search for error must be classified as philosophical rather than scientific. The stern refusal of the evolutionary Establishment to encourage its membership to challenge its own assumptions disqualifies it as a valid scientific undertaking.

This is why convergence is so neglected a topic. It presents a challenge in two ways. It is inimical on the one hand, as we have already noted, to the current dependence on morphology for the drawing up of evolutionary lines of descent by paleontologists in the form of phylogenetic trees, without which no textbook on the subject would be considered suitably dressed. And it is inimical, on the other hand, to the current abhorrence which most naturalists have towards the slightest admission of any kind of vitalism in living organisms, which would encourage the belief that Nature "knows what it is about" in a purposeful sort of way. That unrelated forms should assume structural parallelisms when they are forced to meet a similar challenge in their environment, implies that the process of change is not a haphazard one resulting from the play of natural selection on chance mutations, but is governed in some quite precise way by an in-built mechanism which is not merely opportunistic (to use a term favored by Simpson) but is clearly purposeful. And the idea of purposeful behavior in the sense which vitalists have seen it, is to be avoided at all costs, because purpose suggests a Purposer and we are at once introduced to the possibility of forces acting independently of, or outside of, the strictly causal framework of physics and chemistry. Such a Force is quite beyond science to deal with and therefore challenges its implied claim to omnicompetence.

Once the implications of convergence began to be understood

---

[6] Cf. Washburn, S. L., "The Strategy of Physical Anthropology," in *Anthropology Today,* ed. A. L. Kroeber, U. of Chicago Press, 1953, p. 718: "The realization has been growing for some years that facts alone will not settle problems and that even the collection of the 'facts' is guided by a complex body of unstated assumptions."

by evolutionary philosophers, it was quietly dropped as a subject for research and for discussion, even though at first when the evidence for it began to accumulate extensively it had been given wide recognition. Had the fact become better known prior to the publication of Darwin's *Origin of Species*, the course of events in the life sciences might have been very different. Prior to 1858 when *The Origin* first appeared, a great deal of attention was paid to the relation between *form* and *function*. It was the glory of many of the mid-nineteenth century natural scientists that they had carried their studies so far along these lines that they were genuinely able to reconstruct with remarkable precision whole animals on the basis of only a few bones, simply because they understood very clearly that form is closely related to function, so that if they once knew what function a structure performed, they could re-create the whole of it on the basis of a comparatively small fragment. Virchow was a master at this. Their influence survived the emergence of Darwinism in people like Wood Jones who continued the tradition of nature study in this sense. But their works suffered neglect by the Establishment which was increasingly influenced by Darwin's obsession with morphology as the key to evolutionary relationships. It is a happy thing that some of these older works, which challenged the basic premises upon which the theory of evolution was built, have begun to appear once more as reprints. Thus Prince Petr Kropotkin's *Mutual Aid* has been reprinted, in which the concept of Nature as red in tooth and claw is severely challenged.[7] More importantly in the present context, Leo Berg's[8] *Nomogenesis* or *Evolution Determined by Law* has now been reissued as a fresh challenge to these basic assumptions by showing the extent to which the phenomenon of convergence is found in Nature at every level of life and in the development of structures which are absolutely essential for the continuance of the organism. Berg is quite aware of the implications and underscores them.

In the next chapter, we shall examine the facts of the case as Berg, and many others, have elucidated them. And in the final chapter we shall see to what extent convergence provides an alternative explanation for the skeletal features of prehuman fossil remains and early fossil man, features which have been almost universally presented as proof of man's animal origin.

---

[7] Kropotkin, Prince Petr, *Mutual Aid: A Factor in Evolution*, Extending Horizon Books, Boston, reprint 1955, xix and 362 pp.

[8] Berg, Leo, *Nomogenesis: or Evolution Determined by Law* (orig. Russian ed. 1922, entitled *Nomogenez ili evolinticiia na osnove zakonomernostei*), tr. J. N. Rostovtsov, Mass. Instit. of Tech., reprint 1969.

Chapter 2
The Fact of Convergence

I T MUST be apparent that if convergence is at all common, many forms which have been used to establish genealogical trees of evolutionary significance may not in fact form trees at all but merely, as Manton[9] put it, "bundles of twigs," quite unrelated in any but the most nonevolutionary sense. The genealogical trees are then entirely fictitious, nothing less than misrepresentations of the course of biological history. One's confidence in these phylogenetic reconstructions cannot be very high.

Darwin himself was uncomfortably aware of this fact. In the sixth edition of *The Origin of Species* he wrote:[10]

> It should not be overlooked that certain strongly marked variations which no one would rank as mere individual differences, frequently occur owing to a similar organization being similarly acted on, of which numerous instances could be given with our domestic production.

In 1876, in a letter to Moritz Wagner, he wrote:[11]

> In my opinion the greatest error which I have committed has been in not allowing sufficient weight to the direct action of the environment, i.e., food, climate, etc., independently of natural selection. . . . When I wrote "The Origin" and for some years afterwards I could find little good evidence of the direct action of the environment; now there is a large body of evidence.

A curious course of events followed publication of Darwin's work. One result was an increasing neglect of the study of the relationships between form and function, due to an almost total obsession with the tracing of supposed lines of descent on the basis of form. Morphology totally absorbed the attention of most students of fossil remains. The second was a counter-balancing search by those

---

[9] Manton, I., *Problems of Cytology and Evolution in the Pteridophyta,* Cambridge Univ. Press, 1950: quoted by I. Knoblock, *Jour. Amer. Sci. Affil.* 5, no. 3 (1953):14.

[10] Darwin, Charles, *The Origin of Species,* 6th ed., 1872, p. 74.

[11] Darwin, Charles, *Life and Letters,* October 13, 1876, iii, p. 159.

146

who opposed Darwinism (not necessarily "evolution" *per se*), for instances of structural parallelism between living forms which had developed in entire independence and were not believed to be linear descendants.

With respect to the first, Sir James Gray, the author of a classical work on animal locomotion, wrote on the theory of natural selection:[12]

> Strange as it may seem, one immediate effect of *The Origin* was a marked recession in the study of animal function. There was, and still is, a tendency for morphologists to ascribe to organs and structures a functional significance for which there was, or is, little observational evidence. In this respect "Evolution in action" (Julian Huxley) is by no means guiltless; it goes a considerable way beyond the physiological facts. Is Dr. Huxley quite sure that the loss of the lateral digits by the ancestors of the horse gave them an "additional turn of speed"?

This same obsession with form irrespective of function led Haeckel to formulate his well-known but now quite discredited theory of recapitulation. Sir Gavin de Beer observed:[13]

> The assumption that developmental stages of a descendant represent adult ancestral types has taken all the longer to disprove because of the facile way in which non-crucial observations have been claimed as evidence in its support. . . . In many cases it can be proved that the developmental history *cannot* represent the phylogenetic history, for the reason that if the adult ancestor resembled the modern embryo, it could not have been functional. . . .
>
> The second and, perhaps, the more important reason for which the theory of recapitulation has impeded the progress of biology is that it has blinded embryologists to the necessity of looking for causal connections (i.e., functional ones) within ontogenetic phenomena.

In other words real or superficial resemblances were, and are still, assumed to be evidence of linear descent or close genealogical relationship, whereas they may be functionally determined parallelisms resulting from the similar response of living organisms to similar stimuli. So de Beer concluded with a quotation by the great embryologist Wilhelm His:[14]

> This opposition to the application of the fundamental principles of science to embryological questions would scarcely be intelligible had it not a dogmatic background. No other explanation of living forms is allowed than heredity, and any which is founded on another must be rejected. The present

---

[12] Gray, Sir James, in a review of Huxley's *Evolution in Action*, under the heading "The Case for Natural Selection," in *Nature*, February 6, 1954, 227; and August 7, 1954, p. 279.

[13] De Beer, Sir Gavin, "Embryology and Evolution," in *Evolution*, ed. de Beer, Oxford U. Press, 1938, pp. 58,61.

[14] Ibid., p. 62.

fashion requires that even the smallest and most indifferent inquiry must be dressed in a phylogenetic costume.

This was written by Dr. His in 1888. Some years later, in respect to the conclusions of physical anthropologists, Wilson Wallis wrote sadly:[15]

Since the day of Darwin, the evolutionary idea has largely dominated the ambitions and determined the findings of physical anthropologists, sometimes to the detriment of the truth.

And there is no doubt whatever that the famous Piltdown fraud could never have succeeded as well as it did but for the fact that Dawson supplied for the experts precisely what some of them believed they ought to have. Piltdown Man was just what the doctors ordered. V. F. Calverton, in his introduction to *The Making of Man* wrote:[16]

The very simultaneity with which Darwin and Wallace struck upon the theory of Natural Selection and the survival of the fittest was manifest proof of the intense activity of the idea at the time. Every force in the environment, economic and social, conspired to the success of the doctrine.

Similarly, A. L. Kroeber wrote:[17]

There was evidently a particular historic concatenation in the world's thought which enabled Darwin's discovery to trigger off consequences so great.

In protest against this landslide of approval of a theory which was surprisingly suited to the *Zeitgeist* (as many and recent historians have pointed out), a number of independent minds set out to take a fresh look at the evidence. Prince Kropotkin reexamined the community of wild life to see whether there really was a "struggle to survive" and whether the fittest only came out on top. He found a very different pattern in Nature and set forth his findings in his *Mutual Aid*. Until comparatively recently it was long out of print. But the tide seems to be changing, and there is now a fresh demand which has justified its reprinting. Similarly, in 1922 Leo Berg wrote his massive and scholarly *Nomogenesis* as a protest against the then unbalanced concern with morphology to the exclusion of function. He would probably today have called his book *Convergence*, for that is

[15] Wallis, Wilson D., "The Structure of Prehistoric Man," in *The Making of Man,* Modern Library, Random House, New York, 1931, p. 75.

[16] Calverton, V. F., in *The Making of Man,* Modern Library, Random House, New York, 1931, p. 2.

[17] Kroeber, A. L., "Evolutionary History and Culture," in *Evolution After Darwin,* Vol. II, U. of Chicago Press, 1960, p. 1.

what it is all about. It, too, has now been republished — surprisingly, by the Massachusetts Institute of Technology. Shortly after this first edition appeared, in 1935 Sir Wilfrid LeGros Clark was willing to admit:[18]

> In the evaluation of the genetic affinities, anatomical *differences* are more important as negative evidence than anatomical *resemblances* are as positive evidence. It becomes apparent that if this thesis is carried to a logical conclusion it will be necessary to demand a much greater scope for the phenomenon of parallelism or convergence in evolution than has generally been conceded by evolutionists. The fact is that the minute and detailed researches which have been carried out by comparative anatomists in recent years have made it certain that parallelism in development has been proceeding on a large scale and is no longer to be regarded as an incidental curiosity which has .occurred sporadically in the course of evolution. Indeed, it is hardly possible for those who are not comparative anatomists to realize the fundamental part which this phenomenon has played in the evolutionary (developmental?) process [query mine].

Yet today one hears very little on the subject, as the encyclopedias indicate. Sir Wilfrid himself, in contributing to the rash of Darwinia which were published in the Darwin Centennial year (1958) wrote:[19]

> Reference should be made to the evolutionary phenomena of convergence and parallelism, for it is well known that these can lead to structural similarities which, taken by themselves, may be misleading. The term convergence is applied to the occasional tendency for distantly related types to simulate one another in general proportions or in the development of analogous adaptations in response to similar functional needs.

What had happened in the 25 or so years to convert Clark's "large scale" phenomena "no longer to be regarded as an incidental curiosity" into an "occasional tendency"? Perhaps it had become increasingly apparent during the intervening years that the admission of the fact of convergence on a large scale was highly inimical to many of the more commonly displayed genealogical trees purporting to show linear evolutionary descent based purely on morphology.

So crucial is morphology that the anthropologist Franz Weidenreich formulated the following principle:[20]

> In determining the character of a given fossil form and its special place in the line of human evolution, only its morphological features should be made the basis of decision: neither the location of the site where it was recovered,

---

[18] Clark, Sir Wilfrid LeGros, *Early Forerunners of Man:* quoted by Rendle Short in *Trans. Vict. Instit.* 66 (1935):255.

[19] Clark, Sir Wilfrid LeGros, "The Study of Man's Descent," in *A Century of Darwin*, ed. S. A. Barnett, Heineman, London, 1958, p. 182.

[20] Weidenreich, Franz, "The Skull of Sinanthropus pekinensis: A Comparative Study on a Primitive Hominid Skull," *Paleontologica Sinica*, N.S.D., no. 10, whole series no. 127 (1943):1.

nor the geological nature of the rock stratum in which it was imbedded is important.

But what does one make of this demand that the evidence of geology be ignored and only physical appearance considered? In the light of the possibility that structure may be entirely the result of environmental or historic circumstances and have nothing whatever to do with geological age, the argument is entirely without validity.

Sir Solly Zuckerman, though fully committed to evolutionary theory, admitted freely:[21]

> Several gene patterns may have identical phenotypic effects (so that) when we deal with limited or relatively limited fossil material, correspondence in single morphological features or in groups of characters does not necessarily imply genetic identity and phyletic relationship.

By the phrase "several gene patterns," Zuckerman is referring to the well-recognized fact that where circumstances "demand" that an animal be equipped with some particular organ (a special kind of eye for example), that organ is apt to appear even though the animal does not share a gene complex which has been responsible for the very same organ in some other species. Thus gene complexes or patterns which differ, can nevertheless lead to the production of similar structures in unrelated animals.

Wood Jones argued strongly that there was some kind of "vital force" in nature which resulted in the emergence of all sorts of specialized structures in animals that enabled their possessors to meet the particular exigencies of their lives. Such structures, he was convinced, could appear "out of the blue," as it were, almost upon demand. He listed many examples in his classic little volume *Trends of Life*, all of which were chosen to demonstrate that in some mysterious way "Nature knew what it was about." Like Leo Berg, and now even more recently Sir Alister Hardy,[22] Jones, too, was persuaded that there was little or no element of chance or randomness about this phenomenon. He wrote:[23]

> Since the acceptance of Charles Darwin's theory of Evolution, many attempts have been made by distinguished biologists (such as Gaskill and Patten) to prove that the Invertebrates did in fact "evolve" into vertebrates; but all the available evidence makes it quite certain that the two great phyla arose in complete independence of each other. . . .
> When ordinary people were told by the dogmatic propagandists of

[21] Zuckerman, Sir Solly, *"An* Ape *or The* Ape?" *Jour. Royal Anthrop. Instit.* 81 (1951):57.

[22] Hardy, Sir Alister, *The Living Stream*, Collins, London, 1965, especially chap. 7, pp. 180ff., "Habit in Relation to Structure."

[23] Jones, F. Wood, *Trends of Life*, Arnold, London, 1953, pp. 74,75.

Darwin's theory of Evolution that so complex a thing as an eye had come into existence by some vague force known as Natural Selection, acting on chance minor structural variations, their credulity was taxed to the utmost. Their faith would probably have failed them completely had they been asked to believe that this random and mechanistic process had produced the vertebrate eye and the invertebrate eye in complete independence; and more than that, had permitted the invertebrates to originate at least three different kinds of eyes in independence, within the limits of their own phylum (the single-focal eye, bifocal eye, and compound eye). Not only eyes, but ears, and hearts, and gills, and lungs, and livers, and kidneys, and brains, and all the rest have been developed twice over in complete independence in the two great phyla.

And as we shall show, Jones' list barely scratches the surface of the less obvious parallelisms that exist. Some hitherto unrecognized or ill-defined law has been at work governing all life. Naturally, in the present climate of opinion, such concepts are too tainted with metaphysics to be encouraged by the Establishment. They are rejected out of hand. Everything must be left to chance. Evolution and Chance are virtually synonymous concepts, and perhaps LeGros Clark (like others) had begun to realize that convergence favored development by law, rather than by chance, too pointedly. It is quite clear that this conviction certainly prompted Leo Berg to write his classical study on convergence and to give it the more precise title: *Nomogenesis: Evolution Determined by Law.* The idea that there might be some law governing the development of living forms throughout the ages is no more frightening, of course, than the concept of the rule of law in physics. But the physical events of the past have not shown any progress from simple to complex, lower to higher, more dependent upon the environment to less dependent on the environment, without conscious purpose to a very high degree of purposefulness, and so forth, in the way that living things have. In this sense there is a direction to the development of life which is not evident in the mere physical order. And the idea of "direction" according to "law," and to a significant extent contrary to the otherwise universal rule of "decay" (entropy), inevitably raises the spectre of purpose. And purpose implies a Purposer. This is where the rub comes. . . .

So pervasive did Berg see convergence to be, that he could write without hesitation: "Convergence and not divergence is the rule, not the exception. This appears to be all pervasive, both among plants and animals, both present, recent, and extinct."[24] And in the latest reissue of his work we find him saying:[25]

From the examples set forth in this section, it is obvious that convergence

[24] Berg, Leo, ref. 8, p. 174 of the English ed., Constable, London, 1926.
[25] Berg, Leo, ref. 8, p. 169 of the M.I.T. ed., 1969.

affects the most important organs fundamental for existence, and not merely external characters.

And again, later:[26]

> From the numerous examples that have been offered in this Chapter, and their number might easily be multiplied, we have shown that convergence affects the most fundamental organs in animals and plants, that the phenomenon is widely distributed, and that points of similarity which have been attributed to common descent are often due to convergence.

Before examining the evidence in more detail, it may be well to note, in fairness to other writers since then, that although convergence is too dangerous a doctrine to give much emphasis to, it is, nevertheless, quite widely admitted by the Establishment. G. G. Simpson[27] was willing to admit:

> In convergence, there occurs the same sort of opportunistic development of one way of life by different groups — in this case those groups being dissimilar (or less similar) in adaptive type to start with. The trend towards greater similarity of adaptation involves . . . converging functional and structural characteristics. The groups may be nearly related or may be only very distantly related. . . . Insects and birds are so distantly related that any particular homology between their parts can hardly be traced, and yet they converge, sometimes quite closely.
> Humming moths (given by Evan Shute[28] as Hawk Moths, Trochilidae chordates) and humming birds are so remarkably alike in habits and functional operation that they are often mistaken for each other if seen only from a distance. Convergence on a grand scale is seen in the comparison of South and North American mammals.

Alfred S. Romer[29] observed that "the development of long spindles to support a dorsal tail occurred in at least two and perhaps five separate lines." And he reported that Radfield had suggested to him these were heat regulating mechanisms. This is most probable, I think. Such a structure is to be observed in the *Dimetrodon*, for example.

Boule and Vallois extended the principle somewhat:[30]

> It would be important to know whether we can not accept the existence of convergence phenomena of biochemical characters, analogous to the convergence phenomena of a morphological order. There is no reason why a similar morphological evolution [development?] in two different groups

[26] Ibid., p. 225.

[27] Simpson, G. G., *The Meaning of Evolution*, Yale U. Press, 1952, pp. 183,184.

[28] Shute, Evan, *Flaws in the Theory of Evolution*, publ. privately, London, Ontario, 1961.

[29] Romer, A. S., in *Genetics, Paleontology and Evolution*, ed. Jepson, Mayr, and Simpson, Princeton U. Press, 1949, pp. 103ff.

[30] Vallois, Henri V., and Boule, Marcellin, *Fossil Man*, tr. M. Bullock, Dryden Press, New York, 1957, p. 573 footnote.

should not be accompanied by a parallel evolution of phenomena ascribable to biochemistry. It seems that naturalists have not given attention to this point (query mine).

As we shall see, biochemists *per se* have given attention to the point, but dyed-in-the-wool evolutionists have not given attention to the biochemists.

In speaking of man's ancestry, Ruggles R. Gates wrote:[31]

> The abundance of convergent types also involves recognition of the fact that groups, such as mammals, which are now regarded as uniform [i.e., descended from a single ancestor] have had a polyphyletic (i.e., independent) origin.

Alfred S. Romer[32] even went so far as to say that "the known presence of parallelisms in so many cases and its suspected presence in others suggests that convergence may have been an almost universal phenomenon." And Simpson seemed to be issuing the same caution against the too hasty assumption of relatedness based on homologies when he said: "Sanger has shown that the insulin composition of sperm whales is identical with that of pigs and quite different from that of sei whales! To be sure, a sequence of only three amino acids is involved, and both differences and resemblances could be accidental without even true convergence, but the lesson is there."[33]

One more example. Herbert Friedman, Curator of the Division of Birds, U. S. Natural Museum, in a paper on ecological counterparts in birds, presents a survey of the extraordinary parallels in unrelated species of birds, including patterns of feeding, call, and nest-building, as well as in coloration and structural details. He said:[34]

> The more complete our knowledge of any given group of organisms, the more such cases come to mind. . . . The number of instances may be extended to a point where it grows wearisome. . . .
> The number of possible permutations and combinations of the different colors and patterns (spots, bars, stripes, etc.) found in birds is far greater than the number of kinds of birds. It is therefore interesting, and probably significant, that there should be as many instances of convergence among unrelated groups as there are. It is all the more intriguing when we find that these similarities in appearance are so often corelated with equally marked similarities in habit.

---

[31] Gates, Ruggles R., *Human Ancestry from a Genetical Point of View*, Harvard U. Press, 1948, p. 3.

[32] Romer, A. S., ref. 29, p. 115.

[33] Simpson, G. G., *Biology and Man*, Harcourt, Brace & World, New York, 1969, p. 38.

[34] Friedman, Herbert, "Ecological Counterparts in Birds," *Sci. Monthly* 63, no. 5 (1946):395-398.

So much, then, for acknowledgment of the fact itself. It is to the work of Leo Berg in particular that we must turn for the most complete examination of the evidence. It indicates some measure of the renewed interest in the subject as a whole that his original work, first published in Russian in 1922, and in an English translation in 1926, is once again available for study in 1970.

Consider a few examples of *organs* and *body fluids*. According to Berg, the placenta, by which the embryo is connected with the body of the mother and by which it receives its nourishment and gets rid of its waste products, has been independently formed in various groups of animals including *Polyzoa* (a certain type of fish parasite), *Peripatus* (nonexternally segmented caterpillars), certain insects and scorpions, the *Tunicata* (sea squirts), certain sharks, certain marsupials, and of course all the placental mammals. Berg noted:[35]

> Everything in the anatomy, embryology, and paleontology of mammals inclines us to share Abel's opinion: the monotremata, marsupiala, and Placentalia are three parallel branches which have arisen independently of one another.

Berg pointed out that chlorophyl and hemoglobin are allied substances, yet they have arisen quite independently as life-carriers:[36]

> Manoilov[37] has discovered a reaction for the discrimination of the blood of man from that of woman; it is remarkable that the same reaction afforded the means of distinguishing the male from the female sex in dioecious plants such as the maple (Acer negundo), the nettle (Lychnis dioica), and Vallisneria.

He commented:[38]

> Such a physiological parallelism indicates that the elaboration of chemical substances (which ultimately affect morphology as well as physiology) is subject to certain laws.

While dealing with blood, it may be noted in passing that C. L. Prosser, in a paper inspired by the Darwin Centennial "celebrations," pointed out:[39]

> Haemoglobins, different in protein but similar in heme, have evolved separately many times — in chordates, a few molluscs, some entomostraeons, certain annelids, numerous holothurians, a few dipteran insects, even some nitrogen-fixing bacteria.

---

[35] Berg, Leo, ref. 8, pp. 214,215.

[36] Ibid., p. 224.

[37] Manoilov, W. W., in *The Medical Gazette* 15 (1923): quoted by Leo Berg.

[38] Berg, Leo, ref. 8, p. 225.

[39] Prosser, C. L., "The Origin after a Century: Prospects for the Future," *Amer. Scientist* 47 (1959):539.

And warm-bloodedness has, of course, appeared twice, independently, in birds and in mammals. The transformation of a cold-blooded animal into a warm-blooded animal involves complexities in the central and peripheral nervous systems which are almost unbelievably complex.

Berg noted that in certain insectivorous plants there has developed a fermenting agent similar to the pepsin of the animal digestive system, to enable it to make use of protein food stuffs; and it is secreted by a corresponding organ.[40] Yet curiously enough, pepsin appears only in the higher animals; its presence in invertebrates is still a matter of doubt.

Berg referred to the development of very similarly structured bifocal eyes in fish and in quite unrelated whirligig beetles.[41] These bifocal eyes allow the beetle to see normally in air but "to keep an eye" under water as well, whereas in certain fishes, the reverse is observed. A horizontal band divides the eye in both cases into an upper and lower portion, the lens of one suitable for seeing in the air and the other in water. Such a complex organ has developed twice, therefore, in total independence.

Furthermore, as Rendle Short pointed out,[42] the eyes of the octopus are precisely like those of most mammals including man, and this parallelism extends to the structure of the cornea, iris, ciliary muscle and processes, and the retina. Yet there is clearly no "evolutionary" connection between these two types of living creatures.

Berg noted:[43]

> Eyes with a lens are independently met with in annelid worms, arthropoda, and cephalopoda. In the latter we meet with retina, cornea, iris, ciliary process, and even (in some) with eye-lids.

Zawarzin[44] referred to eyes as "a principle of structure connected with the faculty of vision common to the entire animal world." For such a structure with all its component parts (blood supply, lachrymal glands, neuromuscular control mechanisms, and associated visual areas in the brain) to have formed so many times in such diverse creatures is surely quite beyond the power of pure chance

---

[40] Berg, Leo, ref. 8, p. 223.
[41] Ibid., p. 221.
[42] Short, Rendle A., "Some Recent Literature Concerning the Origin of Man," *Trans. Vict. Instit.* 67 (1935):253.
[43] Berg, Leo, ref. 8, p. 221.
[44] Zawarzin, A. A., *Studies in the Histology of the Sensory Nervous System and Optical Ganglia of Insects* (in Russian), St. Petersburg, 1913, vi and 192 pp.

acting via natural selection upon random changes in the gene complex. This is faith in miracles indeed.

Concerning such strange phenomena as luminosity or phosphorescence Berg remarked:[45]

> The luminous or phosphorescent organs, enigmatic as to function and origin, developed independently in the most diverse groups of marine fishes such as sharks (Spinax and others), in the stomiatidae, the scopalidae, and in antennariidae, and others.

Such a remarkable defense weapon as the ability to give a very powerful electric shock has also appeared independently in three water-living animals: the Electric Eel (a U.S. freshwater species), the Torpedo (widely distributed in the oceans), and Malapterurus in Africa.[46]

Again, speaking of defense, quills have been developed independently by otherwise harmless creatures such as the Australian monotreme Anteater (locally called "Porcupine"), the true rodent porcupine (*Hystrix*) that is common to Europe and North Africa, the South American porcupine (*Synetheres*), also the common hedgehog, and the small prickly Ericulus of Madagascar.[47]

In his book *Animal Weapons*, discussing defense at a time of complete helplessness, Philip Street remarked on a case of parallel development in insects in the larval stage:[48]

> Convergent evolution, by which two completely unrelated types of animals evolve similar structures for a similar purpose quite independently of each other is an extremely interesting phenomenon. There is certainly no possible connection between the various types of tube worms and the larvae of the caddis fly, yet these larvae, usually referred to as caddis worms, construct tubes for their protection which are remarkably similar to those produced by marine annelids.

So much for organs or structures: the same picture applies to whole animals. David Lack, speaking of the Australian fauna, said:[49]

> Australia was colonized by marsupial mammals which, in the absence of placental forms evolved into fox-like, wolf-like, mole-like, squirrel-like, rabbit-like, rat-like, anteater-like, and flying squirrel-like forms, which resemble, often closely, their counterparts among the placental mammals of other continents.

Yet they are not related to them.

---

[45] Berg, Leo, ref. 8, p. 219.

[46] Short, Rendle A., ref. 42, p. 253.

[47] Jones, F. Wood, ref. 23, p. 80.

[48] Street, Philip, *Animal Weapons*, MacGibbon & Kee, London, 1971, p. 37.

[49] Lack, David, *Evolutionary Theory and Christian Belief*, Methuen, London, 1957, p. 65.

From Sir Alister Hardy's work *The Living Stream*, the following illustrations will show how remarkably close in structural detail such parallels may be.[50] The desert rat and the Jerboa (see Fig. 4) are clearly responding to environmental pressures by developing the same exceptional overall form, which enables them to move quickly in loose sand by jumping like a kangaroo rather than by running. The Tasmanian wolf skull cannot be told apart from the skull of the North American or European wolf (see Fig. 5).[51] The range of variability in both overlaps. Even more remarkable is the close similarity between the placental and marsupial moles (see Fig. 6), which have developed almost identical "digging" feet, nose and mouth configuration, eye structure, and ear openings designed to prevent particles entering the ear hole.[52] Yet these two creatures are not related. G. G. Simpson[53] has given an illustration of the structural framework supporting the wing of a bat and a fly, and believes it is another example of convergent development to meet a shared engineering problem. Wood Jones stated it very succinctly:[54]

> It seems therefore certain that structures which have developed for the satisfaction of these common needs may bear a considerable likeness to each other, although the animals manifesting them may be utterly unrelated by kinship or descent. Since so many basal needs are common to all animals and these functional needs are satisfied by the development of appropriate structures, it is to be expected that a common ground plan of parts and organs might be detected. . . .

Homologies are then neither due to chance nor to descent, but to a built-in design factor.

It might be argued that we do not have direct evidence that substantial changes in structure can be attributed to environmental factors. But we *do* have such evidence. For example, the phenomenon of hornlessness in normally horned cattle is observed when herds are moved into areas in which hornlessness is already known. Such cattle are found in Europe, Africa, and South America.[55] Again, Swiss cattle moved into Hungary developed longer horns and longer legs, such as the native cattle have. In another instance, cattle brought from the Bavarian Alps into the crown estate of Altenburg in Hungary not only developed the longer horns common to the area,

---

[50] Hardy, Sir Alister, ref. 22, p. 202.
[51] Ibid., p. 201.
[52] Ibid., p. 200.
[53] Simpson, G. G., ref. 27, p. 182.
[54] Jones, F. Wood, ref. 23, p. 71.
[55] Berg, Leo, ref. 8, p. 241.

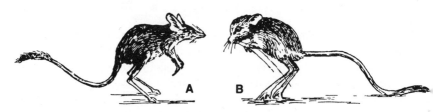

Fig. 4. (A) The marsupial jerboa (*Antechinomys laninger*) and (B) the placental jerboa (*Dipus hirtipes*), redrawn respectively from Troughton's *"Furred Animals of Australia"* and the *"Cambridge Natural History."*

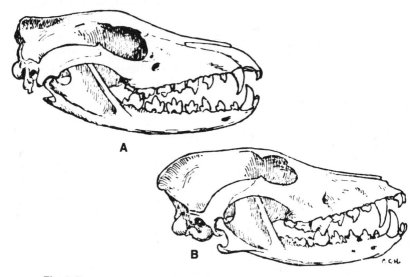

Fig. 5. The marsupial Tasmanian wolf (*Thylacinus cynocephalus*), with (A) its skull compared with (B), that of the placental wolf (*Canis lupus*), drawn to the same scale, from specimens in the Oxford University Museum.

Fig. 6. (A) The marsupial mole (*Notoryctes*), redrawn from the *"Cambridge Natural History,"* and (B) the placental mole (*Tlpa europe a*), drawn from a photograph.

but their horns became harder and acquired a peculiar lyrelike form characteristic of the local Hungarian breed, and the skull became narrower.[56] Such structural differences often form the basis by which modern taxonomists distinguish species and genera, and even higher orders of classification. The investigators believed that these changes were entirely due to the effects of the Hungarian climate and soil. They were not due to interbreeding.

Fishes (*Zoarees viviparus*) transferred from Ise Fjord to Roskilde Fjord in Denmark, a few degrees of latitude, increased the number of vertebrae, the average rising from the native mean of 108 to a higher mean of 114.6 vertebrae.[57] The stocks did not mix with fish already in the new area. Similarly, land molluscs of different genera have developed parallel shell forms, markings, and decorative patterns in entire independence.[58] The list could be extended to the point of boredom. But it works both ways. Unlikes may become like, and likes may come to differ — actual relationship or lack of it is not necessarily reflected by the terminal result. This applies also to apes and men, though the actual data we have shows rather that the human skull more readily degrades towards an apelike form than that the ape skull becomes humanlike. If size is ignored, certain now extinct apes did develop over a long period of time, it is held, into a more manlike form including the acquisition of partial erectness, somewhat reduced brow ridge development, and a more humanlike tooth pattern as a whole. Such changes are possible and may have been due to environmental factors with secondary influences, resulting from changes in food habits as ambient conditions modified the local fauna and flora which comprised the food supply.

In the next chapter we shall examine the extent to which the human skull may be "degraded" structurally until it resembles more nearly the ape skull. Such factors as climate, diet, and certain cultural habits which relate to eating (the presence or absence of knives, for example) can be shown to effect changes in cranial morphology. These brutalize the appearance but do not provide justification, in the absence of any other guide, for supposing that fossil men were phylogenetically nearer to the apes than to modern man.

---

[56] Ibid., p. 280.
[57] Ibid., pp. 281,282.
[58] Ibid., p. 247.

Chapter 3
The Implications of Convergence for Human Origins

I
T IS well known that the human skull is plastic enough that it may, *in the adult stage*, be modified towards a more apelike form if the eating habits of the ape are simulated in one way or another by man. The question bears examination because many of the skulls of early man have undoubtedly been deformed in the direction of the ape skull for what Portmann[59] would have termed "historical" (as opposed to genetic) reasons. Such deformation can occur within a single lifetime. It is, of course, not inherited by the offspring, but if the conditions of life persist over several generations, chances are that a few skulls will be preserved as fossils whose configuration might give the impression that their owners were not far removed *by descent* from an apelike subhuman ancestor, whereas, in point of fact, no such relationship need be postulated.

Wilson D. Wallis observed years ago:[60]

> The evidence of prehistoric human remains does not in itself justify the inference of a common ancestry with the apes. We base this conclusion on the fact . . . that practically all the changes in man's structure traceable through prehistoric remains are the result of *changes in food and habit.*
>
> The most notable changes are found in the skull. Briefly the story of changes is to: a higher frontal region, increased bregmatic height, smaller superciliary ridges, increased head width, less facial projection, decreased height of orbits and a shifting of the transverse diameter downward laterally, a more ovoid palate, smaller teeth, diminished relative size of the third molar, shorter, wider and more ovoid mandible, decrease in size of condyles, decrease in distance between condylar and coronoid processes, and in general greater smoothness, less prominent bony protruberances, less of the angular-

---

[59] Portmann, A., "Das Ursprungsproblem," *Eranos-Jahrbuch* (1947):19: "One and the same piece of evidence will assume totally different aspects according to the angle — palaeontological or historical — from which we view it. We shall see it either as a link in one of the many evolutionary series that the paleontologist seeks to establish, or as something connected with remote historical action. . . . Let me state clearly that for my part, I have not the slightest doubt that the remains of early man known to us should be judged historically."

[60] Wallis, Wilson D., ref. 15, pp. 69ff.

ity and "savageness" of appearance which characterizes the apes. This is evolution in type, but the evolution is result rather than cause. . . .

Practically all of these features of the skull are intimately linked together so that scarcely can *one* change without the change being reflected in the *others*, some features, of course, reflecting the change more immediately and more markedly than do others. If we suppose that man's diet and his manner of preparing food have changed, we have an index to most of the skull changes, provided that the dietary change has been from uncooked or poorly cooked to better cooked food, and from more stringent to less stringent diet. Development of stronger muscles concerned with chewing will bring about the type of changes which we find as we push human history further back into the remote past.

Change is most marked in the region in which *chewing muscles* function. With tough food and large chewing muscles is associated a large mandible with broad ramus, large condyles, heavy bony tissue. . . . Larger teeth demand more alveolar space and there results a more prognathous and more angular mandible. The more forward projection of the teeth in both upper and lower alveolar regions is in accordance with the characteristics of animals which use the teeth for the mastication of tough food, and no doubt is a function of vigorous mastication.

The adjacent walls of the skull are flattened and forced inward as well as downward, producing the elongation of the skull. The temporal muscles reach far up on the skull, giving rise to a high temporal ridge: they extend forward as well as backward, giving a more prominent occipital region, and a more constricted forward region, resulting on the forehead region of the skull in the elevation of the superciliary ridges and intervening glabellar region. Projecting brow ridges are associated with stout temporal and masseter muscles and large canines.

The facial region is constricted laterally and responds in a greater forward projection, one result being that the transverse diameter of the orbits is thrust upward outwardly, giving the horizontal transverse diameter which characterizes the apes and which is approximated in pre-historic men and in some contemporary dolichocephalic (long headed) people. In young anthropoid apes, when chewing muscles are little developed and there is little constriction in the lateral region posterior and inferior to the orbits, the transverse diameter of orbits is oblique as in man, being elevated to the horizontal, when temporal muscles develop and function more vigorously, thrusting in and upward the outer margin of the orbits. Constriction of outer margins of orbits produces the high orbits which we find in apes, and to a less marked degree in prehistoric human remains.

One issue of the Ciba Symposia was devoted to a study of Eskimo life. The subject is particularly a propos in the present context because these extraordinary people are often considered rather precise "models" of paleolithic man. Writing in this issue, Erwin Ackerknecht pointed out:[61]

The cheekbones and jaws of the Eskimo are very massive, possibly under the influence of the intense chewing he has to practice, which also results in a

---

[61] Ackerknecht, Erwin, Ciba Symposia 10, no. 1 (1948):912.

tremendous development of the chewing muscles. Eskimo teeth are often worn down to the gums, like animal teeth, from excessive use.

Fig. 7 shows a characteristic Eskimo male face, with the skull form outlined to show that the greatest width is at the jowls and not in the temple region. The head of Gainsborough's *Blue Boy* in Fig. 8 however, shows how a refined diet tends to produce a head form of another kind with the greatest width in the temporal region.

It has been also pointed out that the Eskimo skull occasionally shows a "keel" along the top, which results directly from the need for a stronger attachment or anchorage for the jaw muscles, which are used much more extensively. This will be noted in Fig. 7, and should be compared with the keel indicated in the skulls of three supposedly human fossils in Fig. 9. It is very clearly marked in the case of the gorilla skull in this illustration.

William Howells pointed out:[62]

> Gorillas have a heavy and very powerful lower jaw, and the muscles which shut it (which in man make a thin layer on and above the temple, where you can feel them when you chew) are so large that they lie thick on the top of the head, about two inches deep, practically obscuring the heavy brow ridge over the eyes which is so prominent on the skull, and giving rise to a bony crest in the middle merely to separate and afford attachment to the muscles of the two sides.

In the Eskimo skull and in the gorilla skull, there is therefore sometimes a certain parallelism, which is in no way any indication of genetic relationship. The explanation of the Eskimo keel is a historical (i.e., cultural) one. Again, we quote Howells on this subject:[63]

> The powerful jaw of these animals in chewing, gives rise to a terrific pressure upwards against the face, and the brow ridges make a strong upper border which absorbs it.

If man is subjected to uncooked food, and forced in the absence of knives to tear it from the bone, the developing muscles will find a way of strengthening their anchorage along these bony ridges. Moreover, if there is not in the diet that which will harden the bone in the earlier years of life when such strains are first encountered, it is inevitable that the skull will be depressed while still in a comparatively plastic state, and the forepart of the brain case will be low and sloping so that it lacks the high vault we tend to associate with cultured man. Thus the massive brow ridges of Sinanthropus, so similar to those of Pithecanthropus, are, as Ales Hrdlicka pointed

---

[62] Howells, William, *Mankind So Far*, Doubleday, New York, 1945, p. 68.
[63] Ibid., p. 131.

Fig. 7. Contrast the form of this Eskimo head with the head of "Blue Boy" in Fig. 8. This drawing is based on a photo reproduced on the cover of Ciba Symposia, Vol. 10, No. 1, and is quite exact in its proportions: (A) a simplified outline; (B) an ancient Eskimo skull, showing the keel (slightly exaggerated) on the top and the front of the head.

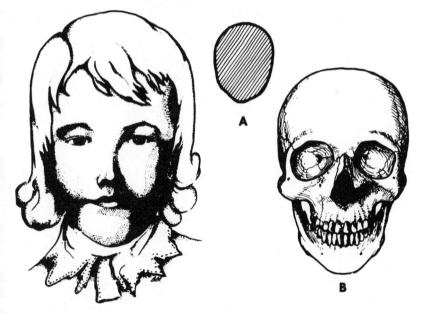

Fig. 8. This head is based on Gainsborough's painting, "Blue Boy," and is drawn to exact scale. It shows clearly the influence of what may be termed a cultured diet. The wide part of the head is at the temples. (A) Cranial outline for comparison with Eskimo head in Fig. 7. (B) Modern European skull.

out some years ago, "a feature to be correlated with a powerful jaw mechanism."[64]

Let us assume, for the sake of argument, that early man was subsequently forced to eat tough food, after an initial family had multiplied and wandered apart; and that this food lacked that which would harden the skull in its formative period of development. Then the strengthening of the chewing and cervical muscles would go hand in hand with building a substructure of bone to provide the necessary anchorage in the form of crests as well as ridges in the front, at the rear, and on the top of the skull. But the skull itself would remain pliable enough that it would undergo considerable distortion. The "keel" which is so noticeable in the case of the gorilla, would naturally tend to appear in this early man, because the muscles would pull the sides of the skull in, under the increased tension (see Fig.10).

When the jaw was used for cracking bones, etc., the chief point of stress would regularly occur at the chin, since the clamping action between the teeth would normally be one-sided. This again led to a certain degree of compensatory thickening. But unlike the apes, man is a talking creature and makes much more use of his tongue. There is reason to believe that the reinforcement of man's chin takes the form of a bony ridge outwards rather than inwards, on this account, and this gives the prominence which is characteristic of the human jaw. The apes and other anthropoids on the other hand have the reinforcement in the form of a ledge which reaches inward instead. This is known as the simian shelf. In some fossils of early man there is some evidence of a simian shelf, and presumably this is a reinforcement in addition to that which is normal for man's chin, by way of compensation for the added load placed upon the structure at this point. Tugging at flesh in the absence of satisfactory "cutlery," or maybe just bad table manners, possibly contributed to the alveolar prognathism which is found in these early remains. The increasing muscle development which rose up under the zygomatic arch naturally forced the latter outwards and it developed a stronger form.

It is quite likely therefore that the functioning of the jaw mechanism determines whether the skull will be depressed or not. The fossil human forms then show clearly that the entire series has been affected to a large degree by the same depressive and compressive forces. Thus if early man were to have been utterly deprived of culture it seems quite certain his fossil remains would have revealed

[64] Hrdlicka, Ales, *Skeletal Remains of Early Man*, Smithsonian Instit. Miscel. Collection 83 (1930):367.

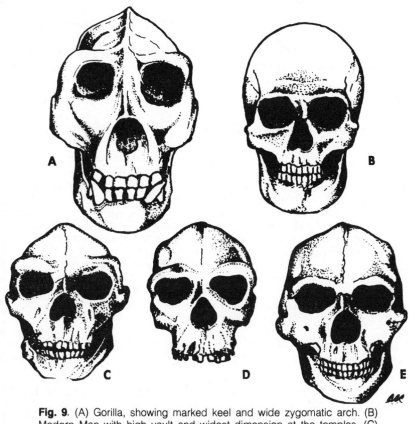

Fig. 9. (A) Gorilla, showing marked keel and wide zygomatic arch. (B) Modern Man with high vault and widest dimension at the temples. (C) Pithecanthropus. (D) Rhodesian Man. (E) Sinanthropus.

Fig. 10. Skulls of a female gorilla (left), a Pithecanthropus (center), and a modern Papuan native (right), viewed from above. The marked formation of the supraorbital ridge and the postorbital narrowness are evident. Such marked differences can almost certainly be attributed to the development of powerful muscles for chewing and biting.

an extreme primitiveness, which might easily be misinterpreted as evidence of a recent emergence from some anthropoid stock. Yet in point of fact, it could happen that individuals might become degenerate at any period in history and leave behind them a cemetery of the most deceptive fossil remains.

Humphrey Johnson remarked in this connection:[65]

> It seems likely that in very early times the human form possessed a high degree of plasticity which it has since lost, and that from time to time such exaggerations of certain racial characters, probably brought about by an unfavourable environment, have occurred. In the Pekin-Java branch of the human family, the exaggeration of the ape-like traits has occurred to a very high degree: it later took place, so it would seem, though not quite so pronouncedly in Neanderthal Man, and has occurred again though to a far lesser extent in the aborigines of Australia.
>
> Some of the low features of the Australians may, as Prof. Haddon thinks, be due to racial senility, and thus the resemblance to Neanderthal Man may be regarded as secondary or convergent. By a wider application of this principle we may consider that "convergence" has played a part in bringing about the resemblance of paleoanthropic men to the anthropoid apes.

If this interpretation of the evidence is correct, it follows that a return to the conditions of diet and life which characterized prehistoric man would be followed by a tendency to move also towards his physical type. Such a resemblance to the ape as is borne sometimes by fossil man would in no way relate to phylogenetic descent. In a given group, the adult male would be more likely to resemble the ape than the infant does (and probably more than the female does, too), yet it could not be argued on this account that the adult was more nearly related to the simian ancestor than the infant or the female. Franz Boas pointed this out many years ago:[66]

> If we bring two organically different individuals into the same environment they may, therefore, become alike in their functional responses, and we may gain the impression of a functional likeness of distinct anatomical forms that is due to environment, not to heredity.

I have said previously that we do not have unequivocal evidence that apelike forms actually evolved into more manlike forms, but we do have evidence of man becoming physically more apelike in cranial bone structure. Indeed, LeGros Clark admitted that this very point has been urged quite seriously and with some force:[67]

---

[65] Johnson, Humphrey, *The Bible and the Early History of Mankind*, London, 1947, p. 89.

[66] Boas, Franz: quoted by Ralph Linton, *The Study of Man*, Appleton-Century, New York, 1936, p. 26.

[67] Clark, Sir Wilfrid LeGros: quoted by Rendle Short, ref. 18, p. 255.

Prof. Wood Jones has pointed out that there *are* some anatomical features which make it easier to believe that the apes are descended from man rather than man from an extinct ape.

He believed that evolution never retraces its steps however. Thus, he argued that such a retrogressive step would never occur. Perhaps, but in structural form and therefore to an uncritical eye, man may "regress" part of the way, though the verb "degenerate" would be much more appropriate. Man has done this, even in comparatively recent times, as Robert Chambers pointed out when recounting the eventual fate of certain poor Irish peasants around 1600 who were dispossessed of their homes under particularly harsh circumstances:[68]

> The style of living is ascertained to have a powerful effect in modifying the human figure in the course of generations, and this even in its osseous structure. About 200 years ago, a number of people were driven by a barbarous policy from the counties of Antrim and Down in Ireland, towards the sea-coast: there they have ever since been settled, but in unusually miserable circumstances.
> And the consequence is that they now exhibit peculiar features of the most repulsive kind, projecting jaws with large open mouths, depressed noses, high cheek bones, and bow legs, together with an extremely diminutive stature. These, with an abnormal slenderness of limbs, are the marks of a low and barbarous condition all over the world.

This is not a case of a single individual, for we have here a whole group of people whose "primitive" appearance resulted entirely from historical circumstance. Undoubtedly they were as far removed from the apes, by descent, as you and I, and were potentially as educable and as intelligent as their contemporaries. If we add cases of isolated individuals who have become "cast out" or lost to society and yet have survived somehow to old age, we have the ingredients of "fossil man." Since in the nature of the case, early man began in one spot, presumably he must have spread under some pressure as population multiplied. At the center, where a larger number of people would encourage the development of higher civilization, fragments would continually be breaking away like pioneers seeking more room and greater freedom. The first small migrant groups would tend to retreat further and further from the center to the periphery as the pressures behind increased, and as they did so they would abandon the well-tried and more familiar accouterments of civilization with which they began and would culturally regress, just as pioneers almost always do at first. The higher their initial estate,

---

[68] Chambers, Robert, *Vestiges of the Natural History of Creation*, Churchill, London, 1844.

the lower would be their last. In time, the struggle would diminish their resources even further, wherever the band was too small or the environment too harsh. A few sole survivors might well perish in frightful isolation along the leading edge of the spreading waves, as old age rendered their continuance impossible. These, at the periphery, may be our "fossil men," *descendants* of civilized human beings, not their *ancestors*.

Arthur Koestler rightly observed,[69] indeed, that longevity might well degrade such individuals even more markedly, till they were quite apelike!

Disease can also play a part. As we know, the first Neanderthal representative was reconstructed as a club-carrying brute creature with apelike stoop and a slouching gait. It is known now that this first specimen was actually a diseased individual.[70] Subsequent finds of Neanderthalers are known to have been quite erect in posture.[71] And there are those who believe Mr. Neanderthal could pass down the street quite unnoticed if he were only correctly dressed, with a suitable haircut (see Fig.11).

Of the effects of disease, Jesse Williams in his *Textbook of Anatomy and Physiology* said:[72]

> Degenerate types show characteristic markings that are known as stigmata of degeneration. Common stigmata are: (1) receding forehead, indicating incomplete development of frontal lobes of the brain; (2) prognathism, a prominence of the maxillae; (3) the Canine ear; (4) prominent superciliary ridges; (5) nipples placed too high; and (6) supernumerary nipples.

Glandular disturbances can likewise have profound effects on the anatomy. Keith[73] attributed a tendency to strong brow ridges to

---

[69] Koestler, Arthur, *The Ghost in the Machine,* Hutchinson, London, 1967, p. 167: "Prolongation of the absolute lifespan of man might provide an opportunity for features of the *adult* primate to reappear in human oldsters: Methuselah would turn into a hairy ape."

[70] The first Neanderthal specimen was evidently suffering from chronic osteoarthritis, an ailment which forced him to adopt a stooped posture. See C. S. Coon, *The Story of Man,* Knopf, New York, 1962, p. 40. Coon said his "bones were rotten with arthritis." See also the report by A. J. E. Cave at the 15th International Congress on Zoology, London, noted in *Discovery,* November 1958, p. 469.

[71] On Neanderthal's normal erectness, see Alberto Carl Blanc and Sergio Sergi, in *Science* 90, supplement (1939):13. These authors reported the finding of two further skulls, with the base of one skull "well preserved, enabling Prof. Sergi to establish for the first time that Neanderthal man walked erect and not with the ape-like posture with head thrust forward as previously believed. The horizontal plane of the opening in the skull shows that the bones of the neck were fitted perpendicular into the opening, showing the posture to be erect as in the present day man."

[72] Williams, Jesse, *Textbook on Anatomy and Physiology,* 5th ed., Saunders, Philadelphia, 1935, p. 49 footnote.

[73] Keith, Sir Arthur: quoted by Sir John A. Thompson in *The Outline of Science,* Vol. IV, Putnam, New York, 1922, p. 1097.

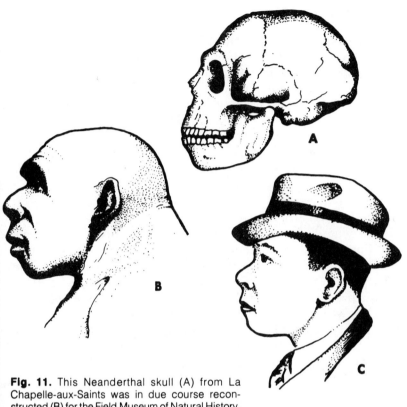

Fig. 11. This Neanderthal skull (A) from La Chapelle-aux-Saints was in due course reconstructed (B) for the Field Museum of Natural History, Chicago, to show how our primitive ancestor looked. It was reconstructed (C) by J. H. McGregor to show how "modern" he really might have been in appearance.

a hyperactive pituitary; whereas underdevelopment of the pituitary may account for a certain flatness of face observed in many European nationals.[74]

Cultural behavior may effect marked changes in the structure of the skull and jaw. Tearing flesh from the bone in the absence of knives tends not only to strengthen the masseter muscles and enlarge the zygomatic arch somewhat as a direct consequence, but also to give a forward lean to the front teeth, both of which features lend a more apelike cast to the face. Indeed, we really have little precise information on the extent to which bone structure may be modified in the absence of a bone hardening diet during infancy.

There is much room for a fresh look at the whole question of the

[74] Keith, Sir Arthur, "Evolution of Human Races in the Light of Hormone Theory," *Bull. Johns Hopkins Hosp.*, 1922.

interaction between form and function. Some of the time being spent rather fruitlessly in an obsession with the establishment of lines of evolutionary descent could perhaps be turned to better account in a new direction. In the interest of truth, it is time that a fresh look was taken at the whole question of the influence of environmental factors (climatic, dietetic, barometric, and cultural) upon the structure of living organisms, especially man.

Most assuredly we live in an age when human wickedness finds many ways to express itself more destructively than ever before. We are probably not more wicked than in other ages, but our civilization has armed us in ways that greatly enlarge our power to do damage. It seems to me that evolutionary philosophy has encouraged violence by its very emphasis on the idea of survival at all costs as the supreme good, thus giving violent action a rationale which justifies it. This model for human behavior is drawn from an erroneous view of animal behavior and a false interpretation of the supposed pattern which is believed to have led to the upward evolution of all life.

Must we not be held responsible, those who know the facts, for failing to apply to this hypothesis the kind of checks which we apply readily enough to other hypotheses that can be much more securely established from the supporting evidence than evolutionary theory has ever been?

As we see man's origin, so we see his destiny. Evolutionary theory is not only bad science, as I see it, but an even worse philosophy.

Part IV
The Survival of the Unfit

Chapter 1
Evolution: An Irrational Faith

IN 1964 George Gaylord Simpson presented the world with a kind of summary of his evolutionary philosophy under the title *This View of Life*.[1] I think it would be difficult to find in current literature any serious work containing so many dogmatic assertions, the strength of which depends so entirely upon the author's personal estimate of the value of his own opinion, nor a like series of pontifical assertions which, in the final analysis, rest upon so small a base of experimental evidence.

It is some measure of the fragility of his state of mind that he has felt it necessary to assure the reader so repeatedly that evolution is a *fact*. On one page alone, containing only twenty lines of type, he repeats the phrase "the fact of evolution" three times, twice within the first four lines.[2] Throughout the book this begging of the issue runs like an unending refrain. Evolution is a fact, not a theory; evolution is one of the few *basic* facts; it is an unassailable fact; a fact supported by all other facts; a fact which only dishonest biologists would argue against.[3] He has to admit that there are a few problems, but "solution of these problems is a triumphant theme of recent research."[4] If ever the sober propriety of true science has been abandoned for dogma, it is here; yet the author uses the word "dogma" only once and applies it to the concept of creation.

Observing the literature carefully over a period of some forty years, it is my impression that the sense of urgency and special pleading in assuring the public that Darwin was right, has increased steadily with the passage of time. At first evolution was presented as a tentative proposal. Then followed a period of facile assurance.

---

[1]Simpson, G. G., *This View of Life*, Harcourt, Brace & World, New York, 1964. Significantly, the subtitle is "The World of an Evolutionist."

[2] Ibid., p. 151. See also p. 193.

[3] Ibid., pp. 10, vii, 62, 40, 51, 63, 151.

[4] Ibid., p. 63.

Now, as this assurance has begun to prove less well founded, we have entered a period of defensive reiteration. A situation has been reached where a small group of men whose names are now household words among biologists, has come to form a kind of College of Cardinals of a new Faith, which to challenge is heresy, the penalty being almost inevitably excommunication from the scientific fraternity. This happens in spite of the increasingly evident fact that virtually all the fundamentals of the orthodox evolutionary faith have shown themselves to be either of extremely doubtful validity or simply contrary to fact. This is true of the argument from homologies as a proof of relationships, from recapitulation as a proof of lines of descent, from the appeal to vestigial organs as a demonstration of progressive change, and now similarly from the whole concept of the struggle to survive and the survival of the fittest — a concept which lies at the root of natural selection. So basic are these erroneous assumptions that the whole theory is now largely maintained *in spite of* rather than *because of* the evidence. But it must be maintained and Pinnock makes a keen observation in this respect:[5]

> The myth of Evolution is so entwined in the current world view that its absurdities are seldom even noticed. It ought to be apparent to the casual observer of the history of science since Darwin, that the theory he propounded, far from becoming better established, is becoming shakier with every passing year. If you ignore for a moment the brainwashing of magazines with a *Time-Life* mentality, and listen to the experts in the various fields, you would soon realize that the data on which this grand hypothesis depends are slender indeed, and capable of a dozen different constructions. . . .
>
> The reason Evolution is believed and taught as a fact is not due to the evidence for it, but rather due to the *need* for it (his emphasis).

As a consequence, for the great majority of students and for that large ill-defined group "the public," it has ceased to be a subject of debate. Because it is both incapable of proof and yet may not be questioned, it is virtually untouched by data which challenge it in any way. It has become in the strictest sense *irrational*. It is now nothing less than a dogma, an article of faith held with strong conviction and based on a logical extension of certain premises which are themselves as yet unproven and may be beyond proof. According to Simpson, those who refuse to accept it are either idiotic, dishonest, or both.

In medieval times, the test of the truth of any proposition was not whether it had received experimental verification but whether it conformed to current orthodoxy. Whatever was agreeable to that

---

[5] Pinnock, Clark H., *Set Forth Your Case*, Craig Press, Nutley, New Jersey., 1967, p. 38.

orthodoxy was accepted as truth and needed no further validation. The position today with respect to the theory of evolution is very much the same. Little, if any, critical examination is applied to any particular piece of information or to any concept which it is felt lends support to it. But information or concepts which challenge the theory are almost never given a fair hearing by the "hierarchy." They are rather apt to be discounted out-of-hand, as Stanley Jaki said: "A successful theory can easily produce a state of mind that fails to recognize the presence of proofs to the contrary."[6]

Evolutionary philosophy has indeed become *a state of mind,* one might almost say a kind of mental prison rather than a scientific attitude. For wherever proof is in the nature of the case either lacking or impossible, the scientific attitude is to maintain an open mind. But this is precisely what the evolutionist is unwilling to allow. He will not admit that any alternative interpretation of the data is possible. Yet the data upon which his faith is postulated is equivocal; it is capable of being interpreted in two entirely different ways. To equate one particular interpretation of the data with *the data itself* is evidence of mental confusion, and this mental confusion leads to some extraordinary propositions.

For example, not long ago it was seriously suggested that man grows a beard because, in the past, it had a survival value. If a man is attacked by an animal which goes for his throat, his beard will tend to trigger the jaw-closing mechanism of the attacking animal prematurely — and thereby save his life. I have not documented this beautiful piece of nonsense, but it was in a perfectly respectable scientific journal. A little reflection will show how flimsy such an argument really is. Half the world's population does not grow a beard, the female half — the half which by nature of their reduced defensive equipment in terms of height and muscular strength ought perhaps to be more in need of a beard than the males! Furthermore, it is primarily Caucasians who grow beards which could conceivably be adequate as a defense of this kind. So that two-thirds of the world's population of males have not been provided selectively with this natural (?) defense against predators. And finally, one might ask, Would dogs or other such attacking enemies exist in sufficient numbers to constitute a threat of adequate dimensions to provide selective pressure enough — and would they attack *adults* only?. . . What kind of sense does it make? That the editor of that journal should take such an idea seriously enough to accept the author's

---

[6] Jaki, Stanley, *The Relevance of Physics,* U. of Chicago Press, 1966, p. 280.

paper for inclusion suggests that the theory of evolution somehow or other is detrimental to ordinary intelligence and warps judgment. It can also lead to some astonishing instances of circular reasoning. In a paper entitled "The Dynamics of Evolutionary Change," G. Ledyard Stebbins wrote this statement:[7]

> To be sure, many examples are known in which a new type of animal or plant appears suddenly and seems to be completely separate in respect to many large differences from any earlier fossil forms.
> To explain these apparent saltations Simpson assumes that the fossil record contains many highly significant gaps.

Consider what this extraordinary statement means. There are many gaps. These gaps are labelled *saltations*. It sounds better than simply calling them gaps. . . . According to Stebbins, Simpson *explains* these saltations by saying there are probably "many highly significant gaps." In short, the many highly significant gaps which are called saltations are explained by the many highly significant gaps. There is surely something wrong with a mind so imprisoned in a theory that it is capable of presenting as a serious contribution to scientific theory this kind of "explanation."

Of course, the most favored explanation of evolution at the present moment is Natural Selection acting upon random mutations within a population. But this explanation, of which Simpson assures the reader that the solution of its remaining problems "is a triumphant theme of recent research on evolution," is now being increasingly called in question, even by those who are themselves confirmed evolutionists. When Sir Julian Huxley published his *Evolution in Action*, a kind of *ex cathedra* pronouncement on the subject of natural selection, Sir James Gray reviewed the book in the English journal *Nature*, noting the fervor with which Huxley "preaches his gospel." Gray put it this way:[8]

> Darwinian orthodoxy demands implicit faith in the efficacy of natural selection operating on chance mutations. Subscribe to this, and all doubts and hesitations disappear; question it and be forever lost. The case for orthodoxy can seldom have been stated with greater cogency and enthusiasm than by Dr. Julian Huxley in "Evolution in Action."
> A few readers, perhaps rather pagan in their outlook, may think it a little strange that, if the case is quite so strong as they are asked to believe, it should

[7] Stebbins, G. Ledyard, "The Dynamics of Evolutionary Change," in *Human Evolution: Readings in Physical Anthropology*, ed. N. Korn and F. Thompson, Holt, Rinehart & Winston, New York, 1967, p. 48.

[8] Gray, Sir James, "The Case for Natural Selection," *Nature*, February 6, 1954, p. 227, in reviewing Sir Julian Hixley's *Evolution in Action*, Chatto & Windus, London, 1953.

still be necessary to argue the merits of natural selection with almost evangelistic vigour.

Gray went on to point out that he is not challenging the concept of evolution itself. This he accepts. What he is challenging is the mechanism by which it is currently explained. And he notes that Huxley himself introduces an anomolous note when he says, "The human species today is burdened with many more deleterious mutant genes than can possibly exist in any specie of wild creature." At that point Gray commented, "It seems a great pity that Natural Selection should have met its Waterloo just when it was most needed."

Contrary to what most laymen think on the subject, it appears, therefore, that natural selection does not necessarily lead to its supposed corollary, "the survival of the fittest." For if mutant genes indicate a deterioration in the organism at a basic level, as is almost universally agreed, then man is perhaps the unfittest of all creatures. And yet he is supposed to be the climax of the evolutionary process, as Wood Jones pointed out with complete justice:[9]

> If, in the ordering of Nature, life on Earth was destined to flourish and multiply, to outfold its forms and increase its varieties, it must be recognized as a tragic failure of its destiny that, so far, it has merely achieved the emergence of the arch-destroyer of life, and the sources of food and shelter necessary for its maintenance.

One might argue, of course, that given sufficient time man will come to grips with this problem and turn out in the end to be Nature's supreme achievement. However, there is more reason to believe that he will go on accumulating and increasing the number of mutant genes that he carries so that by the time he ought to be preparing to take his place as its paramount chief he may be so deteriorated as to be totally unfit. Moreover, there are even now signs that the complexification of his central nervous system has already begun to bring about his downfall just on a purely neurophysiological basis. Speaking on this matter, Raymond Pearl pointed out:[10]

> Proportionately 2.5 times more mammals than birds and reptiles die from causes affecting the nervous system. The corresponding figure for the more primitive of human groups is about 18.0. That for the most highly civilized and culturally advanced human groups is about 27.5.
>
> In other words it appears that in the evolutionary progress from reptiles and birds to the most advanced sorts of men, the relative mortality assignable

---

[9] Jones, F. Wood, *Trends of Life*, Arnold, London, 1953, p. 18.
[10] Pearl, Raymond, *Man the Animal*, Principia Press, Indiana, 1946, p. 9.

to breakdown of the central nervous system has been multiplied more than twenty-seven fold.

These figures are not to be regarded as absolutely precise appraisals, but roughly they do indicate something of the biological price that man has to pay for his high-toned brain.

Interestingly enough, an editorial appeared in the English journal *Endeavour* that proposed that history bears out this progressive deterioration. Writing on "The Future of Man," Holmyard, after suggesting that there was little evidence of any improvement in man's intelligence over the last six or seven thousand years, felt it necessary to point out that there is some evidence in the opposite direction:[11]

There is, however, another possible factor to be considered. Hitherto there is no sign that the progress of science is being hindered by the limitations of the human brain, but we may legitimately surmise that sooner or later a stage will be reached when the mind is inadequate to effect further advance.

The continued existence of warfare may perhaps be taken as an indication that this stage has indeed already been arrived at, so far as morals and ethics are concerned; its eventual attainment in the quest for scientific knowledge would then be equally sure.

If worthiness is an aspect of fitness, it is suddenly becoming increasingly apparent that the epitome of evolutionary processes is no longer either fit *or* worthy to survive. Man shows no improvement physically or mentally, nor in behavior. At the end of his book, John Greene, still an evolutionist, recognized this fact and asked the question:[12]

Is man in truth a kind of Prometheus unbound, ready and able to assume control of his own and cosmic destiny? Or is he, as the Bible represents him, a God-like creature who, having denied his creatureliness and arrogated to himself the role of Creator, contemplates his own handiwork with fear and trembling lest he reap the wages of sin, namely, death? The events of the twentieth century bear tragic witness to the realism of the Biblical portrait of man.

Natural selection is a meaningless concept unless it leads to the survival of the fittest and to the elimination of the unfit. The fitness of all forms of life (apart from man), by and large, impresses the naturalist everywhere he looks. It impressed Darwin. It could be evidence of the hand of God; or it could be evidence of some natural law which sees to it that all unfit forms are eliminated, constantly, unfailingly, being given no chance to perpetuate their kind. Darwin thought he had discovered this mechanism, the struggle to survive,

[11] Holmyard, E. J., "The Future of Man," *Endeavour*, January 1946, p. 2.
[12] Greene, John C., *The Death of Adam*, Iowa State U. Press, 1959, p. 338.

leading to the survival of the fittest. And the very temper of the times in which he lived prepared the public to welcome a concept which seemed to justify the ruthless exploitation of the weak by the strong, a philosophy deeply engrained as a consequence of the Industrial Revolution.[13] In his autobiography, Andrew Carnegie, who made his fortune in steel, described as follows his conversion to evolution on reading Darwin and Spencer:[14]

> I remember that light came as in a flood and all was clear. Not only had I got rid of theology and the supernatural but I had found the truth of evolution. "All is well since all grows better," became my motto, my true source of comfort. Man was not created with an instinct for his own degradation, but from the lower he had risen to the higher forms. Nor is there any conceivable end to his march to perfection. His face is turned to the light; he stands in the sun and looks upward.

Ashley Montagu observed in connection with Big Business that John D. Rockefeller (who certainly should have known better) said, "The growth of a large business is merely the survival of the fittest. . . . This is not an evil tendency in business. It is merely the working out of a law of nature and a law of God." Montagu commented:[15]

> Darwinism was offered as no mere apology. It was more positive than that, it was a validation, a biological justification for competition. This doctrine has become part of the behavioral equipment, the system of overt beliefs, of almost everyone in the western world today. . . .
>
> This view of life is completely false. Yet it largely motivates the conduct of most persons in the western world. And it has brought man into the sorry state of personal, interpersonal, and international conflict in which he finds himself today.

It seemed so entirely proper, and the arguments which Darwin used to support the concept so very reasonable, and the evidence which he *selected* to illustrate how it works in Nature so convincing, that very few people paused long enough to ask whether it was really true.

In retrospect, we can see now that many of the catchphrases with which he bolstered his thesis ought to have been challenged from the very beginning. Is Nature really in a constant state of warfare? Do animals overpopulate the territory they occupy so that many of them are constantly on the border of starvation and only the

---

[13] Calverton, V. F.; *The Making of Man*, Modern Library, New York, 1931, p. 2. He said, "Every force in the environment, economic and social, conspired to the success of the doctrine."

[14] Davidheiser, Bolton, *Evolution and Christian Faith*, Presb. and Reformed Publ. Co., Nutley, N. J., 1969, p. 350.

[15] Montagu, Ashley, *On Being Human*, Schuman, New York, 1951, p. 22.

very fit survive? Is it true that animals are entirely "selfish" and that they are neither altruistic nor interdependent? Do only the fit survive?

The fact is that, little by little, a more careful examination of what goes on in Nature has shown that the answer to every one of these questions is negative. It is the object of this paper to give some of the evidence now available that Nature does not necessarily eliminate or "select out" the unfit, a circumstance which naturalists in their desire to find a mechanism for evolution for a long while tended to overlook. Nature is *not* in a state of constant warfare. Animals do *not* under normal circumstances overpopulate the territory they occupy. Cooperation and interdependence in the community life of animals is not a *rare* thing, but seems rather to be an essential part of the very fabric of it. The whole concept of natural selection, which is still so fundamental to current evolutionary theory, only makes sense if we assume that it eliminates the unfit and that this process of elimination results from struggle of some sort. But what is becoming increasingly apparent is that there is as much cooperation as there is struggle in Nature, and indeed probably more. The unfit often survive, and when they do it is not infrequently because members of their own species actually *assist* them to do so.

In short, the premises of evolutionary theory are about as invalid as they could possibly be. Yet this new knowledge has made only a very small dent in the armor of current biological orthodoxy. If evolutionary theory was strictly scientific, it should have been abandoned long ago. But because it is more philosophy than science, it is not susceptible to the self-correcting mechanisms that govern all other branches of scientific enquiry. Nevertheless, it can only be a matter of time before there *must* come some pretty fundamental revisions. Although he had in mind certain problems in connection with the part played by mutations, Waddington admitted, even in this regard, at the Alpbach Symposium in Switzerland, "I think we are going to see some extraordinary changes in our ideas about evolution pretty soon."[16] But at present — no matter how frequently the old foundations are undermined by further knowledge, only to be replaced by alternative foundations which in their turn prove equally insecure — belief in evolution remains unshaken, whereby we may know that it is indeed a dogma.

In the next two chapters, some of the basic assumptions relative to the supposed operation of Natural Selection are reexamined in the

---

[16] Waddington, Sir C. H., "The Theory of Evolution Today," in *Beyond Reductionism*, ed. A. Koestler and J. R. Smythies, Hutchinson, London, 1969, p. 392.

light of certain facts about the web of life which have tended to be ignored or overlooked. And it will be seen that these facts stand clearly against not only the theory of evolution *per se*, but also against the extension of this theory as a key to the understanding of human behavior.

Chapter 2
Natural Selection: Fact or Fancy?

Is Nature Really in a Constant State of Warfare?

IT IS truly amazing how, once an idea has seized the public mind because it suits the temper of the times, it is almost impossible to dislodge it. It must have been apparent to millions of ordinary people who had any firsthand knowledge of Nature at all that the picture proposed by Darwin of a state of chronic warfare was completely unreal. Obviously, Nature has not essentially changed since Darwin's time, so the behavior we see in the open country, whether in Canada or England or Africa, is what it was in those days. And we do *not* see animals constantly battling with each other. The supposed "struggle" for existence is comparatively mild. Animals establish their territories rather with enthusiasm than viciousness. Nature is far from "red in tooth and claw," as Tennyson pictured it.

One of the first naturalists who had the opportunity to study Nature at first hand over a period of many years was the Russian prince Petr Kropotkin. Petr was born in Moscow in 1842 and came of a family belonging to the highest stratum of Russian aristocracy. His home life was filled with love and gentleness, and though his mother died when he was very young, her extraordinary gentleness and affection stayed with her children all their lives. Although his father owned very many serfs, it is evident that they were always treated with exceptional kindness, and Petr himself in his writings again and again returns to the gentility and great-heartedness of these common people. He was educated for a military career, but his real interests were in geography, zoology, botany and anthropology — more particularly with special reference to Siberia. So Petr sought and obtained a commission in a Siberian regiment where he seems to have spent more time in the study of nature than in the study of warfare. Indeed, his work in zoology from 1862 to 1866 is considered outstanding.

Under the influence of Darwin's *Origin of Species*, which had come into his possession a little while before he went to Siberia,

Kropotkin tells us in the very first paragraph of his book how eagerly he looked for "that bitter struggle for the means of existence among animals belonging to the same species, which was considered by most Darwinists (though not always by Darwin himself) as the dominant characteristic of the struggle for life, and the main factor of evolution."

The book to which reference is made above is his *Mutual Aid,* which was published by Kropotkin in 1902.[17] This appeared first as a series of articles in the English journal *The Nineteenth Century,* the first installment appearing in 1890. The book, in which these papers were bound together, appeared subsequently. It should be carefully borne in mind that this work was the result of close observation in Nature, observation initially stimulated by a search for evidence to bear out Darwin's thesis that a constant struggle went on between living forms. The result, however, was a total repudiation of the whole concept of struggle.

At first he found himself in an area where there was no pressure of numbers, where there was a paucity of life, where underpopulation, not overpopulation, was the distinctive feature of the area. Here he found that there was no "fearful competition for food," which was an article of faith with most Darwinists. So he attributed his failure to validate Darwin's basic thesis to the fact that there were too few animals in northern Asia to fulfill the requirements of adequate competitiveness.

But when he sought out particular localities in which there was a superabundance of animals, he found that even here there was no evidence of the kind of struggle which Darwin postulated:[18]

> Wherever I saw animal life in abundance, as for instance, on the lakes where scores of species and millions of individuals came together to rear their progeny; in the colonies of rodents; in the migrations of birds which took place at that time on a truly American scale along the Usuri; and especially in a migration of fallow-deer which I witnessed on the Amur, and during which scores of thousands of these intelligent animals came together from an immense territory, flying before the coming deep snow, in order to cross the Amur where it is narrowest — in all these scenes of animal life which passed before my eyes, I saw Mutual Aid and Mutual Support carried on to an extent which made me suspect in it a feature of the greatest importance for the maintenance of life and the preservation of each species. . . .

It should be noted that Kropotkin still believed this kind of mutual aid did contribute to "further evolution." He was quite convinced

---

[17] Kropotkin, Prince Petr, *Mutual Aid*, Extending Horizon Books, Boston, 1955, introduction, p. vii.
[18] Ibid., p. viii.

Darwin's main thesis was correct, but his own observations continually and in every way, and most emphatically, drove him to the conviction that struggle in itself did not lead to improvement. Indeed, struggle, when it became critical due to local famine had the effect only of *impoverishing* the animals involved, both in vigor and in health, so that, as he said, "No progressive evolution of the species can be based upon such periods of keen competition."[19]

He found himself forced to reject completely the view that competition was essential to improvement:[20]

> I was persuaded that to admit a pitiless inner war for life within each species, and to see in that war a condition of progress, was to admit something which not only had not yet been proved, but also lacked confirmation from direct observation.

Kropotkin was quite willing to admit that there is within each species a certain amount of real competition for food "at certain periods." But he was very doubtful from his own studies at first-hand in overpopulated areas where the competition is carried on to the extent argued by Darwin, whether what competition there *was* played the part assigned to it in the evolution of the animal kingdom. He felt that Darwin was weakest when dealing with this point, which was, after all, so crucial to his whole thesis. So he wrote:[21]

> If we refer to his paragraph entitled, "Struggle for Life most severe between Individuals and Varieties of the same Species," we find in it none of that wealth of proofs and illustrations which we are accustomed to find in whatever Darwin wrote. The struggle between individuals of the *same* species is not illustrated under that heading by even *one single instance* (my emphasis): it is taken for granted; and the competition between closely allied species is illustrated by but five examples, out of which one at least (relating to the two species of thrushes) now proves to be doubtful.

So, Kropotkin asked, "To what extent does competition *really* exist within each animal species? Upon what is the assumption based?" And his whole book is a striking demonstration of the doubtfulness of Darwin's basic proposition in this respect. Yet so powerfully had Darwinism captured public imagination that very few people were either aware of or paid the slightest attention to Kropotkin's writings. Nevertheless, what he reported has continued to be of such interest that *Mutual Aid* has constantly been reprinted and is constantly running out of stock. (The latest reprint apparently was undertaken in 1972 by the New York University Press.)

---

[19] Ibid., p. ix.
[20] Ibid.
[21] Ibid., p. 61.

This happy practice of reprinting some of the older works has fortunately helped to offset the distressing tendency of publishers of new works to favor only the printing of pro-evolutionary literature, a not unnatural reaction to public demand, since they have to stay in business by making a profit. But it has had the unhappy effect of confirming in the public mind the supposition that there *is* nothing to be said against evolution.

Fortunately, Kropotkin's work stimulated others to take a fresh look at the evidence. And some of these, even though they remained confirmed evolutionists, nevertheless produced works, the cumulative effect of which *must* in the end serve to undermine the whole evolutionary fabric. I am thinking, for example, of W. C. Allee's book, *The Social Life of Animals,* a work which, as might be supposed from its title,[22] sets out to demonstrate from evidence acquired since Kropotkin's time that Nature is not a series of warring states but a remarkably well-balanced cooperating society of animals and plants.

In this last work and in another book of similar nature entitled, *On Being Human,* by Ashley Montagu, we may find an answer to another question asked in the previous chapter.[23]

Do Animals Really Overpopulate Their Territory?

Most people, when they go to see pictures of animals in the wild, expect to see large numbers. So animal photographers not unnaturally take their cameras where the animals are numerous. The consequence is that one inevitably has an impression of "the wild" as teeming with animal life. In the Rockies we imagine that everywhere there are flocks of mountain goats or other such creatures; in Africa vast herds of zebra, giraffe, and even elephants. In point of fact, this impression is the result very largely of selective photography. So also, the inexperienced cameraman or the impatient amateur comes away with one or two pictures showing a few animals together — only after days of searching and a substantial number of false alarms leading to wasted footage. Even where man has not been the most common predator and where the fear of him has not spread the alarm upon his approach, it is likely to be the occasional animal, the curious and unafraid, which will provide the amateur naturalist with his best opportunity.

The fact is that very few parts of the earth are in any way

---

[22] Allee, W. C., *The Social Life of Animals,* Beacon Hill Press, Boston, 1938, p. 233.

[23] Montagu, Ashley, ref. 15, p. 118.

crowded with animals. The total number of birds per acre in most parts of the world is very small and has been calculated out by weight as being only a few pounds. Thus there may be a number of very small birds whose total weight is a few pounds, or one or two larger ones whose total weight is about the same. But the density of individuals is very low. This is not true, of course, where a small island standing alone as a refuge in a vast expanse of ocean is occupied by a tremendous number of birds or other shoreline animals. For here the population per acre must take into account the territory over which these animals feed — which is, of course, *far* greater than the area of the island itself. It should also be remembered that in terms of freedom of movement birds enjoy a third dimension of dispersion, altitude.

This is not to deny that birds flock together in vast numbers, a fact which would seem to challenge the available food supply. Nevertheless, there is very little fighting among such flocks unless they are hedged in by man. And even here, as has been shown for geese, when the animals are resting they will orient themselves as far as possible so that each individual has a certain minimal free space, or "facial distance" as it has been called, in front of it.[24] And though it may take some time for a large flock to settle down in this way, the birds respect this "individual need" and avoid conflict. Even if, due to a wire fence, crowding is extreme, it has been noted that the peripheral individuals will all turn outwards taking up a position which allows them to achieve the required facial distance by looking through the wire fence and thus give the central birds a better chance to achieve a position of no conflict. It seems, therefore, that even under unnaturally stressful conditions most animals will do all they can to keep the peace.

Prior to man's interference, it appears that Nature is seldom crowded. But wherever man has gone, he has been Nature's great disturber, either exterminating animals entirely or forcing them to crowd together unnaturally. Among species in which internicene warfare has been observed, rats are probably preeminent. Yet rats are in a special category, since they spread with man and compete chiefly where men are crowded together. Due to historical circumstances, therefore, it has often come about in the past that man's chief acquaintance with behavior patterns within species of animals other than himself has been badly distorted because of his own influence on these same species. In former times the rat population

---

[24] McBride, Glen, "The Conflict of Crowding," *Discovery*, April 1966, pp. 16-19.

was much greater than it now is, and city people commonly derived their picture of Nature from these unnaturally congested creatures.

Such crowding and its accompanying competition is not characteristic of animals in the wild, even where the environment might be expected to encourage it because of its abundant food supply. Kropotkin's initial researches were conducted in Siberia, which did not seem to him to constitute a sufficiently favorable environment for large numbers of animals. Nevertheless, he noted that many regions enjoying a far more congenial climate than Siberia are equally underpopulated. For example, along the shores of the Amazon River, in spite of the fact that food is plentiful as evidenced by the great variety of mammals, birds, and reptiles, these are very widely scattered, and it is only rarely that animals are seen in any numbers. The fact is even more strikingly observed in the forests of Brazil which afford ample food for birds and yet, like the forests of Asia and Africa, are not overpopulated but rather underpopulated.[25] The same is true, according to Kropotkin, of the pampas of South America, which, although so admirably suited to herbivorous quadrupeds, affords the observer with an astonishingly small number of visible animals. Indeed, to one observer, W. H. Hudson, only one small ruminant was seen in this immense grassy area. Land birds are also few in species and numbers. By contrast, millions of sheep, cattle, and horses introduced by man now graze upon a portion of these prairies.

That areas can, under human husbandry, support far larger populations of animals clearly suggests that the numbers to be found there naturally are not being held down by competition. Nature does not naturally overpopulate; if anything, it underpopulates.

Even so many years after the publication of *The Origin of Species*, the average city dweller still has the impression that every inch of ground is teeming with life in such a way that there is constant conflict between individuals for the available food supply. The country man, on the other hand, is well aware of the fact that for almost all species the distribution is sparse, thinly spaced. One may have to search to find a live representative, and as a rule one would have to *scrutinize* the area keenly to find any dead animals.

Yet if Darwin's picture had any truth behind it, the open country ought to be teeming with competing animals and the competition itself ought to result in many corpses lying around. Moreover, among those species which are highly gregarious, such as

---

[25] Kropotkin, Prince Petr, ref. 17, pp. 309,310.

rabbits in a local warren, or gophers, or any creatures which *are* found in comparatively large numbers here and there, there is no evidence whatever that their crowding has in itself led to a progressive change in form. Yet, according to Darwin, the consequence of this crowding should be just that, namely, progressive change, leading to improvement of the species as a whole. It sounds reasonable enough, but what has become more apparent as research among natural communities of this kind has been extended, is that such competitive crowding has precisely the opposite effect than was supposed by Darwin. It leads to the elimination of the extremes and the perpetuation of the norm. The odd or exceptional individuals tend to be either destroyed or bred out by being overwhelmed by the sheer numbers of the common types. Leo Berg, after a discussion of the imagined effects of the supposed struggle for existence pointed out that careful students of nature[26]

> could not observe any perceptible difference between the individuals which have survived and those which have perished. As far as may be judged from the available data, *natural selection cuts off deviations from the standard by destroying extreme variations* (his emphasis).

He then gave some illustrations from both animals and from plant species, and concluded:[27]

> All the foregoing renders it doubtful whether mortality in natural conditions possesses selective value, i.e., is contributing to evolution: as a rule, individuals approaching the standard survive, and all those which deviate therefrom perish, no matter whether their distinguishing characters are retrogressions or give promise of being able to advance.
>
> Selection in natural conditions thus not only does not assist evolution, but appears in fact to be a hindrance thereto.
>
> Such an opinion was held by Korshinsky: "The struggle for existence, and selection connected with it, is an agency tending to restrict the development of forms already produced by checking further variations, but never contributing to the production of new forms. It is a principle antagonistic to evolution."

Some years ago the animal ecologist Charles Elton pointed out that this absence of evolutionary change in crowded areas applies equally to plants. He wrote:[28]

> Only in certain intertidal communities of the sea do we find that animals have reached the limits of space that will hold them. . . .

---

[26] Berg, Leo, *Nomogenesis*, Mass. Instit. of Tech. Press, 1969, pp. 63,64.
[27] Ibid., p. 64.
[28] Elton, Charles: in a report quoted as originating in *Nature*, September 23, 1969, but not verified. See also his "Animal Numbers and Adaptation," in *Evolution*, ed. Sir Gavin de Beer, Oxford U. Press, 1938, pp. 127-137.

What are the commonest objects meeting the eye in such spots? The answer is mussels and seaweed. If there is a struggle for existence, mussels and seaweed are thus in the very midcentre and vortex of it. Evolution should here be proceeding at top speed. What are the facts?

The eminent professor J. Ritchie, in his presidential address to the Zoological Section of the British Association in August, 1939, handed down the latest bulletin about mussel evolution. He said, "the edible mussel (*Cardium edule*)) has retained its specific characteristics for two millions of years or more, its genus in a wide sense lived 160 millions years ago in the triassic."

And as for the seaweed, those existing today are not in any way different from those found in Cambrian and Silurian seas — which according to the evolutionists themselves date back to at least 500 million years.

In terms of numbers, the prize must certainly be given to insects where one might therefore suppose that competition would be most keen and evolution most in evidence. Estimates show that insect species probably represent half of all species known, and in terms of total numbers of individuals they are possibly four-fifths of the world's population. One would expect to find even less similarity between living specimens and their fossil ancestors (by reason of the very pressure of numbers) than one finds between living reptiles and *their* ancestors, where, because of the smaller populations involved, there ought to have been very little pressure towards change. In point of fact, precisely the opposite is the case. Our reptile world is very different from the ancient world, but our insect world is remarkably similar, a fact noted by Charles Brues:[29]

In general the picture we get from two surveys spanning the past 70 million years is that of a decline in primitive types of insects, a gain in the relative abundance of the specialized orders, and some substantial changes in the rates of certain groups of the total population. But by and large the insect population of today remains remarkably similar to that of an earlier age. All the major orders of insects now living were represented (with little or no change indicated) in the Oligocene Forest. Some of the specific types have persisted throughout the 70 million years since then with little or no change, indicating a pronounced fixity that gives little promise of adaptive change in the future. Furthermore, the insects of that age already showed great variety; indeed, in some groups that we have been able to compare in detail, we find a greater diversity in the Oligocene insect fauna than in the present one.

This means simply that there is no real evidence of progressive diversification into the present. The truth is that in various ways God seems to have so arranged things that when severe conflict within a species is imminent, due to a scarcity of food, migratory instincts

---

[29] Brues, Charles, "Insects in Amber," *Sci. American,* November 1951, pp. 60f.

lead a sufficient number of the community to go somewhere else. The idea of constant warfare within the species is not borne out. In fact some creatures, which would have a hard time to migrate any distance, such as wingless aphids, if raised on an inadequate diet actually develop wings and fly away.

The *spread* of animals, in so far as it is not accomplished by human disturbance, is generally assumed to be due to real overpopulation, that is, to the pressure of numbers. However, Charles Elton has observed:[30]

> The studies of Middleton on the introduced American gray squirrel in England, and of Harrisson and Hallom on the great crested grebe, also in England, have shown that spreading takes place equally in years of abundance and in years of scarcity; in other words, a great deal of spreading may be due to local movements at the edge of the range and not to the pressure of numbers in the ordinary sense.

In order to float his theory, Darwin had to find some basis for selective pressures *within* a species. Warfare between species was, he argued, of significance in favoring animals whose structure gave the predator an edge in powers of capture, or the preyed-upon an edge in the powers of escape. This is how the horse got his longer legs, he suggested. But the real effect of natural selection was supposed to be taking place *within* a species as a result of conflict between members of the same family or herd. But the way in which animals gradually spread does not support this concept at all, because the so-called territorial imperative leads rather to the expulsion of unwelcome members of the species than to their destruction. The expelled animals merely take up residence somewhere else: they are not destroyed. Fighting over territory in the vast majority of cases results in little or no bodily injury, as J. P. Scott put it: "The occurrence of destructive fighting within a species tends to be extremely rare."[31] Again:[32]

> Animal society in the natural habitat shows very little harmful destructive fighting, even under conditions of great stress, as when . . . subjected to general starvation. On the contrary, such societies exhibit behaviour that would in human terms be called cooperative or even altruistic.

Moreover, it is not the strong that throw out the weak as a rule, but the original settler who drives out the latecomer, and the term

[30] Elton, Charles, *The Ecology of Animals*, 3rd ed., Methuen's Monographs in Biological Subjects, London, 1951, pp. 71f.
[31] Scott, J. P.: reviewing "The Natural History of Aggression" (a reported symposium), *Science* 148 (1965):820.
[32] Ibid., p. 821.

"latecomer" applies equally to later generations, i.e., younger animals. The courage of an animal is not dependent on its physical fitness, its size, or its age, apparently, but upon its sense of proprietorship. So, provided it remains within its home base, a weak unfit specimen may drive out the stronger, fitter member of its own species. The term "survival of the fittest" becomes meaningless, until one defines what one intends in any particular situation by fitness.

Recent evidence from the study in their natural environment of those species which are supposed to be nearest to man (gorilla, chimpanzee, and orangutan) indicates that they do not fight with one another even for territory.[33] The impression which Darwin seems to have had of Nature as a battleground may well have arisen from the fact that he limited his observations very largely to animals in captivity. In a recent work by Claire and W. M. S. Russell entitled[34] *Violence, Monkeys and Man,* the authors show very clearly from some fifteen field studies undertaken in natural conditions that aggressiveness between monkeys and apes living together is *rare.* By contrast when the same species are kept together in captivity, aggression between cage-mates is frequent and sometimes severe. Evidently, they conclude, food shortage is not the cause; unnatural crowding itself would appear to be at the root of the trouble. And animals see to it that crowding is avoided in Nature, unless it is normal to the species.

It seems clear enough that there is something basically wrong with Darwin's Malthusian picture of Nature as being in a state of antagonism as a consequence of the imbalance between the numbers of animals in any given area and the food supply there. In the first place, animals for the most part appear to be widely dispersed, and they maintain their dispersion by territorial instincts which lead them to defend their home country only by driving away to a distance unwanted trespassers of their own species. Such trespassers are not killed as a rule nor even seriously injured. The end result is that the population density is maintained at a low level. And yet this does not have the effect of weeding out those animals which are slightly less capable and favoring those which are more capable of survival, because the real strength of the individual to defend his own territory depends not upon his size or his fitness, but upon his

---

[33] Montagu, Ashley, Letter to the Editor under the heading "Animals and Man: Divergent Behaviour," in *Science* 161 (1968):963.

[34] Russell, Claire, and Russell, W. M. S., *Violence, Monkeys, and Man,* Macmillan, New York, 1968: reviewed by V. Reynolds under the heading "Cures for Human Violence," in *Nature,* January 4, 1969, p. 99.

distance from the geographical center of it. A very superior individual of any given species trespassing outside his own territory and into the heart of the territory of an inferior individual of the same species will almost always be put to rout because, in Nature, the courage and tenacity of the defendant is normally found to be far greater than that of the trespasser. This has been observed and reported time and again. The sickly animal at home has many times the courage and energy of the trespasser, bursting with vitality though he may be.

One can observe this, if one lives in the country, by studying the behavior of little creatures such as chipmunks. The defender is full of valor the nearer he is to the center of his homeland. When he chases a trespasser, he has all the edge at first, but this edge slowly diminishes as the chase carries him further from the center. If the trespasser is being chased toward his own home, he, in turn by contrast, will begin to develop greater courage until there comes a point at which he is no longer trespassing. The chase, meanwhile, may have carried the original homeowner out of his own territory. Suddenly becoming aware of this, his courage evaporates, he hesitates for a moment, and then somewhat fearfully turns around and runs back to safety. As soon as this happens, the original trespasser for a moment is in the ascendant until the situation has once again reversed. And so one may see two chipmunks chasing each other furiously nose to tail, A to B, until the boundary is crossed, and then B to A with the same vigor until the boundary is crossed in reverse. Robert Ardrey noted:[35]

> A proprietor's confidence is at its peak in the heartland, as is an intruder's at its lowest. Here the proprietor will fight hardest, chase fastest. That confidence, however, will wane as the proprietor approaches his border and vanish as he crosses it. Having entered his neighbor's yard, an urge to flee will replace his urge to fight, just as his neighbor's confidence and fighting urge will be restored by the touch of his vested soil.

So these creatures maintain a certain distance without doing violence to each other by a means which allows the weak to survive as well as the strong, and the countryside is not, as a consequence, loaded to the bursting point with animals competing for the available food. As Ronald Good and many other naturalists have been pointing out with increasing emphasis in recent years, Nature is a beautiful system of balanced harmony. In his review of *Natural Communities* by Lee R. Dice, Good notes with satisfaction the gradual

---

[35] Ardrey, Robert, *Territorial Imperative*, Delta Books, New York, 1966, p. 90.

change that is taking place in the interpretation of Nature by more recent authorities:[36]

> The third and deepest reason for dissatisfaction is our failure to abandon outmoded biological conceptions, and this has two main aspects. More important, because of its profound significance to the wild in general, is what may be called the "nature red in tooth and claw" fallacy. One would imagine that the influence that such a belief has had on human affairs in the past half-century would at least raise doubts about its validity; but even more odd is the apparent continuing failure to admit that the very existence of a science of "natural communities" belies it. For if nature was indeed as the poet (Tennyson) described it, its condition would be chaotic and in a perpetual state of disequilibrium. If there is nothing else to thank Dr. Dice for, there is the support his book gives to the view that nature is essentially a state of beautiful and delicate balance to which each and every member makes its due, but only due, contribution.

In the second place, Darwin was quite wrong in applying certain principles which he derived from Malthus. Malthus had said, among other things, that animals raise more offspring than they need to do to maintain their kind. This constantly challenges the available food supply. But in commenting on this, Medawar showed its essential fallaciousness:[37]

> The catch in this Malthusian syllogism, pointed out years ago by Fisher, lies in its major premise. So far from producing a vastly excessive number of offspring, most organisms produce just about that number which is sufficient and necessary to perpetuate their kind. . . .

And where, by contrast, there *are* tremendous numbers of animals, such as rabbits, insects, birds, or even fishes, all the evidence points to the conclusion that among these species there has been virtually no evolutionary change. So, if evolution has ever occurred, it seems to have nothing to do with population density or natural aggressiveness among animals. L. L. Whyte pointed this out:[38]

> The decisive evolutionary steps, the branching-out into many different types, seem to have occurred just when the ecological niches were relatively empty, as in the conquest of land by vertebrates. . . . These explosive phases seem to have happened when competition was at a minimum rather than a maximum.

Commenting, Bertalanffy says that "the identification of evolution

---

[36] Good, Ronald: in a review of the book by Lee R. Dice, *Natural Communities*, Ann Arbor, Mich., in *Nature*, July 11, 1953, p. 46.

[37] Medawar, Sir Peter B., *The Uniqueness of the Individual*, Basic Books, New York, 1957, p. 14.

[38] Bertalanffy, Ludwig von, "Chance or Law," in *Beyond Reductionism*, ref. 16, p. 68.

with adaptation is therefore by no means proved. It is a debatable point, not an *a priori* principle of evolution."

Chapter 3
The True Harmony
of Natural Communities

Are Animals Always Selfish and Competitive?

IT IS an interesting reflection upon the way in which our minds work that we should evince a convenient mental blindness to evidence which conflicts with strongly held convictions. Our attention is filtered. Were it not so, we might perhaps find ourselves almost totally unable to form any convictions at all. So we pay a price for what, after all, provides tremendous stimulus. The view that Nature is in a state of warfare, individual against individual, has led to most people being very largely unaware of the fact that animals upon occasion do sacrifice themselves for one another. In a recent book *Human Evolution,* two of the contributing authors make this observation:[39]

> The whole human pattern of gathering and hunting to share is unique to man. In its small range a monkey gathers only what it itself needs to eat at the moment; the whole complex of economic reciprocity that dominates so much of human life is unique to man.

This statement would probably be unchallenged by the general public who have come to accept a view of Nature as being composed entirely of individuals fighting for their own survival in a completely selfish way. Yet if it were not for a tremendous power of control which the pundits of evolution hold over what many publishing houses publish, there is no doubt that an entirely different side of what goes on in Nature would become equally well known — and probably read with far greater interest and enjoyment. For it has been known for a very long time that animals cooperate in helping each other quite widely in Nature and often at some cost to themselves. They may deliberately gather food in order to share it with other members of their own species who for one reason or another cannot help themselves. And I am not thinking now of the feeding of

---

[39] Washburn, S. L., and Lancaster, C. S., "The Evolution of Hunting," in *Human Evolution*, ref. 7, p. 74.

194

the newborn, but of adults helping other disabled adults. Nor do I have in mind only cases where domesticated animals help one another, though it occurs here also. In the English journal *Country Life*,[40] a case was reported of one man who owned a spaniel and an alsatian. The spaniel apparently gradually went blind, and as its eyesight failed, the alsatian took over its guidance, stopping frequently when they journeyed together to make sure the spaniel was all right. In due course the spaniel went totally blind. Thereafter, the alsatian would take her gently by the ear and guide her wherever they went, in the field, in the house from room to room, and even up and down stairs. The spaniel trusted the alsatian so completely that they would go romping together on long country walks even among the trees.

But perhaps domesticated animals are not properly representative of Nature in the wild. Yet the same altruistic interdependence has been reported here too. Driving along a country lane at night, one correspondent in *Country Life* tells how his carlights picked up two rats running down one of the wheel tracks ahead of him.[41] Having a strong dislike of rats, he accelerated at once and ran a wheel over them. Then he stopped his car, being a humane individual, intending to finish them off should either of them be still alive but wounded. To his amazement, one rat, though quite unharmed, did not run away. In its mouth was a long straw which was also held in the mouth of the dead animal, and the survivor was quite blind. The two rats were evidently companions, the "seeing" rat being his blind mate's *seeing eye*, guiding his mate with a straw held between them.

Kropotkin was aware of a number of reports of similar nature.[42] He referred to J. C. Woods' narrative of a weasel which picked up and carried away an injured comrade in a time of danger. He referred to a certain Max Perty who observed rats feeding a blind couple. He told of a reported instance of two crows feeding in a hollow tree a third crow which was wounded, and which apparently had been wounded several weeks previously. He referred to cases where other crows have been reported as caring for blind comrades, in some cases as many as two or three such helpless fellow crows.

Even Darwin himself was aware of these things. He recorded an observation by a Captain Stansbury who during a journey to Utah saw a blind pelican which was being fed, and well fed, by other

---

[40] *Country Life*, October 26, 1967, p. 1069.
[41] *Country Life*, February 2, 1967, p. 245.
[42] Kropotkin, Prince Petr, ref. 17, p. 59.

pelicans upon fishes which had to be brought a distance of thirty miles.[43]

There is one case in which, within a species, provision is made by the stronger members for the weaker ones in a way which is rather wonderful. I have in mind the wheeling of birds taking off together before beginning a long flight. In his *Social Life of Animals*,[44] W. C. Allee pointed out that this habit during flight allows the younger, aged, or weaker birds to reach the proper altitude at a more leisurely pace and yet within the same time frame by the simple device of arranging that the stronger birds will describe a larger circle as they gain altitude. Thus as they spiral into the air, they travel a greater distance than the weaker members of the flock and so all reach the same altitude without undue dispersion. It has been observed that during flight, if dispersion of the flock is excessive the stronger fliers will wheel several times until the other birds have been able to catch up again. It is true that, in this instance, the action probably does not endanger those creatures who decide to delay their flight somewhat for the benefit of their weaker brethren, so that there is no altruism involved, or self-sacrifice. Nevertheless, one must admit here to a certain built-in sensitivity which renders Nature by and large a cooperative and not merely a competitive web of life.

Closer observation of Nature has suggested to naturalists that there are probably far more instances of cooperation between animals than of conflict. Not only is this true between individuals *within* a species, as in all the above instances, but it is true between species. Conrad Limbaugh related the following example of the Pederson shrimp off the coasts of the Bahamas:[45]

> The transparent body of this tiny animal is striped with white and spotted with violet, and its conspicuous antennae are considerably longer than its body. It establishes its station in quiet waters where fishes congregate or frequently pass, always in association with the sea anemone. . . .
>
> When a fish approaches, the shrimp will whip its long antennae and sway its body back and forth. If the fish is interested, it will swim directly to the shrimp and stop an inch or two away. The fish usually presents its head or a gill cover for cleaning, but if it is bothered by something out of the ordinary, such as an injury near its tail, it presents itself tail first. The shrimp swims or crawls forward, climbs aboard and walks rapidly over the fish, checking irregularities, tugging at parasites with its claws and cleaning injured areas. The fish remains almost motionless during this inspection and allows the shrimp to make minor incisions in order to get at subcutaneous parasites. As

---

[43] Darwin, Charles, *The Descent of Man*, Merrill & Baker, London, rev. ed. 1874, p. 166; and L. H. Morgan, *The American Beaver*, n.p., 1868, p. 272.

[44] Allee, W. C., rev. 22, p. 146.

[45] Limbaugh, Conrad, "Cleaning Symbiosis," *Sci. American*, August 1961, p. 49.

the shrimp approaches the gill covers, the fish opens each one in turn and allows the shrimp to enter and forage among the gills. The shrimp is even permitted to enter and leave the fish's mouth cavity.

Local fishes quickly learn the location of these shrimp. They line up or crowd around for their turn and often wait to be cleaned when the shrimp has retired into the hole beside the anemone.

So many illustrations of this can be found in marine life that Conrad Limbaugh concluded:

> From the standpoint of the philosophy of biology, the extent of cleaning behavior in the ocean emphasizes the role of cooperation in nature as opposed to the tooth-and-claw struggle for existence.

Darwin stated categorically that if one single instance of real and complete interdependence between two species could be demonstrated, he would be willing to abandon his theory, for such interdependence could not be (he felt) accounted for upon evolutionary principles. But, as we know, when many such instances began to be reported to him, he did not abandon his evolutionary ideas. Such interdependences are so numerous and are now so familiar to naturalists — between birds and reptiles, between birds and mammals, between fishes of different species, between insects and plants (pollination by bees) — that it would be tiresome to record them.[46]

The effect of our misconceptions regarding Nature as a battle ground, a view to which Darwin contributed in no small fashion, has been most unfortunate in terms of human behavior. W. C. Allee noted many years ago in another of his works:[47]

> Today, as in Darwin's time, the average biologist apparently still thinks of a natural selection which acts primarily on egoistic principles, and intelligent fellow thinkers in other disciplines, together with the much-cited man-in-the-street, cannot be blamed for taking the same point of view.

In spite of the fact that Naturalists are increasingly insisting upon the harmony of Nature, there is still no question that an element of "savagery" *seems* to remain. Predators still pounce upon and rend their struggling victims, victims which give every appearance of suffering. But it is not absolutely certain that this appearance of suffering is an indication of actual inflicting of pain in the sense that man hurts his fellow. Some years ago Crowther Hirst studied this matter in the only way accessible to man that is really capable of

---

[46] Materials illustrating this point will be found in *The Wonders of Life on Earth,* Lincoln Barnett and the editors of *Life,* Time-Life Inc., New York, 1960, pp. 228-241.

[47] Allee, W. C., "Where Angels Fear to Tread: A Contribution from General Sociology to Human Ethics," *Science* 97 (1943):520.

giving a decisive answer to the question, Is Nature cruel?[48] He interviewed personally, or corresponded with, or studied carefully all available records written by, those who had been attacked or mauled by animals. He was able to examine some 60 instances, mostly reporting the experience of travelers, missionaries, or big game hunters, who had been severely injured in this way. Only two of them experienced any pain at the time of the attack, and he felt that in these particular instances the circumstances were rather special. Of the balance, he was able to state with assurance the rather surprising fact that not one of those mutilated experienced any pain at the time, even though their injuries were gross in some cases.

Others have written in a similar vein, expressing the view that the struggle of animals is a reflex which is triggered by unwanted restraints imposed by the predator.[49] This aspect of the matter has been discussed at greater length in another Doorway Paper.[50] The shedding of blood seems unavoidable in the present economy of Nature, but in the wild it does not appear that animals inflict pain upon each other in the way that man does. I have said, *in the wild*, because where man has interfered and, by domestication of either the predators or their prey, upset the normal operation of animal instincts, or for his own selfish reasons has crowded creatures together unnaturally, or disturbed the balance in some other way, what are normally swift, necessary, and comparatively merciful killings become prolonged, meaningless, and vicious.[51]

Surprisingly enough, it now appears that even within a living organism the healthy may be assisting the sick. Graham Chedd in an article entitled, "Cellular Samaritans," remarked upon recently reported instances of cooperation between cells, where one cell is temporarily unable to function properly. He wrote:[52]

> Living cells are rather selfish individuals, even those which have to subjugate themselves to the organism as a whole. But in the last two weeks, two papers have been published which report very different examples of an unexpected and remarkable help-your-neighbor cooperation among cells. In both instances, a cell which is metabolically incompetent to deal with a given situation is helped out by a neighboring competent cell.

---

[48] Hirst, J. Crowther, *Is Nature Cruel?* James Clark & Co., London, 1899.

[49] Wood, Theodore, "On the Apparent Cruelty of Nature," *Trans. Vict. Instit.* 25 (1891):253-278.

[50] Part II, "Nature as Part of the Kingdom of God," in Doorway Papers, Vol. III.

[51] Foxes will kill domesticated hens indiscriminately, but not wild fowl; wolves will kill domesticated sheep indiscriminately, but not wild goats. The responsive behavior of the domesticated animals is apparently unnatural, and the predator's behavior is accordingly disturbed.

[52] Chedd, Graham, "Cellular Samaritans," *New Scientist*, October 31, 1968, p. 256.

One report concerns like cells, cells of the same "race." The other is apparently a straight case of "Good Samaritanism": cells of one species aiding cells belonging to a different race altogether.

In complete contrast to this picture of cooperation, R. E. D. Clark pointed out that Darwin applied the principle of competition even to the buds on the branches of a tree which he viewed as engaged in a mad scramble to see which of them could best appropriate the available supplies of sap.[53] In Germany the concept was carried even further. A book entitled *The Struggle of the Parts of the Organism*, published in 1881, proposed that the general shape and structure of organisms was *determined* by the struggle of the various cells with one another. Organisms arose as the result of cells fighting and competing. According to Clark, Romanes and others "hailed this as a discovery of gigantic importance." Darwin even imagined that molecules themselves were engaged in the same struggle.

By and large, naturalists as a whole increasingly commend to the reader a view of Nature that is very different from the picture presented to us over the past 80 years or so, as the result of Darwin's *Origin of Species*. Ardrey said:[54]

It is fruitless to attempt to explain everything in the natural world in terms of selective value and survival necessity. There are times when one can only record what is true, and dissolve in wonder.

Yet for all that, these same naturalists still cling tenaciously to the theory of evolution. It is the mechanism which is today under question. Perhaps in time it will be more widely recognized that any theory firmly held in the absence of a satisfactory mechanism is held by an act of *faith*. And when this act of faith is camouflaged in order to present it as though it were an unquestionable fact, it becomes nothing less than *dogma*. It is no longer science.

Do Only the Fit Survive?

I have read somewhere that a number of years ago a group of competent aeronautical engineers were asked to design a flying vehicle of a certain size with a certain wing span, a stated degree of maneuverability and speed, and of a certain body shape. They were also given a fairly accurate specification as to the available power and rate of fuel consumption. After some months, they concluded that the task was quite impossible. The limitations placed upon the

[53] Clark, R. E. D., *Darwin: Before and After*, Grand Rapids International Publ., Mich., 1958, p. 98.
[54] Ardrey, Robert, ref. 35, p. 175.

principles of design were far too severe. It was then pointed out to them that, scaled down, all the specifications were precisely met in the common bumblebee — which ought therefore, according to the best informed principles of aeronautical engineering, be quite unable to fly.

The fact is that Nature somehow delights to do the impossible. I would prefer to restate this and say rather that God is full of surprises. If the conclusions of evolutionists had any basic validity, then a great many creatures in the web of life ought to have disappeared long ago, and some other creatures ought still to be around.

Take the case of the common shrew as an example. The long-tailed shrew *Cryptotis parva parva* is the smallest known mammal, weighing about four grams, approximately one-seventh of an ounce (according to some, only one-tenth of an ounce). Being a mammal, it must maintain its body temperature within a very narrow range regardless of environmental conditions. In order to do this it has to be eating constantly. Medawar said:[55]

> Even when studied under conditions particularly conducive towards repose, this species of shrew ate its own weight of worms and insects daily and would have died of starvation if food had been withheld for as little as 12 hours.

For comparative purposes, this would mean that a man of average weight would have to eat somewhere around 150 pounds of food per day or, let us say, 40 pounds for breakfast, 50 pounds for lunch, and 60 pounds for supper. As a matter of fact even this would not fill the requirement, for the shrew and the man could obviously not contain this much food if taken as a "lump sum," as it were. It could only be managed by eating *all the time* — which is precisely what the shrew has to do, or very nearly so. So that in terms of survival the shrew must surely be the most "unlikely" animal in existence. According to Baldwin, since the animal must rest and cannot be food-hunting for twenty-four hours a day, it actually has to ensure for itself this total food intake not in a period of twenty-four hours but of twelve hours approximately. Consequently, it is not unfair to say that in practice it must eat twice its weight every day. Baldwin commented on this:[56]

> Although only a slight increase in size would relieve its hunger pinch, it ceased to evolve long ago, having reached its pre-determined mature phenotype.

This proves that Natural Selection has had nothing to do with the size

---

[55] Medawar, Sir Peter B., ref. 37, p. 110.
[56] Baldwin, James L., *A New Answer to Darwinism*, publ. privately, Chicago, 1957, p. 69.

increase in species. Despite its severe handicap, selection has not been able to add a fraction of an inch to its size in 55 million years.

By its very size the shrew may be, to some extent, protected from the observation of predators. But there are many creatures which are quite conspicuous and yet, though virtually helpless in defending themselves, have nevertheless also survived. The Australian koala is certainly one of the most helpless of all wild animals, since he can neither fight nor run. In the presence of man he has no defenses whatever. And yet in Nature his defenselessness, his unfitness in the struggle of life, has apparently had no bearing whatever on his continued survival. Some species, like the opossum which is considered to be one of the most stupid animals in the world and which probably has the smallest brain relative to body size of any mammal species, survives — and may in fact be still extending its range — because of its fecundity.[57] But this is not true of the koala, which bears only one cub at a time.

By contrast with such creatures as these, which it might be argued ought not to have survived as a species, there are not a few creatures whose structure is such that by all normal standards of judgment they ought never to have disappeared. Such a case perhaps is the *Glyptodon clavipes*, a mammal found as a fossil in Brazil. This creature was protected by armor somewhat like a cross between a tortoise and an armadillo, though much larger, being about 10 feet long. W. K. Parker remarked,[58] "Why such a form as the Glyptodon should have failed to hold his ground (in the evolutionary struggle for existence) is a great mystery; nature seems to have built him, as Rome was built, for eternity." However, it is always possible in such a case as this in which a species seems to have come and gone, to postulate that disease, climatic change, or some other cause than strife between animals may have brought it to extinction.

The trouble is that the evolutionists will, when it suits their purposes, argue that in spite of its defenses, other circumstances may bring about its extinction, whereas in spite of its lack of defenses certain circumstances will allow it to survive. By adopting this principle one can in fact support virtually anything. If a species with notable defenses has survived, one can say that it has survived on that account. In the struggle to survive its better defenses gave it an advantage. But as soon as one comes on a creature well equipped for

---

[57] Moore, J. N., and Slusher, H. S. (eds.), *Biology: A Search for Order in Complexity*, Zondervan, Grand Rapids, Mich., 1970, p. 457.

[58] Parker, W. K.: quoted by McCready Price, *Common-Sense Geology*, Pacific Press Publ. Assoc., California, 1946, p. 214.

defense, which nevertheless did *not* survive, one immediately has to account for its extinction by saying that it was unfit in some other way. As has been pointed out time and again, fitness is *judged* by survival, and is not the *cause* of it. The phrase "survival of the fittest" becomes mere tautology. It has to be admitted that the catch phrase becomes vacuous, for it simply means that for whatever the reason, regardless of size, fertility, strength of defenses, immunity to disease, or environmental change, some animals survive and some don't. This is merely a statement of fact; it is not an explanation, and contributes nothing to theory. As we noted previously, Medawar's criticism of current evolutionary theory is that it is flexible enough to be able to explain anything, to be able to explain why A equals B, and why A *doesn't* equal B. W. H. Thorpe said:[59]

> The (natural) selectionist's argument is one that can be expanded or elaborated to cover anything that may conceivably have happened during the evolution of animals and plants. If selection is taken as an axiomatic and *a priori* principle it is always possible to imagine auxiliary hypotheses — unproved and by nature unprovable — to make it work in any special case.
> But as von Bertalanffy points out, this procedure corresponds exactly to that of epicycles in the Ptolemaic system: if planetary motion is *a priori* cyclic, then any orbit, however seemingly irregular, can be explained by introducing more epicycles.

An excellent example of the meaninglessness of this kind of theorizing was borne out by a report of a simple experiment carried out by one scientist among a number of his colleagues. J. C. Fentriss of the University of Rochester's Brain Research Center became involved in the study of two British voles.[60] He was intrigued to find that one species of vole would "freeze" on sighting a moving test object representing a predator to it, whereas the other species, under the same circumstances, would run for cover. The species which adopted the habit of freezing lived in the open where no cover existed, whereas the other one lived among the trees and bushes.

Just as an experiment, Fentriss reported his findings to a group of zoologists asking them for an evolutionary explanation. But he did this after he had reversed the behavior of the open-field and woodland species, reporting that the woodland species froze when frightened and the open-field species immediately ran in search of cover. From this group of zoologists he received rationalized evolutionary explanations of equal force. The answers he received were convincing enough, and had they been quoted in a textbook

---

[59] Thorpe, W. H., "Retrospect," in *Beyond Reductionism*, ref. 16, p. 430.
[60] Fentriss, J. C., *Scientific Research*, November 1967.

would have been considered authoritative. In point of fact, of course, they were completely wrong.

This may not be a fair test in the minds of many people since the data supplied were incorrect. Yet having been told how these two species supposedly behaved, it does seem that competent and unbiased zoologists ought to have given the matter second thoughts and to have questioned whether the original data had not been misreported. At any rate, so strong is the bias of a mind completely convinced, that a sufficient measure of self-criticism may be entirely lacking. Dependence upon logic is all very well provided that one starts with the truth. Charles Kettering warned, "Beware of logic. It is an organized way of going wrong with confidence."[61]

Wood Jones argued for years that, contrary to popular opinion, a great many of Darwin's conclusions were not based upon observation but upon the logical extensions of a basic idea which had captured and imprisoned his mind. That his premises were at fault has become increasingly apparent, and this applies with particular force to his concept of the "survival of the fittest." A few years ago, L. R. Richardson of the Department of Zoology in Victoria University College (New Zealand), wrote an article which he entitled significantly, "The Survival of the Unfit," a title that provided the inspiration for the present paper.[62] He wrote:

> Nearly one hundred years ago, Darwin published his theory of the way in which evolution takes place. Through simplification and dramatization, there is now firmly planted a general belief that evolution is controlled by a "natural law" known as the Survival of the Fittest. Such a law is recognized as operating in our own daily life and is accepted as a primary principle in commerce: the fit survive, the weak fail.
>
> The present day zoologist has available a wider knowledge than did Darwin and his immediate supporters, sufficient to leave some zoologists with the highest degree of doubt that there is any such law as "survival of the fittest" operating under ordinary conditions in nature.

Richardson then went on to describe how any zoologist who studies animals in the field will come upon many crippled creatures thriving along with their normal fellows. He spoke of five-legged frogs as not being uncommon, or frogs lacking one foot; and of many sea gulls likewise lacking one foot or having a broken or crippled leg. He spoke of rabbits, foxes, wolves, and dingoes that have lost a foot in a trap as being not at all uncommon. And, in passing, we may just add

---

[61] Kettering, Charles: quoted by R. M. Ritland, *A Search for Meaning in Nature*, Pacific Press Publ. Assoc., California, 1970, p. 40.
[62] Richardson, L. R., "The Survival of the Unfit," *New Zealand Listener*, September 26, 1952, p. 8.

personally that we have not infrequently seen one-legged chick-adees, even in the severest Canadian winter, which were able to look after themselves at a feeding-station, where as many as twelve other species came constantly. One winter we had two such chick-adees, and our impression was that both of them had developed a certain dominance in terms of pecking order over their fellows.

Richardson also wrote:[63]

> Any student of fish knows of many cases where mutilated and otherwise crippled animals not merely survive but flourish in spite of their impairment. In my own experience I have found a minnow with no jawbones to support the soft tissues of the jaw; many cases of fish blind in one eye; even one fish which had been totally blinded; and many cases of fish with permanent distortion of the backbone so that they were hump-backed, or wry-backed, and swam as clumsily as do the most grotesque breeds of goldfish. An extreme example was a fish whose whole tail was bent permanently at a right-angle to the body. Many of these and other cases were congenital deformities, and the animal had therefore survived essentially from birth to adulthood deformed in this way.

Richardson then dealt with a second category of animals, crippled by mutilation. Here he spoke of fish with part or all of the tail bitten off; one particular fish with about one third of its body bitten away; a full grown crayfish which had lost all except one of its legs; and other such instances in which it is hard to see how the animal could possibly survive, and yet in which it had indeed survived. Thus he observed:[64]

> This survival of crippled and deformed animals in the wild has profound implications. It paves the way to reinvestigation of such ideas as adaptation and perfection in nature. . . .
> Darwin explained such perfection as resulting from the struggle for existence, in which the better fitted survived to reproduce. The less suited were progressively eliminated in the competition with their fellows. The evidence shows that the intensity of competition necessary for the control of evolution in this way does not exist under natural conditions, otherwise cripples could not survive.

Richardson pointed out, furthermore, that whereas selective pressures are supposed to guarantee only the survival of fishes which are appropriately streamlined for effective predation or escape, this principle constantly breaks down in sea life. As he said, in many species the tail fin "is not a primary organ of locomotion and we can attach no functional value to it." He thought that there was no possibility yet of attributing efficiency to the many ornate and

---

[63] Ibid.
[64] Ibid.

grotesque kinds of tail which occur in some of the more exotic fishes:[65]

> They are not developed as swimming organs, and so may develop to any size or shape so long as they do not interfere with the activities of the fish. On the analysis of this and many other examples, we begin to see that ornateness and variety of structure is in fact associated with an absence of useful value.

So he concluded that the operation in Nature of a law of survival of the fittest would not produce a rich variety of animal structures, but would tend towards monotony and probably simplicity. Hence we reach, in his words, "a reasonable doubt that such a law operates in nature, a conclusion which is in agreement with the fact of the survival of the unfit."

Conclusion

It does not seem to me at all unlikely that the older naturalists had a much better understanding of things when they were quite willing to suppose that God delighted in beauty and variety in His handiwork, and introduced them entirely because of this delight — trusting that man would have sense enough to share it with Him. The millions of flowers whose sheer beauty increases the more closely they are examined and which bloom as often where man does not see them as where he does, and whose form can hardly contribute to their survival *per se* must surely be indicative of His prodigality in this respect. That we have an esthetic sense which we have reason to believe the animals do not share must surely suggest that God's thoughts are not altogether unlike our own in such things. Man has done himself no great service by attempting to repaint the fabric of Nature in colors which make it more like a battle scene than a display of God's perfection. It can only be a matter of time, surely, before people will rebel against this distorted view of Nature and once more seek to rediscover the wisdom and power of God in creation. When this time comes, our greater knowledge of Nature will so enormously enhance our sense of wonder and delight that the famous Bridgewater Treatises will be rewritten to the even greater glory of God.

---

[65] Ibid.

Part V
Is Man an Animal?

The question What is man? is probably the most profound that can be asked by man. . . .

I do not mean to say that the biological study of man or even that the scientific study of man in terms broader than biological can here and now, if ever, provide a satisfactorily complete answer to the question. . . .

The other, older approaches . . . theology . . . and other non-biological, non-scientific fields can still contribute, or can now contribute anew.

— *George Gaylord Simpson,*
Biology and Man

Introduction

I S MAN *really* an animal? To many people the answer must seem obvious. To ask the question at all is naive. Of course he is! Yet there are many informed people who would say with more caution, "Yes, man is an animal, but he is far *more* than an animal."

When it is asked in what ways he is more than an animal, it is customary to list such things as his possession of culture, his powers of abstract reasoning, his use of language, and possibly his self-consciousness: and then to add a few important anatomical differences, such as his permanently erect posture, and his possession of truly opposable thumbs combined with wide-angle stereoscopic vision. By reason of these man becomes a unique creator of culture.

Yet for all this, the feeling persists that such specialized features single man out as unique not so much because he is the only animal which has them, but because he has them in forms so much more highly developed than other creatures do. As we shall see, animals can communicate with one another by a kind of language; they learn from one another and *use* tools — which gives them a sort of culture. Some animals seem to be self-conscious at times. A few animals can stand erect, and some apes can even run erect for short distances. And a few species are able to oppose their thumbs in grasping things. So it could be said that man is, after all, only quantitatively different, different in degree but not *essentially* different in any classificatory sense.

But even a quantitative difference can reach such proportions as to constitute a new order of life, and it is recognized today that man really is in a category by himself for this very reason, as Dobzhansky put it:[1]

Perhaps the most satisfactory way of describing man's status is to say

---

[1] Dobzhansky, Theodosius: quoted by Herman K. Bleibtrue, "Some Problems in Physical Anthropology," in *Biennial Rev. Anthrop.*, Stanford U. Press, 1967, p. 255.

that he is unique in having a unique combination of abilities, rather than in the possession of any single unique ability.

In this way, quantitative differences, when they grow very large, become qualitative differences.

Yet Dobzhansky would still be the first to deny that man had anything other than an animal origin. If he is qualitatively different now, it is because of the accumulation of special abilities. But this accumulation was a quite natural process, to be explained ultimately in neo-Darwinian terms, Natural Selection acting upon random mutations. There is nothing supernatural about man's uniqueness.

On the other hand, the Bible clearly sets man apart in the final analysis not by pointing to his achievements, but by constantly emphasizing the fact that he is a fallen creature with a capacity for redemption, a redemption which involved the Incarnation. The answer to the question "What is man?" cannot be found without taking into account the fact that God Himself came into this world as Man and "visited him" (Ps. 8:4) in the person of His Son, the Lord Jesus Christ, in order to secure his redemption. God "objectified" Himself as a Man, in human form, as Oken put it.[2] Humanity was uniquely designed for this purpose, not merely for God's pleasure, but for His Self-expression; and this design involved not only his spiritual capacity, but his physical form and his intellectual endowment as well. This is what makes man unique and something quite other than animal in nature.

If the Bible is correct in saying that man is a fallen creature (and it never says this of any animal), that sin has affected not merely his spiritual nature, but also his mental faculties, so that he can neither be wholly right in his motivations nor completely sound in his thinking, it must be clear that man cannot define true humanness by studying himself as he now is. Just as the man whose vision is faulty cannot fit himself with corrective glasses unless he has the help of someone who is not similarly afflicted, so if man's perceptive abilities are at fault he cannot obtain a true picture of himself either — without outside help. He requires some yardstick external to himself, some standard of reference with which to compare himself, and thus to correct his definition of what humanness really is. Or, alternatively, such knowledge must come to him through Revelation. It cannot stem from his own reflections upon himself. But we believe that in Jesus Christ we have a dual revelation, a revelation of what God is like (John 14:9), and also a revelation of the nature of true manhood.

---

[2] Oken, Lorenz, *Lehrbuck der Naturphilosophie*, n.p., 1810, p. 26.

Sherrington's justly famous little book *Man on His Nature*[3] may give us useful leads, but it can only speak to us about what man is now. It cannot tell us what he was *unfallen*. Yet it is unfallen man whom we see in Jesus Christ, with powers humanly expressed, both of a spiritual *and* a physical nature, which we no longer possess in our present state. He perceived things we do not perceive. He claimed spiritual powers (and demonstrated them) that are totally beyond us. He used His body in ways entirely outside our capabilities — when walking on the water for instance. He had dominion over the forces of Nature beyond our wildest dreams — as when He stilled the wind and storm for example, or multiplied the loaves and fishes. He healed diseases by a mere command and thus utterly negates our finest medical skills by a simple act of will. And He did these things as Man in a human body, and He promised His disciples that they should do even greater things (John 14:12).

God's definition of what it really means to be a man is not our definition. God's design for man was not the creature we now see in ourselves. All we see in ourselves is but a pale shadow of true manhood, a marred spirit in a diseased body inadequately informed by a mind suffering from the noetic effects of sin. Man is a fallen creature, fallen not merely in spirit, but in mind and in body also.[4] His body is no longer the same body which God designed and created for him. We cannot know this except by revelation, but that revelation is explicit enough in stating that in crucial ways man's body is not now like Adam's. It suffered permanent damage in its organization in Eden, and it will not recover its proper constitution until the resurrection. It looks like a reasonable fascimile, but it received a mortal wound in the Fall, which has made it a shambles of its original stature even though its potential is still truly remarkable. It has not altogether lost its uniqueness in many significant ways, as we shall see in the next chapter. But in the meantime man is not really *man* any longer. C. S. Lewis put it so well:[5]

> The process (of the Fall of Adam), was not, I conceive, comparable to mere deterioration as it may now occur in a human individual; it was loss of status as a species. What man lost by the Fall was his original specific nature. . . .
> This condition was transmitted by heredity to all later generations, for it

---

[3] Sherrington, Sir Charles, *Man on His Nature*, Cambridge U. Press, 1963, 300 pp. Sherrington himself falls into the trap of "nothing-but-ism." Man's mind, he said, "is nothing more than the topmost rung continuous with related degrees below" (p. 156).

[4] On man's body as a fallen organism: see Part II, "The Nature of the Forbidden Fruit," in the Doorway Papers, Vol. V.

[5] Lewis, C. S., *The Problem of Pain*, Macmillan, New York, 1948, pp. 70,71.

was not simply what biologists call an acquired variation. It was the emergence of a new kind of man; a new species, never made by God, *had sinned its way into existence*. . . . It was a radical alteration of his constitution.

The fact is that we are faced with an anomaly in the natural order, for man is a creature who seems in many ways to be bound within its framework and yet is alien to it, lording it over the rest of the created order as though he were its acknowledged crown and yet clearly quite unequipped to conduct this lordship successfully. He has a potential and an inclination for the exercise of dominion which he somehow cannot fulfill. The climax of the supposed evolutionary process has been the production of a creature which has none of the in-built wisdom that has made the rest of the created order such a successful web of life. *Homo sapiens*, man the wise, is the greatest fool among God's creatures and demonstrates his lack of perception in the very classification which he has given himself as *sapiens*.

It is all very well to attribute this disastrous failure to some overcomplexification of his central nervous system, as is sometimes done.[6] *If* man arrived on the scene by some evolutionary process, this might be the explanation except that it is without logic since natural selection, which is the driving force in evolution, supposedly operates to eliminate every venture in Nature which is not in some way an improvement over the existing order, as Wood Jones put it:[7]

> If, in the ordering of Nature, life on earth was destined to flourish and multiply, to outfold its forms and increase its variety, it must be recognized as a tragic failure of its destiny that, so far, it has merely achieved the emergence of the arch-destroyer both of life and of the sources of food and shelter necessary for its maintenance.

The appearance of man as he is, is more logically explained by supposing that he is indeed the crown of creation and ought indeed to have proved himself to be its prime benefactor, but that something then went wrong which turned all his potential for good into an equal potential for evil. He is in fact sick in a way that none of the other animals are ever capable of being. But he is also redeemable in a way that none of the other animals are. In the final analysis, he is a creature unlike any other, not so much because he has certain faculties which are superior to theirs, but because he is capable of sin and of being redeemed, which no other animal ever is. There is, therefore, something about him which places him in a class entirely by himself. His destiny is different: his spirit goes upward to

---

[6] Overcomplexity of the central nervous system: E. J. Holmyard, "The Future of Man," *Endeavour*, January 1946, p. 2.

[7] Jones, F. Wood, *Trends of Life*, Arnold, London, 1953, p. 18.

God who gave it whereas the spirit of the beast goes downward to the earth (Eccl. 3:21). And in keeping with this fact, his origin is also different, not because he was created (for the animals were also created), but because he was created in the image of God (Gen.1:26).

Moreover, as we have seen, man had to be redeemed by a method which would allow God Himself to enter physically within the framework of His own created order and become Man in a form appropriate to His deity and without doing violence to His own Person as Creator.[8] No animal form below man would have sufficed for such an extraordinary event as the Incarnation of God Himself. Only a special creature, special both as to his spirit and as to the body which housed that spirit, could appropriately serve such a plan. Thus, man stands midway between the angels which have no bodies and are not therefore redeemable by such a *mode* of redemption and the animal world which has no spirit capable of sin which would create a *need* for redemption. Man is both more than an animal by reason of his creation, yet less than an animal by reason of his Fall. He is, in fact, something unique to which the term "animal" is not really applicable at all.

This paper is a study of man's assessment of himself apart from revelation, and then a consideration of the light we have from revelation, the revelation of true man in the person of Jesus Christ.

---

[8] The Incarnation: see Part IV, "The Virgin Birth and the Incarnation," in the Doorway Papers, Vol. V.

Chapter 1
The Uniqueness of Man

Once man is put together, everything else falls into place.

—Ana Maria O'Neill
Scientific Monthly
(February 1946)

WESTERN MAN'S assessment of himself in relation to the animal kingdom has passed through several phases. Within the context of the Christian view, man saw himself as so unique that it did not occur to him to enquire into the possibility of a relationship with the animals in any derivative sense; he merely shared God's world with them. But toward the end of the 17th century, western philosophy became enthralled with the idea that *all* living things were directly related in the form of what was called a Great Chain of Being.[9] Between each link in this chain, the distance was infinitesimally small, so small as to be really nonexistent. Just as Nature abhorred a vacuum in the physical order, so equally did Nature abhor discontinuity in the stream of life.[10]

At first it was not a question of the evolution of one thing out of another, but rather the feeling that God, of necessity, could not but fill out the chain with no missing links, since His creation would otherwise have been incomplete and imperfect by reason of the gaps it would contain. The chain was believed to begin with the minerals, merging into plant life, then on into animal life, thence to man, and then, logically, on into angelic forms, and up to God Himself. There were no missing links, nor were there any jumps. The universe was a smooth incline from nothing up to God, not a ladder with steps. Even the concept of species was denied. Only our ignorance led us to suppose that the chain was not complete.

During the 18th century, the idea that each successive form

---

[9] Lovejoy, Arthur O., *The Great Chain of Being*, Harper, New York, 1960: the Study of the History of an Idea.
[10] Ibid., p. 181.

could have emerged or *evolved* without discontinuity from the form below it, rather than being directly created, began to be tentatively proposed. In the 19th century the concept of evolution, much as we find it today, was crystallized. What Darwin contributed more specifically was the provision of a mechanism by which the evolutionary process was carried forward progressively by *natural* means, without the need for supernatural intervention at any stage.

And so man passed from his superior position as a unique creation to the lesser position of being only a link in a chain, a link which was not essentially of any greater importance than any other link. He had become part and parcel of the natural order, made of the same stuff, accountable in the same terms, obedient to the same physical laws, and destined to the same end.

But there is now some evidence of a change in sentiment, a reaction to this oversimplification. Man still seems to be a part of the chain, and yet he is not a part of it. Something new seems to have emerged with the appearance of man that has almost the quality of a break in the chain. Let us look at man's present assessment of his own position and the growing tendency to abandon the view that he is really "nothing but" a link in the Great Chain of Being, though admittedly the most complex link to emerge so far.

As an example of nothing-but-ism carried to its extreme, we have a statement such as this one quoted by Viktor Frankl:[11]

> Man is nothing but a complex biochemical mechanism powered by a combustion system which energizes a computer with prodigious storage facilities for retaining encoded information.

Today, the practice of reducing man to mere physics and chemistry is not quite so popular as it was. Even so, one may still find authorities who delight in oversimplification and seem determined to reduce man's self-esteem by saying that he is nothing but "a made over ape," as Montagu and Brace do.[12] G. Gaylord Simpson objected on principle, and quite rightly, to the tendency to reduce man by such a simple formula to a mere descendant of some other animal:[13]

> These fallacies arise from what Julian Huxley calls "the-nothing-but" school. It was felt or said that because man is an animal, a primate, and so on, he is *nothing but* an animal or *nothing but* an ape with a few extra tricks. It is a fact that man is an animal, but it is not a fact that he is nothing but an animal.

[11] Frankl, Viktor: quoted by Arthur Koestler, *Beyond Reductionism*, Hutchinson, London, 1969, p. 403.

[12] Brace, C. L., and Montagu, Ashley, *Man's Evolution*, Macmillan, New York, 1965, p. 53.

[13] Simpson, G. G., *The Meaning of Evolution*, Yale U. Press, 1952, p. 233.

Let us assume for the moment that man *is* an animal but with some highly significant extras, and see what these extras are, according to the experts. One of the earlier lists of this nature was composed by Linnaeus.[14] He recognized in man six aspects in which he was a unique mammal — theological, moral, natural, physiological, dietetic, and pathological. This is an interesting list because it anticipates some areas of investigation which his immediate successors tended to neglect, namely, the dietetic and pathological ones. Raymond Pearl in his book *Man the Animal*[15] in fact ignored these two aspects even though he referred to Linnaeus' listing. Pearl thought that man's uniqueness is especially reflected in his habitually upright posture, his large brain, his capacity for articulate speech, and his longer life span.

Ales Hrdlicka in his monumental work on *The Skeletal Remains of Early Man* argued that man branched off from some primate predecessor and became truly human as soon as he developed the ability to shape stones and other objects, adopted a habitually upright posture thus completely liberating his hands, experienced a reduction both of the canine teeth and of the jaw itself, developed a relatively large brain, employed articulate language, experienced a dawning self-consciousness, and increasingly refined his social relationships.[16]

Ashley Montagu in his *Introduction to Physical Anthropology* listed 21 features in which man differs from *all* (his emphasis) other primates. These features have reference to anatomy, as follows:[17]

Fully erect posture
Bipedal locomotion
Legs much longer than arms
Comparatively vertical face
Great reduction in projection of jaws
Great reduction of canine teeth
Absence of a bony diastema in upper jaw for the reception of the tip of the canine tooth
Prominent nose with elongated tip (i.e., elongated beyond the nasal bone)
Outward rolled mucous membrane of lips
A well marked chin
A forward lumbar convexity or curve
Nonopposable great toe, set in line with other toes

---

[14] Linnaeus: quoted by Raymond Pearl, *Man the Animal*, Principia, Indiana, 1946, p. 4.
[15] Pearl, Raymond, *Man the Animal*, Principia, Indiana, 1946, pp. 4ff.
[16] Hrdlicka, Ales, *The Skeletal Remains of Early Man*, Smithsonian Instit., 1930, p. 11.
[17] Montagu, Ashley, *Introduction to Physical Anthropology*, Thomas, Springfield, Ill., 1945, p. 43.

Foot arched transversely and from front to rear
Relative hairlessness of body
Absence of tactile hairs
Brain more than twice as large as the largest nonhuman primate brain
The occiput projecting backwards
Highly rolled margin of the ear
Absence of premaxillary bone from the anterior aspect of the face
Iliac fossae or blades of pelvis facing one another
Longer growth period

He then remarked about this list: "There are, of course, many other features in which man differs respectively from the prosimiae (pre-monkeys), the monkeys, and the apes. With respect to more qualitative features man differs from the nonhuman primates in the following potentialities or traits: (1) the capacity for symbolic thought, (2) articulate speech, and (3) the development of a complex culture."[18] He commented: "It is in the possession of these . . . potentialities, and in their active realization and transmission, from generation to generation, that man qualitatively differs so very greatly from all other primates, and the possession of which enables him to become a human being."

In one of his essays, Julian Huxley also made a list of the characteristics which he believed to be unique to the human species:[19]

Language and conceptual thought
Transmission of knowledge by written record
Tools and machinery
Biological dominance over all other species
Individual variability
The use of the forelimb for manipulating purposes only
All year round fertility
Art, humor, science, and religion

It will be noted that there are differences in emphasis in these lists. Raymond Pearl had a particular interest in problems relative to man as a creature who is now beginning to crowd the world with his numbers, and such factors as fertility and longevity especially concerned him. The list composed by Hrdlicka, who spent much time in field work, not unnaturally singles out those marks of humanness which would appeal to the eye of the archaeologist/anthropologist. The list of the more strictly physical anthropologist, Ashley Montagu, reflects his interest in total anatomy. The list proposed by

---

[18] Ibid., pp. 43f.
[19] Huxley, Sir Julian: quoted by Arthur Koestler, *The Ghost in the Machine*, Hutchinson, London, 1967, p. 297.

Huxley begins to place more emphasis upon the cultural aspects of manhood. It was not that Huxley was disinterested in physical anthropology, for he did draw up a table of comparative bone lengths for man and the manlike apes, with the intention of showing that man falls within the range of these apes and to demonstrate that the apes often differ more from one another than some one of them differed from man. His table is shown below.[20]

Limb/Spinal Column Proportions
of Man and Man-like Apes

	Spinal Column	Arm	Leg	Hand	Foot
European Man	100	80*	**117**	26*	35*
Gorilla	100	115	96	36	41
Chimpanzee	100	96	90	43	39
Orangutan	100	**122**	88*	**48**	**52**

All figures are in percentages, the spinal column in each case being 100 percent. Asterisks mark minimum values, bold face maximum.

Commenting on this, A. L. Kroeber remarked:[21]

> If such a relationship held for all or most traits, it would tend to suggest that man should be classified in the group of the apes rather than alongside of it, much as the reconstructed family trees have already suggested.
>
> However, what Huxley in the ardor of his argument did not note is that, in the proportions cited, man is regularly at one end of the ape scale at either the maximum or the minimum of the joint range.
>
> This gives us pause, because it seems to suggest that man does after all stand off on one side by himself.

To these anatomical differences, Weidenreich in his *Apes, Giants and Man* added certain others:[22]

1. The long bones of the lower limb, especially the thigh bone, are longer in man than the long bones of the upper limb, especially the humerus, while in anthropoids the conditions are reversed.[23] It is

---

[20] Huxley's table is taken from A. L. Kroeber, *Anthropology*, Harcourt & Brace, New York, 1948, p. 56.

[21] Kroeber, A. L., *Anthropology*, Harcourt & Brace, New York, 1948, p. 56.

[22] Weidenreich, Franz, *Apes, Giants and Man*, U. of Chicago Press, 1948, p. 6.

[23] This reversal of limb proportions does not apply to the prosimians: see A. H. Schultz, "Primatology in Its Relation to Anthropology," *Current Anthropology*, ed. W. L. Thomas, U. of Chicago Press, 1956, p. 49.

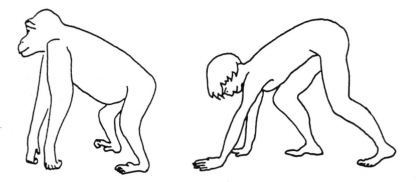

Fig. 12. Difference in posture between ape and man on all fours.

this fact which makes the gait of man attempting to walk on all fours so completely different from that of other animals. (Fig.12) Other quadrupeds stand higher at the shoulder than at the seat but when man attempts this posture his stance is almost ludicrously difficult — even in the infant.

2. The human trunk is short in proportion to the lower limb while, here, again the conditions are reversed in anthropoids.

3. The human vertebral column is curved in a complex way alternately forwards and backwards while in anthropoids it is either straight or uniformly curved backwards.

Such features as these, as we shall see in Chapters 2-4, contribute enormously to the flexibility of the human body and its ready adaptability to many different postures which can be maintained for long periods with comparative ease. For a culture-bound "animal" whose activities both at work and at rest are tremendously varied, such features play an important role.

There are a few other anatomical differences which these particular authorities have not mentioned but which are of great significance to man as a creator of culture. All animals other than man have either four feet or four hands. The primates use the two hind hands habitually as feet, supporting only part of their weight on the fore hands. In spite of unknown centuries of supposed "natural selection," these hind hands have never become reorganized into true feet. The anatomical form of the human foot is significantly different as we shall see, thereby making man unique in this respect in the possession of two perfectly functional feet and two amazingly adept hands.

Another anatomical uniqueness in man is what has been called a wasp waist, a waist which not only provides him with greater trunk flexibility but also allows him (and her) to wear clothing as adornment in an extraordinary variety of designs, supported from the waist as readily as from the shoulders. The chimpanzee at the circus may be dressed like a person but severe limitations are placed upon the chimpanzee clothing manufacturer by the fact that everything must be hung from the shoulders. In terms of self-expression, clothing is capable of adding a whole dimension to the cultural life of man. And as Julian Huxley was wise enough to note, nudity does not become adult man except on rare occasions and for a short time in life, whereas clothing tremendously enhances his stature and adds grace in an infinite variety of ways. It is as though he were designed to allow for this.

Though many animals have very graceful *necks*, those animals which are supposed to be man's nearest relatives, do not. The structure of man's neck is such that by balancing the head centrally, the *foramen magnum* being well forward, the demand for powerful muscles which make the neck massive and indeed almost non-existent as a flexible junction between head and shoulders, is largely eliminated: so the head can move freely on the shoulders in a way which is quite foreign to the head movements of most of the other primates.

There are some highly significant differences between man and all other animals in the degree of dependency of the newborn both in terms of the achievement of physiological maturity and in terms of individual safety against attackers. The young of virtually all other species can fend for themselves in a remarkably short time whereas the extended period of human dependency results in a situation where a number of members of a single family will continue *as a family*, even when the age spread is quite extensive. In terms of interpersonal development, and combined with the very slow rate of maturing of the brain itself in man (by contrast with animals), there is a greatly prolonged period of educability which is entirely missing in all other species. All these are actually related and in a unique way have a combined effect upon individuation.

Man has a temperature regulating system whicn is truly unique and has rendered him a completely ubiquitous creature without the territorial restrictions which seem to apply to all other species. And perhaps, not unrelated in a sense, is the fact that he alone is omnivorous while other creatures are naturally (that is, except under special stress) either herbivorous or carnivorous. Man can live equally well on a purely carnivorous diet if necessary as the Eskimo has done, or equally well on a herbivorous diet as many Eastern people have done who are virtually dependent upon cereals such as rice.

In terms of social organization, there are a tremendous number of highly significant differences between human and animal societies, human societies being essentially organized along cultural lines and animal societies along biological lines. And one very significant difference which lies at the root of the structure of these two contrasting types of social organization is the great importance which the male assumes in human society. In virtually all animal societies the role of the male is exceedingly limited, and in many cases the male is scarcely a part of the society at all, being either ejected by it or voluntarily withdrawing.

Such, then, are some of the clues that we are to pursue and explore in greater detail in the following chapters. The kind of parallelisms which encourage the writing of so many books for popular consumption which seem to delight in reducing man and his society to the terms of animal life have undoubtedly contributed greatly to the blurring of the fundamental lines of distinction which actually put the two into very different categories. The parallels, however, merely look promising, but actually at one time greatly hindered fruitful research by blinding even the experts to these critical differences, in much the same way that the generative idea of evolution was formerly applied mistakenly to virtually every aspect of historical development to the detriment of the truth. The distorting effect was recognized by cultural anthropologists in due time, and it has since been almost everywhere acknowledged as an unfortunate mistake.

Let us then examine these differences with care, that the significances of them in answering the question "What is man?" may become apparent.

Chapter 2
The Human Brain:
Its Size and Its Complexity

IF INDIVIDUAL features of human anatomy and physiology are considered separately, and are compared separately with parallel features found in the animal world, a fairly good case might be made out for the derivation of man by evolution from some animal, presumably among the primates. But if the features of man's anatomy and physiology are taken as a whole, viewed in relation to each other and seen as an integrated unity, the situation is rather different. Virtually every one of the anatomical and physiological features listed in the previous chapter are found singly in rudimentary or developed form somewhere else. And even some of man's characteristic social and cultural forms of behavior are reflected, randomly distributed, among different species also in rudimentary forms.

What I am particularly anxious to make clear, however, is that no single animal, nor any single species, exhibits these features as a whole. Individuals and species can be found which have one or several of these features, but not *all of them.* An awareness of these facts will help us to avoid attaching importance to differences in structure, etc., beyond what is proper in the light of the evidence. At the same time, it will help us to see more clearly that it really is the combination of features which has made man such a unique creature.

If the same Designer and Architect formed the animals as formed man, it should surely not be at all surprising to find that successful "solutions" to problems faced by all living things are used over and over again in different contexts. And this is precisely what we do find.

All living things are chemically organized according to a single basic pattern involving the same nucleic acids, peptides, and amino acids, though not necessarily making the same selection. In his contribution to the symposium published under the title *The Origins of Prebiological Systems,* Peter T. Mora suggested that the amazing similarity in the biochemical processes of living systems implies that life originated only once.[24] There is, however, an alternative implication: namely, that having designed a perfectly effective biochemical process, the Creator thereafter employed it as a basis for every living form that He created. Uniformity in this respect would therefore just as likely be evidence of a single Architect at work, as evidence of the evolution of a single chance product. In the same vein it should be pointed out that all striated muscle is also built on an almost identical pattern in all living things. In this connection, J. D. Bernal draws the same kind of conclusion that Mora drew: viz., that such "an ingenious device," to use his term,[25] can surely have been invented only once and must therefore have been inherited by all the different phyla from the first prototype, "probably to perform ciliary motion." As in the previous case, it may just as well be evidence of a master design being reemployed many times.

When we look at the anatomy and physiology of man, we see plenty of evidence of this reemployment of successful design features already used elsewhere. The similarity of many of the vital organs of living organisms is in no way necessarily evidence of descent. The appearance of almost identical eye structures in the octopus and in mammals should be sufficient demonstration of this fact. Consequently, certain design features in one species that serve a particular purpose may be found in another species in very similar form, yet serving a somewhat different purpose. When we compare man with the animals which are structurally most like him, and are therefore presumed to be most nearly related, we are driven by some compulsive thought process of the human mind to arrange the structures in some kind of ascending or descending order and to assume that this order represents degrees of relatedness. We may tend to do this even when we do not accept the theory of evolution. We make the assumption that a larger brain is a later brain because we recognize that this happens as the infant grows into the adult. We also tend to assume that anything which looks more complex *is* more complex, because in most man-made products this is the case.

And so in considering the relationship between man and the primates from which he is supposedly evolved, it may be well to look into a critical organ (the brain) and a critical anatomical feature (the

---

[24] Mora, Peter T., "The Folly of Probability," in *The Origin of Prebiological Systems,* ed. Sidney W. Fox, Academic Press, New York, 1965, p. 45.

[25] Bernal, J. D., "Molecular Matrices for Living Systems," in Sidney W. Fox, ref. 24, p. 79.

ability to stand erect), and see to what extent the differences are important. And it may be said, in anticipation, that although we do not yet know exactly why the size of the human brain is so much larger than that of the ape brain, we have a somewhat better idea of why man's erect posture is of such great importance. The two combined, however, make all the difference in the world in terms of the potential of man by contrast with that of his supposed nearest relatives.

The feeling that brain size or surface complexity is of crucial importance in terms of intelligence or mental capacity and that man excels in both, has plagued anthropological research for almost a hundred years. Indeed, so compelling is this conviction that anthropologists are guilty not infrequently of either doctoring or distorting the evidence in order to close the gap between man and ape, by raising the cranial capacity or brain size of potential *missing links*, or reducing the cranial capacity of very early man.

It will be helpful to have some basic figures, drawn from a number of sources, which will give an overall picture of size ranges of primate brains. Zuckerman gave the following cranial capacities:[26]

Female chimpanzee	366 ± 6.5 cc.
Male chimpanzee	399 ± 7.0 cc.
Female gorilla	466 ± 10.4 cc.
Male gorilla	543 ± 4.3 cc.
Pithecanthropus erectus	1026 ± 34.2 cc.

The Australopithecines, represented by a number of supposedly separate genera (*Paranthropus, Pleisianthropus*),[27] which were hailed as missing links but are now believed to come a little too late in the geological time scale as currently held, were of particular interest to evolutionists because their cranial capacity was believed to be between 450 and 550 cc., which, combined with their much debated erectness of posture, seemed to fit rather well between other primates and man.

Modern man shows an extraordinarily wide range of cranial capacities. There are records of capacities as low as 800 cc. in individuals of normal size though only found among idiots;[28] and it is commonly agreed that man is not mentally normal with a cranial

---

[26] Zuckerman, Sir Solly, "*An* Ape or *the* Ape," *Jour. Roy. Anthrop. Instit.* 81, parts 1 and 2 (1952):63.

[27] Australopithecines: J. T. Robinson, "The Origins and Adaptive Radiation of Australopithecines," in *Human Evolution*, ed. N. Korn and F. Thompson, Holt, Rinehart & Winston, New York, 1967, p. 296.

[28] Ibid., p. 284.

capacity of less than 900 cc. This figure is sometimes referred to as the Cerebral Rubicon for *Homo sapiens*. Human dwarfs are known with brain volumes which may not exceed 300-400 cc. These are not normal dwarfs but are known as *nanocephalic* or "bird-brained" dwarfs.[29] Their smaller brain of course means far fewer functioning brain cells even than in many chimpanzees, yet they are quite capable of learning language and although usually mentally defective, their behavior is still quite specifically human. In referring to these individuals, David Pilbeam remarked, "This clearly underlines the important point that it is brain structure rather than brain size which is so important in species-specific behavior."[30] I think there is some reason, as we shall see, to question whether even brain structure is important in any specific way, though it may be that the protein composition of the brain substance itself is species-specific.

Occasionally one sees the cranial capacity of the gorilla given as 685 cc. which comes close to the minimum for *Homo sapiens* (although idiotic).[31] It should be noted, however, that this was one single gorilla measurement, and though the figure has been quoted many, many times and often taken as a norm for gorillas, to my knowledge it has never been duplicated. The use of the figure illustrates how strong the temptation is to fill out the series from animals to man. Weidenreich placed the gorilla's cranial capacity at only 620 cc., and he gave the average for the whole anthropoid group as being "only 415 cc."[32]

As we have said, brain weights among human beings vary enormously. In giving measurements of brain size for contemporary man, it is customary to use grams rather than cubic centimeters, but for reasons which it is not necessary to enter into here, the two forms of measurement in this case are virtually the same. The average for the adult male European is about 1375 gm. whereas the brain of Turgenev, the Russian novelist, weighed 2021 gm.[33] It was exceeded by that of only two others so far recorded: one was an imbecile. Then there is the record of a laborer whose brain weighed 1925 gm. and a bricklayer, 1900 gm. The brain weight of Gambetta, the famous French statesman, was only 1294 gm., or less than the average

[29] Human dwarfs: W. E. LeGros Clark, "Bones of Contention," in *Human Evolution*, ref. 27, p. 305.

[30] Pilbeam, David, *The Evolution of Man*, Thames & Hudson, London, 1970, p. 202.

[31] Clark, W. E. LeGros, ref. 29, p. 305. In fairness, Clark gives this figure for *a*, not *the*, gorilla.

[32] Weidenreich, Franz, ref. 22, p. 11.

[33] Turgenev, Gambetta, etc.: George Dorsey, *Why We Behave Like Human Beings*, Blue Ribbon Books, New York, 1925, p. 11.

European. A woman's brain is slightly smaller than man's, and the largest woman's brain recorded was 1742 gm. — she was insane. Another woman's brain of large size weighed 1580 gm., and she also was insane. It is some evidence of the unimportance of brain size that the brain of Anatole France weighed only 1017 gm. while the brain of Bismark weighed 1807 gm.[34]

When we come to review fossil man, we meet with some surprises. While certain of the supposedly earliest fossils fall nicely into place, some of them do not do so. As we have seen, Pithecanthropus erectus was given a capacity of 1026 cc. by Zuckerman but somewhat lower (900-1000) by William Howells.[35] The same authority gave a figure for Sinanthropus of 1150 cc.[36] Th.s seems to be in the right kind of ascending scale. But then Solo Man,[37] who was placed only just above Pithecanthropus erectus in the evolutionary scale by Howells, had a cranial capacity of 1300 cc. — which is essentially modern man's. Once again the order seems to be "satisfactory," but then something goes wrong. For Solo Man is considered to have been contemporary with Neanderthal Man, and Neanderthal Man had a cranial capacity which in several specimens was in excess of 1625 cc., which is far *above* modern man.[38] Two other primitive fossil skulls, *Wadjak* and *Boskop,* had cranial capacities, respectively, of 1550-1650 cc. and 1800 cc. which is even higher.[39]

Because we happen to have some cultural remains of his which are in every way remarkable, Cromagnon Man is generally considered the high point in the development of *ancient Homo sapiens.* Yet Cromagnon had a slightly larger brain capacity than Neanderthal — 1590-1660 cc. — which is 15 percent larger than ours.[40] It might be doubted therefore (if we are guided merely by cranial capacity) whether modern man is really an advance on his ancestors. Cromagnon could be the high point of *modern Homo sapiens,* too.

The actual significance of brain size is being called into question, and so also is its structural form or surface complexity. Consider these facts. Julian Huxley was satisfied that the evidence demonstrates that a larger brain is a better learning organ than a

[34] Bismark: Stanley Cobb, "Brain and Personality," *Amer. Jour. Psychiatry* 116, no. 10 (1960):938.

[35] Howells, William, *Mankind So Far,* Doubleday, New York, 1944, p. 138. Throughout this section, values given by different authorities vary, since measurements often involve certain imponderables such as skulls distorted out of shape by the ground.

[36] Ibid., p. 144.

[37] Ibid., p. 179.

[38] Neanderthal Man, cranial capacity: William Howells, ref. 35, p. 166.

[39] Wadjack and Boskop Man: William Howells, ref. 35, p. 192.

[40] Cromagnon Man: Ashley Montagu, ref. 17, p. 92.

smaller one, though the learning process may take longer.[41] In a nutshell, his argument is that an *absolutely* larger brain (i.e., not larger relative to the body itself) will have a *relatively* as well as an absolutely larger number of cells in its cortex. A larger number of cortical cells makes more elaborate learning possible. The experiments upon which Huxley based this were conducted by the German biologist, Rensch. The data apply equally well not only to higher animals like birds, but even to beetles. By contrast, Zeuner reported that brain size becomes smaller with domestication, in spite of the fact that domestication almost certainly is accompanied by some enrichment of the environment, at least for the dogs which were the subject of his report.[42] He explained this as being the result of atrophy of some senses which become less important. Mention is made of an enriched environment here because Rozenweig found that in rats, at least, an enriched environment leads to cortical enlargement as well as increased convolution.[43] Leakey, as though to confuse the issue even further, reported the finding that some notable scientists have smaller cranial capacity than some notable pugilists.[44] Is it possible that the pugilist's brain enlarges in some area that has to do with his fighting capacity whereas the scientist's brain diminishes without duly compensating for the loss in some other area related to thinking?

Actually, it appears now that there is less certainty than previously even about the validity of "localization theories" i.e., the idea that certain parts of the brain are set aside for certain functions. Years ago, Ralph Gerard, in attempting to localize in the brain such functions as the faculty of speech, etc., wrote: "It remains sadly true that most of our present understanding of mind would remain as valid and useful if, for all we know, the cranium was stuffed with cotton wadding."[45] This was written in 1946. Similarly, R. E. D. Clark noted that according to K. S. Lashley, no part of the upper brain is vital, but one part may take over the functions of another with relative ease.[46] The debate continues and even a symposium on localization of function in the cerebral cortex held in Oxford in 1954 came up with no altogether clear cut evidence of such area speci-

[41] Huxley, Sir Julian, *Evolution in Action*, Chatto & Windus, London, 1953, p. 99.

[42] Zeuner, F. E., "Domestication of Animals," in *A History of Technology*, Vol. I, ed. Charles Singer et al., Oxford U. Press, 1954, p. 348.

[43] Rosenzweig, Mark R., et al., "Brain Changes in Response to Experience," *Sci. American*, February 1972, p. 22.

[44] Leakey, L. S. B., a panel on "Man as an Organism," in *Evolution After Darwin*, Vol. III, ed. Sol Tax, U. of Chicago Press, 1960, p. 168.

[45] Gerard, Ralph, "The Biological Basis of Imagination," *Sci. Monthly*, June 1946, p. 487.

[46] Lashley, K. S.: quoted by R. E. D. Clark in *Science and Religion* 1, no. 5 (1948):223.

ficity, except that language seems to be organized in the left hemisphere in those who are congenitally right-handed, and *vice versa*. *Science News* reported in 1966 that a man suffering from brain cancer had *his entire left cerebral hemisphere* removed and, contrary to all medical expectations, regained some ability to speak, write, comprehend speech, and move his right limbs.[47] The report said, "The brain may have a much greater capacity to reorganize itself than was believed." There *are* neural connections between areas of the brain and bodily functions, but if these areas are damaged or destroyed, other areas seem to take over. One of those who took part in the case (Dr. J. A. B. Bates) showed that even though such connections do seem to exist, precisely the same responses are obtained by stimulation of the white fibers of the cortico-spinal column as by stimulation of the gray matter itself.[48] It was felt that the position he took on this implied a radical break with the traditional doctrine of the hierarchical organization of function in the central nervous system.

A. Irving Hallowell, in a contribution to a Darwin Centennial Symposium, made this significant remark:[49]

> So far as integrative functions are concerned, the present weight of evidence appears to focus upon the influence exercised by the masses of nerve cells in the upper part of the brain stem upon the more recently evolved cortical areas. An older notion that the cortex itself was of prime significance because it was somehow "the seat of consciousness" no longer seems to make complete neurological sense.

He then added this footnote:[50]

> Popular tradition, which seems to be largely shared by scientific men, has taken it for granted that the cortex is a sort of essential organ for the purposes of thinking and consciousness, and that final integration of neural mechanisms takes place in it.
>
> Perhaps this is only natural since there has been an extraordinary enlargement of the cortex in the human brain, and, at the same time, man seems to be endowed with intellectual functions of a new order.
>
> However, the whole anterior frontal area, on one or both sides, may be removed without loss of consciousness. During the amputation the individual may continue to talk unaware of the fact that he is being deprived of that area which most distinguishes his brain from that of the chimpanzee.

[47] *Science News* 90 (December 24, 1966):555.
[48] Bates: referred to by O. L. Zangwill, "Localization in the Cerebral Cortex," *Nature*, October 16, 1954, p. 719.
[49] Hallowell, A. Irving, "Self, Society and Culture in Phylogenetic Perspective," in *Evolution After Darwin*, Vol. 2, ref. 44, p. 344.
[50] Hallowell: quoted by W. Penfield and T. Rasmussen, *The Cerebral Cortex of Man*, Macmillan, New York, 1950, pp. 204-206, 226.

The most complete study in condensed form of which I am aware, of the relationship between brain size, both absolute and relative, and surface complexity was written by Weidenreich in a paper entitled "The Human Brain in the Light of Its Phylogenetic Development." It is difficult to summarize such a compact statement of the facts of the case, but we shall make an attempt. As a kind of introduction to his analysis of the data, Weidenreich observed:[51]

> Some time ago I came across a pamphlet published in 1934, which was written by an English physician. In the author's opinion, the only factors that determined man's evolution since his beginnings as a primitive primate are environment and natural selection.
> But his starting point is the premise, "Cranial capacity is a fairly accurate measure of the mental status from the most primitive primates to *Homo sapiens*." The self-confidence with which this statement is made is typical.

Weidenreich then admitted candidly that we do not know of any fact which proves that mere increase in size of the brain is tantamount to an advance in mental ability. Indeed, increase of body size is normally accompanied by an increase in brain size, so that the elephant has a brain that weighs almost 5000 gm. and the brain of a whale may reach 10,000 gm. And yet for all that, *in proportion to the weight of the body*, the whale has a much smaller brain than man. This might seem to give man the edge, until it is discovered that the dwarf monkeys of South America, the marmosets, far surpass man in this respect, having 1 gram of brain per 27 gm. of body substance, whereas man has 1 gram of brain to 44 gm. of body substance.[52] And man is surpassed even more in these proportions by the capuchin monkey with one gram of brain substance for 17.5 gm. of body substance. It is as Weidenreich observed,[53] "Therefore, neither the absolute nor the relative size of the brain can be used to measure the degree of mental ability in animals or in man."

He then turned to the discussion of the surface pattern of the hemispheres and noted that primates and man do not differ from other mammalian orders with regard to the presence and abundance of the wrinkle system:[54]

> We are lost again if we suppose that the number of complexity of the

---

[51] Weidenreich, Franz, "The Human Brain in the Light of Its Phylogenetic Development," *Sci. Monthly*, August 1948, p. 103.

[52] The fact is well known: see Adolph Schultz, "The Specializations of Man and His Place Among the Catarrhine Primates," in Cold Spring Harbor Symposia on Quantitative Biology 15 (1951):45. Also Sir Solly Zuckerman, "Myths and Methods in Anatomy," *Jour. Roy. Coll. Surg.* (Edinburgh) 11, no. 2 (1966):92.

[53] Weidenreich, Franz, ref. 51, pp. 104,105.

[54] Ibid., p. 106.

wrinkles is co-related with progress or perfection of mental faculties.

The Capuchin monkey, which many experimental psychologists regard as equal in docility (i.e., educability) to any highly gifted chimpanzee, possesses an almost smooth brain surface, whereas the chimpanzee has a wrinkled one that comes close to that of man.

The whale and its relatives, however, again steal the show. They have the greatest number and finest wrinkles all over the hemispheres, and the most intricate arrangement in the whole animal kingdom.

He thus concluded that all the recorded facts indicate that neither the size nor the form of the brain, nor the surface of the hemispheres or their wrinkled pattern in general or in detail, can possibly furnish a reliable clue to the amount and degree of general or special mental qualities. So there it is. Weidenreich said:[55]

> In the face of all these facts, it is hard to understand why people cannot get rid of the idea that mere size or configuration of a special convolution or fissure must give a clue to the mental qualities in general and to those of certain individuals in particular. . . .

From the anatomical point of view, it must be rather obvious, therefore, that the uniqueness of man cannot be tied to the organ of *brain,* though there is no question that it *is* related to his capacity of *mind,* as K. A. Yonge observed:[56]

> It is in the ability to think about thinking that man regards himself as unique in the animal kingdom. It is not simply in his ability to think, that he can claim uniqueness, although he is vastly superior. Animals show their ability to associate one past experience with another and, as a result, to arrive at some plan of action. The rat learning his way through the maze, the chimpanzee figuring out a means to obtain the food out of arm's reach, the dog herding sheep. . . . This, for purposes of this Paper, is evidence of thinking. But man can think about thinking.

Thus it is easy to confuse the *brain* of man with the brain of the animal, and say that in this respect man is merely a superior animal. But it is not possible to compare the *mind* of man with the mind of the animal, for they appear to be in different categories. Konrad Lorenz wrote:[57]

> The central nervous system of animals is constructed differently from ours, and the physiological processes in it are also different from what happens in our brain. These qualitative differences are sufficient to make us conclude that whatever subjective phenomena may correspond to neural processes in animals must be considerably different from what we, ourselves, experience.

---

[55] Ibid., pp. 106,107.

[56] Yonge, K. A., "Of Birds, Bats and Bees: A Study of Schizophrenic Thought Disorders," *Canad. Psychiatric Assoc. Jour.* 3, no. 1 (1958):1.

[57] Lorenz, Konrad, *On Aggression,* Bantam Books, New York, 1967, p. 202.

In summary, then, there is no precisely defineàble way in which man's brain can be considered anatomically superior to the brains of animals below him. Neither in its size nor in its surface complexity does its uniqueness seem to lie. That there is a *qualitative* difference, however, is almost universally agreed. But to define this qualitative difference is in a sense an impossible task. Where is the decisive point at which the uniqueness of *any* "different" thing becomes determinate? Who can really tell?

Most assuredly, man's *mind* is vastly different, no matter how similar his brain cells may be to animal brain cells. So, somewhere, some other factor has added a dimension which is missing in the animal world. We can see the *effects* of this dimension at once. And in a small way we can also discern some of the reasons why this added dimension was effective in man where it almost certainly could not have been effective in any other animal. A certain combination of anatomical features in the design of his body as a whole has allowed the special potential of his mind to express itself in unique ways. These features, anatomical though they are, have effects far removed from any mere biological advantage. They have permitted not merely the creation of a superior technology — for some animals build houses and construct dams, which are forms of technology of a sort — but a whole series of cultural phenomena: language and art, social organization in which the individual may *consciously* sacrifice himself for the good of others, philosophy and science, ceremony and worship. . . . And above all, and most significantly of all, these features have provided an entirely appropriate channel for the revelation of God in Christ by incarnation in a truly human form.

Chapter 3
The Erectness of Man

I T HAS often been said that man's hands are an extension of his mind. When we come to deal with speech we shall see that this is profoundly true. In the meantime, let us consider the fact that his hands are what they are anatomically, and serve the purposes they serve culturally, because of man's erect posture. And here, again, it would be easy to suppose that his erectness is not essentially different from that of a number of other creatures, except that he retains it as a normal posture, whereas animals adopt it only for short intervals. The situation is, however, more complex than this, with many factors being involved — among which are the structure of his feet, the structure of his spinal column and pelvis, the relative proportional length of his limbs, the structure of his neck, and even the configuration of his windpipe and voice box.

In an attempt to minimize the significance of man's erectness, it is well known that Thomas Huxley falsified a diagram. in which he showed four skeletons, three of the primates of increasing size standing in line behind a skeleton of a man.[58] His object was to indicate that man was not the only creature who could stand upright. But in order to emphasize his point, he posed the animal skeletons in an unnaturally upright position — as Weidenreich points out, a position which is not at all characteristic of them — whereas man was put in an equally unnatural position with slightly bent knees (Fig.13a). Although some of the primates do maintain an upright position for a short time, it is generally held that no animals (other than birds) remain erect for more than a total of 25 percent of their waking life, and this 25 percent is made up, for the most part, of brief interludes lasting only a few minutes at any one time. And the

---

[58] Huxley, Thomas: see Franz Weidenreich, ref. 22, p. 6; and for Huxley's *Apologia*, see *Dawn*, September 1931, p. 267.

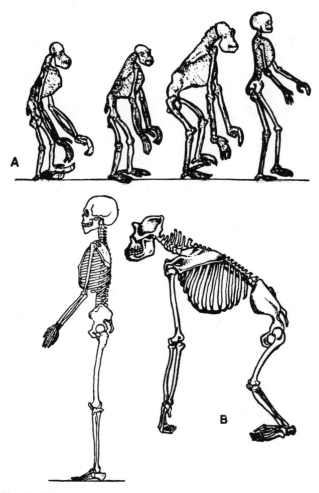

Fig. 13. (A) Thomas Huxley's doctored diagram; (B) the true posture of man and ape.

Fig. 14. The human and ape "foot" contrasted.

primates stoop forward even when erect (Fig.13b), whereas man is truly vertical.[59] A great deal more is involved in sustained erect posture than merely a decision to stand up. Animals which are forced to remain in an upright position for an undue length of time may lose consciousness. The classical experiments on this were carried out by Leonard Hill in 1895.[60] Or, if they do not actually faint due to the fact that their circulatory mechanisms are not adjusted for this kind of change, then they very quickly become fatigued and will fight to regain a normal horizontal position. F. G. Parsons,[61] writing in the *Encyclopedia Britannica* observed, "There is a greater gap between the musculature of man and that of the other primates than there is between many different orders, and this is usually traceable either directly or indirectly to the assumption of the erect posture." But in his *Descent of Man*, Darwin did not appreciate this.[62] To him the change from quadrupedal to bipedal gait presented no difficulty. He wrote, "We see . . . in existing monkeys a manner of progression intermediate between that of a quadruped to a biped." What Darwin was not giving adequate recognition to is the fact that the other primates do not actually have *feet* to walk on. They walk on their hands. As we have already noted, animals have either four hands or four feet, a fact which gave rise to the older term *quadrumana*, as opposed to *quadruped*. The feet of the apes are very poor feet: they are really hands, with opposable thumbs and quite capable of grasping. Man's feet are very different in structure, so different in fact that Dudley J. Morton, in a paper "Human Origin," observed:[63]

> In so far as my own studies would enable me to judge, I endorse Wood Jones' statement to the effect that "if *missing links* are to be traced with complete success, the feet, far more than the skull or the teeth or the shins, will mark them as monkey or man."

As will be seen in Fig. 14, the foot of man and of the orangutan (which was given its name because it looked so much like an old man) are quite different in outline, and — which is even more important — quite different in their anatomical structure (see also Fig.15). In man the great toe is bound in by a ligament to the other four toes. In the apes the four toes are bound together, but the big toe is strictly a thumb. Moreover, with respect to maintaining an erect

[59] Schultz, Adolph, ref. 52, p. 38.
[60] Hill, Leonard: reported in *Jour. Physiol.* 18 (London, 1895):15f.
[61] Parsons, F. G., in *Encyclopedia Britannica*, 1953 edition, Vol. XV, p. 990.
[62] Darwin, Charles, *The Descent of Man*, Merrill & Baker, New York, rev. ed. 1874, p. 59.
[63] Morton, Dudley, *Amer. Jour. Phys. Anthrop.* 10 (1927):195.

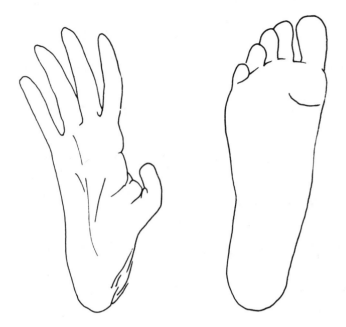

Fig. 15. The plantar aspect of the ape and human foot, the former belonging to an adult orangutan, and the latter to a nine-year-old girl.

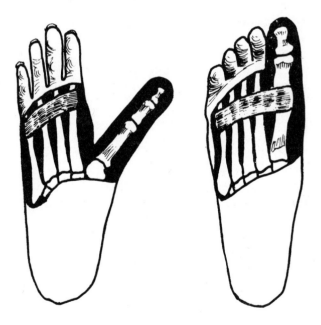

Fig. 16. Oversimplified diagram of the ape and human foot, showing the difference in transverse metatarsal ligament. After Wood Jones, *Man's Place Among the Mammals* (Fig. 147).

posture at rest, it is important to notice that there is an arrangement of muscle associated with the *linear aspera* in the human lower limb by which, in conjunction with a special knee joint, man is able to lock his leg in a permanently straight position, more or less restfully. The ape's lower limb does not have this feature and must therefore maintain truly erect posture only by considerable muscular effort. S. L. Washburn, in a paper entitled "Analysis of Primate Evolution," remarked, "Changes from a foot of such a sort (as the ape foot) to the human foot would not involve any major evolutionary changes. After all, the joining of the first metatarsal to the second by a ligament may well account for a great many of the features which differentiate the foot of men and apes."[64] It seems to me that this is naive, for a "thumb" such as we see in Fig. 16 to be suddenly bound by an entirely new structure to the rest of the toes, thus converting a hand into a foot, is just as difficult to imagine occurring by a series of stages as any other of the major evolutionary changes which the same writer would undoubtedly admit — for example, the balancing of the head on the shoulders in man. It is a completely transforming change with tremendous cultural significance for man, for it allows him to be completely free to use his hands for manipulative rather than balancing or locomotive purposes. The contact of the two feet with the ground is entirely different.

In this connection, Vallois wrote:[65]

> In spite of the existence of some transitional grades of structure observed in certain monkeys and man, all these characters are practically so definite that there can be absolutely no confusion between the most highly developed of living monkeys and the lowest of living men.

The genuine importance of erectness of posture for man is witnessed by the almost desperate effort on the part of physical anthropologists, such as LeGros Clark, to prove that hominoid forms such as the Australopithecines actually walked erect. The controversy over this question has raged for twenty years. And, to my mind, the greatest antagonist to the idea, Sir Solly Zuckerman, has also been the most thorough in his analysis of the data.[66] In paper after paper he has shown, simply by the presentation of factual data,

---

[64] Washburn, S. L., "Analysis of Primate Evolution," in Cold Spring Harbor Symposia on Quantitative Biology 15 (1951):72.

[65] Vallois, Henri V., and Boule, Marcellin, *Fossil Man*, tr. M. Bullock, Dryden Press, New York, 1957, p. 76.

[66] Zuckerman, Sir Solly, ref. 26, pp. 57-68: with an adequate bibliography of W. E. LeGros Clark's papers on the subject.

that LeGros Clark and those who have followed him are guilty of wishful thinking. The very title of one of Zuckerman's papers on the subject, "Myths and Methods in Anatomy," is an indication of what he feels about Clark's interpretation of the data.[67]

One of Zuckerman's strongest arguments is the analysis which he made of the relative position of the *foramen magnum* in the Australopithecine skulls which are complete enough to allow for its location. For the nonexpert, Fig.17 will show how this point of connection between the spinal column and the base of the skull is found to be increasingly more forward, i.e., more centrally located, as one moves from the dog (A), to the chimpanzee (B), to man (C). The Australopithecines show a *foramen* position which is essentially apelike as in (B). Moreover, careful measurements show that the plane in which this opening lies faces toward the back in the Australopithecines but toward the front in man, a fact which shows that the spinal column meets the ape skull from slightly behind (see Fig. 18). But it meets the human skull from slightly forward by taking a curve in the neck or cervical region, which is not found in the apes, but which contributes to the flexibility of the human neck. This fact relates to the difference in configuration between man's spinal column and that of all other animals below him. Fig.19 shows that man's spinal column is complex, compounded of several curves reversed; the ape spinal column is either almost a straight line or a simple backward curve as shown. As we have noted in the first chapter, this compound form allows man to assume a restful condition in a remarkably wide variety of physical postures. He can sit, stand, and lie in an almost infinite number of ways and maintain these positions for a remarkable length of time, a fact which has great importance to man as a culture-bound creature.

In any case, the Australopithecines are no longer considered as ancestral to man, and the possibility that they actually achieved any culture is felt by many authorities to be very slim indeed. The finding of flint weapons of a very crude kind with their remains is equivocal, for archaeologists have actually found pieces of pottery among the bones of some extinct lemurs, perhaps the very pots they were cooked in — but hardly the handiwork of the lemurs themselves. Since we know that the hunter may leave some at least of his weapons beside his prey, the Australopithecine apes may have been the prey of truly human hunters in view of the fact that even by conventional

[67] Zuckerman, Sir Solly, ref. 52, pp. 87-114.

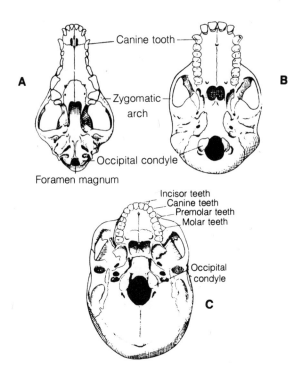

Fig. 17. Basal aspect of skull of dog (A), chimpanzee (B), and man (C). The darkened area is the opening into the skull termed the "foramen magnum." In man it is almost centrally located, the spinal column thus balancing the head with least stress in a vertical position.

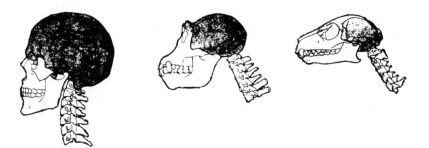

Fig. 18. A companion drawing to Fig. 17, showing how the spinal column supports the skull in man, ape, and dog.

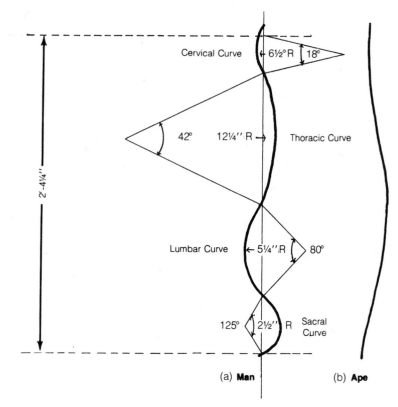

Cervical Curve   6½°R 18°

42°   12¼″ R →   Thoracic Curve

2′-4¼″

Lumbar Curve   5¼″ R   80°

125°   2½″ R   Sacral Curve

(a) **Man**   (b) **Ape**

Fig. 19. The data given are from actual measurements. (From lectures of Prof. George Huntington.)

evolutionary standards of dating they were probably contemporary.[68]

Preoccupation with the determination to find some intermediary creature between the apes and man that walked with a stoop was responsible for the tremendous number of reconstructions of Neanderthal Man, which are still to be found in popular and serious books and museums. In these he is shown brutelike, slouched, and often (appropriately, of course) hairy and carrying a club. It is a curious fact of history that the first Neanderthal man to have been discovered did, indeed, walk with a stoop. Later on other Neanderthal specimens were found who walked as completely erect as modern man does. The first of these was reported in 1939 in *Science* under the name of Sergio Sergi.[69] Since then, more careful examina-

[68] *The Living World of Animals,* ed. H. L. Matthews et al., Reader's Digest Publ., London, 1970, p. 214.

[69] Sergi, Sergio, *Science* 90, supplement (1939):12.

tion of the bones of the first Neanderthal has revealed that he was a pathological specimen, afflicted with osteoarthritis, which forced him to walk with a stoop.[70] But because Neanderthal Man was thought to be a kind of missing link and because in the popular mind he is still looked upon in this guise, even the best scholars yield to the temptation to picture him in this way. Carl O. Dunbar, in his 1966 edition of an oft quoted *Historical Geology*, has a full page illustration of "old man Neanderthal" with a note reading: "Note the slouched posture and compare with Fig.386."[71] Fig.386 reinforces the slouch by being juxtaposed to a skeleton of modern man. Concession is made to the reader, however, as follows:[72]

> Although Neanderthals stood upright, their carriage was more like that of a great ape than that of living man, because the spine lacked the fourth or cervical curvature and the thigh bones were sigmoidally curved in compensation.

That *healthy* Neanderthals maintained a truly erect posture is now almost universally accepted by physical anthropologists. Moreover, Neanderthal Man is sometimes found in association, as contemporary, with modern man. And sometimes modern man is even found preceding Neanderthal Man at the same site.[73]

In view of the tremendous importance of his truly erect posture to man as both a culture-creating being and a creature with spiritual aspirations, a word needs to be said about the claim which is often made that he achieved his erectness by an evolutionary process which is still incomplete, and that he suffers considerably, physiologically speaking, as a consequence of this incomplete process of development.

To my mind, the most thorough single paper on this question was written by F. A. Hallebrandt and E. B. Franseen, entitled "Physiological Study of the Vertical Stance in Man."[74] The following brief extracts will give a useful summary of this paper that runs into some thirty-six pages. The authors stated in introducing their subject:[75]

> Many clinical papers in the current literature on posture indicate that

[70] Neanderthal Man and osteoarthritis: C. S. Coon, *The Story of Man*, Knopf, New York, 1962, p. 40.

[71] Dunbar, Carl O., *Historical Geology*, Wiley, New York, 1966, p. 450.

[72] Ibid., p. 449.

[73] Neanderthal Man preceded by modern man, notably in the finds at Fontechevade: G. W. Lasker, *Evolution of Man*, Holt, Rinehart, & Winston, New York, 1961, pp. 118, 119.

[74] Hallebrandt, F. A., and Franseen, E. B., "Physiological Study of the Vertical Stance in Man," *Physiol. Rev.* 22-23 (1943):220-225.

[75] Ibid., p. 221.

stance defects may result ultimately in a variety of malfunctions including lessened respiratory efficiency, prolapse of the abdominal viscera, impairment of digestion, pressure and derangement of the pelvic organs, dysmenorrhea, haemorrhoids, varicose veins, constipation, cyclic vomiting, foot strain, backache, neuritis, and arthritis. Barring orthopedic disabilities, few of the etiologic associations are based on demonstrable fact. . . .

Almost from their first enunciation these now firmly entrenched concepts have been questioned. Many observations throw doubt on their validity.

The authors then proceeded to examine the evidence pro and con for each of these supposed consequences of man's having adopted a supposedly unnatural animal posture. That some of these ailments result from minor skeletal malalignments they found difficult to believe on the basis of evidence as tenuous as that usually presented.[76]

They then give some thought to the question of the supposed increase in energy cost which is assumed to be involved in maintaining a vertical position. Figures are given for the actual increase in oxygen consumption when a test subject changes from a horizontal to a vertical position and their conclusion was that the cost is very small indeed: "From this point of view, normal standing on both legs is *almost effortless*" (my emphasis).[77] In summing up this aspect of the study they said, "Standing is cheap in terms of metabolic cost. . . . The remarkable indefatigability of relaxed standing has not been fully explained."[78] Perhaps the explanation is that God made us this way. . . .

Even with regard to circulation, some rather surprising findings have been reported, including the fact that stroke volume is significantly reduced in the vertical stance but heart rate increases, thus compensating for the reduced venous return flow from the lower extremities due to gravitational effects.[79]

The authors reported extensive evidence that both erect posture *and* prolonged recumbance are equally conducive to the formation of kidney stones, so it cannot be argued that man's excretory system has been upset by a presumed subsequent assumption of erectness. And provided that free postural sway is allowed, gastric secretory curves are indistinguishable in the vertical body from those in recumbancy.[80]

---

[76] Ibid., p. 223.
[77] Ibid., p. 231.
[78] Ibid., p. 248.
[79] Ibid., pp. 232,234.
[80] Ibid., p. 237.

Although in an erect posture man finds himself at a disadvantage in terms of gravity, since the base upon which he stands is quite small, yet apparently compensatory mechanisms of various kinds automatically cancel mechanical disadvantages of the vertical position, so that gravitational stresses are counteracted easily in the majority of normal men.[81] The phenomenon of standing is elaborately protected by a multiplicity of cooperating reflexes.

I think it is also worth noting in passing that a careful study of factors involved in the *size* of man, made by F. W. Wendt, lead him to the conclusion that man is actually the tallest creature which could reasonably walk upright on two legs.[82] Any creature larger would be in grave danger of upset, with serious consequences to himself. A man approximately six feet tall, if he trips, will have a kinetic energy upon hitting the ground of anywhere from twenty to one hundred times greater than a small child learning to walk. If a man were twice as tall as he is now, his kinetic danger in falling would be so great (thirty-two times greater than it now is) that it would not be safe for him to walk upright at all. Larger animals can become taller because they are more stable on their four legs. Interestingly enough, Wendt also showed that if man were much smaller, his cultural attainments would have been tremendously limited due to his greatly reduced striking power as a craftsman. His analysis of the total situation suggests that man is, indeed, "an optimum size."

The consequences of man's orthopedic capabilities are tremendous. Some of them are very obvious. Some of them are not so obvious but are, if anything, even more important. The importance of the freedom of his hands needs little laboring, though we shall explore this further in dealing with man as a creator of culture, in which his hands become in a very real sense an extension of his mind. Sir Charles Bell wrote eloquently about the refinements and the potential of the human hand.[83]

> We have (in the hand) the consummation of all perfection as an instrument. This, we perceive, consists in its power, which is a combination of strength with variety and extent of motion; we see it in the forms, relations, and sensibility of the fingers and thumb; in the provisions for holding, pulling, spinning, weaving, and constructing; properties which may be found in other animals but which are combined here to form this most perfect instrument.

Bell might have mentioned such complex exercises as those involved

---

[81] Ibid., p. 247.

[82] Wendt, F. W., "The Size of Man," *Amer. Scientist* 56, no. 4 (1968):400-413.

[83] Bell, Sir Charles, *The Hand: Its Mechanism and Vital Endowments As Evincing Design,* 3rd ed., Bridgewater Treatises, Pickering, London, 1834, p. 231.

in typing at high speed or, even more remarkably, in playing the piano. The close association between mind and hand in both is evident from the fact that skill enables the individual to forget about the hands entirely. You will know, if you type by touch, that one will have no immediate picture, in reflection, of the actual position of letters on the keyboard. One has to "discover" them, as it were, in one's imagination if one is not in the presence of a typewriter by acting as though one were typing a word, and if a typographical error is made, it may be several words on before some subconscious part of the mind signals to one that an error has been made. The message passes straight from the copy to the typescript through the mind and the fingers as though mind and hand were really a single transfer channel. This nervous connection, which accompanies the liberation of the hands by reason of man's erectness, has been recognized as one of the most important aspects in the total situation. William L. Straus has said:[84]

> Any further studies of posture and locomotion — whether bipedal, bimanual, or quadrupedal — must necessarily be physiological as well as anatomical. Too often have posture and locomotion been thought of in terms of skeleton and muscle alone. Yet these are essentially effector organs, for it has been clearly demonstrated that the central nervous system is the prime controlling agent.

In the first chapter we listed, among other things, man's possession of truly opposable thumbs combined with wide-angle stereoscopic vision. The point has often been remarked upon by others. Sir Solly Zuckerman, in an article dealing with man's social evolution, wrote:[85]

> According to many authorities, the one unique character which was most prominently concerned in our prehuman development, and without which we should not have evolved to the human level, is our dual possession of stereovision and fully opposable thumbs. This combination exists in no other animal.

Kenneth Oakley underscores the combined effect of these two features:[86]

> Man owes much of his skill to his visual powers, and yet apes and many monkeys have eyes capable of refined stereoscopic and colour vision. Man is, however, psychologically distinguished by his capacity for close visual atten-

---

[84] Straus, William L., "Primates," in *Anthropology Today*, ed. A. L. Kroeber, U. of Chicago Press, 1953, p. 77.

[85] Zuckerman, Sir Solly, "The Influence of Hormones on Man's Social Evolution," *Endeavour*, April 1944, p. 80.

[86] Oakley, Kenneth P., "Skill as a Human Possession," in *A History of Technology*, Vol. I, ref. 42, p. 12.

tion and for prolonged *co-ordination of eye and hand* (my emphasis). These are reflections of cerebral rather than ocular functions. Convergence of the eyes upon handwork is largely dependent upon conscious concentration — in other words, it is under the control of the cortical motor areas, which act in response to coordinated impulses from the eyes.

It has been reported that chimpanzees can learn to use their hands under the direction of their eyes for long enough to thread a needle, but in general the attention that an ape can give to manipulating an object is very fleeting. Furthermore, the erect posture of man, and the fact that his skull is poised above the top of his spine instead of being slung in a forwardly projecting manner as in apes, make it easier for him to pay close attention to any point over a wide field of vision.

It is not without significance that among the very earliest artifacts of man are to be found needles of quite refined design (see Fig.20), and Genesis 3:7 indicates that the very first cultural activity of man after the Fall was to sew clothing for himself.

One of the less well recognized results of truly erect posture in man is its effect upon his powers of communication. The neck structure allows a certain configuration of the windpipe and vocal organs which permits men to talk easily to one another while maintaining the natural and normal position of the head. Both speaking and singing are possible for man without any such straightening out of the head and neck as must occur in other animals when they give voice.[87] One only has to observe the mooing of a cow, or the howling of a dog to realize that considerable change of head position from the normal is required before they can vocalize. Adolph Schultz, in a paper entitled "The Physical Distinctions of Man," remarked upon the fact that the human head does not have a position relative to the spine similar to that in all nonhuman primates: "The profound phylogenetic change in this relation between head and spine in man can be understood only as an ontogenetic specialization. . . ."[88] I would omit the word *only*. After all, this is surely the way God made man in the first place, for very good reasons. In passing, it might be noted that the other class of animals which maintain a normal erect posture, namely, the birds, can also sing without changing their head position.

Furthermore, the refined jaw structure of man may also contribute to his ability to speak. In the apes (as in man) the chief stress placed upon the bone structure of the jaw in chewing hard substances or cracking nuts on one side of the mouth only is concentrated at the chin. The very powerful jaw muscles in the gorilla are

---

[87] Kahn, Fritz, *Man in Structure and Function*, Vol. I, Knopf, New York, 1960, p. 73.
[88] Schultz, Adolph, "The Physical Distinctions of Man," *Amer. Phil. Soc. Proc.* 94 (1950):445.

Fig. 20. Some bone needles found by Karl Absalon at Vestonice, Moravia, "dated" 30,000 years old.

Shelf   **Chin**

Fig. 21. The so-called simian shelf in the ape jaw, contrasted with the human chin.

met with a corresponding mechanical strengthening of the jaw at the crucial point of stress by a "flange" of bone which penetrates inwards as shown in Fig.21. It is widely accepted that this so-called simian shelf, and it is found I believe in all the apes, has the effect of considerably reducing the freedom of movement of the primate animal tongue by restricting the area available for muscles.[89] The number of sounds which the apes can make is therefore more restricted than in man. In a paper on cultural evolution, Julian H. Steward, while agreeing that the origin of language is still quite unexplained, nevertheless saw it as significant that man is *capable* of speech thanks to the speech and auditory centres of his brain, but also "thanks to his jaw and tongue structure."[90] This is no doubt true, but the evidence is not altogether unequivocal, as will be seen above.

The same need for strengthening exists, of course, on the human jaw but in this case the flange projects outward instead, leading to the characteristic formation of the human chin, thus allowing considerably more freedom for the tongue. Man's powers of vocalization

[89] Howells, William, ref. 35, pp. 78,79.
[90] Steward, Julian H., "Cultural Evolution," *Sci. American,* May 1956, p. 72.

are, as a consequence, far greater than in the primates, and he makes full use of this capacity both to share his ideas and to express his emotion.

It has been argued that by balancing the head on top of the vertical column, optimum conditions exist for removing waste products of metabolic activity in this most important area. It is also customary to equate the enlargement of the brain with the assumption of erect posture in man. While I am personally persuaded that God made man upright in the first place, I think it is not at all unlikely that in some way to be yet clearly demonstrated, the size and complexity of man's brain is related to the position of that organ with respect to the rest of his body. S. W. Britton, reflecting the evolutionary view of man's supposed biological history, wrote:[91]

> Man alone stands erect with little or no functional disturbance . . . contemporaneous with development of orthograde progression, the human brain showed its greatest growth and differentiation. The force of gravity exerted linearly through the body significantly influenced conformation and growth.
>
> Delicately balanced arterial reactions, better oxygenation, and enhanced venous removal of metabolic products became possible in the head end. Special sensory and cerebral mechanisms have probably benefitted, particularly through improved circulatory conditions.

The erectness of man is therefore of tremendous importance as an extension of his mental capacities and to give those mental capacities freedom of expression.

It seems also that man is a creature who, by habit, in a way "looks up," and he does this to an extent that few if any other animals do. Their vision seems bent upon the ground; man's is directed otherwise. It is as though his very structure is a reflection of the fact that *his* spirit "goeth upward," whereas the spirit of the beast "goeth downward to the earth" (Eccl. 3:21). His very physical posture itself in some way corresponds to his spiritual nature. Man was truly upright as God made him (Eccl. 7:29), but in the end he becomes bowed down (Ps. 37:3,6), with the weight both of years and sin. The Lord encouraged His people to "straighten up" as they saw the day of their redemption approaching (Luke 21:28), for such is the meaning of the original, as though the very position of the body could symbolize the posture of the soul — as indeed it does!

It is perhaps significant that in grief, sorrow, and crying, man tends to double forward, using muscles which bow him down; but in joy and laughter and praise, he straightens up, indeed even bends

---

[91] Britton, S. W., *Science* 11 (1950):445; under Abstracts of Nat. Acad. of Sciences.

over backwards, using muscles which more than straighten him up. His very worship, as John R. Howitt pointed out, bows him before his Creator in contrition, but then leads him to lift up his head in praise.[92]

[92] Howitt, J. R., "Man the Upright," *Creation Res. Soc. Annual,* 1968, pp. 46-48.

Chapter 4
The Ubiquity of Man

Comparative Defenselessness of Man

MAN IS surely the most defenseless of all creatures, unless armed artificially.[93] He appears to have no dependable instincts for self-protection.[94] What natural defenses he can muster from within himself are puny compared with those of animals. And there is no evidence that early man was very different from ourselves, so that we cannot blame this deficiency altogether on a cultural heritage which tends to supply us with substitute defenses. The strength of animals relative to human strength is tremendous. A chimpanzee, for instance, has something like three to five times the strength of man, though considerably less weight (120 lbs).[95] The fact of man's helplessness in terms of self-defense has been remarked upon by many writers, not a few of whom have seen in it, quite rightly, one of the reasons for his ability to exercise dominion over the rest of Nature. For in lieu of natural equipment he has been granted superior intelligence and learned to arm himself accordingly.

Years ago Sir William Dawson made this statement:[96]

> It is, in animals below man, a law that the bodily frame is provided with all necessary means of defence and attack, and with all necessary protection against external influences and assailants.
>
> In a very few cases, we have a partial exception to this. A hermit-crab, for instance, has the hinder part of its body unprotected; and has, instead of armour, the instinct of using the cast-off shells of molluscs; yet even this animal has the usual strong claws of a crustacean for defence in front. There are only a very few animals in which instinct thus takes the place of physical

---

[93] It is possible that honors in this respect may have to go to the koala bear which, I have read, is completely without defenses.

[94] Animals appear to know when to stand and fight, and when it is wiser not to do so. This is particularly true of birds, as noted by Alexander F. Skutch, "The Parental Devotion of Birds," *Sci. Monthly*, April 1946, p. 369.

[95] Noted by R. A. Gardner, *Science* 165 (1969):664.

[96] Dawson, Sir William, *The Story of Earth and Man*, Hodder and Stoughton, London, 1903, p. 365.

contrivances for defence or attack, and in these we find merely the usual unvarying instincts of the animal. But in man, that which is the rare exception in all other animals becomes the rule. He has no means of escape from danger compared with those enjoyed by other animals, no defensive armour, no effective weapons for attacking other animals.

These disabilities should make him the most helpless of creatures, especially when taken with his slow growth and long immaturity. His safety and his dominion over other animals are secured by entirely new means, constituting a *new departure* in creation. Contrivance and inventive power, enabling him to utilize the objects and forces of Nature, replace in him the physical powers bestowed on other animals.

Obviously, the structure of the human being is related to this, and so related to it as to place man in a different category altogether from any other animal.

The evidence from antiquity, from the study of fossil man and his cultural remains, indicates that man has always had to depend upon his intellect rather than his physical strength or natural defensive weapons. If man had not fallen, it is my belief that he would not have had to defend himself against other animals at all, but would have achieved dominion over them by a kind of power akin to moral force. Even yet there are among us individuals who seem to have retained something of this power over animals. It would be an interesting question for debate to ask whether many of the defensive instincts of animals would have been necessary if sin had not entered into God's creation, and therefore whether they were conferred upon them by God as soon as man's sin began to disrupt the natural order. Fabre, with the true insight of a devout naturalist, recognized animal instinctual behavior as "inspired activity."[97]

But returning to early man, a keen student of civilization, Vere Gordon Childe, wrote:[98]

> Man is now, and was apparently even at his first appearance in the Pleistocene, inadequately adapted for survival in any particular environment. His bodily equipment for coping with any set of conditions is inferior to that of most animals. He has not, and probably never had, a furry coat like the polar bears for keeping in the body's heat under cold conditions. His body is not particularly well adapted for escape, for self-defense, or hunting.
>
> He is not, for instance, exceptionally fleet of foot, and would be left behind in any race with a hare or an ostrich. He has no protective colouring like the tiger or the snow leopard, nor bodily armour like the tortoise or the crab. He has no wings to offer escape and give him an advantage in spying out and pouncing upon prey. He lacks the beak and talons of the hawk, and its

---

[97] Fabre, Henri: quoted by W. R. Thompson in a Convocation Address: "The Work of J. Henri Fabre," *Canad. Entomol.* 96, nos. 1 and 2 (1964):70.

[98] Childe, Vere Gordon, *Man Makes Himself*, Thinkers Library, Watts, London, 1948, p. 23.

keenness of vision. For catching his prey and defending himself, his muscular strength, teeth and nails are incomparably inferior. . . .

As Kipling said, man is indeed "a poor naked frog." And yet man has a vast superiority, for all his weakness and in spite of the Fall. He did not entirely lose in Eden the power to obey the command to have dominion over the earth. The processes of civilization are really only exhibitions of this ability expressed in terms of fallen man. During World War II, C. E. M. Joad, a man who thought deeply about the events of his day, wrote a little pamphlet entitled *For Civilization*. His opening paragraph reads as follows:[99]

> Wherein are to be found the distinctive characteristics of our species? In what, that is to say, do men differ from and excel the beasts? In swiftness or ferocity? The deer and the lion leave us far behind. In size and strength we must give way to the elephant and the whale; sheep are more gentle, nightingales more melodious, tortoises longer-lived, bees more co-operative, beavers more diligent. The ants run a totalitarian State much better than any Fascist.
>
> The truth is that our bodies are feeble and ill-adapted to survival; they are the prey to innumerable diseases, their enormous complexity means that things can go wrong in a vast number of ways, while so poorly are they equipped against the vagaries of the climate that it is only by clothing ourselves in the skins of other animals that we can survive.

All these things are true, but not the whole truth, and Dawson, Childe, and Joad from their different points of view would at once acknowledge this. It is true that man is not supplied with natural defenses against potential enemies, but he does have a brain and hands which allow him to design vastly superior weapons for himself. It is true that he is naked, but these same hands and brain allow him to devise clothing which gives him the ability to live where other animals cannot live, except under his protection. He may indeed be slow to move, yet these same hands and brain have made him more mobile and faster than any other creature. And though he may apparently be ill-protected against the vagaries of climate, he is nevertheless, physiologically speaking, quite uniquely equipped to maintain his deep body temperature within remarkably narrow limits over an extraordinary wide range of external conditions of temperature, pressure, and humidity. And as we shall see, in his diet he is further exceptionally fitted to live in any part of the world.

Many years ago Alexander Macalister, professor of anatomy in the University of Cambridge, wrote a paper entitled "Man, Physiologically Considered," in which he was careful to note that

---

[99] Joad, C. E. M., *For Civilization*, Macmillan War Pamphlets, London, 1940, p. 3.

there are many features of man's anatomy and physiology which contribute to the use he has made of his superior brain:[100]

> While it is thus power of mind, not power of body, which gives to man his supremacy, yet, in all respects, *man's bodily organization is fitted to enable him to use to the best advantage his mental endowments.*
>
> If he conceives in his mind the plan of making a weapon, his prehensile hand with its sensitive skin and its independently moving and opposable thumb can fabricate it. His sinuous backbone and completely extensile lower limbs enable him to stand upright with perfect stability, with an ease and perfection competent to no other animal; and thus his forelimbs, relieved from all necessity to act as organs of progression, are perfectly disengaged for work. . . .

His very weakness has in the providence of God served to enhance man's chief glory, his power to think things through. But his superior mental abilities had to be supported adequately to find expression through the other members of his body, and his body needed to be organized in a number of ways uniquely to make this possible. It was God's intention that he should fill the earth and govern it, and there is little doubt that when this command was given, the climatic conditions on earth were not fundamentally different from what they are today in that while there were zones where the temperature was moderate and laid little stress on the body, there were other zones where man was going to experience considerable heat stress or cold stress. It may be perfectly true that if Paradise had not been lost, the world's climate would have been uniformly temperate, though this would involve tremendous geophysical modifications. But undoubtedly God knew what man would do and that he would face in the end the task of filling a world in which climatic extremes would exist as they do now. He must therefore have been designed, to begin with, with the capability of making the necessary physiological adjustments in order to occupy these challenging zones. No other animal was designed, it seems, for such ubiquitousness.

Next, let us just consider the nature of territoriality of animals other than man; then, the significance of man's uniformity of physical type in spite of his wide dispersal and often long isolation; and finally, all too briefly, the complex mechanisms by which man maintains his deep body temperature at the optimum level to allow the exercise of his full potential as a thinking creature within an exceptional range of external conditions. This study will serve to

---

[100] Macalister, Alexander, *Man Physiologically Considered*, Vol. 7, no. 39, Present Day Tracts, Relig. Tract Soc., London, 1886, pp. 6,7.

demonstrate that this mechanism in man is in certain fundamental respects quite different from the mechanism which serves somewhat the same purpose in animals, and this will underscore at the same time the fact that it is easy for the inexpert to suppose that because the mechanisms look alike they are in fact the same.

Man the Free-roaming Creature

First, consider the extent of animal territories. Every increase in our knowledge of this subject only tends to confirm that all animals have limited territories, which they mark out rather specifically. Often more than one species will occupy a single area, but each species marks out its territorial boundaries in defiance of other members of its *own* species. In the case of social animals, the territory owned by the individual may be quite small. Birds, especially sea birds, may claim only space sufficient to land upon and lay their eggs. But other animals, like some of the large cats, may dominate territories covering a number of square miles. Just as an illustration of the kind of spread involved, the weasel may claim from two to nine acres, a male stoat up to eighty-five acres, martens about one square mile, a waterbuck anywhere from forty to five-hundred acres, some bears, ten square miles or more, and a pride of fifteen lions, thirty or more square miles.[101] The territory of animals which migrate should not strictly include their corridors of migration which they merely pass through, but must be limited to their range of wintering or summering. The primates nearest in form to man claim territorial rights over far less territory, the proportion working out to about two and one-half chimpanzees per square mile, for example.[102] The Sifaka monkeys in Madagascar occupy about three acres each.

Social animals that live in colonies seem to crowd their environment, but apparently, except under stress, they do not actually compete severely for the food supply. Herds of animals may live with herds of another species, serving as sentinels for one another but not competing for the available food because their diets are different. I think it is amusing that evolutionists who believe that Nature has advanced itself by the very fact of competition are also able to turn around and show that evolution has often had the reverse effect, i.e., limiting competition. So we have a situation in which competition leads to evolution upwards while evolution tends towards the elimination of competition. Thus a magnificent volume, *The Living World*

---

[101] *The Living World of Animals*, ref. 68, pp. 56, 58, 59, 101, 106.
[102] Ibid.: chimpanzees, p. 198; Sifaka monkeys, p. 215.

of Animals, under the editorship of L. H. Matthews and others, has this enlightening paragraph:[103]

> This concentration of animals (in Africa) does not lead to the severe competition between species for food that might be expected, because each has his own preferences even when several different species graze upon the same plant. Red Oat grass, for instance, is eaten by the zebra, the wildebeest, and the topi, but each feeds upon it at a different stage of the plant's growth. This limited competition, *the result of evolution* (my emphasis), has permitted a great variety of animals to fit into the environment; every species has its niche, from the smallest insect to the elephant.

Not only are animal territories rather precisely defined, but the geographic distribution of species tends to be equally well defined, except where man has interfered and taken domesticated animals with him. Of the primates, the gorilla is confined to a small tract of West Africa about the size of France. The chimpanzee, although ranging over a larger district of Equatorial Africa, still does not extend beyond the region limited by the parallels 12° north and south latitudes, and in this belt is only found between the sea coast on the west and the meridian of Lake Tanganyika on the east. The orangutan is limited to the islands of Sumatra and Borneo.[104]

Washburn and Lancaster, in a paper on the evolution of hunting, remark upon the difference between the territory occupied by men who hunt as opposed to animals which hunt:[105]

> Social groups of non-human primates occupy exceedingly small areas, and the vast majority of animals probably spend their entire lives within less than 4 or 5 square miles. Even though they have excellent vision and can see for many miles, especially from the tops of trees, they make no effort to explore more than a tiny fraction of the area they see.
>
> Even for gorillas the range is only about 15 square miles, and it is of the same order of magnitude for savanna baboons; they refuse to be driven beyond the end of their range and double back. The known area is a psychological reality, clear in the minds of the animals. Only a small part of even this limited range is used, and exploration is confined to the canopy, lower branches, and bushes, or ground, depending on the biology of the particular species. . . .
>
> In marked contrast, human hunters are familiar with very large areas. In (one) area studied . . . eleven waterholes and several hundred square miles supported a smaller number of Bushmen than the number of baboons supported by a single waterhole and a few square miles in the Amboseli Reserve in Kenya. The most minor hunting expedition covers an area larger than

---

[103] Ibid., p. 96.
[104] Macalister, Alexander, ref. 100, p. 5.
[105] Washburn, S. L., and Lancaster, C. S., "The Evolution of Hunting," in *Human Evolution*, ref. 27, p. 73.

most non-human primates would cover in a lifetime. Interest in a large area is human.

It is not unusual for a single Eskimo family to occupy for hunting purposes a territory stretching for 200 to 300 miles. Moreover, unlike any other species, man seems by nature a wanderer and an explorer, to whom no part of the globe does not have an appeal in one way or another. Man is truly ubiquitous.

Comparative Absence of Physical Variability

For all his ubiquity man has not, even in those earlier periods of history in which population was thin and tribes were often isolated for centuries, developed varieties of the species *Homo sapiens* to anything like the extent that animals have. It is true that in one area of the world, Africa, we do have Pygmies whose average height is perhaps four feet six inches, and Nilotic Negroes whose average height may be around seven feet, but in terms of body mass the difference between the Nilotic Negroes and the Congo Pygmy is far less than, for example, the difference between the St. Bernard and the Chihuahua. Moreover, this apparent limitation in terms of variability within the family of man has made it possible for all races to interbreed freely. In the case of the St. Bernard and the Chihuahua,, for example, interbreeding is not successful for physical reasons unless artificial means are used. And if the mother is the Chihuahua, she apparently cannot bear her pup sired by a St. Bernard because of its size at full term.

Within the animal kingdom other factors may result in *psychological* blocks to successful mating — the time of heat of varieties of a single species too-long separated may not be in register; sometimes the block is apparently due to unacceptable body odor caused by a difference in diet. The inflexibility of the period of heat among species, an inflexibility which is governed by their need to bear their young at an appropriate time in the year, is said by some authorities to be responsible for the extinction of at least some species in early Pleistocene times when it is held that great climatic changes were taking place.[106]

Experience shows, by contrast, that none of these barriers exist between members of the human species, though they may be brought together from the ends of the world for the first time in human history. Mankind as a species has not a restricted "season of

---

[106] Slaughter, W. H., "Animal Ranges as a Clue to Late-Pleistocene Extinctions," in *Pleistocene Extinctions,* Vol. VI of Proc. of 7th Congress of the International Assoc. for Quaternary Research, ed. P. S. Marten and H. E. Wright, Yale U. Press, 1967, p. 155.

heat," such as characterizes all other species. And this fact has tremendous importance, as we shall see in the next chapter. The potential for interbreeding successfully seems to me to indicate that, unlike other animals, man was uniquely designed from the beginning to be able to go anywhere in the world without becoming a genetic isolate.

Although I cannot find myself in agreement with Teilhard de Chardin, he is certainly correct in underscoring the importance of this fact for man:[107]

> By climatic and geographical influences, varieties and races (of animals) come into existence. Somatically speaking, the *fanning out* (of man) is present continually in formation and perfectly recognizable. Yet the remarkable thing is that its divergent branches no longer succeed in separating.
>
> Under conditions of distribution which in any other initial phylum would long ago have led to the breakup into different species, the human verticil as it spreads out remains entire, like a gigantic leaf whose veins, how ever distinct, remain always joined in a common tissue. With man we find independent (interfertility) on every level. . . .
>
> Zoologically speaking, mankind offers us the unique spectacle of a species capable of achieving something in which all previous species had failed. It has succeeded, not only in becoming cosmopolitan, but in stretching a single organized membrane over the earth without breaking it.

It is clear, then, in a way which has never been demonstrated for animals, that every variety of man is "made of one" (Acts 17:26, where the word "blood" is probably not part of the original text). And this true unity of such a far-flung race guarantees that throughout history One Man could always be recognized as a true representative of all men, without exception.

Another notable circumstance with respect to animal populations is the interesting fact that according to our present understanding, animal species remain remarkably stable in terms of the number of individuals constituting each particular species. Were it not so, of course, their territories would have to increase or they would have to become progressively more crowded. Darwin saw that all organisms possess the potentiality for increase, a potentiality not merely for arithmetical multiplication but geometric. It was this belief that led him to assume that Malthus' essay on *human* population growth must also apply to animals. He therefore postulated an unending

---

[107] Teilhard de Chardin, Pierre, *The Phenomenon of Man*, Collins, London, 1959, p. 241. A more "orthodox" authority, G. G. Simpson, has remarked upon the same circumstance: "Regardless of the diversity of races, it is obvious that all men resemble one another much more than any of them differ from each other. They all share the basic quality, anatomical, physiological and psychological, that make us human, *Homo sapiens*, and no other species that is or ever was" (*Biology and Man*, Harcourt, Brace & World, New York, 1969, p. 87).

struggle to survive, with the triumph of the fittest. We know now that this was an entirely erroneous extrapolation from human to animal population growth. Sir Julian Huxley himself underscored the fact that for various reasons this population growth does not materialize, and so he observed, "In spite of the tendency to progressive increase, the numbers of a given species actually remain more or less constant." Subsequently, he wrote:[108]

> With our much greater knowledge of ecology, we know today that many species undergo cyclical and often remarkably regular fluctuations, frequently of very large extent in their numbers.

At this point, he referred to the work of Charles Elton, and although I do not have the work he refers to, I do have a similar work by that author in which he underscored this interesting finding, and after giving some specific illustrations, concluded:[109]

> All this goes to support the idea that there is some important principle involved in the stability of the total number of species in an animal community.

Elton was speaking in this case not of the number of individuals in a species but the number of species in a given area. This is a fact which has been recognized for a long while: namely, that when any particular species dies out, some other species will move in to fill the ecological niche which has thus become vacant. But they do not overpopulate it. So the web of life is preserved intact, and the total number of animals as a consequence remains remarkably constant. The pattern of human population growth is quite otherwise. Were it not so, man would never finally "fill the earth." But did those constraints against *animal* population growth not exist, it could very well be that the animals, rather than man, would have usurped his dominion long before this.

In the meantime, evidence has recently come to light that, again, unlike human beings, animals are somehow able to control their own numbers, not by killing off unwanted children as it were, but by producing fewer offspring. This has become apparent, for example, of the elephant population in the Murchison Falls area of Western Uganda in Africa.[110] Where one section of this particular population has had its territory reduced by the extension of farming,

[108] Huxley, Sir Julian, *Evolution and the Modern Synthesis*, Harper, New York, 1942, p. 15.

[109] Elton, Charles, *The Ecology of Animals*, Methuen, London, 1950, p. 20. See also his "Animal Numbers and Adaptation" in *Evolution*, ed. Sir Gavin de Beer, Oxford U. Press, 1938, pp. 127ff.

[110] Animal population stability: Robert Ardrey, in a series of two articles on the subject in *The Globe and Mail*, Toronto, September 30 and October 1, 1971.

the elephant population has somehow diminished by a change in the birth rate. The normal spacing for calves is four years; in this potentially overcrowded area it has risen to nine years. No one knows the mechanics of this, though it has recently been recognized that the same thing may happen in other parts of the world. In an English woodland, if the number of great-tits doubles, in the next season the egg clutch size will be reduced by two. In an Iowa marshland, if muskrat numbers rise too high, then the mother muskrat produces fewer embryos or reabsorbs them.

Man the Omnivorous

Another factor which contributes to man's unique ubiquity is his willingness and ability to accept a vegetarian or meat diet with equal ease. There are millions of people who for centuries have been to all intents and purposes vegetarian, such as those in the Far East who depend upon cereals (rice, etc.). By contrast, there have been branches of the human race, such as the Eskimo people, who were not completely but almost entirely meat eaters. At certain seasons of the year they probably had some fruits in the form of wild berries. The human body, therefore, can be nourished equally well by either form of diet.

By contrast, as Loren C. Eiseley says, "All of the existing great apes are essentially vegetarian, and indeed the arboreal bracchiators have no other consistent source of food."[111] Whether these creatures could successfully adopt a carnivorous diet without completely changing their character, or at least becoming no longer interfertile with members of their own species who remain vegetarian, it is difficult to say. It is known that in at least one branch of the primates, a number of animals have changed their diet from a herbivorous to a carnivorous one due to man's disturbance of their natural environment. Eugene Marais pointed out that up until about 1860 the wild baboons in Africa fed on insects and roots.[112] In a manner of speaking, they were therefore already omnivorous, though insects as part of a diet do not usually qualify the eater as a carnivore. But the drying up of the continent due to man's bad farming management, forced these animals to look for liquid to drink from new sources, and they started killing goats just to suck the milk from their udders. In time they began attacking all kinds of domestic animals and eating them for food.

---

[111] Eiseley, Loren C., "Fossil Man and Human Evolution," in *Current Anthropology*, ref. 23, p. 73.

[112] Marais, Eugene, *My Friends, the Baboons*, Methuen, New York, 1939, p. 1.

This is an exceptional circumstance, not a natural one. And the fact remains that virtually no other animal bearing some similarity to man is equally capable of living on either a vegetarian or a meat diet. This is of great importance to man, for there are areas of the world where vegetables are simply not available (for example, desert areas and the high Arctic) unless they are imported. The settlement by man of such areas would therefore have been altogether impossible unless he had been omnivorous by nature. Man's constitution is therefore such that in this also he is uniquely equipped to fill the earth and subdue it in a way that no other creature is.

We come, then, to one further aspect of human constitution which is easily overlooked but is of equally profound significance for man in the light of his original commission. This has to do with the means by which he maintains his body temperature.

Man the Supreme Homeotherm

Although all animals, whether cold-blooded or warm-blooded, must have *some* temperature regulation in order to sustain life, there are ascending degrees of regulation as we move up the scale of complexity in animal form. The cold-blooded animals are not strictly *cold*-blooded. They are so constituted that within certain limits their body temperature floats with the environmental conditions, and the amount of energy they have fluctuates accordingly. They are sluggish and virtually defenseless when the environmental temperature falls below a certain level, because energy is derived in the animal body by the "burning" of food stuffs and this burning process becomes very inefficient at low temperatures. Obviously, such creatures must be able to prevent a fall below a certain point, otherwise they would lack energy even for digestion and other vital processes. They can, however, sustain a fall in deep body temperature far below that of warm-blooded animals. This is an advantage to them in terms of survival where they are not in danger of attack from other animals, but it severely limits their potential for accomplishment. The next level seems to be found in those animals which, although they are able to maintain their body temperature quite close to that of man, nevertheless have the ability to allow their temperature to fall everywhere in the body except in certain vital organs. There are animals which can hibernate. They reduce the demand of their body for energy to an absolute minimum for long periods of time and pass into a state of dormancy. But when the external environmental temperature rises above a certain point, some mechanism awakens them and they become as active as any other warm-blooded animal, thereafter maintaining their body temperature throughout the season of warm weather as other warm-blooded animals do throughout the year.

There is a third class of animals, among which man *seems* to be but one among many, which have an in-built thermoregulatory system. Except under very extraordinary circumstances and with extreme rarity, this system maintains the body temperature as a whole within a degree or two of some norm — in mammals around 98° F. and in birds a few degrees higher.

I have emphasized the word *seems* in connection with man, because in point of fact his thermoregulatory system is quite unique and involves several mechanisms which are not found in other animals in spite of appearances to the contrary.[113] Briefly, the system works somewhat as follows: When the human body is threatened with a fall in temperature, the first line of defense is what is called peripheral vasoconstriction, in which the circulating blood is prevented from flowing through the tiny capillaries immediately at the skin surface and is short-circuited back into the venous return flow system through special channels (anastomoses). As a result, it does not reach the surface where it would be chilled by radiation loss and by conduction to the cold surface. The effect is that the skin turns white. At the same time, this white skin acquires approximately the insulating value of cork by the reduction of its fluid content and correspondingly lowered conductivity.[114]

If this first line of defense proves insufficient, the body initiates a second defense mechanism, namely, the tightening up of skeletal muscles, especially in the limbs. This muscle tension generates heat metabolically and can actually double the resting metabolism of the body. It also, of course, accumulates waste from the breakdown products of the metabolism and results in the feeling of stiffness and ache that is experienced after exposure to the cold for a sufficient length of time. Muscle tension is maintained by the asynchronous firing of nerve impulses to the muscles.

If this second line of defense mechanism still proves inadequate, then the asynchronous firing of nerve impulses is synchronized and the muscles begin to contract in unison. We experience this as shivering. And if shivering is allowed (one should not try to suppress

---

[113] As Douglas J. H. K. Lee put it, "Man is supreme as a homeotherm." See "Heat and Cold," in *Ann. Rev. of Physiol.* 10 (1948):368.

[114] E. F. DuBois gives the specific conductivity of epidermis, subcutaneous, fat, and muscle tissue when not bathed in sweat water and in a condition of vasoconstriction as 0.00047 to 0.00050 gm. cal./sec./cm²/cm., compared with the specific conductivity of cork, which is 0.0007.

it), metabolic heat generated within the body may be increased threefold.

We therefore have a dual mechanism for maintaining the body temperature against a fall which involves muscular activity *and* a shift in circulation. Animals shiver, but it does not appear that they have the human defense of a closed-down peripheral circulation to reinforce its effect. It should be understood that the circulation of the blood is of crucial importance in the matter of temperature regulation, acting rather like a hot or cold water system in a house, the fluid itself forming the heat reservoir and by its circulation providing a highly efficient heat exchanger.

When the body is threatened with a temperature *rise*, a threat which incidentally is far more dangerous to man, a somewhat different mechanism is set in motion. The first line of defense is, again, a change in the circulation of the blood at the periphery. In this instance, miles of tiny capillaries are opened up and the blood floods through them very close to the skin surface. This is known as vasodilatation, and the visual effect is that the skin reddens. It happens in the cheeks very rapidly under emotional stress (i.e., blushing). Certain drugs like alcohol will also produce the same effect of reddening in the face and neck. A rise in body temperature due to an increase in environmental temperature is immediately counteracted by this peripheral vasodilatation. The mechanical effect is now to allow the blood to cool at the surface. Deep body heat is thereby transported and eliminated by radiation and conduction from the skin surface.

If this should prove insufficient, a second line of defense is at once initiated, a line of defense which, contrary to popular opinion, is believed to be unique in man. This is technically known as thermogenic sweating. The thermostat in the body appears to be situated in the hypothalamus which is bathed in blood and responds to minute changes in blood temperature.[115] A rise of $0.01°$ C in hypothalamic temperature is sufficient to initiate sweating when the set point has been reached.[116] During sweating, the body surface becomes bathed in a watery fluid expressed to the skin surface via some two million sweat glands, where it evaporates. The evaporation of water occurs only where the ambient air is able to absorb the

---

[115] Custance, Arthur C., "The Existence, Nature, and Behaviour of the Set-point in the Human Thermostat," DREO Report 622, Def. Res. Bd., Ottawa, 1970, 36 pp.

[116] For a fuller discussion: T. H. Benzinger, "The Human Thermostat," in *Temperature: Its Measurement and Control in Science and Industry*, Vol. III, no. 3, Reinhold, New York, 1963, pp. 637-665.

water vapor. When this can be 100 percent effective, the amount of heat removed from the body under certain circumstances can be extraordinary since the body has the ability to sweat copiously. In our own experiments, we have not infrequently observed that men can lose five or six pounds (up to three liters) of body water by this means within a single hour. This is under extreme conditions of heat stress, but it can be sustained for a surprising length of time without ill effect provided that the water is replaced. Very little rise in body temperature will occur under these conditions. The moment sweating is prevented by the use of drugs which suppress it[117] or is made valueless because the water expressed to the skin surface cannot evaporate, deep body temperature will begin to rise precipitously — and with fatal results.

These two mechanisms of handling heat and cold contribute fundamentally to man's ability to live in the Arctic or in the tropics with comparative ease. On the whole, he sustains the thermal stress better when it is negative, i.e., when there is a threat to the reduction of his body temperature.[118] He is better in the cold than in the heat, though not always as comfortable. Being such a creature as he is, man prefers to feel warm. But in point of fact, he is in much greater danger from heat and is likely to be much less energetic both physically and intellectually. He therefore tends to overcompensate against the cold by heating his buildings more than he really needs to do, thus reducing his acclimatization to the cold, a circumstance which only increases his sensitivity to it and his distaste for it. Nevertheless, he is uniquely equipped to maintain the temperature of his vital organs, especially his brain, at an optimum level for fruitful and energetic employment.

His body is exceptional in this regard. Many animals have sweat glands, some of them in the mouth (like dogs), some of them over the whole body surface (like horses), but in Nature no animal has the ability to prevent a temperature rise in times of heat stress which is comparable to man's. In spite of appearances to the contrary, the sweating of horses is initiated for quite other reasons and serves a cooling function only by accident and with nothing like the efficiency that it serves in man.[119] Physiologically, the sweating of

---

[117] Custance, Arthur C., "A Method of Measuring the Effect of Drugs on Sweating as a Function of Time," *Canad. Med. Assoc. Jour.* 95 (1966):871-874.

[118] Custance, Arthur C., "Stress-Strain Relationship of Man in the Heat," *Med.Services Jour. Canad.* 23, no. 5 (1967):721-726.

[119] Sweating of animals: see, for example with respect to horses, Stephen Rothman, *Physiology and Biochemistry of the Skin*, U. of Chicago Press, 1955, p. 166. Also, H. M. Frankel et al., "Effects of Type of Restraint upon Heat Tolerance in Monkeys," *Proc. Exper. Biol. and Med.*

horses is not thermogenic at all, that is to say, it is not initiated by a rise in *temperature* in the animal but is due to the increase in adrenalin in the animal's bloodstream as a result of violent exercise. In Nature the animal would not sweat, because it would not exercise itself as man exercises it. In addition to this, the circulatory adjustments of which the human body is capable in response to temperature fluctuation is not known in any other animal.[120] Thus man has clearly been *built* to maintain his body temperature against challenges with which no other species is likely to be faced in Nature. These circulatory adjustments involve a tremendously complex neuromuscular activity for which the human body seems to be expressly designed, and one can only suppose, therefore, that God knew what would happen to man after he fell and made provision beforehand for just such a contingency, a provision which He did not have to make when He designed all the other creatures which were to share his world but not share his ubiquity.

Conclusion

The whole body of man has, therefore, clearly been designed to support and enhance the uniqueness of his mind. Mind, tongue, and hand have somehow been structured in a very remarkable way to give coordinated expression to the sum total of human potential: to the power of reflection, of communication, and of creation; in fact, at one and the same time, of having dominion over the rest of God's creation and yet of worshiping the Creator. But it is not merely the structure of his brain and the anatomy of his body which have made these things possible. Man's uniqueness goes deeper than this. In some not yet clearly understood way, his whole physiological organization and the very special quality of his spirit have together played a part in leading inevitably to the kind of culture that he creates as a framework for his own self-expression and restraints, and — in the final analysis — the kind of redemption he needs and is capable of apprehending by faith. We next look first at the kind of culture he has

---

97 (1957):339-341; C. H. Wyndham, "Role of Skin and Core Temperatures in Man's Temperature Regulation," *Jour. Appl. Physio.* 20 (1965):36; J. D. Hardy, "Summary Review of Heat Loss and Heat Production in Physiologic Temperature Regulation," NADC-MA-5413, U. S. Naval Air Dev. Center, Johnsville, Pa., October 1954, 12; and "Control of Heat Loss and Heat Production in Physiological Temperature Regulation," Harvey Lectures Series 49, Academic Press, New York, 1953-54, pp. 247-252; Sir Charles Lovett Evans, "The Autonomic Nervous System," *Brit. Med. Bull.* 13, no. 3 (1957):154,199.

[120] Circulatory adjustment in man: see on this, for example, R. H. Fox and O. G. Edholm, "Nervous Control of Cutaneous Circulation," *Brit. Med. Bull.* 19, no. 2 (1963):110-114; Stephen Rothman, ref. 119, p. 257.

created and why it has almost inevitably taken the form it has. Then we look at his combined need for and capacity for salvation, a truly unique need and capacity which apparently has never applied to any other of God's creatures, whether angel or animal.

Chapter 5
Man the Culture Maker

A FEW years ago, it was held that in the assessment of the fossil remains of manlike forms, the crucial question to ask was, Did these creatures use tools or weapons? The use of such artifacts was a kind of *cultural* Rubicon. If the answer was Yes, the fossils were said to be human regardless of the morphology. The crucial test in the minds of many physical and social anthropologists was a cultural one, because it was held that man was the only culture-creating animal, and tools and weapons are cultural artifacts.

Now, in this context, Culture is defined as "learned behavior" by contrast with the patterned behavior of animals in their natural state, which is instinctive. This definition breaks down where birds have learned, for example, to open milk bottles — as they are still doing in England — which is clearly not instinctive behavior. But the definition is still essentially correct. Ruth Benedict pointed out that an ant colony reduced to a few members would automatically reconstruct its whole system of patterned behavior with virtually no loss, whereas the human race, similarly reduced, would lose 99 percent of its culture. For ant behavior is instinctive, whereas human behavior is learned.[121] Let us look at some of these elements of culture which have been considered diagnostic of true humanness and see to what extent these are really determinative.

Man the Toolmaker

Early in the history of anthropology it had been claimed that the use of tools was limited to *Homo sapiens,* but it soon became increasingly apparent that a remarkable number of animals also used tools of one kind or another, both of stone and of wood. It had been known for a long time that birds used sticks to pry out insects in cracks in

---

[121] Benedict, Ruth, *Patterns of Culture*, Pelican Books, New York, 1946, p. 11.

wood, but since birds were never candidates as precursors of man, the fact was not considered to conflict with proposed markers of humanness. One of Darwin's finches, for example, uses cactus spines to pick out insects in crevices in tree trunks.[122] It is also known that the burrowing wasp, *Ammophila*, uses a small pebble as a hammer to pound down the soil over its nest of eggs.[123] But insects are not precursors of man either. More recently, an Egyptian vulture, *Neophron percnopterus*, has been observed to break open ostrich eggs by *throwing* a stone held in its beak at the egg shell.[124] The bird's aim is quite good.

But in some mammals even more complex tool-using has been observed. For example, floating on its back in the water, a sea otter will place a slab of rock fifteen or twenty cm. in diameter, collected from the sea floor, on its chest. Then, holding a small mollusc shell in both forepaws, it repeatedly strikes it on the stone with full swings until it is able to break it open.[125] Polar bears apparently have been reported using quite large stones or blocks of ice as weapons. According to Reclus, in an early issue of *Nature* (1883), J. Rae reported seeing a polar bear lying in wait on an elevated point for an unsuspecting walrus or sea calf gambolling on the beach immediately below. When one came within range, the polar bear hit it on the head by aiming his weapon very skillfully.[126] Coming a little closer to man, morphologically speaking, baboons are known to use natural implements such as stones or sticks which happen to be at hand.[127]

It is therefore quite possible, for example, that the Australopithecines with whose fossil remains there was evidence of stone tools or weapons of a simple design, usually referred to as

---

[122] Darwin's finches: David Lack, "Darwin's Finches," *Sci. American*, April 1953, p. 68.

[123] Burrowing wasps: Kenneth P. Oakley, ref. 86, p. 2.

[124] Vultures: Jane and Hugo van Lawick Goodall, "Use of Tools by Egyptian Vulture, *Neophron percnopterus*," *Nature*, December 24, 1966, p. 468.

[125] Sea-otter: Kenneth P. Oakley, ref. 86, p. 5.

[126] Polar bears: Elie Reclus, *Primitive Folk*, Scott, London, n.d., p. 17.

[127] Baboons: on this see panel discussion on "Physical Anthropology and the Biological Basis of Human Behaviour," in *An Appraisal of Anthropology Today*, ed. Sol Tax et al., U. of Chicago Press, 1953, p. 263, An excellent study has been published by Philip Street, *Animal Weapons*, MacGibbon & Kee, London, 1971. See also on this, K. R. L. Hall, "Tool Using Performances as Indicators of Behavioural Adaptability," in *Human Evolution*, ref. 27, p. 178. Wilbert H. Rusch, "Human Fossils," in *Rock Strata and the Bible Record*, ed. Paul A. Zimmerman, Concordia, St. Louis, 1970, p. 149: he mentions that chimpanzees may sometimes crush leaves and use them as a sponge to soak up water from a cavity. It has recently been argued that chimpanzees in the wild may actually manufacture tools. But R. L. Holloway held that "the fashioning of termiting sticks and other reported tool-making activities on the part of chimpanzees do not represent the imposition of arbitrary forms on the environment," by which is meant actual *creation* of tools out of raw materials (see "Culture: A Human Domain," *Current Anthropology* 10 [1969]:395-407).

"pebble-tools," could have been using these as baboons use stones and quite by chance have fractured them so that they appear to have been consciously worked whereas in fact the working of them might have been accidental. On the other hand, it is also possible that these associated simple weapons were manufactured deliberately by hunters for whom the Australopithecines were the prey. Man may have killed these apes for food or in self-defense, or in taking over their territory.

So the mere employment of tools is not decisive. If birds by experience learn to use the right kind of sharp instrument to flush out insects, deliberately choosing this piece of wood and rejecting some other piece that is too large, it is hard to see why an intelligent ape might not also choose a piece of stone which already happened to have a cutting edge. There is also some question in the minds of anthropologists about the basis of judgment of a very simply worked flint in determining whether it has accidentally come by its form or been deliberately worked. Many of the eoliths found in France and elsewhere by such early archaeologists as Lartet and others were later rejected as purely accidental, though to a predisposed eye they appeared convincing enough.[128]

So the issue has now been refined a little, and humanness is not considered to be established merely by the presence of tools, but only by determining whether the tools are genuinely man-made. But there are times when this is very difficult to do. Of course, tools with symmetry or complex working are almost certainly man-made and not the work of other primates below man. But, so equivocal can very *simple* tools be in this regard that some authorities would attach very little significance to them unless there *is* also evidence of fire. Thus the search is made for other lasting evidences of the presence of man, such as charred remains that signify the use of fire. Coon held that "the use of fire is the only open-and-shut difference between man and all other animals."[129] And there seemed little likelihood of this being disputed.

Man the Firemaker

The use of the evidence of fire as proof of the presence of man is

---

[128] Lartet: see A. S. Barnes in *Amer. Anthropolog.* 41 (1939):99; and more recently, Henri V. Vallois and Marcellin Boule, ref. 65, pp. 98-109, for a discussion. At the time when the issue was a very live one, a paper entitled "Eolithic Implements," illustrated with a number of plates (some even in color), was presented by R. A. Bullen, which appeared in *Trans. Vict. Instit.* 33 (1901):191-225.

[129] Coon, C. S., ref. 70, p. 63.

not really confused by the fact that we know now that animals *may* use fire just as they use tools. For example, apes may go to a human hearth after its native maker has left it and warm themselves by it.[130] Whether any ape has ever thought to poke the fire to improve its heat output, is a moot question. Negatively speaking, we do not have any record of a dog, lying beside the fire in an English home, getting up and putting another log on it to maintain it. And it seems even safer to say that no animal ever deliberately lit a fire to keep warm by. It seems clear, therefore, that the presence of a hearth is absolute evidence of the presence of true man.

Nevertheless, the *absence* of any evidence of fire is not unequivocal evidence of the absence of man, since some primitive people, even in recent times, apparently never learned or had forgotten how to make fire for themselves. According to Radcliffe Brown, the Andaman Islanders did not make fire when he studied them between 1906 and 1908,[131] and somewhat more recently Patrick Putnam around 1940 found that the Pgymies of the Ituri Forest could not make fire for themselves.[132] Almost certainly man alone *makes* fire, though man is not *alone* in using fire.

Man the Speechmaker

We turn, therefore, to another aspect of culture which is considered to be diagnostic, but even this proves to have its limitations for prehistory. This is the use of language; and as Herskovits rightly observed, "Language (is) the vehicle of culture."[133] One can nicely juxtapose two observations by well-known authors here. Von Humboldt wrote, "Man is man only be means of speech, but in order to invent speech he must be man already."[134] One may couple this with the following statement by A. L. Kroeber: "Culture, then, began when speech was present, and from then on the enrichment of each meant the further development of the other."[135] While some people use only the most primitive of tools which, if found in isolation, would barely be recognized as such, and while some whole tribes lack the ability to make fire and must continue without it until they

[130] Greene, John C., *The Death of Adam,* Iowa State U. Press, 1959, p. 180.

[131] Radcliffe Brown: quoted by Ashley Montagu, *Man's First Million Years,* Mentor Books, New York, 1958, p. 158.

[132] Patrick Putnam: quoted by C. S. Coon, *A Reader in General Anthropology,* Holt, New York, 1948, p. 327.

[133] Herskovits, Melville, *Man and His Works,* Knopf, New York, 1950, pp. 440ff.

[134] W. von Humboldt: quoted by Charles Lyell, *The Antiquity of Man,* 4th ed., n.p., 1873, p. 518.

[135] Kroeber, A. L., ref. 20, p. 225.

can obtain it from some neighbor, no tribe or people has ever been known which did not have a language. And, as it turns out, often the more primitive the tribe, the more complex the language.[136] As a matter of fact, in the light of present knowledge, it seems that language more often proceeds from the complex to the simple and not in the reverse direction.[137] Thus we can say unequivocally that any creature that *uses speech to converse* is clearly a human being.

But this raises two open questions. The first is, Do animals actually have language, which we have not recognized because we don't happen to speak in the same way? Or to put it in another way, Is speaking a uniquely *human* faculty? The second question is whether there is any way in which we could tell for certain whether a particular fossil cranium belonged to a speaking creature or a dumb one. Unless we can tell this, the use of speech diagnostically for true man doesn't help us in dealing with prehistory.

When Broca in 1865 discovered, as a result of war wounds, that damage in a specific area of the brain results in disturbance of speech, he "localized" a speech area in the brain. As a consequence, it was hoped that an endo-cranial cast of sufficient refinement should provide evidence of the ability to speak or otherwise on the assumption that the impression would adequately reflect the formal configuration of the brain itself and thereby allow accurate assessment of its potential by indicating the full development of this area. There was confidence that such studies would give some evidence of the owner's powers of speech. Added to this, it was believed that a careful analysis of the inside of the jaw should provide further confirmation of the adequacy and refinement of the tongue muscles used in speaking. Between the two, it was felt that fairly firm statements could be made: "This individual probably had the power of speech, but this individual did not." Analysis of many of the more famous fossil remains of early man or proto-man was at once undertaken along these lines, and whether Neanderthal Man or Cromagnon Man could speak or not was energetically discussed at the time.

For example, the absence of a little process of bone in the middle

---

[136] A. L. Kroeber remarks in this connection, "Dictionaries compiled by missionaries or philologists of languages previously unwritten run to surprising figures. Thus the number of words recorded in Klamath, the speech of a culturally rude American Indian tribe, is 7,000; in Navaho, 11,000; in Zulu, 17,000; in Dakota, 19,000; in Maya, 20,000; in Nahuatl, 27,000. It may safely be estimated that every existing language, no matter how backward its speakers are in their general civilization, possesses a vocabulary of at least 5,000 to 10,000 words. Kroeber then adds this note(!): "Jesperson, who allows 20,000 words to Shakespeare, and 8,000 to Milton, cites 26,000 as the vocabulary of Swedish peasants." See ref. 20, p. 231.

[137] Kluckholm, Clyde, *Mirror for Man*, McGraw-Hill, New York, 1949, p. 149.

of the lower jaw to which some of the muscles of the tongue are attached was believed to prove that the Canstadt Race could not speak. Cromagnon Man, however, was more advanced since he had this little process and therefore could. We were taught this in university courses in the early 1930s. It seemed to reinforce the validity of the usual lineup of primitive men from apelike to *Homo sapiens*. What we, as students, did not know at that time was that the whole idea had long since been shown to be without foundation. By 1888, Sir William Dawson of McGill University had already shown the fallacy of this argument. After consultation with Wesley Mills, Professor of Anatomy in that university, he appended this note at the appropriate place in one of his works dealing with early man:[138]

> Though the muscles attached to the genial tubercles (the Genio-hyoid and Genio-hyo-glossi) are the most important in the greater movements of the tongue as when it is protruded from the mouth, yet many minor movements, such as those concerned in speech, are possible in the absence of the functional activities of these muscles.
>
> The clearest evidence that the tongue itself is neither the sole organ of speech nor even an *essential* organ of speech, is derived from the fact that after the removal of the tongue, as complete as may be, speech is so far possible as to be intelligible though not perfect, the dentals especially being indistinct; yet there is good utterance.
>
> I myself, many years ago, followed a case of excision of the tongue, and was surprised at the degree of perfection of utterance attained even in a few weeks after the operation.
>
> A comparison of even a few lower jaws of man shows that these genial tubercles vary very much in size, in some cases being but indifferently marked. . . . So that, altogether, I should myself hesitate to infer that men in whom these tubercles were absent had been without the power of speech. . . .

Today, the point is seldom, if ever, discussed. The argument simply has died for lack of evidence. Even at the time of our course of lectures, Wilson D. Wallis was reiterating that "the anatomist cannot tell from an examination of the skull of modern man whether or not the possessor had speech; much less from fossil skulls."[139] Or more recently, in 1948, Weidenreich wrote:[140]

> The claim of paleoanthropologists to the effect that Neanderthal or Peking Man was right handed or left handed, was able to speak, or write, or could only stammer, all deduced from shallower and narrower, or deeper and broader impressions on the inside of the brain case, have no scientific basis. . . .

---

[138] Dawson, Sir William, *Modern Science in Bible Land*, Dawson Bros., Montreal, 1888, p. 225 footnote.

[139] Wallis, Wilson D., "The Structure of Prehistoric Man," in *The Making of Man*, ed. V. F. Calverton, Modern Library, New York, 1931, p. 65.

[140] Weidenreich, Franz, ref. 51, p. 107.

Furthermore, it is now known that manlike apes such as the chimpanzee are not prevented from speaking because they lack the necessary tongue muscles. They *ought* to be able to speak, if it is *merely* a matter of these particular muscles. As early as 1916, W. H. Furness, in attempting to teach articulate speech to both the orangutan and chimpanzee, observed, "I found that the first difficulty to be overcome is their lack of *use* of lips and tongue in making their emotional cries."[141]

Now, there are several things that must be said to qualify this observation. And the crucial importance of speech for man requires that we look at the subject a little more carefully. In the first place, Furness would be the first to agree that one cannot speak usefully of "teaching articulate speech" in this context. For thus far the most elegant and imaginative programs have only reinforced at every turn the fact that nonhuman primates *do not* and probably *cannot* speak. They can communicate in remarkable ways, as we shall see, but the power of speech is not, apparently, within their reach. They are dependent upon the use of signs, just as other animals have elaborate means of communication by the use of signs, the only difference with these primates being that they can evidently be taught to use a large number of signs deliberately — which they would never use in their own natural environment — in order to communicate with man. But they do not *speak*, apparently because they *cannot* speak. Let us look at the evidence.

A number of attempts have been made over the past forty years to bring up a chimpanzee from infancy in a home environment, treating it precisely as though it were a member of the family, subjecting it to the same disciplines as other children, the same encouragements, and as far as possible the same stimuli. Every attempt was made to induce speech as is normally made to induce speech in a human child. The best known of these experiments were those made first by the Kelloggs[142] (1933), by the Hayeses[143] (1951), by the Gardners[144] (1967), and finally by Premack[145] in 1969.

The Kelloggs named their chimpanzee Gua. Essentially, for our

---

[141] Furness, W. H., "Observations on the Mentality of Chimpanzee and Orangutan," *Proc. Amer. Philos. Soc.* 55 (1916):281-284. On lip form see E. H. Lenneberg, *Biological Foundations of Language*, Wiley, New York, 1967, especially pp. 37-52.

[142] Kellogg, W. N., and Kellogg, L. A., *The Ape and the Child: A Study in Environmental Influence on Early Behavior*, McGraw-Hill, New York, 1933, reissued by Hafner.

[143] Hayes, K. J., and Hayes, C., *The Ape in Our House*, Harper, New York, 1951.

[144] Gardner, R. A., and Gardner, B. T., reported in "Teaching Sign Language to a Chimpanzee," *Science* 165 (1969):664-672.

[145] Kellogg, W. L., "Communication and Language in the Home-Raised Chimpanzee," *Science* 162 (1968):424.

purposes in this paper, their findings may be summed up by saying first that although in the wild and when domesticated the chimpanzee may be very vocal and give expression to a number of emotional cries when angry, excited, or in need, it is a remarkably *silent* animal otherwise. In an experimentally controlled environment in which the home-raised chimpanzee is given the same linguistic and social advantages as a human baby, the chimpanzee displays no evidence of vocal *imitation*. Despite its generally high level of imitative behavior, it never spontaneously copies or reproduces human *word* sounds. W. N. Kellogg noted that neither in their own previous experiments, nor in those undertaken by R. M. Finch, nor in those undertaken by N. Kohts (Moscow), was there the slightest evidence of any attempt on the part of these animals to imitate speech or to reproduce any human vocalizations:[146]

> Moreover, no ape has ever been known to go through the long period of babbling and prattling which, in the human baby, seems to be the necessary pre-requisite to the subsequent articulation of word sounds. Vocalized play of this sort was absent in (our) chimp, who made no sounds "without some definite provocation which in most cases was obviously of an emotional character."

The end result of the Kelloggs' experiment was that they succeeded in getting Gua to signal to them by sign language what she wanted. For example, pushing away her cup meant "enough"; holding the genitalia meant the need to go to the toilet; biting or chewing at the. clothes or the fingers of the experimenter meant "hungry"; removing the bib from her neck meant "finished eating"; hanging on the hand of the experimenter meant "swing me"; and so forth. Of speech, that is, the use of *words* for communication, there was no evidence whatever.

The Hayeses had better success. They were able to teach their chimpanzee, Vicki, to say *mamma* by manipulating her lips as she said *ah*. It took a long while to achieve this and she still persisted in putting her own forefinger on her upper lip. Later the words *papa*, *cup*, and possibly *up* were added to her repertoire. In 1916 Furness had, by a similar means, succeeded in training an ape (this time an orangutan) to say *papa* and *cup*, also by manipulating the lips.

The facial mobility of man has often been remarked upon. It is quite tremendous. Few animals can alter their features except to snarl. Chimpanzees have considerable facial expression, but appearances may be deceiving. What looks like a smile may not indi-

---

[146] Furness, W. H., ref. 141, p. 281.

cate pleasure at all. At any rate, the effect of the muscles in the chimpanzee face may seem to be similar to man's, but the functions of these muscles are actually quite different.[147] The lack of adequate control of lip movement evidently *contributes* to the chimpanzee's inability to mimic the sound of words.

Kellogg summed up his impression of the work of the Hayeses by saying:[148]

> The most important finding of the Hayeses was perhaps not that their chimp could enunciate a few human sounds. It lay rather in the discovery that these sound patterns were extremely hard for the ape to master, that they never came naturally or easily, and that she had trouble afterwards in keeping the patterns straight.

Of their own experiments, Kellogg concluded that the chimpanzee could respond correctly to a number of simple commands in spoken human language and achieved this slightly ahead of a child of the same age. But having done this, by the end of the first three years the chimpanzee seemed to have reached its limit of learning capacity, just at a time when the child, which had been its companion, began to forge ahead at a tremendous speed. These simple commands were such as the following: "no, no," "come here," "close the door," "blow the horn," "don't put that in your mouth," "go to daddy," "go to mamma," "go to Donald," and so on.

Two important conclusions emerge: first, neither Gua nor Vicki learned to speak in the ordinary sense (Vicki's four words were not really being used as *words*), and secondly, the ape's mind can clearly discriminate the intent of sentences in which the succession of sounds is distinguishable and will respond to them — such as go to *daddy*, *mamma*, or *Donald*. But understanding, not reproduction, is the limit of achievement. A horse or a dog will also respond to commands.

The experiments of the Gardners were much more sophisticated and clearly gained a great deal from the experiments of their predecessors, the Kelloggs and the Hayeses. In their report in *Science*,

---

[147] Weinert, H., in *An Appraisal of Anthropology Today*, ed. Sol Tax et al., U. of Chicago Press, 1953, p. 25. See also William Howells, ref. 35, p. 79. R. J. Andrew has a very useful paper on this subject entitled "Evolution of Facial Expression." His title is odd in a way, because what he succeeds in doing, to my mind, is demonstrating rather clearly that "facial expression" in man, even when it approximates quite closely that of apes or monkeys, conveys a completely different message and is an expression of entirely different inner feeling. Andrew's paper carries the blurbs "Many human expressions can be traced back to reflex responses of primitive primates and insectivores." But this is surely presumption. If muscles serve an absolutely different function in so far as, on his own showing, Andrew traces the human smile (an expression of good will) to the animal's snarl (a preparation for battle), can one properly speak of causal connections at all? (*Science* 142 [1963]:1034f.)

[148] Kellogg, W. L., ref. 145, p. 424.

they pointed out that although the Hayeses spared no effort to teach Vicki to make speech sounds, she nevertheless succeeded in a period of six years only in learning four that approximated English words. They, too, noted that while the vocal apparatus of the chimpanzee is very different from that of man, the vocal *behavior* of the chimpanzee is even more so:[149]

> Chimpanzees do make many different sounds, but generally vocalization occurs in situations of high excitement and tends to be specific to the exciting situation. Undisturbed, chimpanzees are usually silent.

The close tie between vocalization (in the sense of giving voice) and emotion is highly significant in dealing with the whole problem of the origin of speech in man. The subject has been discussed in summary fashion in another Doorway Paper,[150] to which the reader should refer for a more extended bibliography. But the point at issue here is that linguists who have concerned themselves with the problem of the origin of speech agree upon this fact, that emotional cries are *not* the foundation of man's speaking capacity, since emotion has precisely the opposite effect. It tends rather to reduce him to a state of speechlessness. The emotional exclamations, *oh, ah,* etc., are involuntary (except when acted, of course), and they have the characteristic brevity of all emotional cries. Cries like, Help! are equally monosyllabic. Cries such as these do not constitute speech: they are formalized *signs* of emotional stress. In emotional language we usually use short words. The feelings of the man who says to a girl "I love you" are easily distinguished from those of the man who says, "I have a tremendous admiration for you." The longer the word, the less its emotional content as a rule; and the greater its emotional content, the less does it reflect the true nature of speech as a means of communication, particularly the communication of ideas. Thus the very fact that these nonhuman primates (which seem so responsive in other ways) nevertheless do not learn to *speak*, seems to be closely related to the fact that *vocalization* is for them an expression of emotion, not of thought.

For this reason, the Gardners adopted the very sensible plan of using something akin to deaf and dumb language which involves no vocalization at all but the use of signs. The results of their experiment fully justify this approach. Their experimental animal, whom they named Washoe, proved herself an apt pupil. Within sixteen months she had learned nineteen signs reliably, with five more in process. By

---

[149] Gardner, R. A. and B. T., ref. 144, p. 664.
[150] Part VI, "Who Taught Adam to Speak?" in the Doorway Papers, Vol.II.

the end of twenty-two months, she understood and used twenty-eight signs in one day, out of a total of thirty-four which she had learned. By the time she was four years old, she had been taught to make reliable responses to more than eighty different signs, though it is not clear whether she actually used all these signs herself. Not only did she make use of signs, but she was able to transfer their value. For example, the sign for "open" she could apply to the unlocking of a cupboard and then to the unlocking of doors, and finally to the idea of turning the ignition key in the car. Occasionally she "confused" the signs a little, like *flower* with *odor*, and *dog* with *barking*. But, as the Gardners put is, "Her signs do not remain specific to their original referents but are transferred spontaneously to new referents."[151]

While I think that we are forced by these results to recognize that part of our problem in accurately assessing the animal mind lies in our inadequate means of communication with them, we must not — for all our surprise — overestimate the animal mind nor underestimate the fundamental difference between animal mind and human mind. In Washoe's case the response was always situational. The signs that were adopted and used by Washoe had to do with, and were used in connection with, personal needs, not with the needs of others. Nor were they used in connection with unrealities, abstract concepts, things merely of interest for conversation, hypothetical things. Conceptual language was not involved. Nor were the signs structured consistently into sentences in such a way as to indicate an awareness of grammatical principles. A child becomes aware of grammar by some unconscious process, and untaught. One can observe this in delightful ways in children, if one is careful. Last summer a little friend of ours, who is about three years old, was talking to me as I climbed out of my car, and suddenly noticed a dead grasshopper at his feet. He looked at it for a moment, and then he said reflectively, "Somebody deaded it." He had learned the difference in meaning between an adjective and a verb, between "dead" and "deaded." He created the verb for himself, quite correctly — though uncommonly. There is no doubt that no one had taught him to do this.

In his review of E. H. Lenneberg's *Biological Foundations of Language* E. A. Weinstein notes that in children there is a normal order of the development of vocalization from crying to cooing, and then to babbling.[152] Single words appear between the ages of twelve to eighteen months, followed by two-word combinations "which are

[151] Gardner, R. A. and B. T., ref. 144, p. 671.
[152] Weinstein, E. A., *Science* 156 (1967):1585.

not random compositions, but constitute a primitive subject predi-
cate organization. They are not imitations of adult speech, but
indicate that certain rules of grammar have been acquired." Even in
brain-injured, deaf, and otherwise handicapped children, though
the rate of language learning is slowed down, nevertheless the same
order obtains.

In other words, Washoe never put her signs together to reconstruct a sentence. Neither did she invent words. There was no
grammar involved. Yet it is grammar that converts a series of sounds
into a form of speech. Furthermore, the use of signs was always
immediately contingent upon circumstance. There was no delay.
Man can sit and think over a situation, take it apart, analyze it into
components each of which he can label separately, and then he can
reconstitute reality and give it expression verbally in a sentence in
which the very organization of the components conveys his understanding. As the Gardners put it, in Washoe's case, there was no
"disengagement from the immediate context."

The Gardners achieved their success by adopting a means of
communication which did not require Washoe to speak, that is, to
attempt the vocalization of words. In commenting on their work, I
think David McNeil of the University of Chicago summed things up
very nicely when he said:[153]

> The Gardner's ape is fascinating, but the few examples of her "speech"
> that I have seen appear to be quite different from the speech of young
> children. The structural arrangement, if there is any, looks unlike anything
> that occurs in the development of language.

Using the same principle of signs developed by the Gardners, a
still more sophisticated series of experiments was conducted by
David Premack and reported under the title, "Language in Chimpanzee?"[154] Premack's program was carried out with an African-
born female chimpanzee whom he named Sarah. She was six years
old when the study began, a fact which suggests that it may not be
altogether true that man's greater learning capacity is due to the
much longer period during which man is anatomically and
physiologically still plastic, although the experience of the Kelloggs
did suggest that some measure of "fixity" began to take place in their
subject at about three years of age.

Premack's experiments seem to have been even more elaborate
than those of his predecessors'. In some ways they force us to credit

---

[153] David McNeil: quoted by Arthur Koestler, ref. 11, p. 317.
[154] Premack, David, *Science* 172 (1971):808-822.

the chimpanzee's mind with even greater potential for communication by such means, because there was evidence of the ability to understand at least *something* of the meaning of sentence structure, the concept of *class* relative to objects, the meaning of the copula (is), of pluralization, of logical connections (if — then), of the conjunction "and" and in a rudimentary way the meaning of symbolization. With respect to this last, Premack rightly asks the question whether it is possible to teach an organism the meaning of symbolization if it does not already symbolize in its own mind. He felt that the training procedures he used were not teaching symbolization, but must have been utilizing a capacity the animal already possessed. Who knows, therefore, what really goes on in the mind of such an animal?

Several of his findings confirm, or seem to me to confirm, previous observations. For example, Premack could not induce Sarah to structure a sentence which was directed altruistically, unless he rewarded her very specifically.[155] Thus she would put down the symbols in the right order for, say, "Mary give Sarah apple," but she was reluctant to put down, "Mary give Gussie [another person familiar to Sarah] apple." She would only do it when she was rewarded with a tidbit she preferred in exchange for the right answer. She could not be sufficiently motivated by a situation which did not reward her personally. It should not be thought, however, that in Nature animals never act altruistically.[156] They do, not only in parent-child relationships, but in fellow creature relationships.

It should be borne in mind that Sarah still did not speak, did not verbalize. She merely manipulated plastic symbols, as a child manipulates alphabet blocks. But she did manipulate them in quite sophisticated ways.

In a study of the vocal tract limitation of nonhuman primates, Philip H. Lieberman et al.[157] concluded that the inability of apes to mimic human speech results from the inherent limitations of their vocal mechanisms. It is conceivable that they have something to say, but they have no way of saying it. "The human speech-output

---

[155] Ibid., pp. 808-810.
[156] For examples, see Part IV, "The Survival of the Unfit," in this volume.
[157] Lieberman, P. H.; Klatt, D. H.; and Wilson, W. H., "Vocal Tract Limitations on the Vocal Repertoires of Rhesus Monkeys and Other Non-Human Primates," *Science* 164 (1969):1187. Another study of the organs of speech has been published: J. Wind, *On the Phylogeny and the Ontogeny of the Human Larynx: a Morphological and Functional Study*, Groningen, The Netherlands, 1970. In reviewing this in *Science* 173 (1971):414, R. O'Rahilly notes the author concludes that "no satisfactory explanation of speech emergence has yet been given."

mechanism should thus be viewed as part of man's species-specific endowment."[158]

Somewhere in the total constitution of man's mind, there appears to be a capacity for the use of symbols which, coupled with his appropriately designed organs of speech, allows him to manipulate his understanding of reality and to discuss it intelligibly with his own kind. It now appears, therefore, that it is man's combined capacities, capacities involving the nature of his mind and his anatomy working together which allow him to acquire and sustain speech and, through speech, to enhance his powers of understanding and communication. So he compounds the fruits of his learning and enormously multiplies his cultural wealth. Somewhere in the process of socialization, self-awareness arises and with it self-evaluation, the ability to assess and judge the actions and motives, in others and in himself.[159] And so the way is opened for him to become, by reason of the divinely implanted spiritual component in his nature, a morally responsible creature.

Thus although tremendous advances have been made in our understanding of the potential for communication in animals below man, the work of the Kelloggs, the Hayeses, the Gardners, and now Premack, with chimpanzees, has underscored the fact that *speech*, the use of the spoken word, is a unique human faculty. The means of communication between animals are much more varied, it seems, than in man, but far less pregnant with potential. Bees use a language of movement.[160] Fishes use a chemical one.[161] Mutual recognition between birds is based on sound as well as visual cues.[162] It has even been found recently that unborn chicks, still in their shells, communicate with each other by clicks and other vocal sounds which have been tape-recorded.[163] Bats, of course, signal to one another in

---

[158] G. G. Simpson, ref. 107, p. 116: "Perhaps we can at least determine when language arose by tracing the anatomical evolution of the vocal apparatus? That line is even now being followed seriously by some anatomists, but I think they are astray. A human brain in a monkey's body would probably mispronounce English words, *but it would certainly produce a language*" (my emphasis). The point is well taken and underscores the fact that unless the brain is human, true language will not emerge whether the *organs* of speech are appropriate or not: and conversely, if the brain is human, language will emerge under the right social conditions even when the organs of speech are faulty. Even the anatomically dumb can employ language.

[159] Mead, George Herbert, *Mind, Self and Society*, U. of Chicago Press, 1948.

[160] Bees: Carl von Frisch's justly famous *Dance Language and Orientation of Bees* has been republished in a translation by L. E. Chadwick, Harvard U. Press, 1968, xiv and 566 pp.

[161] Fishes: "The Chemical Language of Fishes," *Sci. American*, May 1971, pp. 98ff.

[162] Birds: W. H. Thorpe, "Perceptive Basis for Group Organization in Social Vertebrates, Especially Birds," *Nature*, October 12, 1968, pp. 124-128.

[163] Unhatched chicks: Margaret A. Vince of Cambridge, in Britannica Book of the Year, 1971, under the heading "Biological Sciences," p. 166.

frequencies beyond the hearing range of the human ear. So animal means of communication are varied indeed. One of the most useful collections of data on the use of signs by animals was produced by Dietrich Burkhardt, Wolfgang Schleidt, and Helmut Altner in *Signals in the Animal World.*[164]

If evolution were a fact, it seems as though it must have somehow miscued by dividing the potential of living creatures in such a way as to reduce the likelihood of their developing the capacity to *speak*. What I have in mind is the fact that in one class of animals, the birds, we find the combination of erect posture, vocal organs which allow for song, and — even more importantly — the ability to imitate a substantial number of words and sentences — as seen in parrots and other bird species. But the ability to communicate by the use of deliberately chosen signs, such as can be acquired by some of the nonhuman primates, appears to be lacking. They thus have the ability to speak, but have nothing to say. By contrast, evolution has produced (supposedly) another class of animals, represented by chimpanzees, which, while they can manifestly learn to communicate with man in a sign language, are evidently not equipped anatomically for speech. They are quite unable to vocalize words as some of the birds are able to do. They thus may possibly have something to say, but can't say it. This seems like a misdirected distribution of capabilities, for we therefore have in one line of development the necessary mechanism for the sounding of words which can only be meaningless; and in an entirely different line of development the mechanism for giving meaning to words which can't be said. In short, only in man do we find these two capabilities united; along with an erect posture that makes conversation easy and natural *face to face*, coupled with a manipulative skill in the hands, providing a unique extension of the mind, and a means of considerable reinforcement to verbal expression.

Although many contributory factors in the anatomy of man are obviously involved, nevertheless it seems pretty clear that the prime source of uniqueness, the seat of ultimate superiority, lies in his mind. Whether mind and brain can be related, as we have for the most part imagined them to be, does not seem to be as clearly demonstrated today as it seemed to be a few years ago. In some way, the whole man appears to be alive with man-soul. Yet it is simpler and more convenient, perhaps, for purposes of discussion to accept for the moment the idea that "mind" is at the root of it all, and by

---

[164] Burkhardt, Dietrich, et al., tr. Kenneth Morgan, Allen and Unwin, London, 1967.

putting the *mind* in quote marks I want to leave it as an open question whether the mind of man encompasses both his intellect *and* his spirit. One thing seems reasonably certain that if we allow the quality of his mind to stand as representative of his humanness, then the mind of man is *not* the same as the mind of an animal, and therefore he himself is not the same as an animal — despite all appearances. In part this is recognized by many writers. Years ago, Briffault observed:[165]

> Between the mental constitution of the rudest savages and that of any animal, including the anthropoids, there is a wide gap, and that gap consists of more than a difference in degree; it amounts to a difference in kind. Primarily that difference depends upon the conceptual character of human mentality.

Conceptual character of human mentality: what does it mean? It means man's ability to create mental images which are not bound to the realities which impinge upon his senses. He can dream of things which do not yet exist: he can imagine situations which are contrary to fact. He can, indeed, tell lies usefully. The early Church Fathers recognized this as one of the special characteristics of man. They pointed out that animals cannot tell lies (though they can, of course, be deceived) and God would not tell lies. Man does. He will speak of negative numbers or of decimals — parts of numbers. He will speak of ten days which never exist at one time, or (in statistics) of the average family as being composed of 3.6 people. Thus he can do impossible things with his mind. His speech is propositional, he can discuss hypotheses and play with his ideas until he invents new things and achieves new understandings. His ability to verbalize allows him to talk about what is contrary to fact and thus often bring to pass things which enormously extend his dominion over the earth — and even beyond the earth. Some years ago in thinking about these things, Henri Bergson wrote:[166]

> The impression arises when we compare the brain of man and that of animals that the difference at first appears to be only a difference in size and complexity. But judging by function, there must be something else besides. . . . Between man and the animals the difference is no longer one of degree but of kind.

All of history confirms this judgment. The difference is absolute, even though there are enough parallels to make it virtually impossi-

[165] Briffault, Robert, "Evolution of Human Species," in *The Making of Man,* ref. 139, p. 762.

[166] Bergson, Henri, *Creative Evolution,* Modern Library, New York, 1944, pp. 200,201.

ble to quantify the difference when its substance is dissected. It is the potential which really clinches the matter.

Conclusion

We begin to see, therefore, something fundamentally new in man, which is not merely the result of the addition of new capacities but seems to arise from a whole new dimension that is somehow in the mind and yet not of it. The whole increasingly becomes more than merely the sum of the parts. Everything about this creature, *Homo sapiens*, is of a piece, each part uniquely contributing. The specialized hands and their nervous connections with an area of the brain seems designedly to be juxtaposed against the centers of speech and motor control of the tongue and voicebox, and the receptive areas of hearing and seeing. There is design here, optimization of the system as a whole, not for the *survival* of the organism (though this is necessary), but for the elaboration of the life of the organism beyond mere survival and often, in fact, to its very endangerment.

Compared with other creatures, man seems constantly at a disadvantage, yet he can dominate them all. Taken singly, his hearing and his seeing are less acute than theirs, his sense of taste and smell are less refined, the speed of reaction of his reflexes and the strength of his muscles cannot compare, his resistance to disease and his powers of recovery from wounds are lower, his rate of reaching maturity and independence in infancy, and even his achievement of "social wisdom" are slower — all these, individually, fall far behind the faculties, abilities, and processes in other animals. It seems, superficially, that none of these have been maximized in man relatively speaking, and some of them, important as they are to animals, seem to be almost rudimentary in him.

Yet in some remarkable way, the total configuration of strength and weakness seem to contribute to rather than detract from his potential for greater things, for a higher position, for greater responsibility, for an entirely new kind of self-realization. His very weaknesses seem to fit him uniquely for fellowship with God.

Now we have already considered some of these more obvious specific qualifications which contribute manifestly to his superiority. Let us now look at some of those which by contrast would superficially seem to be a handicap to him — though in point of fact, they are not. Let us examine the significance for man of his slowness in reaching physical maturity and his long dependency in childhood, the role of the male in the human family, his progressive complexification of his social relationships, his ability to achieve personal individuation, the factors governing breeding in animals and in man, his dietary unwisdom, his susceptibility to disease and slowness in healing, his strange drive to order, arrange, and organize, and finally his willingness to sacrifice the temporal for the transcendental and his need for and capacity for redemption. In all these things, as we shall see, man stands apart by himself.

Chapter 6
The Expression
of Humanness in Man

I N THIS chapter I draw attention to some significant factors in the development of a human being which do not appear in the animal world. Superficially, they look like mere extensions of animal behavior. When analyzed more carefully, it will be seen that they are not. If a student begins with the assumption that he will find the explanation of human behavior in the animal world, he will discover in due course that he has been mistaken. Those who have matured in their study and have honestly faced the evidence will already have discovered the inadequacy of such an assumption. It is in the textbooks which are written for younger students and for the public that the most misleading statements in this regard are to be found. In works of a more serious nature a different picture emerges. Let me illustrate this with a series of quotations, before entering into a detailed consideration of this chapter under more specific headings.

Writing in *Science* in 1945, Alexander Novicoff said:[167]

Man's social relationships represent a new level, higher than that of his biological make-up. Man's behaviour differs from that of other animals because of his possession of body structures, notably the highly developed nervous system, which make thought and speech possible and whose functioning is profoundly affected by social and cultural influences. . . .

The study of animal behaviour cannot be a substitute for the study of man's behaviour. As we establish the likenesses in behaviour of animals and men, we must simultaneously investigate the fundamental qualitative differences between them. . . . Animal societies never rise above the biological level, only man's society is truly sociological.

Anyone who has tried to teach biological change to college students knows the barriers to learning that have been created by the identification of animals with men throughout the student's lifetime.

This observation underscores an important point. For reasons which

---

[167] Novicoff, Alex, "The Concept of Integrated Levels and Biology," *Science* 101 (1945):211-213.

are complex, man does not build his society along the lines of biological expedient. Let me quote from a more recent source on this point. David R. Pilbeam, reviewing a book by P. V. Tobias, *The Brain in Hominid Evolution*,[168] challenged his view that this unique creature, man, really emerged in his present form because he became a tool-maker. Pilbeam felt otherwise:

> There is more to human cultural behaviour than the ability simply to learn, or to chip flint. Our behaviour differs from the learned behaviour of all other animals, including chimpanzees, in such important ways as to render descriptions of non-human primate learned behaviour as examples of "crude and primitive culture" potentially highly misleading.
>
> Human cultural behaviour involves a very special form of learning, depending upon learned rules, norms, and values which vary arbitrarily from one culture group to another. . . .

About the only thing that can be said that is universally true of human behavior is that it is *noninstinctive*. As a consequence, like Cleopatra's charms, it has "infinite variety." When you have a single species producing an infinite variety of cultural patterns, even where those varied patterns are found to have developed in virtually identical environments, then you obviously have a species that is not like any other species in Nature. Bertalanffy had this to say on the subject:[169]

> According to von Uexkull's doctrine, the organization and specialization of an animal is decisive for what enters into its ambient world. Of the great cake of reality, an animal cuts a slice, so to speak, of what becomes stimuli, to which it reacts in correspondence with its inherited organization. The rest of the world is non-existent for that particular species.
>
> In contrast to the organization-bound ambient of animals, "Man has a universe," to use an expression of Gehlen. Any section of the world, from the galaxies that are inaccessible, to direct perception and biologically irrelevant, down to the equally inaccessible atoms, can become an object of interest to man. . . .
>
> Precisely because he is lacking organic and instinctual adaptation to a specific environment, he is able to conquer the whole planet from the poles to the equator. So man creates his own ambient, which is what we call human culture.

In one of the flood of Darwin Centennial volumes which appeared from 1958 on, Ernest R. Hilgard in *Theories of Learning*, observed:[170]

---

[168] Pilbeam, David, in *Science* 175 (1972):1101.

[169] Bertalanffy, Ludwig von, "A Biologist Looks at Human Nature," *Sci. Monthly*, January 1956, p. 35.

[170] Hilgard, Ernest, *Theories of Learning*, 2nd ed., Appleton-Century, New York, 1956, p. 461.

There have emerged (in man) capacities for re-training, re-organizing, and foreseeing experiences which are not approached by the lower animals, including the other primates. No one has seriously proposed that animals can develop a set of ideals that regulate conduct around long-range plans, or that they can invent a mathematics to help them keep track of their enterprises. . . .

There are probably a number of different *kinds* of learning which have emerged at different evolutionary periods, with the more highly organized organisms using several of them. It is quite probable that these different kinds of learning follow different laws, and it is foolhardy to allow our desire for parsimony *to cause us to overlook persisting differences* (my emphasis).

We have, then in man a new kind of learning. In point of fact, man's kind of learning actually leads him to *ignore* experience, to live in an unreal world. No animal does this. As we shall see, because animals learn by experience, the older animal is almost certain to be the wiser animal. This is by no means true of man. Yet his very foolishness has enormously enriched his experience. In fact, it is probably the basis for one form of human behavior which must surely be unknown in any other animal, namely, laughter. We can find, as we shall see, some *evidence* of culture in animals, including art; and of course we find a gamut of emotions from the sheer joy of life of the young colt or the spring lamb to the grief of a dog which has lost its human companion. But we do not observe laughter.

One final quotation: Clifford Geertz, in a paper entitled "The Transition to Humanity," had this to say:[171]

Some students, expecially those in the biological sciences — zoology, paleontology, anatomy, and physiology — have tended to stress the kinship between man and what we are pleased to call the lower animals. They see evolution as a relatively unbroken, even flow of biological processes, and they tend to view man as one of the more interesting forms life has taken, along with dinosaurs, white mice, and dolphins. What strikes them is continuity, the pervasive unity of the organic wild, the unconditioned generality of the principles in terms of what is formed.

However, students in the social sciences — psychologists, sociologists, political scientists — while not denying man's animal nature, have tended to view him as unique, as being different, as they often put it, not just in *degree* but in *kind*.

Man is the toolmaking, the talking, the symbolizing animal. Only he laughs; only he knows he will die; only he disdains to mate with his mother and sisters; only he contrives those visions of other worlds to live in which Santayana called religions, or bakes those mud pies of the mind which Cyril Connolly called art.

He has, the argument continues, not just mentality but consciousness, not just needs but values, not just fears but conscience, not just a past but a history. Only he, it concludes in grand summation, has culture.

[171] Geertz, Clifford, "The Transition to Humanity," in *Human Evolution*, ref. 27, p. 114.

I'm not sure Geertz himself accepts this demarcation altogether, but it is a beautiful summary of a position to which I subscribe and which the rest of this chapter explores analytically. And it leads us, in the end, to man's unique possession of conscience and spiritual aspiration, his need for redemption *and his capacity for it*, which is the subject matter of the final chapter of this paper.

Let us, then, turn first to an analysis of man's culture.

Home and Hearth – Uniquely Human

All mammals have some form of family life. The young are born in varying states of dependence upon their parents for food, shelter, warmth, protection against enemies, and discipline. But the period of dependence is comparatively short, in some cases exceedingly so, and this brevity is related to the fact that in all animals, except man, the time to maturity relative to the total life-span is *much* shorter. This seems to be governed partly by the speed with which the young mature and become self-sufficient, and perhaps partly because the maturing process is reached more quickly the educability of the young comes to an end far sooner.

The consequences of these two circumstances are, first, that the family unit in the animal world tends to be ethereal for any particular brood. The young are very quickly and very deliberately ejected from the home, even from the territory, being forced thereafter "to go it alone" and actually being unwelcome any longer around the house, as it were. Secondly, from experience with apes, and indeed with many other animals, it has by and large been found that any training in performance which is not natural to the animal must be done very early, before the animal's brain seems to have become "crystallized." We have noted already, the Kelloggs found that at three years of age their experimental chimpanzee had reached her graduation point, whereas the human subject, which was sharing the chimpanzee's experience, was just beginning to accelerate his learning processes. Indeed, in the normal course of events, it is likely that he would go on learning, actively, in the sense of formal education for perhaps another twenty years. In terms of total life-span, the average human being is still highly teachable for from one-third to one-half of his normal life whereas the chimpanzee does most of his learning in what is probably less than one-tenth of his normal life. Since learning is cumulative and not merely additive, a program of education conducted actively for twenty years has not merely seven times the potential of the ape, but some much greater factor entirely.

Eric H. Lenneberg, in his study on the physiological basis of the human faculty of speech, attributes man's ability to use language to the slow maturing of his brain:[172]

> Species differ in their embryological and ontogenic histories. Brain-maturation curves of *Homo sapiens* are different from those of other primates. Man's brain matures much slower, and there is evidence that the difference is not merely one of a stretched time-scale, but that there are intrinsic differences. Thus man is not born as a foetalized version of other primates; the developmental events in his natural history are *sui generis*. The hypothesis is advanced that the capacity for language acquisition is ultimately related to man's peculiar maturational history. . . .

Not only does the animal's mind reach a static maturity sooner, but its whole body reaches mature stature more rapidly. Man at birth is approximately 5 percent of his mature weight; at fourteen he is about 60 percent; and he must reach the age of twenty before he will be 90-95 percent of his final size.[173] By the time they are one year, other animals will have reached 60 percent of their adult size, and by the time they are three years old 90-95 percent of adult size. In other words, their growth is relatively accelerated — something like seven times compared with man. In some animals the acceleration in growth rate is much greater than this. Samuel Brody said "Pre-pubertal percentages of sheep and goats which have the same mature weight as man is *sixtyfold* that of man."[174]

Brody examined the effects of the decelerated growth rate for man in terms of experience and observed:[175]

> The large and highly developed brain affords reflective power and furnishes the basis for speech and writing, the long growth period affords opportunity to learn, and the long life span affords time to reflect and to develop traditions, all of which are pre-requisite for the development of religion and science.
>
> Moreover, the long human childhood period of dependency on parents stimulates socialization, the rearing of children of different ages simultaneously (a uniquely human characteristic) reinforces socialization, with charity and tolerance on the part of the stronger towards the weaker children, and the mental consciousness of the involved relationships leads to the development of group morals.

Robert Briffault emphasized the matter of slow maturing in terms of educability:[176]

> The question is sometimes mooted whether young gorillas or chimpanzees might not by careful training be taught to speak. . . . The brain of the

[172] Lenneberg, E. H., *Biological Foundations of Language*, Wiley, New York, 1967, p. 179.
[173] Brody, Samuel, "Science and Social Wisdom," *Sci. Monthly*, September 1944, p. 207.
[174] Ibid., p. 209.
[175] Ibid.
[176] Briffault, Robert, ref. 165, p. 768.

young anthropoid grows too quickly; it is formed, it has lost its malleability before the time required for such an education.

This was written in 1931, long before the Kelloggs and their successors reported their experiences. Briffault has proved to be quite correct in his prognostications. It is true that Premack did not begin his program of training of Sarah until she was six years old and he had surprising success, which might seem to contradict what we have been saying. It is possible that Sarah was an exceptional animal. Or it is possible that if she had begun her training in infancy, she, too, would have reached her capacity within three years. Perhaps her brain, in so far as some kind of speech area was involved, was in this area still "uncommitted," to use Penfield's apt expression. Nevertheless, the experience of other trainers of animals which can learn to respond to human commands bears out the statement that their learning capacity falls off very rapidly as soon as they reached, for them, adolescence.

In his paper, Samuel Brody had a scattergram (Fig.22) showing the relative growth rate of nine animals (cow, pig, sheep, rabbit, fowl, rat, mouse, guinea pig, and dove) contrasted with the growth rate of man. In the interest of simplicity, I have traced his curves but omitted all the symbols which he used to show the actual scatter for the different species. The point O represents the point of birth for the animal species. The points C and B represent the time of conception and the time of birth for man. The difference between these two curves *in childhood and adolescence* (up to 14 years of age in man) will be seen to be quite fundamental.

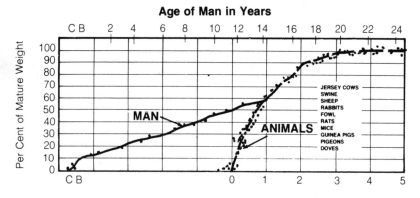

Fig. 22. Scattergram showing the relative growth rates to maturity for man and ten other animals. Redrawn after Brody (*Science*, September 1944, p. 207).

This fact has been recognized for many years, of course, but many textbooks are strongly biased toward human evolution and they tend to omit information of this sort, because it requires explaining and evolution has not come up with an explanation. But commenting on the form of such curves, Bertalanffy had this to say:[177]

The time curve of growth in mammals, fish, crustaceans, clams, and other classes follows a pattern which is characterized by the fact that it approaches a final weight by way of an S-curve. These characteristic growth curves as well as different ones found in different groups such as insects and snails, can be explained and predicted by a theory of "growth types and metabolic types."

Since its pattern is essentially the same, the growth of different species, such as a fish, a mouse, an elephant, or man can be represented by the same curve shape. Only the scales of unit of time and size are different.

In such comparison, only one organism, man, makes an exception. In its first part, the human growth curve is distinguishable from that of all other animals in that a growth cycle seems to be added so that the *infant* period is greatly prolonged, and the steep almost exponential increase in size as is characteristic for early post-embryonic growth curve may appear to be an insignicant detail but it has tremendous consequences.

Thus animals run swiftly through the period of the somatic and behavioural growth, and sexual maturity is soon reached. In contradistinction, the characteristic shape of his growth curve gives man his uniquely long period of growth and opportunity of a long period for learning and mental development. It is an indispensible pre-requisite of human culture.

Not only does the human organism mature more slowly, but by comparison with the bodies of other animals like him, it does not mature *at all* in some respects, or only very late in life. For some reason, the human body retains its youthful stages into adult life. This is known technically as paedomorphism, and Sir Gavin de Beer wrote at some length on the phenomenon in man. In his *Embryos and Ancestors*,[178] he gave a chart showing for example, how the relationship between the head, neck, and spinal column has retained in man the configuration which it has in the embryo. In animals, the head section swings through ninety degrees in order to bring it into the right position for an animal which is to carry its body horizontally. As we have seen, the position of man's head and neck with respect to the organs of speech is very important, making it possible for him to communicate while maintaining a natural position. Thus, even in this respect, the changes which take place in the maturing of animals carries them away from the likelihood of acquiring the same capabilities that man has as an adult. The whole design and struc-

---

[177] Bertalanffy, Ludwig von, ref. 169, p. 36.
[178] De Beer, Sir Gavin, *Ancestors and Embryos*, Oxford U. Press, 1951, p. 56.

ture and growth pattern of man is of a piece, looking to the future potential, and in the meantime involving him in a period of dependency through extended immaturity, which results in the development of family relationships which are not reflected in any other species.

Goldenweiser attaches great importance from the cultural point of view to this protracted dependency relationship in the life of the human infant:[179]

> We know then that there is culture and that it comes to man in the process of education. But even this is not enough for an exact understanding of what it is that happens here. One of the differences of what occurs in the case of any animal on the one hand, and in that of man on the other, is the rate at which they grow up.
>
> With variations, as between animal and animal, their young mature very fast. It is a matter of mere months. So fast do they mature that were there much for them to learn and had they the ability to do so, they could not, on account of the very shortness of the period separating birth from relative maturity. . . .
>
> Fortunately for the animal, its life is planned differently. It is equipped by nature with a large assortment of instincts or reactive complexes which make their appearance almost ready for action and which develop perfect form after relatively few experiences. . . .
>
> The factor in human life on the other hand, which makes acquisition of vast knowledge and the accumulation of experience possible for the young, is the so-called prolonged infancy in man.

It is evident, therefore, that man has not been provided with such instincts as animals have for a very good reason. His pattern of behavior has been left "open" and not instinctive. This means that he *must* learn for a longer period before he can become independent, but it also means that he is free to a larger extent in his behavior and therefore *responsible* for it in a way which animals never are.[180]

It is also important to underline the significance of the fact that children of different ages mature together. To my knowledge this never happens among animals because the young are ejected from "home," not only before the next brood is born but probably before the mother becomes pregnant again. In some cases this is because she does not come to heat until her family has left home, and in other cases it is because the male is not allowed in the home while the young are still dependent on the mother.

Now, the fact that we have a group of children growing up at different stages of development is of great importance in the forma-

---

[179] Goldenweiser, Alexander, *Anthropology*, Crofts, New York, 1945, p. 39.

[180] For a discussion regarding moral responsibility of animals, see Part VI, "The Extent of the Flood," in the Doorway Papers, Vol. IX.

tion of personality, as Samuel Brody pointed out. The fact of diversity of age within a single cohesive family has implications for the structure of society. In the animal world there may be a number of offspring growing up together but they will all be of the same age, and for the most part they are likely to be the same size. The very idea that any one of them might be responsible for the safety or well-being of a younger sibling can never arise in this situation. The whole idea of being responsible for one's fellows begins to arise in a child's mind, not because it becomes aware that the parents are responsible for *it*, but because it is made aware of its own responsibility for others. Edward Sapir underscored the significance of the "family" situation for the development of social organization as a whole. He rejected an older view that the organization of the family evolved out of the kind of promiscuous clan structure in which, at first, everybody made their own way with no special attachments or responsibilities:[181]

> A more careful study of the facts seems to indicate that the family is a well nigh universal social unit, that it is the nuclear type of social organization *par excellence*. So far from a study of clans, gentes, and other types of enlarged kinship groups giving us the clue to the genesis of the family, *the exact opposite is true*.

In case the point should be missed and in view of its importance, it is worth underscoring. Since family life in the human sense cannot be derived directly from anything in the animal world, it was at one time felt necessary to account for it through an intermediary stage. Herds of protomen became herds of men with perhaps a herd leader but no breakdown into small family units which were in any way recognized or protected as such by the group. Such recognition and such protection was then supposed to have emerged later. A study of primitive people suggests that this is entirely unrealistic. Moreover, there is some evidence that family life is as old as fossil man. The finds at Choukoutien (China) and at Es Skhul (Palestine) both seem to imply the same kind of family life. Several adult males were involved in a single setting, and at least in the case of the former, all were killed at the same time — men, women, and children. Jacobs and Stern wrote:[182]

> The absence of a stable family unit has been claimed for early Pleistocene eras, but no convincing arguments . . . have been adduced. All of the economically most primitive societies known are characterized by monogamous families, with rare but permissible polygamy or polyandry.

---

[181] Sapir, Edward: quoted in *Selected Writings of Edward Sapir*, ed. David C. Mandelbaum, U. of California Press, 1949, p. 336.
[182] Jacobs, M., and Stern, D. J., *Outline of Anthropology*, Barnes & Noble, New York, 1947, pp. 151f.

> The lower the technological level, the greater need there appears to have been for a family of two persons, one a man who had relative freedom of movement, the other a woman who did not have to hunt or fish and who could therefore bare and nurse her baby.
>
> It follows that the monogamous family thus existed from the very beginning of culture — that is to say, from eolithic or earliest paleolithic times. . . . The monogamous family and not promiscuity was, then, in all likelihood the earliest form of family, and it has remained the dom. ant form in all societies.

Goldenweiser was even more specific and added that there is no evidence whatever for any concept of communal ownership of *any* kind of property at all, whether things or persons. He said, "The patent facts do not at all support the *a priori* conception which must be regarded as one of the *ad hoc* concoctions of the evolutionists, who were looking for something less specific than individual property . . . and found this in communal ownership."[183]

Another factor which indicates that family life in the sense of broad interdependence between parents and children is unique to man, is the fact that fertility in the human female tends to decline or cease at such an age in her life span that she is not likely to have children so late in life that she cannot perform the role of mother until the child has reached an adequate stage of independence — more particularly perhaps where female children are involved. Parents will therefore live long enough under normal circumstances to raise all the children to maturity.[184] Since the process of maturing in animals is so much faster, fertility can be extended later in life. I believe this is generally found to be the case. For example, C. R. Carpenter mentioned a case of a female gorilla in a state of advanced senility which was found to be carrying an infant when shot.[185]

In the animal world, the raising of a brood cannot be compared with the raising of a family in the world of man. Normally, in the latter, both man and woman play a role of equal importance in terms of discipline, protection, feeding, and education. In the animal world the role of the male is entirely different in those species that might be supposed to serve as prototypes for man. Among birds, both sexes will care for the young, but this is something of an exceptional circumstance. Certainly such a shared responsibility is not reflected among the primates, and cannot possibly be the basis of human behavior.

---

[183] Goldenweiser, Alexander, ref. 179, p. 147.

[184] Swartout, Herbert O., "The Meaning of the Origin and Activities of the Human Body: Control of Growth and Aging in the Human Body," *Bull. Creation, the Deluge, and Related Sci.* 4, no. 5 (1944):71f.

[185] Carpenter, C. R., "Life in the Trees: The Behavior and Social Relations of Man's Closest Kin," in *A Reader in General Anthropology,* ref. 132, p. 21.

The Role of the Male in the Human Family

I cannot do better than quote Ralph Linton on the role of the male in the human family:[186]

There is no point at which present day man departs more widely from the general primate condition than in the male's assumption of responsibility for and care of his offspring. Even the anthropoids seem to leave the care of the young almost entirely to the females, although the males may exhibit good-natured curiosity or even play with them.

Other authorities would go further than this and say that in the great majority of animal societies the male is actually *antisocial*. In some instances this is so marked that the females take steps to incapacitate the males in one way or another. In termite societies and other such insect communities, the males are "sterilized," only just enough "unsterilized" males being left to guarantee the continuance of the breeding process. Even among domesticated animals where males and females are kept together unnaturally, it is a common enough observation that one can easily create a herd of cows, but a herd of bulls would be unthinkable. The only way in which males can be added successfully to the herd is by castrating them.

The primates reflect the same pattern of rivalry, the old or stronger male builds his harem and drives the other males to the periphery. This is particularly true in the breeding season for the species. Once this season is over, the males are apt to be excluded even from their own harem and either form bachelor societies or become loners.

William M. Wheeler of Harvard, in a paper entitled "Biology and Society," written years ago, remarked:[187]

Owing to the decidedly unsocial character of behaviour (of the male) which manifests itself almost exclusively in voracity, pairing, or fighting with other males, he is always so to speak socially more or less indigestible. There seems to be no reliable record, at least among the lower animals, of a male providing food for the female or the young, or even protecting them.

Indeed, after pairing, the sexes seem to become indifferent or even hostile to each other, and the female retires to bear, suckle and rear her young in a safe lair or retreat which she alone establishes. She thus forms a family with her young of both sexes, and in advanced life may become the leader of a herd consisting of several such female-offspring families (this is true of ruminants, elephants, cetaceans, etc.). . . .

The unsocial character of the male reveals itself even more clearly, both among the lower mammals and the anthropoid apes, when he becomes

[186] Linton, Ralph, *The Study of Man*, Appleton-Century, New York, 1936, p. 148.
[187] Wheeler, William M., in *Sci. Monthly*, October 1934, p. 295.

senescent and impotent and wanders away from the herd or troop, to lead the life of a rogue.

It was at one time customary to view primitive cultures as representative of a stage of social organization halfway between the anthropoids and modern man. But it was very quickly apparent that the argument did not hold, for among primitive people family relationships are far more carefully hedged about and precisely defined than in our own more advanced (?) society. And as far as the role of the male is concerned, so much importance is attached to providing every child with a father who is recognized as such that even where the actual physical father has not been established, some official father *must* be provided. Moreover, in some societies where, until comparatively recent times, the role of the father in procreation or the fact of "physical paternity," to give it its proper anthropological name, was not even recognized (which was the case among the Trobrianders and some Australian aborigine tribes, for example), even here a father *had* to be apportioned, as it were, to each child.[188] Manifestly, therefore, in human social organization, the role of the father was not established on a biological foundation. It seems to be based on something more profound. It could be that it goes back to Adam and God's appointment, in order to provide a paradigm for our relationship to God Himself.

Complexification of Social Relations

Social organization and Culture are quite distinct concepts. Culture is learned, rather than instinctual behavior, but social organization may be entirely instinctual, as it is with insects. Kroeber observed, "The presence of cultureless societies among insects is an aid in distinguishing the two concepts in the abstract."[189] It is estimated that there are some 10,000 insect societies in which the organization is highly complex.[190] Referring to the behavior of ants, Ruth Benedict observed:[191]

> The queen ant, removed to a solitary nest, will reproduce each trait of sex behaviour and each detail of the nest. The social insects represent nature in a mood when she was taking no chances. The pattern of the entire social structure Nature has committed to the ant's instinctive behaviour. There is no greater chance that the social classes of an ant society or its patterns of

---

[188] Physical paternity: see Part VII, "Light From Other Forms of Cultural Behavior on Some Incidents in Scripture," in the Doorway Papers, Vol. II, pp. 290-292.

[189] Kroeber, A. L., ref. 20, p. 34.

[190] Wheeler, William M., ref. 187, p. 291.

[191] Benedict, Ruth, ref. 121, p. 11.

agriculture, will be lost by an ant's isolation from its group, than that the ant will fail to reproduce the shape of its antennae, or the shape of its abdomen. For better or for worse, man's solution lies at the opposite pole. Not one item of his tribal organization, or his language, or his local religion, is carried in his germ cells.

Under human influence, animals can be taught different patterns of behavior, but, as Schneirla pointed out, the learning process is stereotyped and rote in character, limited to the individual and the given situation. Unlike human societies where knowledge is cumulative, "such special learning of each society (of animals) dies with it."[192] The important point here is that human learning processes are cumulative and transferable, that is to say, they are not necessarily tied to the situation in which the learning occurs, but can be broadly applied. The experiments of Z. Y. Kuo with cats and rats illustrates that learning dies with the individual.[193] He showed that cats could be trained to play with rats rather than to kill them, but he also showed that cats could be conditioned to be *afraid* of rats. But the kittens of these cats so differently conditioned, when raised in isolation, all became rat killers when they grew up. Lorenz pointed out:[194]

> In animals, individually acquired experience is sometimes transmitted by teaching and learning, from older to younger individuals, though such true tradition is only seen in those forms whose high capacity for learning is combined with a higher development of social life. True tradition has been demonstrated in jackdaws, Graylag geese, and rats.
>
> But knowledge thus transmitted is limited to very simple things, such as path finding, recognition of certain foods, and of enemies of the species, and — in.rats — knowledge of the danger of poisons. However, no means of communication, no learned rituals, are ever handed down by tradition in animals. In other words, animals have no Culture.

The matter of path finding as learned behavior is difficult to assess because a number of social animals leave a trail of scent. The animal which picks up this scent is not really following the trail by imitation, and learning is not strictly involved. This has been demonstrated for many animals and insects. With respect to rats, the situation is rather exceptional because it has been found that when a colony of rats come across a new food, only one of the rats will eat it while the others look on. The rest of the rats will not touch the new

[192] Schneirla, T. C., "Problems in the Biopsychology of Social Organization," *Jour. Abnorm. and Soc. Psychol.* 41 (1946):385-402.

[193] Kuo, Z. Y., "The Genesis of the Cat's Responses to the Rat," *Jour. Compar. Psychol.* 11 (1930):1-30.

[194] Lorenz, Konrad, ref. 57, pp. 64f.

food for two or three days but will observe its effect on the single rat who has eaten it.[195] Since rats are rather unique in that they inhabit areas only where man is and therefore are introduced to new foods provided by man, their behavior is in some sense unnatural and cannot be taken as an example of what occurs in Nature among other species.

In man, culture and social organization seem to go hand in hand, and both are learned: even in family organization in so far as the roles of mother and father are concerned, the behavior patterns normal to a society are learned. The roles may be reversed (as in the Tchamuli), combined or blurred (where all are alike, mother and father, as among the Mundugumor or the Arapesh), or even ignored entirely (as among the Alorese).[196] What we suppose to be the instinctive and therefore predetermined role of the mother as opposed to the father is evidently not instinctive, in spite of general impressions to the contrary. It may be entirely absent; even mother love may be lacking.[197] Under circumstances which occur not infrequently, a mother may not love her newborn but reject it. Scripture asks the question, "Can a woman forget her suckling child?" (Isa. 49:15). The answer is, Yes, she may, according to Scripture itself.

It is difficult to know exactly what goes on in the mind of a natural mother, whose culture differs radically from ours, but judging by the fact that in a time of famine such people will eat their newborn babies apparently without hesitation, seems to indicate the absence of the kind of attachment between mother and child which we assume to be instinctive. Such behavior has been reported from a number of primitive cultures. Daisy Bates mentioned it several times in her study of the Australian aborigines.[198]

One of the most difficult factors about human culture is to understand why man insists upon elaborating it to the point where it is not only no longer useful, but often positively dangerous, as Susanne Langer observed:[199]

> To contemplate the unbelievable folly of which (men) the symbol-using animals are capable, is very disgusting or very amusing, according to our

---

[195] Garcia, John, "The Faddy Rat and Us," *New Scient. and Sci Jour.*, February 7, 1971, p. 254.

[196] Reversed roles: Margaret Mead, *Sex and Temperament in Three Societies*, Mentor Books, New York, 1952; and Cora DuBois, *The People of Alor*, U. of Minnesota Press, 1944.

[197] Mother love: see Robert Briffault, "Group Marriage and Sexual Communism," in *The Making of Man*, ref. 139, p. 497.

[198] Bates, Daisy, *The Passing of the Aborigine*, Murray, London, 1966: first publ. in 1938.

[199] Langer, Susanne, *Philosophy in a New Key*, Mentor Books, New York, 1942, p. 27.

mood: but philosophically it is, above all, confounding. How can an instrument develop in the interests of better practice, and survive, if it harbors so many dangers for the creature possessed of it?

Linton wrote at some length about this anomaly, admitting that the reason why men have gone on amplifying culture generation after generation is still an unsolved problem:[200]

If Culture, like the social heredity of animals, were simply a means of insuring survival for the species, its progressive enrichment might be expected to slow down and ultimately cease. . . . Every society has developed techniques for meeting all the problems with which it was confronted passably well, but it has not gone on from there to the development of better and better techniques along all lines. Instead, each society has been content to allow certain phases of its culture to remain at what we might call the necessity level while it has developed others far beyond this point. . . .

Even in the case of tools and utensils where the disadvantages of such a course would seem most obvious, we have plenty of examples of quite unnecessary expenditure of labour and materials. Hundreds of tribes ground and polished their stone axes completely, although such instruments cut no better than those ground at the bit and are actually more difficult to haft. . . .

In rare cases the elaboration of certain phases of Culture is even carried to the point where it becomes activ, y injurious and endangers the existence of the society. Many Eskimo tribes rohibit the hunting of seals in summer. Although this meant little under ordinary circumstances, there were times when it was highly injurious. It is said that if land game failed, a tribe would often starve when there were plenty of seals in sight. . . .

The natives of Australia in some parts of that continent appear to be obsessed with social organization and prohibit marriage between many different classes of relations. It is said that in one tribe these regulations were worked out to the point where no one in the tribe could properly marry anyone else. . . . This tendency towards unnecessary and in some cases injurious elaboration of culture is one of the most significant phenomena of human life.

It requires little imagination to see this happening in our own culture with grave consequences not only to ourselves but to mankind. The future looks gloomy indeed. It would almost seem that man has now organized and elaborated his culture for the elimination of himself.

John H. Hallowell rightly observed, "With man, economic desires are never merely the expression of the hunger or the survival impulse in human life."[201] The lion's desire for food is satisfied when his stomach is full. Man's desire for food is more easily limited, but the hunger impulse is subject to the endless refinements and perversions of the gourmet. Shelter and raiment serve entirely other pur-

---

[200] Linton, Ralph, ref. 186, pp. 86-90.
[201] Hallowell, John H., *Religious Perspectives in College Teaching: Political Science*, Hazen Foundation, New Haven, n.d., pp. 17,18.

poses, man's coat never being merely a cloak for his nakedness, but the badge of his calling, the expression of an artistic impulse, a method of attracting the opposite sex, or a proof of a social position. His house is not merely his shelter, but becomes an expression of his personality and the symbol of his power, position, and prestige.

It is a curious thing that this drive towards complexification seems to be almost a drive toward suicide. Individually, very few primitive people commit suicide, and as a rule they tend to do so only when old age has brought their powers of contributing as expected to their society to an unacceptably low level. In such cases suicide becomes part of the cultural pattern and is not frowned upon. By adopting this "out," they are actually redeeming themselves. But in our complex civilization suicide does not have any socially redeeming features about it; it is only an acknowledgement of despair and total failure. The primitive may seek and receive the help of his own fellows to end his life in a culturally acceptable way.[202] With us, such behavior is totally unacceptable. Nevertheless, every year the suicide rate goes higher and higher as our civilization becomes more complex, a circumstance which suggests that the complexification of culture may have something inherently inimical to man about it. We suppose that culture evolved by the same kind of natural process as everything else that is assumed to have evolved from the simple to the complex. But no animal society ever deliberately elaborates its organization to the point where it endangers the species. It should not be supposed that primitive societies are incapable of such complexification. This is obviously not the case, as Linton pointed out with the Australian aborigines, whose culture is otherwise the simplest known to us in modern times. Moreover, research has shown that primitive languages consistently turn out to be more complex than modern languages, when they are adequately studied. So somewhere there is in man a tendency which has become entirely harmful to him and in fact may very well endanger his existence as a species. Other animal species have disappeared when their environment changed or as a consequence of the predatory habits of man, but no other species has deliberately followed a course of increasingly complicating its patterns of behavior to its own increasing detriment. Arthur Koestler attributed this to a fault in the mechanism of man's mind, a mechanism which he considered to be faulty not because it is too limited, but because its potential is altogether too great for man to control himself. He would not have

---

[202] See, for example, the Yahgans as reported by Thomas Bridges in *The Story of Man*, ref. 70, p. 97.

suggested such a thing, but to me this looks like clear evidence of the Fall, sin, which has disrupted human nature in its every aspect — physiologically, spiritually, and intellectually. Koestler wrote:[203]

> When we say that mental evolution is a specific characteristic of man and absent in animals, we confuse the issue. The learning potential of animals is automatically limited by the fact that they make full use — or nearly full use — of all the organs of their native equipment, including their brains. The capabilities of the computer inside the reptilian and mammalian skull are exploited to the full, and leave no scope for further learning. But the evolution of man's brain has so wildly overshot man's immediate needs that he is still breathlessly catching up with its unexploited, unexplored, possibilities.

It is well known that neurologists estimate that even at the present stage we are using only 2 or 3 percent of the potentialities of the brain's built-in "circuits."[204] It seems as though man is operating, therefore, at an *exceedingly* low efficiency in terms of his potential. Either he was made this way, which would be a solecism in Nature, or he is a fallen creature. In either case, since animals were not made this way, operating as they do probably at near 100 percent mental efficiency relative to their capacity, man is in a class by himself. Presumably if he had not fallen, he could safely have complexified his culture perhaps to fifty times what it is without the slightest ill effects ensuing.

Individuation

In the present context, by the word *individuation* I have in mind underscoring the quite exceptional degree to which in man, the individual may develop a uniqueness of character which marks off one person from another. Even in cultures which frown upon "being different," there are individuals who stand out as exceptional people. Their endowment seems to mark them out as "great" when judged by the standard of the rest of their community. The human potential seems to have encompassed within itself a tremendous range of variability in terms of personal differences between individuals, and this far exceeds anything that is found among the animals within a species which have not been interfered with by man.

In domestication, by selective breeding man has produced varieties of particular species which have markedly different character from other varieties, as different as the bulldog is from a spaniel, for example, or a Clydesdale from a thoroughbred race horse. These

[203] Koestler, Arthur, ref. 19, p. 229.
[204] Koestler, Arthur, *The Sleepwalkers*, Hutchinson, London, 1959, p. 514.

animals differ not merely in physique but in temperament. But if one compares bulldogs with bulldogs or spaniels with spaniels, or any other variety with members of its own variety, one finds a uniformity of character which makes it possible to predict animal behavior in a way that is totally impossible in man. The unpredictableness of a human individual and the predictableness of the animal has been underscored by Chesterton's famous remark: It makes good sense to ask the young child what he's going to be when he grows up, because that is virtually impossible to predict; but it is quite unnecessary to ask a puppy what he's going to be when he grows up, because we know. It seems as though God has assigned to each species of animal a place in the total economy of things, and a form and a disposition entirely appropriate to that place.

It may be objected that there are notable animals in a herd or a pack — born leaders, as it were. But as far as I have been able to discover from a fairly wide search of the literature on herd leaders, there is pretty well unanimity of opinion about the nature of this kind of leadership. In 1832 the English jurist, John Austin, published his famous *Province of Jurisprudence Determined.*[205] He was one of the founders of University College, London, and its first professor of jurisprudence. And although almost everyone disagreed with his thesis, he had a profound influence on the thought of his day, and on people like John Stuart Mill. Essentially, his view was that all laws, properly so-called, are commands addressed by a human superior to a human inferior, and that the system or institution of government by law evolved from this basis. It was a kind of "great man" view of history. The curious thing is that most disagreed with him because they could not see any evidence for such a "great man" thesis among animals, and it was felt that such a view made man too exceptional.

The position regarding animals has not changed. One can legitimately speak of "great apes," but one cannot speak of a *great* ape. It has been pointed out many times that herd leaders are not commanders in the sense that human leaders are.[206] They function really as special sense organs for the group, that is, for the herd, the flock, or the pack. They watch and listen, while the rest of the members tend to the other businesses of life. The group reactions of the herd are not responses to commands, but rather group reflexes set off by stimuli transmitted through the leader, acting as a sensory receptor for the group. There is a sense in which the "leader" of a wolf pack may maintain a certain hierarchy by establishing superior-

---

[205] Austin, John: quoted by Raymond Pearl, ref. 15, p. 115.
[206] Herd leaders: Raymond Pearl, ref. 15, p. 115.

ity as a fighter, but it is a transient leadership, and he may very easily be displaced by some other member of the pack who showed no special character up to that moment and who may later return to the position of being merely a follower when another leader takes over. The leadership appears to be transient and must at least quite often be the result of almost an accidental victory in a fight, which was equally unplanned.

In his *Territorial Imperative*, Ardrey referred to some experiments by C. R. Carpenter who established a colony of rhesus monkeys on an island in the West Indies.[207] Groups marked out territories, and one of these groups was led by a male of very strong dominance, which continually led his followers into neighboring preserves with much success. When this male was experimentally removed, the group no longer trespassed, so that he was clearly a leader. When restored to the group, again trespassing went on as before. Ardrey observed that Carpenter's experiments were impressive evidence of leadership, but he pointed out that later research revealed that in rhesus life the conditions which Carpenter established were artificial because territory is not normally defended at all.

By and large, animals of a species have a distinct character that can be described, and the vast majority of the members will fit the description. There is a uniformity that seems to be native to the species. Now and then some accident gives rise to a single exceptional animal, but it seems to be a rare event. With human beings such uniformity is found only among primitive people, but for reasons which should be noted briefly because it really has nothing to do with their potential for individuation. The uniformity of character is the result of a particular situation.

Primitive people have always tended to show more respect for Nature and for animals than highly civilized man. Western man has customarily attributed this to some kind of spiritual kinship, a kinship most of us have lost and therefore look upon with some nostalgia. The sense of community with Nature appeals to the tired city dweller every now and then, though not as a steady diet, or he would move to the country. Actually *primitive* man (a very unjust epithet really) is not so much in *communion* with Nature much of the time as he is in awe of it, or envious of its self-sufficiency. In reports of those who knew the Eskimo years ago in his "unspoiled" times, we read of his reverence before the capture of his prey, but then are surprised at his almost insane delight after the prey has been sub-

---

[207] Ardrey, Robert, *Territorial Imperatives*, Delta Books, 1966, p. 279.

dued. He often took a kind of savage pleasure in proving his mastery over it by a display of cruelty toward it that was rather unnecessary. Later he might feel it wise to apologize to the dead animal or to the Creator. The fact is that primitive man saw and envied the strength, or wisdom, or skill of the creatures he hunted — or which hunted him — and he was impressed with the precariousness of his own position. As long as he was the weaker element in some particular situation, it was necessary to be humble, but the moment he had the upper hand, he could exult in being for a short time superior.

As an illustration of what I mean, consider the following incident which was told to me by a man who had spent some time in the Arctic. An Eskimo who had a number of dogs trained to pull his sleigh and whose hunting trips often took him a hundred or more miles away from home, on one occasion got lost in a storm because his dogs wandered from a track which they normally followed quite regularly. His friends had often observed how well he treated his dogs and how there seemed to be a good working relationship between him and them. Such dogs do not normally make pets, but he had apparently got as close to this as ever happened. When he discovered his dogs had followed the wrong trail, he was furious and started to whip them. The dogs became excited and frightened, and then a little vicious. He suddenly dropped his whip, ran back to the sleigh, got his gun and shot them one by one, every single one of them, shouting a great victory cry as each animal fell over in its tracks. He then turned his back on the whole outfit and walked the full hundred miles to his own camp with a sense of high elation. In his own mind he had proved his absolute mastery of the situation.

Most primitive people live precariously, partly because they occupy areas that the more civilized members of the human race have not yet taken over, because of its inhospitability. Such people, over the centuries, have learned how to adjust themselves, their behavior, and their needs to the limited resources of their environment. The margin of survival is often very small. As a consequence, these people become highly conservative and are very reluctant to upset the pattern of living. Given the superior weapons of the White Man, all the caution, which was often mistaken for some sense of communion with Nature, is apt to be lost very quickly. With horses and firearms, the Indians probably did as much as the White Man to bring the buffalo, on whom he had depended for centuries, almost to extinction.

The point here is that in any society which lives in a precarious position, it is not wise to rock the boat. Individualism is therefore suppressed. Every member of the community must be trained to conform to the established way of life with as little disturbance as possible. A small tribe with little margin of survival cannot support individualism. Yet, for all that, now and then great individuals do arise in such societies, strong enough and with sufficient character and intelligent enough to ignore the taboos and bring about radical changes in their own culture. Such men may displace hereditary chiefs and become leaders by sheer will-power and sustained personal initiative.

In the animal world, the situation at first appeared similar, but closer study has suggested that this is not so. In the first place, animals do not live in a consciously precarious condition. They belong in the web of life. Instinct guides them to avoid certain dangers, to eat certain foods, to respect neighbor's rights, and to seek no goals that are not natural for them or proper for them individually. It is well known in England that foxes will not molest natural prey in the immediate vicinity of their own home base. And these neighbors, whether birds or rabbits or any other like potential sources of food, know this instinctively and do not therefore live in constant fear. Of this sort are the checks and counterbalances in Nature. Accordingly, it is not on account of any fear of disturbing the *status quo* that exceptional individuals are discouraged from emerging as such. It is simply not in the nature of animal species other than man to individuate.

To be a leader, one must have followers. Among animals this "following" seems to be instinctive. There is a kind of tension between any individual who strays out from the group and the rest, which either causes him to double back or leads the other animals to suddenly follow.[208] Quite by chance any one individual can stray and be followed, thereby becoming a leader, purely by accident. Konrad Lorenz described an interesting little experiment conducted by Erick von Holst who operated on the brain of a minnow in order to destroy the animal's tendency to stay with the rest of the fishes. As a consequence, whenever this brainless minnow did actually stray, it did not have the same sudden urge to return to the shoal, and the end result was that the rest of the shoal immediately set out after him. As Lorenz put it, "By virtue of its deficiency, the brainless animal had become a dictator."[209]

In conclusion, I suggest that *Homo sapiens* is in some unique way

---

[208] One often observes a beautiful *V* formation of Canada geese suddenly breaking off and reforming when some particular goose seems to have decided to leave the line.

[209] Lorenz, Konrad, ref. 57, p. 140.

equipped to become individual in his person, in a way which does not apply to other animal species. This does not make every man great, but in a remarkable way it does make every man unique. Even physiologically, this uniqueness exists and is reflected in the fact that skin grafts cannot be made from person to person (except, of course, in the case of monozygotic twins), whereas the same operation has readily been performed from animal to animal, providing that they are of the same species.[210] Only in primitive societies where extreme conservativism has tended to take over for circumstantial reasons does individuation seem to be minimal, but the potential is there — as we can see at once in the so-called "emerging nations."

It has been said that when God makes the mold in which to cast an individual, He breaks the mold when the work is done. I think it must be true.

The Impulse to Breed in Man and in Animals

In animals, mating and the impulse to breed are virtually synonymous. In man the impulse to breed has been sublimated, and in normal human male-female relationships it is no longer the only bond which holds them together. It has become only one of several contributing elements in the expression of what we call love, a term which is indeed difficult to define but which, perhaps ideally, is most directly equated with a willingness to make self-sacrifice. As such, it seems to be essentially a human relationship, though there is no question that some animals that have become domesticated will deliberately give expression to it by sacrificing themselves — as dogs have been known to do. I think it is safe to say that *within* a species, that is, between members of a single species, love as a basis of relationship is uniquely human.

In animals, the drive to breed is almost, if not entirely, the basis of all social organization. It is the fundamental regulatory mechanism which controls their behavior, whether social or antisocial. The behavior patterns of animal communities are predetermined and regulated by the reproductive cycle of the female. This, in turn, is chemically controlled but is in some way responsive to environmental conditions. Thus among species which live under environmental conditions that do not favor the raising of young at certain seasons of the year, it has been observed that the period of heat is governed by the gestation period in such a way that the young

---

[210] Medawar, Sir Peter B., *The Uniqueness of the Individual*, Basic Books, New York, 1957, pp. 148,176,177. See also R. A. Reisfeld and B. D. Kahan, "Markers of Biological Individuality," *Sci American*, June 1972, pp. 28-37.

will be born when environmental conditions provide the best opportunities of surviving birth and reaching a stage of comparative independence. Samuel Brody wrote:[211]

> Species that evolved and are living in regions with wide seasonal temperature fluctuations confine their breeding activity to a sharply limited interval of the year. . . .
> Shifting of the animal to another lattitude correspondingly changes the breeding date. Shifting the animal to the tropics, where fluctuations in temperature, light, and food supply are insignificant, or domesticating it so that its food supply, warmth, and light are uniform throughout the year, often abolishes the seasonal breeding rhythm.
> Thus, whereas wild cattle breed in the autumn only, domesticated cattle breed throughout the year. Whereas wild fowls produce only one batch of perhaps half a dozen or a dozen eggs in the spring, domestic fowl may produce eggs throughout the year.

In Nature, the optimum breeding season is regulated by factors which are not directly under the control of the individual animal. Even domestication does not alter this fact, it only broadens the range of conditions under which the mechanism is triggered. This mechanism governs also the migration schedules of birds, the periods of separation of males and females among mammals for a large part of the year, and the antagonisms and the bonds between the sexes and within a sex. It is, in fact, pervasive in regulating animal behavior.

In man, the situation is uniquely different. In an article entitled, "The Influence of Hormones on Man's Social Evolution," Sir Solly Zuckerman pointed out:[212]

> There is one major difference of a negative kind between us and the rest of the zoological group to which we belong. . . . It is our freedom from the rigorous internal chemical control of reproductive functions, such as is experienced by apes and monkeys, and even more so by other mammals. Recent research into the physiology and chemistry of the hormones which control reproduction — the hormones of the anterior lobe of the pituitary gland, and the steroid hormones of the gonads — shows that this freedom must have been vital to our emergence as *Homo sapiens*.

He then pointed out that the rhythm of life in most wild animals is rigidly fixed by the periodicity of the reproductive processes. The entire life of most mammals, he argues, is constrained by the periodic functioning of the sex organs. He summed this up by saying:[213]

> The worlds of such animals, already restricted to their immediate environment and immediate present, are thus rigidly determined by an internal

---

[211] Brody, Samuel, ref. 173, p. 206.
[212] Zuckerman, Sir Solly, ref. 85, p. 81.
[213] Ibid., p. 82.

chemical control, whose bonds cannot be broken; what they do next and their social relationships are both pre-ordained.

This internal chemical control is not as strict in the world of apes and monkeys, but, as far as is known, it is still sufficiently powerful to dominate the lives of almost all species.

Moreover, Zuckerman pointed out that the relationships of the females to the males within each family unit, and of the females to each other, are controlled by the alternating periods of heat of a female. He concluded: "From all this man has been freed," and to it must be attributed "the stabilization of the family unit."[214]

When we examine the relationships that appear in man, we find a fundamental difference: the time of heat and the time of ovulation no longer coincide, and indeed the former seems to bear no relationship whatever to the latter. G. W. Corner of the Carnegie Institute, writing in the *British Medical Journal*, noted in this connection:[215]

> There is a strange difference in the outward expression of these two events, between the human species and other mammals. . . . In animals commonly observable to us (mouse, rat, guinea pig, etc.) sexual activity of the female is restricted to a limited period at the time of ovulation. In the human female a very different pattern exists. The event of ovulation is not marked by any outwardly observable sign, nor by a surge of erotic responsiveness. This great recurrent crisis in the human life process is silent and occult.

Corner then examined briefly the evidence for the existence of any peak of sexual response and sought to relate it to the chemical events which are occurring in the female body. He then concluded:[216]

> Although in the human species the *corpus luteum* phase begins with no outward sign, its conclusion is marked by a conspicuous event, namely, menstruation. Exactly the opposite condition prevails in those animals in which oestrus and the ovulation phase are physically evident. . . .
>
> In the case of the human female, however, the peak of sex response occurs at the very time when both oestrogen and progesterone are at or approaching their lowest level in the cycle. We must therefore assume either that the rhythm of endocrine control differs from what we know in other animals, in the face of all the similarities in the cyclic histology of ovaries and uterus between the human and other species, or (which is more probable) that in women endocrine control of sex arousal has become subordinate to other factors, presumably neuropsychological, which culminate not at the time of ovulation, but shortly before menstruation.

Now the effect of freeing of human behavior and responsiveness in this matter from hormonal control has been to throw the responsi-

---

[214] Ibid.

[215] Corner, G. W., "The Events of the Primate Ovarian Cycle," *Brit. Med. Jour.*, August 22, 1952, p. 403.

[216] Ibid., p. 405.

bility for restraint upon the individual himself. The sexual drive, being liberated from chemical control, had to be placed instead under some other kind of control in order to make social organization possible, otherwise chaos would have resulted in family life and consequently in social life. This has had tremendous repercussions in human society. Robert Lowie pointed out some of these:[217]

> The admirable researches of Yerkes, Carpenter, and others about the sex life of the anthropoid apes do not directly help us (in understanding our own problems). . . .
> The sociologist has to cope with the fact that every known society discriminates among forms of sexual intercourse. *Biologically,* rape, incestuous unions, fornication, concubinage, companionate, civil, and ecclesastical marriage are not distinguishable. *Sociologically,* the several forms of mating are outlawed, reprobated, condoned, accepted, or definitely approved. The forms enjoying the highest approbation constitute "marriage" in a given society. . . .
> A chasm, then, yawns between man's sex life and that of the gorilla or the chimpanzee. The question is not at all whether the gorilla may turn out to be monogamous or polygamous: the question is whether gorilla society countenances, punishes, or otherwise judges the sexual activity of its members.

So we are once again forced to recognize the absolutely fundamental difference between the impulse to breeding which is instinctive and governed entirely by chemicals, and the desire to breed which in man has been separated from purely chemical control. Once again, man seems to be in a class by himself. How did this come about? Of course, the evolutionists cannot admit a separate creation for man, but they do admit, much as Humboldt admitted for the possession of language, that man must have been truly man as soon as this dissociation occurred. What caused it to occur is a mystery. And just as we know that the most primitive of societies from whom evolutionists hopefully expected to be able to draw some conclusions regarding the twilight period when man was "becoming" human, threw no light whatever on the origin of language since primitive man has had more complex forms of speech than highly civilized man, in the same way — as Lowie pointed out — "Extremely primitive tribes are monogamous, very advanced societies permit polygamy."[218] Thus we do not find promiscuity among the very people who are supposed to give us some clues about human nature and behavior in this twilight period. It looks as though man was created as he now is with the freedom and therefore the responsibility that he now has in the matter of his sex life.

---

[217] Lowie, Robert, *Social Organization,* Rinehart, New York, 1949, p. 87.
[218] Ibid., p. 229.

There is another, more specifically physiological, difference between man and all other animals which shows up as soon as we begin to attempt to apply to man the breeding principles and practices which work so well with animals. From the point of view of eugenics it has often seemed desirable to be able to improve the race selectively by mating individuals who seem to have superior characteristics. Hitler actively supported research along these lines in the hopes of producing a superrace. I'm not sure whether any adequate report has ever been made of these experiments, but certainly in the rest of the scientific community very little hope of success is placed in such experiments. The fact is that man seems to be afflicted with more deleterious mutant genes than any other species. If an attempt is made to inbreed the members of a family who by chance have produced a number of outstanding individuals and who are therefore assumed to have some measure of genetic superiority, the results have proved most disappointing. Raymond Pearl wrote:[219]

> In absolute numbers the vast majority of the most superior people in the world's history have in fact been produced by mediocre or inferior forebears. And furthermore, the admittedly most superior folk have been singularly unfortunate in their progeny.

Pearl believed that any analogy drawn between human breeding and livestock breeding is in part both specious and misleading. Inbreeding with animals may and often does lead to the rapid, sure, and permanent improvement of a strain of livestock. But as he said, "When the results of human breeding are interpreted in the light of the clear principles of the progeny test (i.e., empirical results), the eugenic case does not fare too well."[220]

So disappointing have been the few such attempts made, that in certain countries even the formation of a Eugenics Society has been virtually suppressed by the scientific community in view of the fact that it is not only in danger of becoming a political tool, but it is almost certainly doomed to failure. In his book *Why We Behave Like Human Beings*, George Dorsey wrote:[221]

> Man could probably breed a race of human beings with the following traits: bald, fat, long chest, short and crooked legs, left handed, six-fingered, fingers and thumb webbed, near-sighted, deaf and dumb, feeble minded, curley hair, cataract, albino, long-lived, and prolific with a tendency to twins. . . . At any rate, these are a few of the so-called Mendelian traits capable of transmission.

---

[219] Pearl, Raymond, *Biology on Human Trends*, Smithsonian Report for 1935, Smithsonian Instit., 1936, p. 339.
[220] Ibid.
[221] Dorsey, George, ref. 33, p. 116.

The fact is that in every primitive society, as well as in the higher civilizations, one of the most rigidly enforced taboos is that regulating the mating of individuals too closely related. Experience throughout history has shown that under normal circumstances such matings rapidly degrade the stock. In small communities, isolated from larger communities, where continued inbreeding has occurred, the incidence of deaf mutism and the number of imbeciles relative to the size of the population is far above the average.[222] Willard Hollander wrote, "Hidden within many of us are recessive genetic factors which, if we had ill-luck to mate with another carrier, would be deadly to our offspring."[223] And again in the same connection Hollander said, "The quickest way to expose lethal traits is by intense and continued inbreeding."[224]

In a paper entitled "A Biological View of Human History," Bentley Glass attempted to indicate the kind of possibilities that there are of multiplying the effects of man's seemingly excessive complement of harmful mutant genes.[225] He certainly did not favor the Christian view that man is a fallen creature, but if in the Fall man began in himself a unique process of deterioration which has been cumulative through the succeeding centuries, we would have some explanation for this unhappy uniqueness. Moreover, that incest was not forbidden until long after the creation would seem to suggest that at the beginning there were no such dangers from inbreeding, because there were few if any mutant genes. The marriage of a brother and a sister might be undesirable for quite other reasons, but it would not be forbidden because of its probably disastrous consequences to offspring. Cain might safely have married a sister — as indeed, he *must* have done.[226]

---

[222] W. L. Ballinger remarked, "Forty-seven marriages between blood relatives produced seventy-two deaf mutes" (*Diseases of the Nose, Throat and Ear*, 8th ed., Lea & Febiger, Philadelphia, p. 823). E. B. Dench stated, "Consanguinity of the parents is among the most common causes, and the greater frequency of deaf-mutism among the inhabitants of mountain districts is probably to be explained by the fact that intermarriage is much more common among such people" (*Diseases in the Ear*, Appleton, 1921, p. 694). And Lajou's *Analytical Cyclopedia of Practical Medicine* states, "Several statisticians have proved that the closer the degree of relationship between parents, the larger was the number of deaf-mute childern born" (p. 450). Curt Stern wrote, "If a gene is a rare autosomal one, it is highly improbable that a woman heterozygous for it will marry a man who also carries it. . . .unless the spouses are closely related to each other" (*Principles of Human Genetics*, Freeman, San Francisco, Cal., 1950, p. 226). It is rather interesting that the effects of such close intermarriage should be found in that area of man's constitution which is so essential for speech, and by which therefore he stands separated from the animals.

[223] Hollander, Willard, "Lethal Heredity," *Sci American*, July 1952, p. 15.

[224] Ibid., p. 60

[225] Glass, Bentley, in *Sci. Monthly*, December 1951, p. 367.

[226] Part VI, "Cain's Wife and the Penalty of Incest," in *Doorway Papers*, Vol. VI.

I can hardly do better than sum up this aspect of man's total uniqueness than to quote some words of John H. Hallowell:[227]

It is the transcendance of man's spirit over the physical and historical processes which distinguishes man from the beast. It is for this reason that man can never be completely comprehended or explained in physical terms alone.

The sex impulse which man shares with the animals is never purely biological in man as it is in the beast. Sex in man is bound up with love, and when man endeavours to make the sexual act a purely biological experience it is only by an act of perversion that he is able to do so.

Only man is capable of *perverting* his natural impulses; animals are not.

Man's Dietary Unwisdom

Nowhere does man better display his ineptitude than in the matter of diet. He is the only creature who eats what is not good for him. He eats when he is not hungry, drinks when he is not thirsty, and does not replace his water loss adequately when he ought to do so. In some strange way, man's senses are out of kilter. His sense of hunger no longer regulates effectively the quantity or type of his food intake, and his sense of thirst is no longer adequately adjusted to the fluid needs of his body. To my knowledge, all the experimental evidence at present available points in precisely the opposite direction with respect to animals. Their discriminating powers can only be described as absolutely fantastic when it comes to choice of diet, and their sense of thirst is precisely adjusted to any water imbalance in their bodies.

It might be supposed that domestication would have upset this discrimination. But apparently it has not done so. As far as I'm aware, the sole exception to this rule might be that horses will drink water immediately after eating oats and thereby endanger their lives rather dramatically, because the oats swell and the animal is choked. If young colts are allowed to take water at will after eating oats, they will tend to avoid this mistake by drinking very little and will not act unwisely when they grow up. It is true that pets will sometimes be led into eating things that violently disagree with them but even here, if they are given half a chance, they will recover themselves by selecting other foods which serve as antidotes.

The powers of discrimination of both domestic and wild animals in choosing the most nutritious foods where there is a selection of varying value in this respect is almost unbelievable. Curt Richter,[228] in an extended article significantly entitled "Total Self-

---

[227] Hallowell, John H., ref. 201, p. 17.

[228] Richter, Curt P., *The Total Self-Regulatory Functions in Animals and Human Beings,* Harvey Lecture Series 38 (1942-43):63.

Regulatory Functions in Animals and Human Beings," a title appropriate indeed for animals but hardly for man, found experimentally that rats would refuse to eat sugar or fat when their bodies were operatively modified so that they could not digest these substances. When they were given increasing quantities of insulin, they ate increasing quantities of sugar made available, precisely adjusting their intake to what was appropriate for their condition. Subsequent experiments with rats have only served to emphasize their powers of discrimination. Paul Rozin of the University of Pennsylvania demonstrated the remarkable ability of the thiamine-deficient rat to sense the deficiency and search for food containing thiamine.[229] The rat would change his eating pattern as the deficiency became evident, abandoning its current diet and exploring new food sources. When placed in an "experimental cafeteria" containing a variety of flavored foods, one of which had adequate thiamine, the rat went into a "testing mode." That is to say, it ate small meals of one new food at a time, spacing its meals several hours apart. It is thus able to locate or identify the food containing thiamine. Rozin says that the rat behaved precisely as would a rational man who had lost all the labels in his medicine cabinet and was feeling ill. In the wild, whenever rats encounter novel food, they will eat a small amount of it and wait before consuming more. Thus they are able to detect poisoned baits while minimizing risk.

Bennett Galef [230] of McMaster University was able to demonstrate something which is perhaps even more surprising — that experimental rats are able to associate the *effects* of a particular food with the food itself, even though those effects do not show up until hours later. Moreover, he showed that this is not because traces of the meal or drink lingered in the mouth or gastrointestinal tract. No visual cues were involved. Coloring the disagreeable food in order to mark it visually, or serving it in a particular form, or on a particular dish, did not provide the cue. In the experiments, such possible visual cues were eliminated by scrambling them constantly. The rats were still able to identify which food was causing its discomfort.

In a fascinating paper entitled "Discrimination in Food Selection by Animals," William Albrecht collected in short compass some of the extraordinary evidence of the sensitivity of animals to the relative nutrient values of the same foods grown in variously enriched soils.[231] This applies both to animals in the wild and to farm

---

[229] Paul Rozin: referred to by John Garcia, ref. 195, pp. 254-255.

[230] Bennett Galef: referred to by John Garcia, ref. 195, p. 255.

[231] Albrecht, William A., "Discrimination in Food Selection by Animals," *Sci. Monthly*, May 1945, p. 350.

animals. He spoke of their discriminating powers as being "uncanny." Among many examples he gave the following, relating to a particular hundred-acre area which was well enriched up to 1936 but then had no further treatment of any kind until the time of the experiments in 1943. The delicacy of the appetite of the cattle kept there is clearly demonstrated by the following factors in the case. No more than 600 pounds of fertilizer was put on the surface of the soil (i.e., only six lb/acre). It was subjected to an annual rainfall thereafter of thirty-five inches for a period of eight years. Nine crops of hay were removed. This "treated" hay was each year "diluted" by being mixed in the proportion of one part in five with other hay taken from untreated fields. In the eighth year the animals were still by-passing the untreated hay in the mixed haystacks. It should be borne in mind that this hay was enriched only to the extent that it came from soil treated eight years previously and since washed by 280 inches of rain. By the ninth year the cattle could still recognize the effects of the original fertilizer if free to graze in the hundred-acre lot, but they no longer recognized it when cut and mixed with the other untreated hay. He concluded:[232]

> In the light of this evidence the animal's choice must be recognized as a refinement of detecting differences in the crop coming by way of the soil that chemistry as yet cannot duplicate.

Similar findings have been reported for wild deer, for hogs, and "very delicate differences are even recognized by chicks," as demonstrated by Weston A. Price. With respect to hogs whose capacity to exercise choice he also described as "uncanny," Dr. Price had this to say:[233]

> When it is now reported that vitamins are generated through microbial activity in the cow's paunch, we may appreciate the soundness of the old practice of hogs following fattening steers in order to gather the undigested corn.

He commented that by and large the evidence shows that in otherwise unmarked patches animals will crop out of a field which has received varying enrichment treatments with such accuracy that they will recreate these patches by close cropping to within an inch or two of the original demarcation line. He spoke of this as an animal detecting instrument with a delicacy such as approaches that of the chemist's spectrograph.

So much, then, for the ability of animals not only to choose what

---

[232] Ibid.
[233] Ibid., p. 352.

is best for them, but also to compensate for vitamin or other deficiencies in their own bodies. Nor do animals overindulge. Only man becomes needlessly fat thereby endangering his existence. I have said "needlessly," because animals do fatten themselves in anticipation of extended periods without food intake. But man does this to his own ill-health and for no other reason than that his appetite has somehow got out of adjustment with the demands of the body. If a man were to eat only just the food that would satisfy the demands of his body, he would be hungry much of the time. One basic reason for this is that his body is so inefficient relative to the bodies of animals. This may well be due to the effects of the Fall. But the mechanism responsible for this lack of adjustment is fairly well understood.

The following statement is an oversimplification. We obtain the energy we need for the work we do by burning food in the body. This generates heat. The experimental evidence, which has been substantiated in hundreds of laboratories, shows that the human body in this respect is only about 20-25 percent efficient. We have established in our laboratories, for healthy young men (army volunteers) doing various exercises and at rest, efficiencies that show considerable variation, running from 16 percent to 36 percent in one case. The high figures were always for men riding a bicycle in a way a curious finding, but one which has been reported by others also.

Animal efficiencies as studied by others, are found to be very high indeed. Fish are somewhere near the top of the scale with approximately 80 percent.[234] This efficiency is established by measuring the work output and comparing this with the oxygen intake, the amount of oxygen being used providing a measure of the actual energy that one *ought* to get out of the human "engine." Even at rest, of course, the body uses oxygen, but the measurement of "work" output is much more difficult. During exercise it is simpler to measure. In either case, what is found is that approximately four-fifths or 80 percent of the potential energy of the oxygen consumed by a man is not turned into "useful" work and must be eliminated as heat. The rise in body temperature initiates the loss of this heat normally by radiation or evaporative cooling. The more a man has to sweat to do the same amount of "useful" work, other things being equal, the less efficient he is. Just as a scale of reference, it might be added that a steam engine is seldom more than 15 percent efficient, a diesel engine around 33 percent, and some highly refined aircraft

---

[234] Efficiency of fishes: "Submarines as Efficient as Fish," item under "Technological Review," in *New Scient.*, June 25, 1970, p. 629.

engines of conventional design 40 percent. Compared with animals, both man and man-made machines are not outstanding. In terms of food intake man eats, theoretically, about four times as much as he should be eating if he were simply an animal. But if he cut down his food intake to one-fourth of what it is, he would be everlastingly hungry.

The same general picture holds for man with respect to his fluid intake. It has been found that the level of dehydration of an animal's body guides it precisely in the control of the amount of water it drinks. Man, by contrast, finds his thirst is quenched when he has only drunk about one-third to one-half of what his body in some stressful circumstances actually needs to replace water lost by the evaporation of sweat. He accepts a severe level of dehydration voluntarily. On the other hand, of course, he may overindulge, to an even greater detriment.

By and large, therefore, man stands apart from the rest of the animal world, as far as we know, both with respect to his appetite for food and his thirst for fluid. This may indeed be simply the consequence of the Fall, but it also has the effect of extending man's potential enjoyment of life in directions which manifestly would never have been likely if eating and drinking were, for him, merely a question of satisfying physiological demands, as it is apparently with all other animals.

Susceptibility to Disease and Slowness in Healing

Man not only appears to have lower resistance to disease of bacterial and viral origin but he seems to be susceptible to more of such diseases. Animals do suffer from disease (including dental caries), but compared with man they are *relatively* disease-free. And as a matter of fact some authorities have suggested that all disease is essentially man-made. It is a little doubtful whether this can be wholly true, but it is possible that man is responsible for the conditions which have allowed most diseases to invade the animal world. Moreover, it has been observed that wounds do not infect where man has never cultivated the soil. Some primitive people perform rather gruesome initiation rites which involve severe insults to the body, but curiously enough the wounds heal without becoming infected in those societies where the soil has never been cultivated.

One thing is fairly clear when comparing human and animal wounds — animal wounds (with some exceptions among domesticated animals) do not need suturing. The animal's skin is loose and does not immediately gape open even when very severe tears occur.

In speaking of this fact in a book appropriately entitled *The Uniqueness of the Individual*, in a chapter with equal appropriateness entitled "The Imperfections of Man," Medawar had this to say:[235]

> If the entire thickness of the integument in the chest region of an adult rabbit is excised over a rectangular area of 100 sq. cm., something that looks superficially like an irreparable injury is produced. But, so far from being irreparable, it requires for its quick and successful healing nothing but the most elementary surgical care. . . .
> The surface area of an adult human being is about 7 or 8 times as great as the rabbit's, but a skin defect of the same absolute size and depth, and the same relative position, cannot by any means be relied upon to heal satisfactorily of its own accord. If left to itself, it will heal painfully slowly and will gather up and scar; a wound of similar size in the leg (which is not so much thinner than a rabbit's trunk) could cause a serious disabling injury if left untreated. . . . Such an injury cries aloud for skin grafting.

So he asked why the rabbit is so accomplished in wound healing and the human being so strikingly poor, and added that the answer hinges upon an understanding of the mechanism of healing as it occurs in the rabbit's skin. He then explained how healing occurs in the rabbit by a process which is ultimately dependent upon the fact that this skin is loose on its body. This is true of most dogs also, domesticated though they are, and it is true of cats, horses, and cattle. When the skin is cut, the wound does not at once pull apart as it does in man. Medawar continued:[236]

> In human beings, the integument is no longer a generous fitting coat, but is much more firmly knit to the tissues below; the intrinsic muscles of the skin are now (was it ever otherwise?) confined to areas of the face and neck, and the skin generally is much more of a piece with the rest of the body.
> The upshot of this new anatomical arrangement is that contracture (the ability of the skin to close the wound by drawing together), so far from being an efficient mechanism of wound closure has become something of a menace; it constricts, disfigures, and distorts, and may yet fail to bring the edges of the wound together.

At the end of the chapter he asked, "What compensating advantage the human being gets from the novel structure of his skin is far from obvious, though it is hard to believe that there is none."[237]

After reading this statement, I wrote to Medawar and asked him whether the tightness of human skin might not be related to the fact that the sweat glands, which are deeper than the skin, express their fluid to the skin surface to provide evaporative cooling through

---

[235] Medawar, Sir Peter B., ref. 210, p. 130.
[236] Ibid., p. 132.
[237] Ibid., p. 133.

a comparatively long thin tube. If the skin was too loosely wrapped around the body, such tubes would have to be unduly elastic or they would be constantly in danger of rupture. Such elasticity would in any case be likely to cause rupture under certain conditions of normal sweating because the fluid pressure in the sweat glands is remarkably high (250 mm. mercury),[238] and not infrequently the orifice of the gland becomes temporarily plugged at the surface. Since man is so entirely dependent upon the effective evaporative cooling of his skin surface via sweat gland activity to prevent deep body temperature from rising unacceptably, any structural feature of his body which interfered with such a mechanism or endangered it would limit his ability to inhabit a large part of the earth's surface where environmental temperatures exceed his normal skin temperature, which is about 80-90° F. Depending upon where it is measured.

Medawar replied to my query very graciously, and though not at once convinced said, "However, I shall ponder upon the matter and allow my subconscious to pass judgment on it." This is fair enough. Man pays a penalty for his ability to live anywhere on the globe, the penalty of a tight skin and certain problems in wound healing. Perhaps if man had not fallen, serious wounds would have been very rare. In any case, man is capable of engineering the necessary repair because of his unique hand and brain combination. The chimpanzee can thread the needle, but man can make the needle and the thread, and use it appropriately to suture the wound — which no animal can do.

One further point. Man's susceptibility to disease and his comparative helplessness when sick in a way that animals are not, is both a curse and a blessing. Washburn and Lancaster, in pointing out how well adapted to their environment animals are and having in mind at the time those animals which live in the African savanna, said:[239]

> Man cannot survive the diseases of the African savanna without lying down and being cared for. Even when sick, the locally adapted animals are usually able to keep moving with the troupe. . . .
>
> Although many humans die of disease and injury, those who do not, almost without exception, owe their lives to others who cared for them when they were unable to hunt or gather, and this uniquely human caring is one of the patterns that builds social bonds in the group and permits the species to occupy almost every environment of the world.

---

[238] Best, C. H., and Taylor, N. B., *The Physiological Basis of Medical Practice*, Williams & Wilkins, London, 1945, p. 627.

[239] Washburn, S. L., and Lancaster, C. S., ref. 105, pp. 74,75.

This is certainly true and probably has far wider application than the authors had in mind — although I think it needs qualification to this extent that there are occasions, exceptional though they may be, in which animals have been known to care for one another in times of injury. Some illustrations of this in birds, dogs, and even rats will be found in another Doorway Paper.[240]

There is no question that in some wonderful way God has blended strength and weakness in man, so that he can be ubiquitous because his temperature regulation has been so elaborately refined, but only at a cost to his capacity for healing — which, in turn, has made him more than ordinarily dependent upon others when wounded. So man takes his unique social organization with him into every part of the world.

Man the Organizer

Grace de Laguna in a paper entitled "Culture and Rationality," gave an apropos observation about man's insistence upon order, reason, and organization in his life, a characteristic that appears to be almost entirely lacking in the animal world except where, purely by instinct, the bee, for example, constructs a symmetrical comb. Such "ordering" is not deliberate, not does it extend to anything else that the animal does. Grace de Laguna wrote:[241]

> Man's rationality is not a higher faculty added to, or imposed upon, his animal nature: on the contrary it pervades his whole being and manifests itself in all that he does as well as in what he believes and thinks.

One might almost say that man does not *have* rationality. It would nearly be true to say he *is* rationality, perhaps in some sense reflecting the sentence construction of the Lord's words, "I *am* the truth" (John 14:6), not "I *have* the truth." I am not equating truth and rationality in this statement: I mean only that in some way the Lord *was* the truth, not merely holding it as part of His being. And in some way man *is* rationality, not merely having rationality. I believe that he is often irrational, but in a strange way even his irrationality has a certain order to it, a certain *rationale*, unless he is, of course, a mental case.

In almost every aspect of man's mental activity he prefers order to disorder, reason to unreason, structure to nonstructure: where they do not exist in his environment, he seeks to impose them. Even in the great move "back to Nature" when the English countryside

---

[240] Part IV, "The Survival of the Unfit," in this volume.
[241] De Laguna, Grace, *Amer. Anthrop.* 51 (1949):380.

was deliberately restructured to look more "natural," a revolt against the influence of some of the great landscape artists like Claud Lorrain, a reaction against the previous tendency to landscape everything in straight lines and symmetrical patterns such as characterized formal gardens after the pattern of Versailles, care was taken not to create chaos, only an ordered disorder — better perhaps, a restrained freedom in the planting of things. Virtually every aspect of his cultural activity reflects this drive, if we can but recognize it. Consider the following tabulation, for which I have no other scholarly authority but my own judgment, yet every article of which could be the subject of a supporting essay:

Man structures time by composing music.
Man structures emotion by writing poetry.
Man structures space by art and architecture.
Man structures quantity by creating mathematics.
Man structures events by writing history.
Man structures experience by philosophizing.
Man structures his sense of justice by formulating codes of law.
Man structures social behavior by custom (which is really the objective of primary education).
Man structures his religious impulses by liturgy and ritual.
Man structures his faith and calls it theology.

Man *must* organize. He cannot allow anything to remain disorderly for very long without either feeling uncomfortable or turning his back deliberately on something that is very deeply engrained in his nature. In this he is removed far from the rest of the animal world. Indeed, so inseparably do we consider this sense of order to belong to truly human activity that we speak of a mind which has something basically wrong with it as beong "disordered." And when it was proposed that we should try to communicate with other intelligences in the universe, the first proposal was that a series of huge fires should be set out in the Sahara Desert in such a way as to mark the corners of a right angled triangle with squares on the three sides. It was believed by H. G. Wells and others at the time that if there were anywhere in the universe other intelligences who had the earth under surveillance, they would understand from the order and logic of the fires that the earth also was inhabited by intelligent creatures. No animal would ever think of communicating by the use of consciously ordered signals or displays of this kind.

In this list above we have essentially the sum of *human* activities as distinct from the accomplishments of animals. Language we have already examined. Among animals music is not believed to be consciously created with infinite variety and elaborated as man creates his music, but is used instinctively and always bound tightly to a given circumstance and a specific message. It is a warning of territorial rights, it attracts the female, or it is an *involuntary* expression of inner feelings of joy, pain, or anger. Because animals do not write, they cannot write poetry or history. Their social behavior is, as we have seen, fixed and conditioned, and if they do happen to add anything to its pattern it is strictly utilitarian. They never elaborate or embroider social activity and sustain it unless it contributes in some specific way to their survival. Man does this even when it has precisely the opposite effect. In spite of certain advertisements a few years ago of some brand food which was believed to be particularly desirable for "thoughtful dogs," there really is no reason to believe that dogs or any other animals philosophize. Philosophy involves unreality, abstraction, the consideration of alternatives to fact, the power to analyze in retrospect experiences long past and to contemplate in prospect experiences which are remote from reality. Animal thought is contingent: they live in the present. This is true even though they may confuse past, present, and future, as when a dog may yelp with pain before the punishing blow falls. There is no evidence that animals have any sense of the presence of God, such as leads men to worship in adoration, in awe, or in gratitude.

Kroeber mentions some examples in which chimpanzees, gorillas, and Cebus monkeys seem to derive pleasure from a form of painting.[242] Just what this means is hard to say. Some recent experiments suggest that chimpanzees like to play around with colored paints, but there is no evidence of harmony, form, or order of any kind in their "creations." They are purely random expressions of some kind of exuberance. I do not think anyone has suggested that they are emerging artists. Bower birds decorate their homes, but again the essence of order and meaning seems to be missing.

There is a report of the ability of birds to "count," but only up to six or seven. And in this case it appears to be more pattern recognition than number comprehension.[243] Munro Fox, in his book *The Personality of Animals,* has a whole chapter entitled "Can Animals Count?" in which he refers to a particular zoo chimpanzee named Sally who learned to pick up four or five straws when asked to, but that was as far as she could count. Above five she made mistakes.[244] He also refers to a pigeon that was taught to pick up five grains of wheat. The bird was then placed before a heap of wheat, in front of

[242] Kroeber, A. L., ref. 20, p. 65.
[243] "Learning in Man and Animals," editorial, *Nature,* June 23, 1956, p. 1147.
[244] Fox, Munro, *Personality of Animals,* Pelican Books, London, 1952, p. 100.

which were piles of one, two, three, and four grains of wheat. Faced with each pile separately, the pigeon ate the grains in front of it and then went to the heap and ate just enough to make a total of five. Fox believes that this is real addition; but actually it could again be simply a pattern of movements which were conditioned leaving the bird in some kind of state of dis-ease until it had completed the circuit of movements. It is very difficult to know whether any of these experiments really demonstrate the ability to count. To my mind, even the quite fascinating experiments carried out with rats by Loh Seng Tsai, reported in *Life* (January 11, 1954), did no more than to demonstrate the rat's ability to recognize a configuration of signs, and only up to three signs in any case. However, the ability of birds to count up to six or seven does not always appear to be merely pattern recognition. Huxley referred to some work done by Otto Koehler, who set jackdaws the problem of taking a definite number of peas out of a series of boxes:[245]

> Surely they mastered this problem fairly easily, but sometimes they made mistakes: and one jackdaw realized his mistake. He ought to have taken 6 peas — 2 out of the first box, then none, 1, 2, and 1 (out of successive boxes).
> He went back to his cage after taking only five. But then he suddenly came back and counted out his task by bowing his head the right number of times in front of each box. When he got to five, he went on to the next box and picked up and ate the one pea he had forgotten.

The behavior of this jackdaw in bowing his head, however, could be taken as indicative of the fact that he had a kind of physiological memory of the number of actions to perform at each station that did not actually involve counting at all. It would be a kind of conditioned reflex. And something told him that he had not completed the performance. . . .

We made some experiments with a cat we once had, who was raising a family of three kittens. When the kittens were old enough that they could half stand up and could raise a loud mewing, we took the mother cat out of the room and lifting the three kittens out of their box, we deposited them in the center of the floor, their box being in a corner of the room. When they set up a great noise, we allowed the cat in, and she frantically dragged off a kitten back into the box. While she was doing this, we quickly removed the other two kittens into another room where their noise was not heard. So long as the mother cat did not hear the noise of their mewing, she was not concerned any further than to rescue the single kitten. On the other hand, if we left one of the two remaining kittens on the floor, it would

---

[245] Otto Koehler: quoted by Sir Julian Huxley, ref. 41, p. 106.

THE EXPRESSION OF HUMANNESS • 319

make such a noise that she would jump out of the box and rescue it also, dragging it back to the box. In the meantime, if we quietly and quickly removed the one she had already in the box, she apparently did not notice its disappearance at all when she got the second one home. It appears that she could recognize the difference between one and none, but not between one and two.

Matthiasson in his Fifth Thule Report, 1921-24, *The Material Culture of the Iglulik Eskimo*, remarked upon the method used by these people to attract caribou within range of their bows. Two men, having sighted a caribou, will proceed to walk away from it. The curious animal will follow cautiously at a distance. One man will suddenly drop out of sight behind a snowbank and remain hidden, while the other one goes on. The caribou unsuspectingly follows, not noticing the absence of one man; and of course, he pays the price. This seems clear evidence of inability to recognize the difference between two and one. Apparently it has also been found that if three men go openly to a hideout for shooting game fowl, the game will fly away from the area. But if one of the men openly leaves the hideout, the birds will unsuspectingly return. Beyond this, efforts to detect the ability to count in other animals have not been successful.

We have, then, in man one further unique character, namely, that of *rationality*, taking rationality in the broadest possible sense to include preference for order, which involves a form of counting, logic, truth, symmetry, and harmony against their respective alternatives. In all these things other animals seem to be totally indifferent wherever they have the power of choice.

Conclusion

Once again, we find that it is not possible to explain man's behavior in terms of animal behavior. Man's home and his role in it, and his relationship with others, are not based on the biological expedients of the animal world. Man displays infinite variety in terms of personality whereas animals have uniformity of character. But most unique in man is the quality of rationality which pervades his whole being. While this rationality opens up such great potential for him, he lacks the wisdom of animals in its exploitation. There seems to be something basically wrong with him, not only in the sickness of his body, but in the harmfulness of his behavior.

Thus we come back to the question first proposed, What is man? In the next chapter we shall examine what I believe to be, at least for the Christian, the most conclusive evidence of all that man is not merely more than, but something quite *other* than, an animal.

Chapter 7
The True Nature of Man
in Jesus Christ

IN THE light of the evidence few will dispute the fact that man is anatomically, physiologically, and — for want of a better term — psychologically, unique; that some strange event somewhere back in the dim and distant past led to the sudden appearance of a creature whose whole being was a new departure from the then course of events in the living world of animals. Evolutionists themselves admit it. It has been referred to as the "critical point" concept.[246] A. L. Kroeber postulated that "the development of the capacity for acquiring culture was a sudden, all-or-none, quantum-leap type of occurrence in the phylogeny of the primates."[247] Susanne Langer put it even more dramatically when speaking of the acquisition of language, the lifeblood of culture:[248]

> Language is, without a doubt, the most momentous and at the same time the most mysterious product of the human mind. Between the clearest animal call of love or warning or anger, and a man's least trivial word, *there lies a whole day of creation* (my emphasis).

Fothergill writing in *Nature* and reviewing two books on evolution, underscored his doubts about the validity of current conceptions regarding the origin of man by quoting the words of Humphrey Johnson who said, "There is a wider difference between a man and a gorilla than there is between a gorilla and a daisy."[249] In some vaguely definable way, we know that the gorilla and the daisy really do belong somehow within the same world frame. Man seems entirely alien. In his book *God's Image in Man,* James Orr quoted a contemporary writer, Fiske, as having said, "While for *zoological* man, you can hardly erect a distinct family for man from that of

---

[246] Geertz, Clifford, ref. 171, p. 114.
[247] Kroeber, A. L.: quoted by Clifford Geertz, ref. 171, p. 115.
[248] Langer, Susanne, ref. 199, p. 83.
[249] Humphrey Johnson: quoted by P. G. Fothergill, in *Nature*, February 4, 1961, p. 341.

the chimpanzee and the orang; on the other hand, for *psychological* man, you must erect a distinct kingdom, nay, you must dicotomize the universe, putting man on one side and all things else on the other."[250] It is quite true.

But it is apparent from history that when the coming of man introduced a sudden leap into a new order of life, it was not without a penalty. Indeed, it has manifestly been as harmful to the whole order of Nature as it has been beneficial, as though something went seriously wrong almost at the very beginning. So totally disrupting has man's presence been that there are those who are prepared to speak of modern man as being "obsolete — a self-made anachronism becoming more incongruous by the minute."[251] Arthur Koestler reflected the view of many thoughtful people when he said, "Something has gone seriously wrong with the evolution of the nervous system of *Homo sapiens*. . . . The delusional streak which runs through our history may have been an endemic form of paranoia built into the wiring circuitry of the human brain."[252]

The assumption is always made by such writers that what has gone wrong is a "mechanical" fault. This may be true actually, though we tend to think of it as more spiritual than physico-electrochemical. But in point of fact, the fruit that was forbidden to Adam but which he ingested may indeed have contained a poisonous substance of some kind that did cause "mechanical failure," a defect since then inherited by all who are his descendants.[253] This is not, of course, to deny the fact that the very act of disobedience *per se* destroyed his communion with God and had equally fatal effects upon his spirit as the fruit did upon his body. The first was immediate, bringing what Scripture calls "spiritual death"; the second was more delayed in its effect, initiating a process which terminated in his physical death. At any rate, between the two, which appear to act synergistically, psychosomatically, and somatopsychically, the spirit on the flesh and the flesh on the spirit, the end result is best described by the simple word *suicidal*, to use James Gall's fitting description:[254]

> What is wrong with man is some disease that has nothing good about it.
> No animal does by nature things which injure its instincts, spoil its enjoyment

[250] Fiske: quoted by James Orr, *God's Image in Man*, Eerdmans, Grand Rapids, Mich., 1948, p. 60.

[251] Melvin, Bruce L., "Science and Man's Dilemma," *Science* 103 (1946):243.

[252] Koestler, Arthur, ref. 19, p. 239.

[253] Custance, Arthur C., Part II, "The Nature of the Forbidden Fruit," in the Doorway Papers, Vol. V.

[254] Gall, James, *Primeval Man Unveiled*, Hamilton, Adams, London, 1871, p. 91.

of life, or shortens its days to no purpose either to itself or its species. The behaviour of predators, which sometimes look savage and cruel in the extreme, and thus reminds us of human savagery and cruelty, really has none of the characteristics of human savagery. The animal is without hate, or revenge, or desire to hurt merely for the pleasure of hurting.

It is possible that no predator ever does actually hurt its prey,[255] and it certainly does no injury to its own nature unless its nature has been disturbed by human interferences. When man acts according to *his* nature, he all too frequently acts self-destructively. The fact is that natural human behavior is diseased behavior. To pretend otherwise, as humanists do, is folly. Man *is* a fallen creature. He is diseased, and the disease is *sin*: the symptoms of the disease are everywhere evident in human wickedness. It makes man essentially murderous in his intent. It is recognition of this fact even within himself that has driven human society to hedge itself about with the restraints which, when well structured, we call Civilization. Murder and civilization emerged together (Gen. 4ff.); it is not something observable anywhere else in Nature. As Arthur Koestler put it, the unique characteristic of our species is that we practice intraspecific homicide both individually and in groups.[256] Animals do not murder or torture one another, nor do they make war as man makes war on his own species. And the assumption, therefore, that man "though occasionally blinded by emotion, is basically a rational animal,"[257] is an assumption that is "untenable in the light of both historical and neurological evidence." Whatever he *is*, man is *not* an animal. . . .

What has happened then? Is this the way man was made? And if not, how *was* he made at first? What was he like before the disease of sin entered? Is man as we see him in ourselves *man* at all? What is true manhood? Why did God create such a creature knowing what the consequences would be, even if the fault for the present situation is ours? Only when we know what man was created *for*, can we really know what man *is*.

A colleague of mine, a French-Canadian organic chemist, walked into my laboratories one day and said, "We've had this thing around the house ever since I was a kid. Any idea what it is?" We both studied it carefully. It was made of wood, obviously shaped by hand, asymmetrical along its axis, and about six inches long. It weighed only a few ounces, and it had been nicely finished with a

[255] Custance, Arthur C., Part IV, "The Problem of Evil," in Doorway Papers, Vol. IX.

[256] Koestler, Arthur, ref. 19, p. 305.

[257] Ibid., p. 324.

good lacquer. I've always felt I was quite sharp at guessing this kind of thing. But I couldn't identify it at all. Apparently nobody else had been able to either — not even at the National Museum! Yet it was not simply a piece of wood that someone had doodled into shape, as a fancy of the moment might have suggested. Without a doubt it had been made for some purpose. There were even unmistakeable wear marks on it in one place that indicated it had actually been used for something. But what had it been used for?

Now there's the point. We could not say what it *was*, because we could not imagine what it was *for*. Knowing what it was made of, its shape, weight, color, size, or any of its other physical or chemical characteristics, still did not tell us what it was, because we did not know what it was for. As far as I know, my friend never did find out. One day, someone will say, "Oh, I know what that was for. . . ." And the problem of identity will be solved.

Nor can we say what man is — even knowing all these things about him, his physical characteristics, his chemical constitution, and even his psychological make-up — unless we know what he is for. But we shall know what man is only when we know what God's object was in creating him. We can see in some measure how each animal fits into the web of life and "makes its due, but only due, contribution to the scheme of Nature."[258] Man, by contrast, seems alien to this whole scheme. As Laura Thompson said, "He is the only one who *could* contribute to the regulation of the whole process of Nature by reason of his position at the apex."[259] Indeed, it has been Julian Huxley's basic philosophy that such was the goal of evolution, to produce a creature who could thereafter consciously direct its course in the future.[260] If this *was* the purpose of the emergence of man, he has certainly dismally failed in his responsibilities. But was this what man was made for? Once again we are back at the question, What for is Man?

Perhaps we can provide some kind of answer by the use of an analogy. If a man builds a house for his animals, he suits its construction to their nature and disposition, besides being guided by what he hopes to do with them. If he happened to be raising snakes in order to extract their venom for research purposes, it would be a house from which they could not escape but in which they would yet thrive. For

---

[258] Dice, Lee, *Natural Communities:* reviewed by Ronald Good, in *Nature,* July 11, 1953, p. 146.

[259] Thompson, Laura, "Basic Conservation Problems," *Sci. Monthly,* February 1949, p. 130.

[260] Huxley, Sir Julian, "New Bottles for New Wine: Ideology and Scientific Knowledge," *Jour. Roy. Anthrop. Instit.* 80, nos. 1 and 2 (1950):20.

his cattle, he could build a house that is large enough to accommodate their greater bulk, with facilities for keeping them fed, warm, and clean, but they must be able to go in and out. Yet he would not need to take the same precautions against their escape as he would have to do with dangerous creatures like poisonous snakes — or destructive animals like pigs, or vagrant ones like horses. For his dog, he would construct a house that in some small measure shared his own home comfort and style, for this is what his dog is likely to do. Thus the nearer he gets to a house for a creature sharing his own likes and dislikes, the more like his own house it will be. For his hired man, he will probably build a house that he himself and his family would be willing to occupy — if he is a man of feeling and concern.

Ultimately, we come to his *own* house. How does he build it? He builds it not to suit his livestock, or his pets, or even his hired man. He builds it for himself. It takes on and reflects his own person in many subtle ways. It is likely, at least in so far as he has the resources and the design ability, to be uniquely suitable for *him* — more suitable for him than for anyone else. When a man hands over such a house to someone else, either by sale or as a gift, it is almost certain that it will be modified by the next resident, thus proving how special in certain respects it was for himself as a habitation.

Now what, then, will God do if *He* decides to build a house which is to be fit for Himself, which in due course will be *His* habitation, a house which is to serve Him for thirty-three years, in which *He* will live and express His character, inhabiting it day and night, constantly, actively, fully, sleeping and waking, being born and dying? It will be a house capable of being so lived in, appropriately and worthily. It will be a house that can sustain the demands of habitability that *He* will make upon it.

It will be beautiful, for obviously God must rejoice in beauty that He should make so many beautiful things in the world, and it will be "flexible" to allow for expression in the face, by the hands, by body movement, of the whole range of human mood from delight to mourning, from solitude to companionship. It must have all the facilities — faculties now, since it is a *body* that we speak of — which will permit movement, expression, communication, gesture, comprehension, display of emotion, and even feelings of weariness, which are necessary for true sympathy of the human lot and to which others can upon special occasion minister. And above all, if the object from the very first was to be not merely for the revelation of God but for the redemption of man, it must be a house of such a nature that it could be deliberately sacrificed, not because it has worn out or was wearing out, but because He who was incarnate in it chose to sacrifice it.

In order that this sacrifice could be truly and wholly an act of will and not something surrendered to inevitably, the house must be a house that would never wear out of itself, never collapse in the course of time as our houses do because it is their nature to do so, for otherwise it would be merely *prematurely* demolished. It *must* be capable of lasting indefinitely, even though it can be deliberately sacrificed. This house had to be of such a nature as to allow an event which was to signify something other than the mere premature breakdown of its structure. The house had to be of such a nature that its demolition could be purely an act of will, unrelated to the condition of the house itself. The same kind of house must be appointed as the habitation of the First and the Last Adam, in order that the conditions of physical life of both might have the same potential. It must be, for God's purposes, a house built with the capability of lasting for ever, even though that capability was twice sacrificed — the first time in Eden by an act of disobedience, and the second time on Calvary by an act of obedience.

Man is not a creature of spiritual significance who merely *happens* to have the kind of a body he does and who might just as easily have been equipped with any other kind of body. He is a creature whose uniqueness from the point of view of his humanness both in terms of culture and spiritual aspiration is as much dependent upon the structure of his body as upon the nature of his spirit. It is quite wrong to imagine that man's body is incidental and that he might have been structured like a giraffe, a dog, a mouse, or even an ape and still have fulfilled the role for which he was created. In 1810, Lorenz Oken said, "God objectified Himself in Man,"[261] and in 1872, Charles Hodge said, "Creation was in order to redemption."[262] Both statements are directly related, and both hinge upon the reality of man's uniqueness both spiritually and physiologically.

This house, this body that is the home of man's spirit, is not just a complex electrochemical machine. It was *designed* from the very first for a special purpose. It was so built that it would properly meet the requirements that God had in mind both for man *and for Himself* in the Person of the Lord Jesus Christ. In due course, it was to make it possible for God to express Himself perfectly in terms of human personality *as a man*. And then, as a man, to sacrifice His life vicari-

---

[261] Oken, Lorenz: quoted by A. O. Lovejoy, *The Great Chain of Being*, Harper Torchbooks, New York, 1960, p. 321.

[262] Hodges, Charles, *Systematic Theology,* Vol. II, n.p. 1872, p. 316.

ously for any man who would believe and appropriate that sacrifice as a full, perfect, and sufficient satisfaction in the face of the divinely appointed moral law, against his own sinfulness, failure, and self-will. God made man's body such that He Himself could assume it for a season as His own proper House — and in the person of His Son, Jesus Christ, could die in it that we who are dying in it even as we live, might be redeemed to live again and forever in a new and even more glorious resurrected "house" throughout eternity, thus exhibiting the grace and love of our Savior God as a matter of personal experience. No mere animal body could have sufficed for such a tremendous purpose.

It is inconceivable that God could have expressed Himself as a Person in any animal. It is only in man's reprobate mind that the idea of God as a serpent, a crocodile, a bull, a wolf, or a bird could have occurred with such force that he would bow down and worship such images, changing the truth of God into a lie and worshiping and serving such creatures rather than their Creator (Rom. 1:23-25). Even to worship God in an image fashioned after man *as he now is* is the expression of a mind that is darkened and foolish.

Yet the Lord Jesus Christ accepted the worship of men without rebuke. And one must therefore assume that the body which was His house, though it looked like ours, was somehow not the same. His body was glorious. His body was made with the potential for unending continuance (Heb. 7:16). There was something in His body which distinguished it from ours and gave it its glory, though it was not different from the body which Adam had at first. He could become weary both in body and in spirit, and we know that He found rest — at least at Jacob's well — by sitting down, a circumstance which implies that gravity could have its effect on that body. And yet He could walk on the water, a circumstance which showed that gravity did not always have an effect on that body. His was a body that had the same needs for food and drink at times, and yet was, perhaps, in some way not totally dependent upon these things as our bodies are. His body was a body so full of energy that those who strove to keep up with Him imagined, in their weariness, that He was obsessed, which, of course, He was. Yet that energy could be depleted and He be aware of it, as when the woman touched His garment.

This kind of body is not in the same category as an animal body. In some way that is impossible for us to analyze, there was a fundamental difference. But neither was it a body the same as our bodies are now, for in the Lord Jesus Christ the world was presented once more with Adam; and between our bodies and the body of Adam before he fell, there is a hiatus as between two different categories of life. One could conceivably make out some kind of case for the derivation of fallen man's body from some animal prototype, though as we have seen in the previous chapters an extraordinary combination of special circumstances has to be postulated to account for the differences. But in order to account for a body such as housed the spirit of the Lord Jesus Christ, which was born uniquely and terminated uniquely, and which reflected in a unique way the body of unfallen Adam as created, one has to search outside the ordinary course of events entirely. As to their bodies, both the First and the Last Adam were miraculously originated. As to the termination, there is this difference also between them and all other living things, namely, that whereas, for animals, death is natural, for man death is unnatural. And for the Lord Jesus Christ death was vicarious and supernatural.[263] At the root of virtually all false systems of theology lies the failure to recognize this fundamental truth.

But in the Fall, man ruined this house in its nature. Death, physical mortality, was introduced into it via the forbidden fruit even as death was introduced into the spirit which inhabits it by the very act of disobedience. If we allow that Adam was the first *man* but that by his Fall he surrendered his true nature as such, what we see now in ourselves is no longer true manhood, but something else. Man now has neither the virtual freedom from disease and fantastically efficiently operating body of an animal, nor the beautifully adjusted instincts which guide the life of every other creature below him. He is corrupted in body and in spirit. If he has any instincts at all, they seem to be instincts of destruction; destruction to himself, his society, and his environment. Something is totally, wholly, wrong with him — even if he were merely considered as an animal. Man is *less* than an animal, lacking in every impulse that is natural as well as healthful for every other creature in its contingent circumstances. He is virtually an alien in the universe, alienated from all other creatures and alienated from God.

Furthermore, unless man is redeemed by the grace of God, he is a lost creature under judgment in a way that no other creature is, whether animal or angel. Redeemed, he is greater than both. But in neither case is he an *animal*. He is in a different category, though his body and his mind show the hand of the same Designer and Architect at work in both himself and the animals. Only *he* was created

[263] Custance, Arthur C., Part VII, "How Did Jesus Die?" in Doorway Papers, Vol. V.

in the image of God, in order that God might one day appear as man. It is useless to ignore the Fall and try to discuss what man is. It is useless to ignore the Incarnation and try to discuss why man was made as he was. It cannot be done.

Man was made *for* God, and as such he had to be a creature with those freedoms which alone would make fellowship with God meaningful. But God knew what the consequences of such freedoms would be and how they must be dealt with. God knew that man would have to be redeemed and that He would have to be the Redeemer. To be the Redeemer, God had to become man in the Person of His Son Jesus Christ. And thus man had to be such a creature that God could assume his form and his nature in order to become his Redeemer without diminishing His own Person. The Incarnation, that God should be manifest as man in Jesus Christ, is the key to the reasons why man has been constructed in his total being in the way he has. This is part of the truth to which the child of God is called to bear witness, a truth the knowledge of which is not to be derived from philosophical reflection on scientific research but only from Scripture.

The evidence of anatomy, physiology, pharmacology, medicine, culture, and language, all tell the same story. Man is an animal only if one merely wants to emphasize what man and animals share in common. And they do share much in common, since the same Creator created them both to share a similar environment. But this ignores all that they do not share in common. It ignores what actually makes man *man*. What constitutes man something entirely other than an animal is the fact that he was not made for the same purpose. Superficially, a small chisel may look like a screwdriver. To argue that either can be used in emergency for cutting wood or for driving a screw does not make them both the same. They were intended to serve different purposes. To confuse them and to ignore differences is not only an insult to the designer, but a confession of ignorance.

The clue to man's identity, then, is in the purpose for which he was made. He was literally "made for *God*." In every sense this is true. It is the reason why he has the anatomy and physiology he has. It is the reason for the special nature of his central nervous system. And, in the final analysis, it is the reason for his Fall and his redemption.

I believe that even in a society which rejects the Gospel, the Church is still called upon to bear witness to the fact that man is not an animal, that man is a unique creature of unique significance in this universe, unique in origin, unique in design, of unique destiny, and, whether *redeemed or unredeemed,* related in a special way to the Creator. This uniqueness stems not only from the circumstances surrounding man's creation and Fall, but also from the fact that after death he will live again to face judgment for what he has been in this life.

Man is not a superior animal but a child of eternity. And I am convinced that the world needs to be constantly reminded of this fact. And it needs also to be reminded that there can be no understanding of "the phenomenon of man" unless his special origin and destiny are recognized fully. Nor can the ills of society be properly diagnosed or any proper provision be made for the real fulfillment of human aspirations even at the ordinary social level unless the true nature of man as a fallen but redeemable creature is acknowledged.